Statistics for Social and Behavioral Sciences

Advisors:
S.E. Fienberg
W.J. van der Linden

For further volumes:
http://www.springer.com/series/3463

Dominique Haughton · Jonathan Haughton

Living Standards Analytics

Development through the Lens
of Household Survey Data

 Springer

Dominique Haughton
Department of Mathematical Sciences
Bentley College
Waltham, MA, USA
dhaughton@bentley.edu

Jonathan Haughton
Department of Economics
Suffolk University
Boston, MA, USA
jhaughto@beaconhill.org

ISBN 978-1-4614-0384-5   e-ISBN 978-1-4614-0385-2
DOI 10.1007/978-1-4614-0385-2
Springer New York Dordrecht Heidelberg London

Library of Congress Control Number: 2011934800

Printed on acid-free paper

Springer is part of Springer Science+Business Media (www.springer.com)

To our parents
Monique and Paul Boudier
and
Helen and Joe Haughton
and to our daughter Isabelle

Preface

The Gallup Organization polls a thousand people every day. The Thailand Statistical Office interviews 3,000 households, using detailed surveys, every month. The amount of digital information doubles every 18 months.

We are, to use a headline from *The Economist*, facing a data deluge. What a contrast to the time when Nobel prize winner Wassily Leontief (1971), in his Presidential Address to the American Economic Association, could complain about a plethora of theory and a dearth of data, and call for a shift to "large-scale factual analysis" (p. 5).

The earliest analysis of household survey data – going back at least to the pioneering work of Seebohm Rowntree (1901) – was largely confined to tabulations. Starting in 1980, the World Bank's Living Standards Measurement Survey project boosted the pace and quality of household survey data gathered in Less-Developed Countries; 89 of the surveys may be downloaded from its Web site, but hundreds more such surveys are now available. By 2002 the project had generated 135 technical papers. This second wave emphasized the use of graphical and regression techniques, nicely summed up in the essential volume by Angus Deaton, *The Analysis of Household Surveys: A Microeconometric Approach to Economic Development* (1987).

We are now experiencing a third wave, with the increasing application of an ever-broadening array of analytical tools – such as directed acyclic graphs (DAGs), Kohonen maps, and propensity score matching – in addition to refinements to regression.

The purpose of this book is to introduce, discuss, illustrate, and evaluate the colorful palette of analytical techniques that can be applied to the analysis of household survey data, with an emphasis on the innovations of the past decade or so. It is conceived as an antidote to an overly narrow view of what constitutes legitimate empirical work, and reflects our own preferences as methodological eclectics.

The term "analytics" means the science of analysis, and in the business world – from which we have borrowed the term – it denotes the use of data, often in large quantities, to improve decision making. We use the term in its widest sense, as the harnessing of data, particularly from household surveys, to improve policy recommendations. It is a large canvas, ranging from the mainstream econometric approach of testing and subsequently revising the sharp lines of model-generated hypotheses – what Deaton (2010, p. 4) calls the hypothetico-deductive method – to the soft brush strokes of some of the atheoretical techniques of data mining and exploratory data analysis. Both painting styles have their place in the gallery of analytics.

This is a gateway book. Most of the chapters begin by introducing a methodological or policy problem, to motivate the subsequent discussion of relevant methods. They then summarize the relevant techniques, and draw on examples – many of them from our own work – and aim to convey a sense of the potential, but also the strengths and weaknesses, of those techniques. The idea is to provide enough detail to allow the reader to take the next steps, but not so much detail as to get bogged down.

To be exhaustive would be too exhausting. For example, we introduce Kohonen maps in Chap. 6, explain how they function, and work through an example. The interested reader will then be well positioned to dig deeper, into a field where more than 5,000 articles have been published.

In writing this book, we have three main audiences in mind. The first is graduate students in statistics, economics, policy analysis, and social sciences, especially, but certainly not exclusively, those interested in the challenges of economic development in the Third World. We would be delighted if this book opens the reader to a handful of new ideas: skim the book, alight on the pages that catch one's fancy, and return to it regularly as a reference and a fount of ideas.

Our second target group is academics, who will likely be very conversant with some of the material in the book, but would appreciate a quick *tour d'horizon* to familiarize them with other interesting, and potentially useful, techniques. This is a book, like Deaton's *Analysis of Household Surveys*, that can serve as a reference work, to be taken down from the shelf and perused from time to time.

Our third audience is practitioners, by whom we mean anyone who works closely with survey data, whether in statistics offices, think tanks, research units, international organizations, central banks, NGOs, businesses – the list is long. We know, from teaching online and internationally, that there are many who, having left the university environment, are not sure how to keep up with new technical developments; we believe the book will help, because it introduces the techniques and ideas without getting too lost in the technical detail.

The Substance

We begin the book with a consideration of graphical methods, because this is often the first step when we are trying to develop a feel for our data. Graphs can be revealing, and they can be helpful in presenting our findings. We start by discussing how to produce a useful histogram, and its continuous-valued cousin, the kernel density. Boxplots are also easy to use and especially helpful when we want to compare the essential features of two or more distributions side by side. The chapter also includes some discussion of violin plots, scatterplots, and bag plots, before turning to presentational graphics. We agree with Gelman et al. (2002) that graphs could productively be used more often when presenting scientific results: The beautiful bubble plot in Fig. 1.13 contains more information than its apparent simplicity would suggest. The final section of Chap. 1 looks at maps, which can now be produced remarkably quickly and easily; the cartogram in Fig. 1.17 shows the distribution of child mortality worldwide, and instantly conveys the locus of the problem.

After graphics comes regression, which we survey in Chap. 2. Seasoned econometricians and other quantitative researchers can skip this chapter, but it is our experience that regression is sufficiently subtle, and the ideas sufficiently slippery, that one needs a quick review of the material on a regular basis. We note the main problems faced in regression, including measurement error, omitted variable bias, multicolinearity, heteroscedasticity, adjustments for clustered data, outliers, and simultaneity, and suggest ways in which these may be dealt with. Thus the chapter includes a discussion of, among other things, instrumental variables, and quantile regression. It is a whistle stop tour, which is exactly what most of us need.

Household survey data almost never come from simple random samples, and in Chap. 3 we address the issues related to sampling, first reviewing the main types – simple, stratified, cluster – and then presenting the essentials of how to determine an appropriate sample size while recognizing the need to trade off sampling with nonsampling errors. We show how to incorporate sample design into the computation of summary statistics – using Stata, the statistical package that we have used most over the years – and summarize the debate on whether to use weights in regression. The last two sections of the chapter ask how best to survey hard-to-reach groups, such as migrants – the main focus of a recent survey in the two main cities of Vietnam – and groups such as jazz players, or prostitutes, where respondent-driven sampling has been quite successful.

In Chap. 4 we move beyond linear regression, first by making the linear specification more flexible, and then by using nonparametric methods to fit curves. This segues into an explanation of multivariate adaptive regression spline (MARS) models, which we apply to a model of changes in consumption spending in Vietnam between 1993 and 1998. We also discuss classification and regression tree (CART) models; both CART and MARS are particularly good at exploring the data for nonlinearities and interactions. We have used a CART model with some success as a first step in helping us specify the functional form of a parametric model of the determinants of short-term malnutrition in Vietnam.

Much of our interest in working with living standards survey data arises from our desire to say something useful for policy purposes. This requires us to be able to say, "if you do X, then Y will happen," which is a causal statement. The question of causality, and more specifically how to conceive of and measure causal statements, is the subject of Chap. 5. The experimentalist school focuses on measuring the "effects of causes," where possible using randomized experiments to try to determine whether microcredit raises spending or flip charts improve exam performance.

The structuralist school worries that the outcomes of experiments leave us with an insufficient understanding of the underlying causal mechanisms, and urge us to pay attention to unearthing the "causes of effects," which may then be generalized to other situations and applied to policy. Taking its cue from Edward Tufte, who famously wrote that "correlation is not causation but it sure is a hint," the causal inference school, seeks to measure causality using a combination of correlations and logic. This approach is essentially mechanical, and the results are usually shown in the form of directed acyclic graphs (DAGs). This is unfamiliar terrain for most economists and policy analysts, which is why we devote much of the chapter to explaining how DAGs are constructed and what we might learn from them.

We often group data, for instance looking at income by gender, region, or quintile. In Chap. 6 we explore in more detail how observations may be clustered. This is an exploratory process, traditionally conducted with hierarchical or non-hierarchical clustering, which can produce beautiful graphs. It is also possible to incorporate more statistical structure using latent class models. The second half of the chapter introduces Kohonen maps, which have become very popular: They typically group observations on a two-dimensional grid, and present the results in the form of gorgeous "maps" – all of which we explain and illustrate here.

In approaching any scientific question, or looking at any data, we almost always have at least some idea of what we expect. If the data showed that richer households bought fewer cars, or poorer households eat more caviar, we would be shocked. Bayesian analysis provides a formal framework for incorporating these prior beliefs, in contrast to the more standard frequentist approach that either ignores them entirely, or locks them into rigid models. Chapter 7 provides an introduction to Bayesian analysis, setting out the ideas, the approach, and an example, and then addressing the problems of eliciting priors, applying posterior predictive checking, combining models in the form of Bayesian model averaging, and determining the appropriate sample size for a survey. This is not the easiest chapter in the book – the intrinsic difficulty of the subject helps explain its still-limited spread beyond trained statisticians – but it is likely to be one of the more useful for nonstatistician readers.

We are rediscovering geography, and recognizing once again that what happens in one area can influence what happens nearby. The presence of spatial dependence has implications for how to specify and estimate regression models – most commonly through the use of spatial weights matrices that measure the strength of the contiguity effects. We illustrate the use of these techniques in Chap. 8, drawing on a study of the spatial pattern of unemployment in the Midi-Pyrénées region of France, where we also present an algorithm for choosing among different types of spatial models.

Although it is still comparatively rare, increasing numbers of household surveys are based on panels, where households are surveyed repeatedly over time. In Chap. 9 we show how panel data can allow for more precise inference, and in many cases can help us tackle the knotty problem of unobserved heterogeneity: if households differ in ways we cannot observe, but these differences – in ability or drive, for instance – do not vary over time, then differenced data can sweep away such effects, laying bare the relationships that we are usually interested in measuring. We illustrate this with an example in which we try to measure the effect on income of loans extended under the Thailand Village Fund, which burst onto the scene in 2002 and by 2004 had become the largest microcredit scheme in the world. Still, panel data are not a panacea; attrition bias can be a problem, and even without attrition, panels become less representative over time.

One of the most important uses of household survey data is to measure poverty, and vulnerability to poverty. Chapter 10 reviews this field, starting with the choice of a measure of well-being, through the construction of a poverty line, to the choice of a summary measure of poverty. We then discuss the robustness of poverty measures, focusing on sampling and measurement error, and explaining the notion of stochastic dominance. After a section in which we consider the problems peculiar to international comparisons of poverty, we consider ways in which vulnerability to poverty – defined as the probability that a household will be poor in the future – may be measured.

We return to an essentially technical issue in Chap. 11, where we look at bootstrapping. This is especially useful when we need to estimate the standard error of a measure – such as the Sen–Shorrocks–Thon index of poverty – and where an analytical formula is not available. The technique can be powerful, especially where the data come from complex samples, and is increasingly straightforward to implement; we illustrate this with an example in which we create a histogram of bootstrapped changes in the poverty rate in Vietnam between 1993 and 1998.

Does a program work? Was a project effective? These are questions addressed by impact evaluation, where we try to compare the actual outcomes, for those who have been "treated," with a counterfactual, which is our estimate of what would have happened in the absence of the program or project. The traditional gold standard is experimental design, or randomization, but in Chap. 12 we show that even this is not without its limitations. It is much more common to use quasi-experimental methods, of which the most popular are propensity score matching, double differences, and instrumental variables. For each of these we set out the principles, consider an example, and review both the strengths and weaknesses. This is a relatively long and detailed chapter, but it has proven to be effective when teaching impact evaluation to graduate students in economics.

Household survey data mainly come from large, complex questionnaires administered to relatively small samples of perhaps 5,000–10,000. This allows one to conduct the analysis at the level of a country or broad region, but not at the level of a small county or district. Yet we would often like to measure, for instance, poverty rates at a "small-area" level, the better to target spending to alleviate poverty. In Chap. 13 we discuss how to do this, first describing a basic synthetic regression model, and then explaining how one might estimate a two-level, or even multilevel, model with random effects. This chapter applies the methods to Vietnam, and includes two elegant maps that result from the analysis.

Perhaps it is fitting that the last chapter in the book, Chap. 14, looks at duration models. In many cases, the time dimension is central to the analysis, such as the interval between one birth and the next, or the time spent unemployed. We introduce the Kaplan–Meier estimator, which allows for an exploratory analysis of duration data, and move on to the Cox proportional hazards model, parametric regression models, and mixture models of two Weibull regressions. As always, this chapter is designed to help the reader take the first steps – enough for the first draft of a solid research paper, even if lifting it to the level required for scholarly publication will always call for digging a bit deeper.

Where We Stand

We come to this book with different perspectives – one schooled in economics where the mindset is one of "model first, then test," the other more comfortable with data mining and letting the numbers speak "for themselves." The tension between these approaches runs throughout the book, and we see this as a virtue. One of us is skeptical that directed acyclic graphs are useful in helping us understand how the world really works, and thinks that the main virtue of Kohonen maps is that they are pretty. The other has yet to find an instrumental variable that looks compelling, and thinks that a lot of highfalutin theory is "nonsense on stilts." We do not try to resolve these debates – we are reminded of the observation by George Box that "essentially, all models are wrong, but some are useful" – but instead set out the techniques and ideas, to help the reader develop an informed opinion.

Together, we have over 50 years of experience working with household datasets, and have written over 200 papers, articles, and reports, over 80 of them in scholarly journals. This book is our take on what we find to be most useful, or at least intriguing or innovative; it also contains what we would like our students to know.

We are grateful to all of those who helped us on the way to this book. All of our more than 150 co-authors have at least some claim to intellectual parentage. Glenn Jenkins started the ball rolling in 1979 by interesting one of us in using survey data to address a practical development problem, in this case whether to build small-scale irrigation projects in Malaysia. In 1994, Mark Sidel encouraged us to work with the General Statistics Office in Hanoi; this, and the ongoing support from Nguyen Phong of the GSO, explains why so many of the examples in this book are drawn from the various living standards surveys undertaken in Vietnam.

We would like to thank our institutions – Bentley University and Suffolk University – for providing research support and sabbatical leaves that helped us get the book written. We are grateful to John Kimmel for trusting us with the project, and waiting patiently for it to progress, and to Marc Strauss for taking up the baton; to Dan Westbrook for reviewing an early draft; and to Maria Skaletsky, Sunida Susantud, Bayar Tumennasan, and Jason Wells for very helpful comments.

References

Deaton, Angus. 1997. *The analysis of household surveys: A microeconometric approach to development policy.* Baltimore: Johns Hopkins University Press.

The Economist. 2010. Special report on managing information. February 27.

Gelman, A., C. Pasarica, and R. Dodhia. 2002. Let's practice what we preach: Turning tables into graphs. *The American Statistician*, 56(2):121–130.

Leontief, Wassily. 1971. Theoretical assumptions and nonobserved facts. *American Economic Review*, 61(1):1–7.

Rowntree, Seebohm. 1901. *Poverty: A study of town life.* London: Macmillan.

About the Authors

Dominique Haughton (PhD, MIT 1983) is Professor of Mathematical Sciences at Bentley University in Waltham, Massachusetts, near Boston, and Affiliated Researcher at the Université Toulouse 1, France. Her major areas of interest are applied statistics, statistics and marketing, the analysis of living standards surveys, data mining, and model selection. She is the editor-in-chief of *Case Studies in Business, Industry and Government Statistics (CSBIGS)*, and has published over 50 articles in scholarly journals, including *The American Statistician, Annals of Statistics, Sankhya, Communications in Statistics,* and *Statistica Sinica.* In 2011, she was elected a Fellow of the American Statistical Association.

Jonathan Haughton (PhD, Harvard 1983) is Professor of Economics at Suffolk University, and Senior Economist at the Beacon Hill Institute for Public Policy, both in Boston. A specialist in the areas of economic development, international trade, and taxation, and a prize-winning teacher, he has lectured, taught, or conducted research in over a score of countries on five continents. His *Handbook on Poverty and Inequality* (with Shahidur Khandker) was published by the World Bank in 2009, his articles have appeared in over 30 scholarly journals, and he has written numerous book chapters and over a hundred reports.

Contents

Chapter 1
Graphical Methods

1.1 Introduction

It is tempting, but wrong, to believe that graphical techniques have little to offer for serious researchers in economics, statistics, or policy analysis. Their true power comes from the ability of the eye to discern patterns in a graph that are not clearly evident from lists of numbers or tabulated statistics. In Tufte's pithy phrase, "graphics reveal data" (Tufte 2001, p. 13).

We explore this theme in the chapter, beginning with the use of basic exploratory graphical methods in Sect. 1.2, considering presentational graphics in Sect. 1.3, and introducing some more recent techniques, including maps, in Sect. 1.4.

With data in hand, the most productive first step is often to explore the data graphically. These graphs do not have to be especially polished and beautiful; rather, they need to be easy to produce and thoroughly informative, a visual scratch pad where we use the power of graphics to get a sense of the shape of variables and the interactions among them.

Following Tufte (2001), the point can be emphasized elegantly with the help of Anscombe's quartet – four data sets, reproduced in Table 1.1, that may be summarized by the same linear model, and where the mean values of the X and Y variables are the same in each case. Yet a graphical display of the data sets (Fig. 1.1) demonstrates how very different they are. Real data do not usually yield such coherent or clear patterns, but a good initial graphical analysis can easily come up with surprises – showing outliers, suggesting a need to use a mixture of distributions, or raising questions about how variables are related.

Graphical techniques are also exceptionally useful in presenting the results of one's analysis, and we agree with Gelman et al. (2002) that they are typically underutilized for this purpose. But presentational graphics require an approach that is quite different from that of exploratory graphics: they serve to communicate ideas to others, and so they need to be more beautiful and more carefully constructed.

D. Haughton and J. Haughton, *Living Standards Analytics*, Statistics for Social and Behavioral Sciences, DOI 10.1007/978-1-4614-0385-2_1,
© Springer Science+Business Media, LLC 2011

Table 1.1 Anscombe's quartet of data sets

I		II		III		IV	
X	Y	X	Y	X	Y	X	Y
10.0	8.04	10.0	9.14	10.0	7.46	8.0	6.58
8.0	6.95	8.0	8.14	8.0	6.77	8.0	5.76
13.0	7.58	13.0	8.74	13.0	12.74	8.0	7.71
9.0	8.81	9.0	8.77	9.0	7.11	8.0	8.84
11.0	8.33	11.0	9.26	11.0	7.81	8.0	8.47
14.0	9.96	14.0	8.10	14.0	8.84	8.0	7.04
6.0	7.24	6.0	6.13	6.0	6.08	8.0	5.25
4.0	4.26	4.0	3.10	4.0	5.39	19.0	12.50
12.0	10.84	12.0	9.13	12.0	8.15	8.0	5.56
7.0	4.82	7.0	7.26	7.0	6.42	8.0	7.91
5.0	5.68	5.0	4.74	5.0	5.73	8.0	6.89
9.0	**7.5**	**9.0**	**7.5**	**9.0**	**7.5**	**9.0**	**7.5**

Notes: Each data set has 11 observations; the means are shown in the bottom row. Every regression line is $Y = 3 + 0.5X$; the standard error of the slope coefficient is 0.118 and its t-statistic is 4.24. In every case, $R^2 = 0.67$
Source: Anscombe 1973

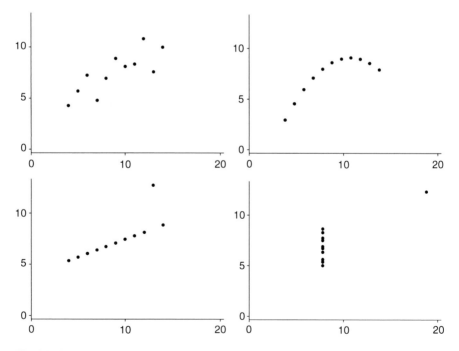

Fig. 1.1 Scatterplot of Anscombe's quartet (*Note*: Data from Table 1.1)

In Sect. 1.3 we review some of the key principles of graphical design, drawing heavily on the work of Tufte (2001), and suggest a few ways in which graphs could be used to make standard tabular presentations more effective.

1.2 Exploratory Graphical Methods

1.2.1 Histograms

A good place to start any analysis is with the most basic of visual techniques. Consider Fig. 1.2, which shows a simple frequency distribution (histogram) of birth weights of children born in Vietnam in 1992–1993. The data come from the Vietnam Living Standards Survey of 1992–1993, which surveyed 4,800 households nationwide and collected information on birth weights for 1,687 children. The graph represented the first step in an analysis by Sarah Bales (1999) of the determinants of low birth weights, and was generated using Stata.[1]

A baby is typically defined as being underweight if he or she weighs less than 2.5 kg at birth. Thus the histogram in Fig. 1.2 alerts us to a problem: an implausibly large number of births are heaped into the 2.5 kg category (and the 3.0, 3.5, and 4.0 kg categories). Indeed, 10.1% of the births were reported as weighing less than 2.5 kg and a further 10.7% as weighing exactly 2.5 kg! The rounding error matters here; the weight of some babies has presumably been rounded up to 2.5 kg, and in other cases the weight has been rounded down to 2.5 kg. So, while it is clear that more than 10.1% of babies are born underweight, but fewer than 20.8%, it is not clear whether it is preferable to define "underweight" as $w < 2.5$ or $w \leq 2.5$ (where w refers to the weight of the baby in kilos). The solution chosen by Bales (1999) was to use both definitions; fortunately, she found that the exact definition of underweight made relatively little difference to the direction and strength of the determinants of low birth weights.

Like a stethoscope, a histogram appears to be a simple tool, but it takes some practice to make it work effectively. The key choice that has to be made is that of the number of classes ("bins") into which to group the data or, alternatively, the width of each class, and this choice is as much a matter of art as of science.

A histogram aims to lay bare the distribution of the underlying data, and the classification of data into bins serves to filter out some of the noise. This is illustrated in Fig. 1.3, which displays four histograms showing the number of individuals covered by the 1998 Vietnam Living Standards Survey, broken down by age. The bottom right panel of Fig. 1.3 has just ten bins, and hints at a unimodal distribution dominated by the large proportion of individuals in the 10–20 age

---

[1] For a tutorial-based introduction to Stata, with examples that use easily accessible household survey data from Bangladesh, see Appendixes 1 and 2 of Haughton and Khandker (2009).

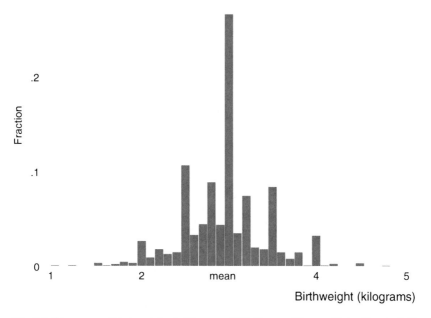

Fig. 1.2 Histogram of birth weights in Vietnam, 1993 (*Source*: Vietnam Living Standards Survey, 1993)

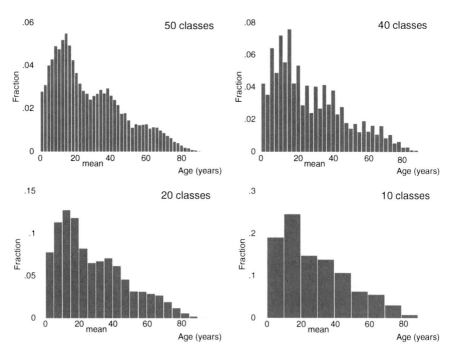

Fig. 1.3 Histograms of ages (in years) for individuals surveyed in the Vietnam Living Standards Survey of 1997–1998, with differing numbers of classes ("bins")

bracket. The top right panel uses 40 bins, and is clearly unsatisfactory; the age interval 0–100 is divided into 40 equal classes, so those aged 0, 1, or 2 are in the first bracket, those aged 3 or 4 in the next bracket, those aged 5, 6 or 7 in the third bin, and so on, in a saw-toothed fashion. This particular problem arises because the age data are integer rather than continuous, but even continuous data are often subject to heaping, as we saw in Fig. 1.2.

We get closer to a sensible pattern with a 20-bin histogram, which suggests a second peak. This is confirmed by the very informative histogram in the top left panel of Fig. 1.3, which uses 50 classes. Turned on its side, this gives half of a population "pyramid." Note, in this context, the dramatic reduction in the number of births since they peaked in about 1972 (i.e., 16 years prior to the 1998 survey), and the shortage of those aged roughly 45–60 – casualties of war, as they would have been in the armed forces in the years up to 1975 – and their children (Haughton 2000).

Are there better ways to choose bin widths other than trial and error? Freedman and Diaconis (1981) argue that if the histogram is to serve as a density estimator, then an appropriate rule for determining bin width is

$$BW_{FD}(x) = 2 \times IQR(x) \times n^{-1/3}, \tag{1.1}$$

where $BW_{FD}(x)$ is the Freedman and Diaconis bin width for variable x, $IQR(x)$ is the interquartile range of x, and n is the number of observations. With more observations we can afford to have narrower bins; with greater variation in x the bins need to be wider.

Other rules have been suggested. For instance, Wand (1997) proposes starting with a "zero-stage rule" that sets the bin width as

$$BW_W(x) = 3.49 \times \left[\min\left\{ s, \frac{IQR(x)}{1.349} \right\} \right] \times n^{-1/3}, \tag{1.2}$$

where s is the standard deviation of the sample.

In the example in Fig. 1.3, the Freedman–Diaconis rule gives a bin width of 1.9, implying 52 bins, while the Wand rule generates a bin width of 2.3, implying 43 bins. Neither rule gives results that are as clean as those with 50 bins, but they would filter the data nicely if one were using truly continuous (rather than integer) data.

Statistical software packages try to help the user by starting with sensible guesses of the appropriate number of bins. Microsoft Excel sets the number of bins equal to $\sqrt{n}$ (rounded to the next integer) or 50, whichever is the smallest. Stata uses an only slightly more complex default, which is

$$\text{Number of bins} = \min[50, \min\{\sqrt{n}, 10 \times \ln(n)/\ln(10)\}]. \tag{1.3}$$

This sometimes works well, but usually some further exploration is called for to produce a sensible histogram.

1.2.2 Kernel Densities

A histogram provides a discretized, nonparametric approximation to the underlying density, but it has three drawbacks: it is not smooth, it depends on the bin widths, and it is sensitive to the choice of end points of the bins. So it is often more useful, or at least more elegant, to work with a smoothed version. This is achieved by estimating a kernel density.

Suppose we have a dataset X_1, X_2, ..., X_n, and array the observations on the horizontal axis of a graph. We are interested in estimating the density, $f(x)$, at any given point x. A natural way to measure the density is by measuring the concentration of observed data points that are in the vicinity of x, say in the interval $x \pm h$, where h is the bandwidth half length. As we move x and its associated interval rightwards along the horizontal axis, we drop points to the left and pick up new observations on the right. The effect on the total number of observations is gradual, hence the smoothing effect.

The process we have described here may be formalized. It generates the naïve (or rectangular) estimate of the density at x, given by

$$\hat{f}_N(x) = \frac{1}{hn} \sum_{i=1}^{n} W\left(\frac{x - X_i}{h}\right) \equiv \frac{1}{hn} \sum_{i=1}^{n} W(z), \tag{1.4}$$

where

$$w(z) = \begin{cases} 1/2 & \text{if } |z| < 1 \\ 0 & \text{otherwise} \end{cases} \tag{1.5}$$

so that

$$\hat{f}_N(x) = \frac{1}{nh} \sum_{i=1}^{n} \frac{1}{2} I(|z| \leq 1), \tag{1.6}$$

where $I(\cdot)$ is an indicator function that takes on a value of 1 if the bracketed expression is true, and zero otherwise.

More generally, we may define a kernel density estimator as

$$\hat{f}(x) = \frac{1}{hn} \left[\sum_{i=1}^{n} K(z) \right], \tag{1.7}$$

where $K(z)$ is the kernel function, calibrated so that the estimator integrates to 1. The naïve estimator puts an equal weight on all the observations in the interval $x \pm h$ when estimating the density of x, which is why the kernel function in this case is referred to as "rectangular." However, it is usually more satisfactory to use a symmetric function that puts more weight on values of X_i that are closer to x, and progressively less weight on values further from x. The widely used Epanechnikov

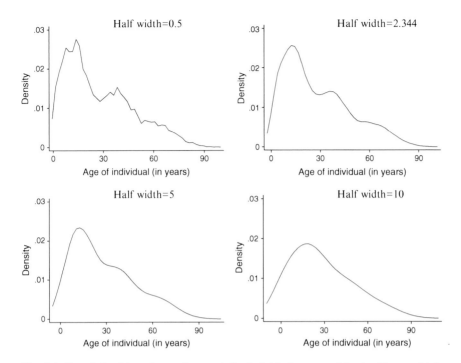

Fig. 1.4 Kernel densities of ages (in years) for individuals surveyed in the Vietnam Living Standards Survey of 1997–1998, with differing half-widths, including the Stata default value of 2.344

kernel is a concave quadratic function with maximum weight at x and zero weights at $x \pm h$. Formally,

$$K_E(z) = \frac{3}{4} \times \left[1 - \frac{1}{5}z^2\right] \Big/ \sqrt{5} \times I(|z| < \sqrt{5}). \qquad (1.8)$$

The principal virtue of the Epanechnikov kernel is that it is the most efficient in minimizing the mean integrated squared error, which is the difference between the true and estimated densities (Stata 2010; Silverman 1986). The Gaussian kernel is also popular, and is given by

$$K_G(z) = \frac{1}{\sqrt{2\pi}} e^{-z^2/2}. \qquad (1.9)$$

In fitting a kernel density we have to choose both the kernel function itself and the bandwidth h. It is generally agreed that the important decision concerns the choice of h, just as the choice of bin width is central to the construction of a good histogram. If h is too wide, the kernel density filters the data too much, and potentially valuable information is lost – compare the bottom right panel of Fig. 1.4, which has a wide bandwidth, with the top right panel, where the bandwidth

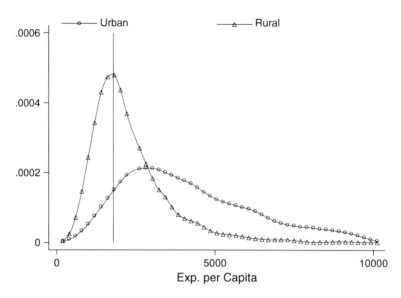

Fig. 1.5 Kernel densities of expenditure per capita for urban and rural Vietnam, 1998. (*Source*: Vietnam Living Standards Survey of 1998)

is narrower. The densities in Fig. 1.4 are based on the same Vietnamese data as in Fig. 1.3, and show the age distribution of the population.

One can also go too far, as the top left panel in Fig. 1.4 shows; in this case the estimated density will not filter out enough of the unwanted noise.

A number of rules have been developed for picking a suitable bandwidth, h. The default value of h used by Stata is given by

$$\tilde{h} = 0.9 \times mn^{-1/5}, \tag{1.10}$$

where n is the total number of observations in the sample, and

$$m = \min(s, \mathrm{IQR}/1.349). \tag{1.11}$$

Here, s is the standard deviation of the sample and IQR the interquartile range. Silverman (1986, p. 48) argues that using $\tilde{h}$ with a Gaussian kernel will yield a mean integrated square error within 10% of the optimum, for a wide range of true densities. However, for multimodal or long-tailed or skewed densities, it is generally accepted that this choice of $\tilde{h}$ is typically too wide, and so oversmooths the density.

To illustrate the use of kernel densities, consider Fig. 1.5, which shows the Epanechnikov kernel densities, using the Stata default values of $\tilde{h}$, for real expenditure per capita in Vietnam in 1998 (424.45 for urban households, 161.60 for rural households). The "taller" density refers to rural households, and it is clear from the diagram that they are poorer, and their expenditures less widely dispersed, than urban households.

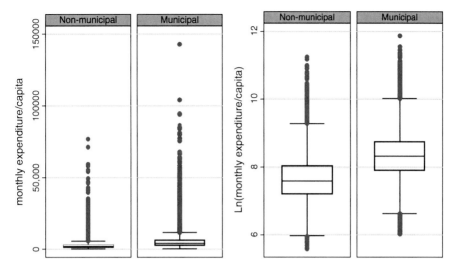

Fig. 1.6 Boxplots of expenditure (and log of expenditure) per capita in rural and urban Thailand, 2004, in baht per month. Based on 2004 socioeconomic survey

The vertical line in the graph shows the basic needs poverty line established by the General Statistics Office at 1.79 million dong of spending per person per year in 1998 (equivalent to about $137 using the exchange rate prevailing at that time). The poverty line in 1998 was close to the modal level of expenditure per capita in rural Vietnam, and so even relatively modest increases in rural expenditures would be expected to shift the rural expenditure distribution to the right and lift large numbers of rural households out of poverty. Indeed this is exactly what happened, and helps explain why the poverty rate in Vietnam fell so rapidly, from 55% in 1993 to 37% by 1998 and 29% in 2004 (Economist Intelligence Unit 2005).

1.2.3   Boxplots

One of the most useful, and straightforward, ways to get a first look at a univariate distribution is with a boxplot – also known as a box-and-whisker plot – a graphical device that was first used by geographers in the 1930s. In Fig. 1.6 we present boxplots showing the level of monthly expenditure per capita for municipal and nonmunicipal areas of Thailand, based on the socioeconomic survey of 2004.

At the heart of the boxplot is a box that shows the 25th percentile (the "lower hinge") and 75th percentile (the "upper hinge"), as well as the median value of the observations. On the upper side of the box one adds a line that stretches to the "upper adjacent value" and ends in a whisker; the whisker extends up to the largest

data point that lies within 1.5 interquartile ranges of the 75th percentile. A similar
line stretches to the lower adjacent value. All values of the variable beyond the
adjacent values (the "outside values") are plotted.

The result is a snapshot of the distribution of a variable that allows one to get a
sense of its symmetry, and the role of outliers. The panels on the left hand side of
Fig. 1.6 plot expenditure per capita, but are dominated by the outside values and
indicate that the distribution is highly skewed – as is generally the case with
expenditure data. The panels on the right hand side of Fig. 1.6 plot the natural log
of expenditure per capita, and are more helpful; although expenditure levels in
urban and rural Thailand overlap somewhat, it is clear that they are much higher in
urban areas. It also appears, at a first approximation, that the shape of the expenditure distribution is similar in urban and rural areas.

Boxplots are exploratory devices, and one must resist the temptation to try to use
them for statistical inference. While it does seem from Fig. 1.6 that expenditure
levels are higher in urban than rural Thailand, the correct way to make a statistically
valid comparison is generally with a t test. In this case the mean log expenditure
level in urban areas is 8.23 (equivalent to 4,855 baht per month), compared to 7.56
in rural areas (equivalent to 2,431 baht), a difference of 0.67, or about 67%. The
standard error of this difference is 0.018, yielding a t-statistic of 37.1 and a p-value
of 0.00, indicating clearly that there is a highly significant difference in expenditure
levels between urban and rural Thailand.[2] We used the log of expenditure per capita
in this case because its distribution is closer to being normal than the simple level of
expenditure per capita, as Fig. 1.6 makes clear.

Boxplots are especially useful when used to compare a limited number of
subgroups, as illustrated in Fig. 1.7. In this case, we wanted to compare the
distributions of (the log of) income per capita for Thai households, broken down
by the five major regions in the country and by gender of head of household. The
boxplots have been sorted by median level of income per capita, and in this case the
outside values have been suppressed in order to get a cleaner and less cluttered
comparison; in large datasets like this one there are likely to be numerous outside
values and they risk overwhelming the boxplot. It is clear from Fig. 1.7 that gender
differences in income distribution are minimal; and that the distribution of income
in Bangkok is higher and relatively less dispersed than in other parts of the country.
The boxplots in Fig. 1.7 are very similar to the trellis plots (or lattice graphs) that
have been developed by Cleveland (1993) and others.

The violin plot combines a boxplot (without the outside values) and a kernel
density, with the latter repeated symmetrically, as shown in Fig. 1.8 (Hintze and
Nelson 1998). The result is an elegant graphic that does, however, lack the
forcefulness of a good boxplot and the interpretative ease of a horizontal kernel
density.

---

[2] These computations adjust for sample stratification and clustering. The boxplots also adjust for
sampling weights.

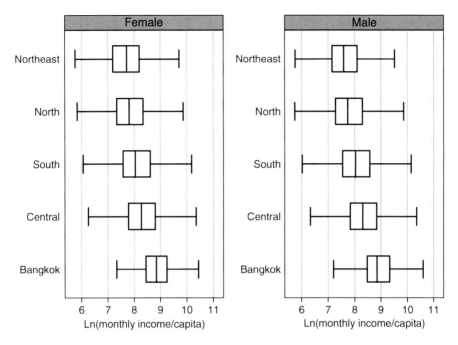

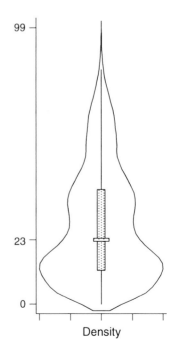

Fig. 1.7 Boxplots of log of income per capita for the five regions of Thailand, by gender of head of household, 2004. (*Source*: Thailand Socioeconomic Survey, 2004. Note that the outside values have been suppressed)

Fig. 1.8 Violin plot of age of individuals surveyed by Vietnam Living Standards Survey of 1998

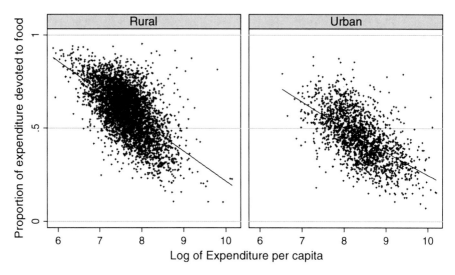

Fig. 1.9 Scatterplots, with best-fit lines, of food expenditure shares against expenditure per capita, rural and urban Vietnam, 1998. (*Source*: Vietnam Living Standards Survey of 1998)

1.2.4 Scatterplots

Most of the graphs used so far have been univariate, designed to get a sense of the distribution of a single variable. While that is an appropriate place to begin, we quickly want to move on to graphs that show how variables are related to each other. The most straightforward of these is the scatterplot, which simply plots each observation using two dimensions. The scatterplots in Fig. 1.9 show how the share of expenditure devoted to food is associated with (the log of) expenditure per capita in Vietnam in 1998, with separate plots for households in urban and rural areas. These graphs also include fitted summary lines (estimated using ordinary least squares).

These plots are dense; together they show 5,999 observations. Yet the eye can clearly pick up some patterns: in both urban and rural areas, the share of spending that is devoted to food falls sharply as expenditure per capita levels rise; this is a good illustration of Engel's Law at work. There is also a good deal of noise, so that households with a given level of expenditure per capita can devote very different proportions of expenditure to food; clearly this implies that other variables are likely to be relevant, and this opens up possible lines of inquiry. It is also clear that urban households are, on average, more affluent, and so spend relatively less on food than rural households.

There is also a hint that as expenditure per capita rises, the fall in the share going to food slows down; this may be inferred from the observation that the fitted line for rural households (who have, on average, lower expenditure) is steeper than the fitted line for the (more affluent) urban residents. Such nonlinearity makes intuitive sense;

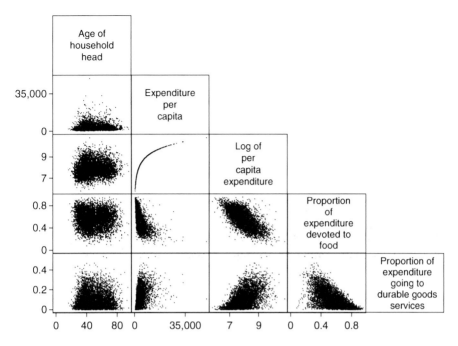

Fig. 1.10 Matrix scatterplot, variables Vietnam Living Standards Survey of 1998

otherwise, simple extrapolation of the linear fitted values would show that very affluent households spend nothing on food! The interesting point here is that simple scatterplots are often useful in suggesting possible functional forms for relationships between variables, an issue to which we return at several points in this book.

When dealing with many variables, it can be tedious to set up numerous scatterplots. An easy shortcut is to use a matrix scatterplot, which produces numerous small-scale scatterplots in a single graph. We illustrate this in Fig. 1.10, which graphs scatterplots for five variables from the Vietnam Living Standards Survey of 1998. A total of 29,995 data points are shown in a small space, and we very quickly perceive that the age of the head of the household appears to be unrelated to household expenditure per capita or to the proportion of spending devoted to food – at least in the simple bivariate comparisons. In passing, note that the emphasis in Fig. 1.10 is on the pattern of the data points, and at this stage we pay less attention to the details of the scale used. Frequently it helps to transform data by taking logs, and this helps in Fig. 1.10, where the share of expenditure devoted to food (and, to a lesser extent, the proportion going to durable goods services) is more clearly related to the log of per capita expenditure than to per capita expenditure itself. Stata produces matrix scatterplots very easily (just type graph followed by a list of variables), but its default is inefficient in that it produces each plot twice; for clarity and efficiency we have suppressed the redundant upper triangle of the matrix.

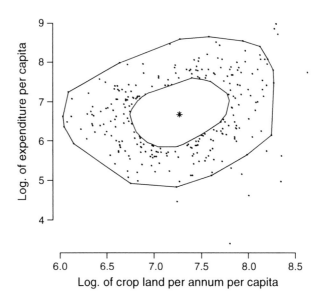

Fig. 1.11 Bagplot of the log of real expenditure (dong per capita) against the log of land cropped (square meters per capita) for ethnic minority households, rural Vietnam, 1998. (*Source*: Vietnam Living Standards Survey, 1998. *Note*: Only households with positive amounts of land are included here)

1.2.5 Bagplots

Scatterplots are generally very helpful, but when there are a large number of observations they can degenerate into a mere blob of ink. To address this problem, it is sometimes helpful to graph a two-dimensional version of the boxplot, called a bagplot. Introduced in 1999 by Rousseeuw et al., the bagplot allows one to visualize the location, spread, skewness, and outliers of two variables together.

In Fig. 1.11 we show a bagplot based on information from the Vietnam Living Standards Survey of 1998. The horizontal axis shows the log of the amount of land, per household member, used for annual crops (such as rice or maize), in square meters, and the vertical axis shows the log of real expenditure (in dong per capita per year). We have excluded the few outlier households with more than 60,000 m^2 of land or per capita annual expenditure above 15 million dong (about US$1,150), and these numbers refer only to ethnic minority households, who mainly live in the more remote and mountainous parts of Vietnam.

The "asterisk" symbol near the center of the graph is the "depth median," which is the two-dimensional analog of the median that is used in the (one-dimensional) boxplot. The depth median is defined as the point with the highest halfspace location depth, and the halfspace location depth of a point is the smallest number of data points contained in any closed half plane whose boundary runs through the point.

Intuitively, a point near the edge of the distribution will have a small halfspace location depth, because it is possible to construct a half plane containing few, if any, points. At the other extreme, for a point in the thick of the distribution it will be difficult to construct a half plane that does not include almost half the dataset.

The inner bag in Fig. 1.11 contains essentially half of the data points, and corresponds to the box in the boxplot. Given a dataset with n observations, define D_k as the set of data points with a halfspace location depth greater than or equal to k. Now pick k such that

$$\text{No. of obs. in } D_k \leq \text{int}(n/2) < \text{No. of obs. in } D_{k-1} \qquad (1.12)$$

and interpolate linearly between D_k and D_{k-1} relative to the depth median.

The outer bag is obtained by inflating the inner bag threefold relative to the depth median; while the value of three is arbitrary, Rousseeuw et al. (1999) argue that it is appropriate, based on their simulation exercises. The values beyond the outer bag are considered to be outliers, although in a large dataset they can be numerous. This bagplot also shows all of the actual data points (outside the inner bag), and was computed using code in R.

From Fig. 1.11 we learn that both underlying variables are right skewed. The inner and outer bags are slightly elongated, hinting at a positive relationship between land ownership and expenditure levels, but the elongation is slight, implying that any such relationship is very noisy. Notice too the restricted range of the horizontal axis; the left side of the inner bag represents just under a tenth of a hectare, and the right side about a quarter of a hectare. There are essentially no large farms in this sample. This is consistent with the traditional image of rural Vietnam as one of a "poor household on a tiny plot of land," a legacy of the way in which land was redistributed after 1950.

1.3 Presentational Graphics

It is not enough simply to do research; it must also be communicated to others with clarity, coherence, and efficiency. Graphical displays can be immensely helpful in helping a viewer get to the heart of the matter, especially when the amount of information is large.

But what makes for excellence in statistical graphics? Edward Tufte, in his classic *The Visual Display of Quantitative Information* (2001), includes the following among his main lessons:

- Show the data, without distorting what they have to say
- Present many numbers in a small space, making large data sets coherent
- Encourage the eye to compare different pieces of data

Table 1.2 Counts and rates of citations in the New York Times, by profession, 1996

Profession	Frequency of recent citations	1996 total employed (1,000)	Relative frequency
Lawyers	8,101	880	9.2
Economists	1,201	148	8.1
Architects	1,097	160	6.9
Physicians	3,989	667	6.0
Statisticians	34	14	2.4
Psychologists	479	245	2.0
Dentists	165	137	1.2
Teachers (not university)	3,938	4,724	0.8
Engineers	934	1,960	0.5
Accountants	628	1,538	0.4
Computer programmers	91	561	0.2
Total	20,657	11,034	1.9

Source: Ellenberg 2000

- Induce the viewer to think about the substance rather than the style
- Reveal the data at several levels of detail, from a broad overview to the fine structure

At a practical level he urges us to produce graphs with a high data density (per square inch), and with a high "data-ink ratio." This latter is defined as the ratio of ink used to represent data-information to the total ink used to print the graphic. One can achieve a higher data-ink ratio by reducing the weight and extent of grids, by keeping axes and tick marks light, by avoiding gratuitous decoration – in short, mainly by working to erase unuseful material. We have tried to follow these precepts in our own graphs in this chapter.

Tufte's own work provides numerous illustrations of excellence in statistical graphics and, to serve as a caution to us all, some wonderfully bad graphs as well.

Perhaps the best advice that one can give is that good graphical communication requires sustained effort and some imagination. When data or results have to be communicated to others, we need to ask whether this might be done graphically, and if so how, and then spend the time required to ensure that the graph does its job.

In this spirit, we borrow from an exercise by Gelman et al. (2002), who asked whether the tables that appeared in articles in the March 2000 issue of the *Journal of the American Statistical Association* might not have worked better had the information been presented in the form of graphs. Following one of their examples, consider the Table 1.2, which appeared in Ellenberg (2000), and which displays the frequency with which different professions were cited in the features section of the New York Times over a period of just over a year in the late 1990s. The table is clear and relatively straightforward, but it also takes a few minutes to understand.

Fig. 1.12 Citations in the
New York Times by profession
and by number employed,
1996. (*Source*: Gelman et al.
(2002). Reprinted with
permission from *The
American Statistician*.
Copyright 2002 by the
American Statistical
Association. All rights
reserved)

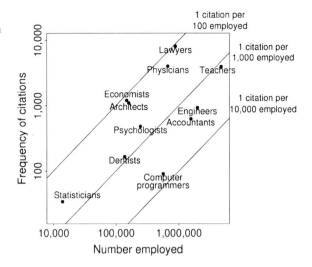

Gelman et al. (2002) created Fig. 1.12 on the basis of these numbers, and it is illuminating: the eye quickly determines which groups have the most citations, which are the most numerous, and which are cited with the greatest frequency. The precise numbers have been lost, of course, but do we really need to know that there were 3,989 citations by physicians, or do we just need to know that physicians are almost as numerous as lawyers, but not cited quite as frequently?

One of the more elegant graphical devices is the bubble plot, which is like a scatterplot except that the size of the points varies according to a third variable. For instance, one might graph infant mortality rates (*y*-axis) against income per capita (*x*-axis) for the countries of the world, where each bubble is scaled in proportion to its population, and possibly colored along a fourth dimension (e.g., country with rapid population growth, no population growth, and so on).

In Fig. 1.13 we present an example based on data from the Vietnam Household Living Standards Survey of 2002, which graphs per capita food consumption on the vertical axis against per capita expenditure on the horizontal axis. Red bubbles refer to urban areas, and blue to rural areas. Each bubble is scaled in proportion to the rural (or urban) population in one of Vietnam's eight regions. The bubbles for Red River Delta Urban (mainly Hanoi) and North East South Urban (mainly Ho Chi Minh City) stand out at the top right; the dominance of the rural over the urban population is clear; and the very poorest areas have relatively small populations.

One can create dynamic bubble plots, where the bubbles can be seen to move over time. Some quite remarkable ones have been created, and narrated, by Hans Rosling, Professor of International Health at the Karolinska Institutet in Stockholm, and the people at http://www.gapminder.org/ (accessed April 2011).

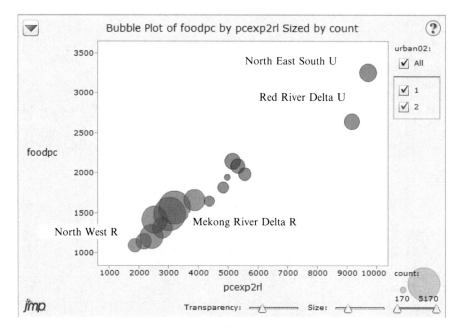

Fig. 1.13 Bubble plot of food per capita against expenditure per capita, by region, separated into urban (*red*) and rural (*blue*), Vietnam, 2002

1.4   Statistics with Maps

It is often useful to display statistical information on maps. This can certainly be done with established packages such as ArcGIS/ArcView or MapInfo, but often one needs software that will allow one to visualize the information quickly and easily, with a more modest investment of time. In this section we suggest a few examples.

Figure 1.14 uses the JMP module of SAS to show how a study clustered the countries of the world in 2000, and again in 2007, using measures of living standards and the level of "digital development" (Skaletsky et al. 2011). Lower numbers represent higher living standards. The most visually striking changes are the improvement in living standards and digital literacy in India, and in Russia and Eastern Europe.

Another useful package is Tableau (http://www.tableausoftware.com, accessed April 2011), which has a relatively user-friendly interface; an example of its "dashboard" is reproduced in Fig. 1.15, which comes from a study by Wang and Meisner (2010) that also serves as a good introduction to the software.

The map in Fig. 1.16 was created with Tableau, and is based on information from almost a score of Investment Climate Assessment (ICA) surveys of enterprises conducted between 2006 and 2009. The firms were categorized into formal, semiformal, and informal, based on whether they had a bank account and/or

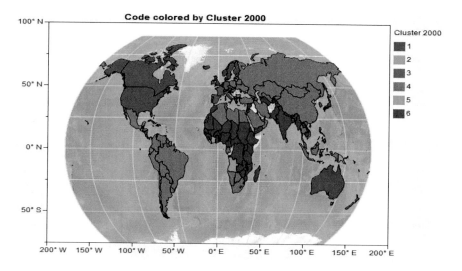

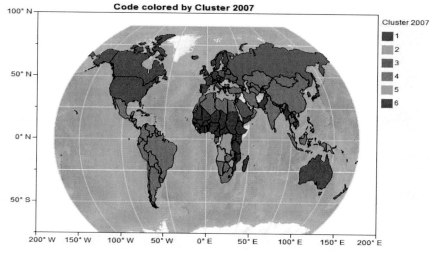

Fig. 1.14 Clusters and their evolution around 2000 and 2007. (*Source*: Skaletsky et al. 2011)

produced accounts (Haughton et al. 2010). Informal firms are particularly promi-
nent in coastal West Africa; formal firms dominate in South Africa and Mauritius.

Our final graphic is a cartogram, which is a map where countries (or other
geographic units) are resized based on a variable other than area. The cartogram
in Fig. 1.17 scales country by infant mortality, and shows dramatically how low
mortality is in Europe, Japan, and North America, and how large it is in Africa and
South Asia. It is becoming easier to create cartograms; Mark Newman of the
University of Michigan has a site with some other fine examples, and free software
(at http://www-personal.umich.edu/~mejn/cartograms/), and Worldmapper has
some fascinating animated examples.

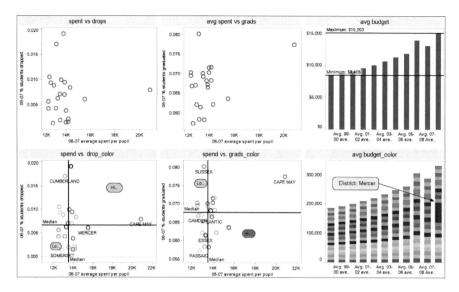

Fig. 1.15 Dashboard of the New Jersey Department of Education Data (*Source*: Wang and Meisner 2010, Table 9)

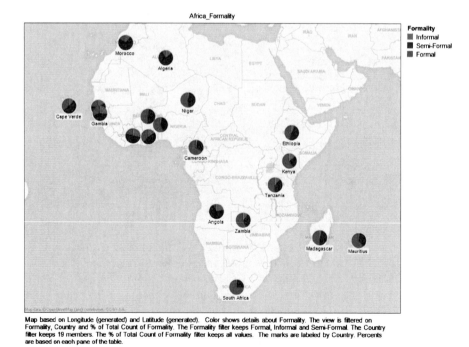

Map based on Longitude (generated) and Latitude (generated).   Color shows details about Formality. The view is filtered on Formality, Country and % of Total Count of Formality. The Formality filter keeps Formal, Informal and Semi-Formal. The Country filter keeps 19 members. The % of Total Count of Formality filter keeps all values. The marks are labeled by Country. Percents are based on each pane of the table.

Fig. 1.16 Firms by degree of formality (informal/semiformal/formal), Africa 2006–2009. (*Source*: Haughton et al. 2010, based on Investment Climate Assessment surveys)

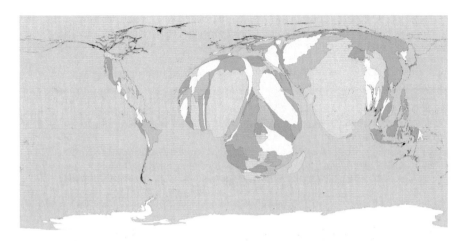

Fig. 1.17 Cartogram of Child Mortality Worldwide, About 2000. (*Source*: Mark Newman, http://www-personal.umich.edu/~majn/cartograms, reproduced with permission)

1.5 Conclusion

It has become relatively straightforward to visualize and explore data using graphical techniques. The central theme of this chapter is that graphical methods should be part of the toolkit of serious researchers. A well-constructed graph, chart, or map can be very illuminating. It can also be helpful when one needs to present results, or make a persuasive case to the reader.

References

Anscombe, F.J. 1973. Graphs in Statistical Analysis. *American Statistician* 27:17–21.

Bales, Sarah. 1999. Determinants of low birth weights. In *Health and wealth in Vietnam*, ed. D. Haughton, J. Haughton, S. Bales, K. Chuyen, and N. Nga. Singapore: Institute of Southeast Asian Studies.

Cleveland, W.S. 1993. *Visualizing data*. Summit: Hobart Press.

Economist Intelligence Unit. 2005. Vietnam: Country Profile. London.

Ellenberg, Jonas. 2000. Statisticians' significance. *Journal of the American Statistical Association* 95(449): 1–8.

Freedman, David, and Persi Diaconis. 1981. On the histogram as a density estimator: L2 theory. *Probability Theory and Related Fields* 57(4): 453–476.

Gelman, A., C. Pasarica, and R. Dodhia. 2002. Let's practice what we preach: Turning tables into graphs. *The American Statistician* 56(2): 121–130.

Haughton, Jonathan. 2000. Ten puzzles and surprises: Economic and social change in Vietnam, 1993–1998. *Comparative Economic Studies* 17(4): 67–92.

Haughton, J., and S. Khandker. 2009. *Handbook on poverty and inequality*. Washington, DC: World Bank.

Haughton, D., J. Haughton, and A. Mbaye. 2010. The informal sector, business climate and firm growth: WAEMU countries in comparative perspective, Université Cheikh Anta Diop, Dakar.

Hintze, J., and R.D. Nelson. 1998. Violin plots: A box plot-density trace synergism. *The American Statistician* 52: 181–184.

Rousseeuw, P., I. Ruts, and J. Tukey. 1999. The bagplot: A bivariate boxplot. *The American Statistician* 53: 382–387.

Silverman, B. 1986. *Density estimation for statistics and data analysis.* London: Chapman and Hall.

Skaletsky, M., O. Soremekun, and R. Galliers. 2011. The changing – and unchanging – face of the digital divide: An application of Kohonen Self Organizing Maps, unpublished, Bentley University, Waltham, MA.

Stata Corporation. 2010. The kdensity command. *Stata manual for release* 11: 816–825.

Tufte, E. 2001. *The visual display of quantitative information*, 2nd ed. Cheshire: Graphics Press.

Wand, M.P. 1997. Data-based choice of histogram bin width. *The American Statistician* 51: 59–64.

Wang, C., and M. Meisner. 2010. Dynamic data visualization. *Case Studies in Business, Industry and Government Statistics* 4(1): 9–22.

Chapter 2
Regression

2.1 Introduction

This chapter reviews the essentials of regression analysis. For most readers it will be a refresher that can be skimmed quickly; it provides a concise, self-contained coverage of topics that are the staple of any good course on econometrics.

The emphasis here is on the issues that commonly arise with household survey data. Most survey data are cross-sectional, with relatively large numbers of observations. Occasionally one encounters panel data, but they are always short panels, with few time periods and many households or individuals; we address the special issues related to panel data in Chap. 9.

Survey data almost never come from simple random sampling. As noted in Chap. 3, there is typically stratification – which calls for the use of sampling weights in computing most sample statistics – and clustering, which reduces the precision of estimation, and needs to be taken into account explicitly, as explained more fully below.

Data collected in household surveys are prone to error. This is true of any data, but some of the variables that are widely used based on surveys, such as household income or expenditure, are particularly difficult to measure with precision (Haughton and Khandker 2009, Chap. 2).

The other salient feature of survey data is that they are almost always incomplete. We rarely have all the variables that we would desire; compromises are inevitable, given the cost of asking questions and the need to choose what to ask. Moreover, some of the most important variables of interest, such as an individual's "ability," may be unobservable, and this has implications for how to proceed with regression.

In the next section we outline the basics of regression, and then consider the problems that arise in the context of household survey data, beginning with measurement error, and then turning to omitted variable bias, multicolinearity,

D. Haughton and J. Haughton, *Living Standards Analytics*, Statistics for Social and Behavioral Sciences, DOI 10.1007/978-1-4614-0385-2_2, © Springer Science+Business Media, LLC 2011

heteroscedasticity, outliers, clustering, and simultaneity. For a more formal treatment we recommend the classic textbook by Greene (2011); an excellent blend of theory and practice, with numerous examples using the Stata software, may be found in the book on microeconometrics by Cameron and Trivedi (2009).

2.2 Basics

The most fundamental use of regression is to summarize and describe patterns in data. To illustrate, consider the scatterplot in Fig. 2.1 (similar to the one in Haughton and Khandker 2009, p. 275), which graphs food consumption per capita against expenditure per capita for 9,189 Vietnamese households, based on data from the 2006 Vietnam Household Living Standards Survey. The problem with the graph is that the data points are so numerous and crowded that it is difficult for the eye to discern any essential underlying relationships.

A regression line goes some way toward solving this problem. The straight line in Fig. 2.1 represents the results of regressing food spending per person on total spending per person. For this example we used Stata – although any statistical software would do the job just as well – with the commands

```
regress food1 exp1
predict food1hat
```

The second command here puts the predicted values into a variable called food1hat, and this is what is actually graphed in Fig. 2.1. The estimated equation is

$$(\text{food spending per person}) = 1.188 + 0.22 \ (\text{total spending per person}).$$

The data in Fig. 2.1 are measured in millions of dong per year; in 2006 the exchange rate was about VND15,000 per US\$. This relationship shows that an extra thousand dong in total spending is associated with an extra 220 dong of spending on food. This is simply an observed association; we are not trying to make a statement about causality – a topic that we address more fully in Chap. 5.

Going back at least to the late nineteenth century, when Ernst Engel first noted the phenomenon based on household budget data collected in Belgium, it is widely accepted that higher per capita expenditure levels are associated with a falling share of spending devoted to food. This idea is captured in Fig. 2.1 by the quadratic curve, which flattens as one moves from left to right. The regression estimate that summarizes this may be written as

$$(\text{food spending per person}) = 0.853 + 0.30 \ (\text{total spending per person})$$
$$- 0.0021 \ (\text{total spending per person})^2$$

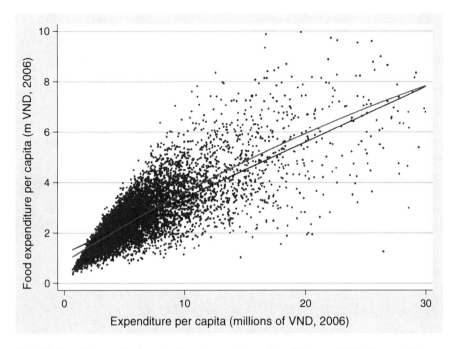

Fig. 2.1 Spending on food graphed against total spending, Vietnam, 2006. *Source*: Vietnam Living Standard Survey of 2006. Variables are in per capita terms. 9,122 observations are shown here; a further 67 are not shown (for readability)

Based on this equation, we find that for someone who is very poor, almost a third of incremental spending is devoted to food, but for those in the top percentile of the distribution the proportion of additional spending associated with food spending is just 0.14.

2.2.1 Inference

While the use of regression to summarize voluminous data is helpful, most researchers are interested in going further, using it for statistical inference. We want to know whether the link between variables is statistically significant, and we often hope to attempt to infer causality, so that we may conduct policy experiments that allow us to answer questions such as "if we were to change variable x, what would happen to variable y?" Indeed Deaton (1997, p. 65) makes the point that the essential thrust of most econometrics is to try to make causal inferences from nonexperimental data.

In order to use regression for inference, a number of additional assumptions are required. In setting these out, we broadly follow the approach taken by Cameron and Trivedi (2009).

Based on theory or intuition or prior practice, we believe that the conditional mean of some "dependent" variable y is given by a linear model of the form

$$E(y|\mathbf{X}) = \mathbf{X}\beta \equiv \beta_0 + \beta_1 X_1 + \cdots + \beta_K X_K. \tag{2.1}$$

Given data on N observations of variables y and $X_1, \ldots, X_K$, we want to estimate the vector of coefficients β.[1] Since the model cannot be expected to fit the data perfectly, we include an (additive) error to give, for the ith observation, the regression model

$$y_i = \mathbf{x}_i'\beta + e_i, \quad i = 1, \ldots, N. \tag{2.2}$$

The true errors (e_i) are unobservable; if we knew what the errors were, they would not be errors! In the classical regression model we begin by making three assumptions about the nature of these errors, and then spend most of our time figuring out how to proceed when we believe these assumptions have been violated. The assumptions are

Classical assumption 1
Exogeneity of Regressors: $E(e_i|\mathbf{X}_i) = 0$.

This says that the errors have zero mean; in addition, we assume that the errors are independent of the $\mathbf{x}_i$ regressors, which may thus be considered to be exogenous. This assumption is essential for consistency in the estimation of the parameters.

Classical assumption 2
Conditional Homoscedasticity: $E(e_i^2|\mathbf{X}_i) = \sigma^2$.

In other words, the errors are homoscedastic – that is to say, they are distributed with a constant variance that does not vary with the regressors.

Classical assumption 3
Conditionally Uncorrelated Observations: $E(e_i e_j|\mathbf{X}_i, \mathbf{X}_j) = 0, \quad i \neq j..$

This supposes that the observations are conditionally independent.

The ordinary least squares (OLS) estimates $\hat{\beta}$ of the coefficients are generated by $\hat{\beta} = (X'X)^{-1}X'y$, and when assumptions 1–3 hold, these OLS estimates are efficient; formally, they are the best linear unbiased estimates (BLUE). In large samples the vector $\hat{\beta}$, which is itself a random variable, is asymptotically distributed as (multivariate) normal, which gives

$$\hat{\beta} \dot\sim N\left(\beta, \operatorname{Var}(\hat{\beta})\right). \tag{2.3}$$

---

[1] Here $\mathbf{X}$ is an $N \times K$ matrix in which each column represents the observations on one of the right-hand variables.

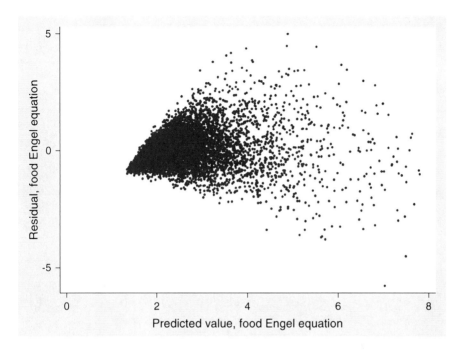

Fig. 2.2 Plot of residuals (*vertical axis*) vs. predicted values of spending on food (*horizontal axis*), Vietnam, 2006. (*Source*: As for Fig. 2.1)

Here $\text{Var}(\hat{\beta})$ is the asymptotic variance–covariance matrix of the estimator (VCE), which itself needs to be estimated by $\hat{V}(\hat{\beta})$. The standard error of $\hat{\beta}_i$ is given by the square root of the ith diagonal element of $\hat{V}(\hat{\beta})$. Most survey samples are large enough for the asymptotic conditions to apply (approximately), allowing one to base inference tests on the normal distribution (for $\hat{\beta}$) or χ^2 distribution (for $\hat{V}(\hat{\beta})$). However, even in these cases, for data on subgroups – such as observations for a province within a country – small-sample tests based on the t and F distributions are typically needed.

Having estimated a basic equation, this is often a good point at which to look at some basic diagnostic plots, which can be very helpful in indicating whether the classical assumptions are likely to apply. A relatively standard graph puts the regression residuals on the vertical axis and the predicted values of the dependent variable on the horizontal axis; if the classical assumptions apply, the observations should appear to form a random cloud. On the other hand, if there is heteroskedasticity, or if the residuals are not independent of one another, it will usually be quite evident at this point because they will form a pattern; for instance, in Fig. 2.2, which is based on a linear regression of the data shown in Fig. 2.1, the scatter of the residuals "opens up" as we move toward the right, a sure sign of the presence of heteroskedasticity (which we discuss further below).

Another useful graph is the *Q–Q plot*, sometimes referred to as a quantile plot or a probability plot. In the version shown in Fig. 2.3 – generated using the qnorm

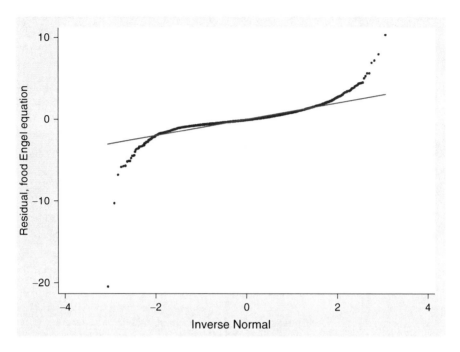

Fig. 2.3 *Q–Q* plot of residuals from food Engel curve, Vietnam, 2006. (*Source*: As for Fig. 2.1)

postestimation command in Stata – the residuals from the linear regression in Fig. 2.1 are sorted from smallest to largest, and the actual quantiles are graphed against the values that would be expected if the residuals were distributed normally. The actual values deviate from the 45° line, which means that the residuals are not quite normally distributed.

2.3 Addressing Regression Problems

Mechanically, it is straightforward to generate regression estimates. In practice, the classical assumptions are frequently violated, and we usually need to adjust our models in order to minimize the harm done by these violations.

2.3.1 Measurement Error

It is all but impossible to measure a variable with complete accuracy – for reasons we discuss more fully in Chap. 3 – and so measurement error is pervasive. For some commonly measured variables, such as household expenditure or income, the error can be large (see Chap. 10). It even applies, in many cases, to variables that we would expect to be able to measure precisely, such as a person's age; in many surveys these values cluster at higher ages, around numbers such as 70, 75, and 80, while avoiding the ages in between.

If the measurement error is in the dependent variable, we observe y^* rather than the true y. If the error is linear, we have $y^* = y+w$, where w is a vector of (presumably random) errors. So instead of

$$y = \mathbf{X}\beta + e \tag{2.4}$$

we observe

$$y* = \mathbf{X}\beta + (e + w). \tag{2.5}$$

A regression based on (2.5) will still yield unbiased estimates of the coefficients – the classical assumptions have not been violated – but the fit will be poorer, so the value of R^2 will be lower. This is because the signal-to-noise ratio has fallen, making inference less precise.

Measurement error in the independent variables is more serious. If we observe $\mathbf{X}^* = \mathbf{X}+\mathbf{w}$ rather than $\mathbf{X}$, then we would base our estimates on

$$y = \mathbf{X}^*\beta + (e - \mathbf{w}\beta). \tag{2.6}$$

Here the coefficient estimates $\hat{\beta}$ will be biased toward 0, because the noise in the $\mathbf{X}$ variables masks the true nature of the dependence of y on $\mathbf{X}$. More precisely, for any single right-hand-side variable,

$$E(\hat{\beta}) = \beta \frac{\sigma_X^2}{\sigma_X^2 + \sigma_w^2} = \beta \left(1 - \frac{\sigma_w^2}{\sigma_X^2 + \sigma_w^2} \right), \tag{2.7}$$

where the σ^2 terms are the true (not estimated) variances. Note that

$$\lim_{\sigma_w \to \infty} E(\hat{\beta}) = 0. \tag{2.8}$$

This means that with greater variance of the measurement error in the x, the estimated coefficient is pushed closer and closer to zero, and we are faced with attenuation bias. Deaton (1997, p. 99) shows how the inclusion of additional correctly measured regressors will generally make the bias worse.

It is not clear how serious these effects are in practice, but here is a simple experiment. Using the observations on 9,189 households from the 2006 Vietnam Living Standards Survey, we regressed the log of food consumption per capita on the log of expenditure per capita. The results are shown in the top panel of Table 2.1, and show a food elasticity of 0.652. Now we introduce an additive random normal

Table 2.1 Illustrating the effects of measurement error

	Coefficient	t-statistic	Adjusted R^2
Panel 1: Dependent variable ln(food/cap)			
Constant	−0.230	−32.7	0.732
Ln(expenditure/cap)	0.652	159.3	
Panel 2: Dependent variable ln(food/cap) + error			
Constant	−0.228	−25.1	0.623
Ln(expenditure/cap)	0.652	122.2	
Panel 3: Dependent variable ln(food/cap)			
Constant	−0.129	−16.9	0.661
Ln(expenditure/cap) + error	0.589	133.9	

Notes: 9,189 observations on households, from the Vietnam Living Standards Survey of 2006. Panel 2 adds an error distributed $N(0,0.2)$ to the dependent variable; panel 3 adds an error distributed $N(0,0.02)$ to the independent variable. The mean value of the dependent variable is 1.606, with a standard deviation of 0.614; for the independent variable these are 0.817 and 0.468, respectively

error with mean 0 and standard deviation 0.2. In the second panel we add the shock only to the dependent variable; the equation fits less well, but the food elasticity remains the same (to three decimal places). In the third panel we add the shock only to the independent variable; again, the equation fits somewhat less well, but now the estimate of the food elasticity falls to 0.589, with an apparently tight 95% confidence interval of 0.580–0.598. Errors of the magnitude introduced here are entirely plausible for measures of income and expenditure; by ignoring them we may be lulled into a false sense of confidence in the precision of our estimates.

2.3.2   Omitted Variable Bias

It is rare that the fit of an equation based on cross-sectional survey data – as measured by R^2 – comes close to 1. In other words, variation in y is not completely "explained" by variation in the X variables. Measurement error aside, this suggests that there may be other explanatory variables, but we have not included them in the model for one reason or another – perhaps they are unobservable (like "ability"), or unobserved (the survey did not ask enough questions), or overlooked. The key point is that some variables, denoted by Z, have been omitted from the regression model. So instead of estimating

$$y = X\beta + Z\gamma + \tilde{e} \tag{2.9}$$

we actually estimate

$$y = X\beta + e. \tag{2.10}$$

In effect we have a compound error term here, because $e = \mathbf{Z}\gamma + \tilde{e}$. This need not interfere with the estimates $\hat{\beta}$ unless the values of the included variables ($\mathbf{X}$) are correlated with the omitted variables ($\mathbf{Z}$), in which case

$$E(\mathbf{Z}\gamma + \tilde{e}|\mathbf{X}) \neq 0,$$

violating the first classical assumption, and making $\hat{\beta}$ biased and inconsistent.

Suppose we are trying to measure the effect of fertilizer on farm rice yields, and estimate

$$y = \beta_0 + \beta_1 X_1$$
$$\text{rice output (kg/ha)} = \beta_0 + \beta_1 \text{ fertilizer input (kg urea/ha)}$$

It is reasonable to think that more-capable and more-dynamic farmers make greater use of fertilizer (so $\mathrm{corr}(X_1 A_1) > 0$, where A_1 refers to ability), and also raise yields in other ways. Thus a better model would be

$$y = \beta_0 + \beta_1 X_1 + \beta_2 A_1 + \tilde{e}.$$

It can be shown that

$$E(\hat{\beta}_1) = \beta_1 + \beta_2 \sigma_{X_1 A_1},$$

where $\sigma_{X_1 A_1}$ is the covariance between fertilizer use and (unobserved) ability. In this case, our estimated $\hat{\beta}$ is too large; it is in effect picking up not only the influence of fertilizer use on rice output, but also some of the effect of ability on rice output.

Since almost every model leaves out some relevant variables, omitted-variable bias is pervasive. But is it destructive? There is no simple answer to this, and no substitute for judgment, necessarily on a case-by-case basis. Unfortunately, many omitted variables are unobservable, so one can only speculate about their possible influence on the coefficient estimates.

With panel data it is sometimes possible to attenuate the effects of time-invariant unobservables. Suppose we have information on the rice crop (y) for farmer i for 2 years ($t = 1,2$), and that as before, the crop depends on fertilizer input (X) and the farmer's ability (A). Then we have

$$y_{it} = \beta_0 + \beta_1 X_{1it} + \beta_2 A_{1it} + \tilde{e}_{it}. \tag{2.11}$$

If A_{1it} ("ability") does not vary over time, then using the time difference operator Δ we have

$$\Delta y_i = \beta_1 \Delta X_{1i} + \Delta \tilde{e}_i, \tag{2.12}$$

and we have purged the data of the unobservable. This is essentially the same as using fixed effects – for instance, a different intercept for each farmer – to sweep away the influence of unobservables. In practice, household-level panel data are relatively uncommon, and the effects of unobservables cannot always be washed out so easily; we return to these issues in Chap. 9, which deals more thoroughly with panel data.

One can test whether more variables should be included in a regression model by adding the variables to the right-hand side and applying an F test of the null hypothesis that the coefficients are zero. An attractive alternative approach to model building is to use an information criterion: models with more variables have a higher likelihood, but some penalty is appropriate in order to ensure parsimony. In Stata, the Akaike Information Criterion (AIC) is given by

$$\text{AIC} : -2\ln L + 2K,$$

where L is the likelihood and K is the number of parameters (including the constant), and the Bayesian Information Criterion (BIC) is defined as

$$\text{BIC} : -2\ln L + K\ln N,$$

where N is the total number of observations. Defined thus, smaller values of the AIC or BIC reflect a "better" model. The AIC tends to overfit, so the BIC is usually the preferred measure (Haughton 1988).

Some scientists, especially in biostatistics, commonly include in their models only variables that are statistically significant at some level (e.g., $p < 0.05$). Stepwise commands, that either trim nonsignificant variables, or add variables from a predetermined list, do this automatically. Most economists prefer to leave, in their models, all the variables that they believe, from theory or experience, to be relevant. This reduces the risk of inconsistent parameter estimates, but also reduces the observed precision of the estimates.

2.3.3   Multicolinearity

Multicolinearity is present when two or more of the right-hand variables in a multiple regression are highly linearly related. In the case where the right-hand variables are completely uncorrelated with one another – i.e., they are mutually orthogonal – then a set of separate simple regressions would yield the same coefficients (except for the constant terms) as a multiple regression that includes all the independent variables. However, this situation almost never arises in practice, which implies that there is nearly always some degree of colinearity among the regressors.

For instance, the nutritional status of a child – measured perhaps by standardized height-for-age, which reflects stunting – may be influenced by the educational achievements of the parents (which we may define as A_M for the mother and A_F for the father). A basic model would then look like

$$y_i = \beta_0 + \beta_1 A_M + \beta_2 A_F + e. \tag{2.13}$$

However, well-educated men tend to marry well-educated women, so A_M and A_F are likely to be correlated (Haughton and Haughton 1997).

Multicolinearity does not hurt the fit of the overall equation, but it makes the coefficient estimates imprecise and inaccurate.

A tight-fitting equation where all the coefficient estimates are barely significantly different from zero is a sure sign that multicolinearity is a problem, as is the case where we cannot reject the null hypotheses that the individual coefficients are zero, but we do reject the null hypothesis that the coefficients are jointly zero. Some researchers find it helpful to look at the *variance inflation factor* for each coefficient; this is defined as $1/(1 - R_{k.}^2)$, where $R_{k.}^2$ is the R^2 of a regression of variable x_k on all the other right-hand-side variables. High variance inflation factors – typically of 5 to 10 or above – indicate that multicolinearity is a potential problem. Before estimating a regression equation, it is good practice to look at a matrix of correlations among the independent variables. High (absolute) correlations indicate the potential for multicolinearity.

While multicolinearity is not a serious problem in time-series data if the goal is forecasting, it is not always easy to know what to do when it appears in other contexts, including with cross-section data. If X_1 and X_2 are highly correlated, it is tempting to leave out X_1 (or X_2), but this is likely to generate omitted variable bias, which would then attribute the wrong amount of influence to X_1 (or X_2). The textbook solution is to try to find more data, but this is not usually realistic, especially with survey data, where one is presumably using all the data that are available. Greater precision may be possible with Bayesian techniques (see Chap. 8), which bring prior information to bear on the problem, or if theory can lead to a clearer specification of the relevant variables. As data become more available, and as variables multiply and data exploration proliferates, the problems posed by multicolinearity are likely to become more common.

2.3.4   Heteroscedasticity

The second classical regression assumption supposes that the errors in the regression model are homoscedastic; in other words, the errors come from a single distribution that is unrelated to any of the independent variables. When the error term does not have a constant variance we have heteroscedasticity.

In household survey data, the assumption of homoscedasticity is unrealistic. It is far more likely that the observations are distributed as in Fig. 2.1; at low levels of the independent variable X the observations are close to the line, but at higher levels of X the errors are more scattered. This is, of course, only one of the many possible forms that heteroscedasticity may take.

The estimated coefficients are not affected by the presence of heteroscedasticity, but the OLS standard errors will be understated, making the coefficient estimates appear to be more precise than they really are.

Sometimes a straightforward transformation of the data solves the problem. For instance, we know that the distribution of income per capita is highly skewed to the right; if income per capita is used directly as a dependent or independent variable,

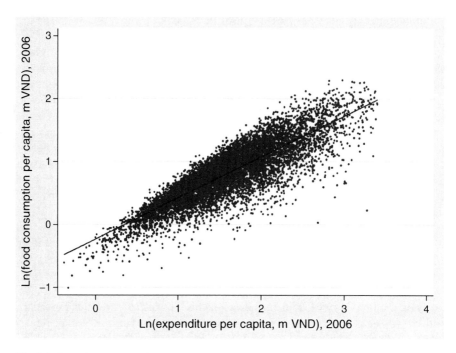

Fig. 2.4 Log of spending on food graphed against log of total spending, Vietnam, 2006. (*Source*: As for Fig. 2.1)

the errors also tend to be skewed (i.e., heteroscedastic). A log transformation of income per capita typically removes most of the skewness, although perhaps not all, since there is some evidence that at the upper end, income follows a Pareto distribution. Figure 2.4 log-transforms the variables from Fig. 2.1; the heteroscedasticity is a bit less apparent, but has by no means all disappeared.

2.3.4.1 Aside: Log Transformations

In passing, it is worth noting that if the dependent variable is in logarithmic form ($\ln y$), care must be taken when predicting values of y. Suppose the model we estimate is

$$\ln y = \mathbf{X}\beta + e. \qquad (2.14)$$

From this we can get the predicted value $\widehat{\ln y} = E(\ln y | \mathbf{X}) = \mathbf{X}\hat{\beta}$, but we are typically interested in recovering $E(y|\mathbf{X})$. It is not correct to take $\exp(\widehat{\ln y})$, because $\exp\{E(\ln y)\} \neq E(y)$.

Cameron and Trivedi (2009, p. 103) point out that (2.14) implies that $y = \exp(\mathbf{X}\beta)\exp(e)$, so

$$E(y_i|\mathbf{X}_i) = \exp(\mathbf{X}_i\beta)E\{\exp(e_i)\}. \tag{2.15}$$

If $e_i \sim N(0, \sigma^2)$, then $E\{\exp(e_i)\} = \exp(0.5\sigma^2)$, where we will need to estimate $\exp(0.5\sigma^2)$. Alternatively, if we assume that the e_i are independently and identically distributed (iid), $E\{\exp(e_i)\}$ may be estimated by $\sum_{j=1}^{N}\exp(\widehat{e_j})/N$. The relevant computations can be done easily enough in Stata, but are not generated automatically.

To illustrate, we return to our earlier example using 2006 Vietnamese household survey data, where we regressed the log of food consumption per capita on the log of expenditure per capita. We have the following (in millions of dong per capita per year):

Mean value of food spending (i.e., y):	2.540
$\exp(\widehat{\ln y})$:	2.467 (incorrect)
$\exp(\widehat{\ln y}) \times \exp(0.5\sigma^2)$:	2.539
$\exp(\widehat{\ln y}) \times \left(\sum_{j=1}^{N}\exp(\widehat{e_j})/N\right)$:	2.536

By failing to transform correctly from logs to levels, our estimate of food spending would be off by about 3% in this case.

2.3.4.2 Testing for Heteroscedasticity

It is possible to test for heteroscedasticity in a number of ways. White (1980) proposed regressing the squared residuals on the regressors, their squares, and their cross-products; a Lagrange Multiplier test for significance then tests for the presence of any statistically significant patterns. In Stata, just type whitetst after running a regression in order to perform this test. It rejects the hypothesis of homoscedasticity for the regressions that are graphed in Figs. 2.1 and 2.4. Breusch and Pagan (1979) allow the researcher to control the variables that are considered likely to cause any heteroscedasticity, but their test is otherwise simple to execute (see the downloadable bpagan command in Stata). With large sample sizes, these tests will often reject homoscedasticity, even if it is not a major problem in practice.

It has now become almost standard practice, when using cross-sectional data, to (at a minimum) adjust for heteroscedasticity using White's estimator. Table 2.2 shows the formula for the variance–covariance matrix in the homoscedastic case (the usual default), and for White's robust estimator. The table also shows the formula for the variance–covariance matrix when the observations may be considered to be clustered, a subject we return to in the next section.

In Stata, the robust estimate of the variance–covariance matrix is obtained by adding vce(robust) to the regress command, as in

```
regress y X1 X2 X3, vce(robust)
```

The adjustment for heteroscedasticity can make a difference, especially when the sample size is not particularly large. Consider the numbers shown in Table 2.3.

Table 2.2 Standard and robust measurement of the variance–covariance matrix

	Variance–covariance matrix – i.e., $\hat{V}(\hat{\beta})$	Stata command
Standard	$s^2(\mathbf{X'X})^{-1} = \left(\frac{1}{N-k}\sum_i \hat{u}_i^2\right)(\mathbf{X'X})^{-1}$	[default]
Robust (White)	$(\mathbf{X'X})^{-1}\left(\frac{N}{N-k}\sum_i \hat{u}_i^2\mathbf{x}_i\mathbf{x'}_i\right)(\mathbf{X'X})^{-1}$	vce(robust)
Clustering	$(\mathbf{X'X})^{-1}\left(\frac{G}{G-1}\frac{N}{N-k}\sum_g \mathbf{x}_g\hat{\mathbf{u}}_g\hat{\mathbf{u}}'_g\mathbf{x'}_g\right)(\mathbf{X'X})^{-1}$	vce(cluster var1)

Notes: Based on a linear regression of the form $\mathbf{y} = \mathbf{X}\beta + \mathbf{e}$ and residuals $\hat{u}_i = y_i - \mathbf{X}_i\hat{\beta}$. In the case of clustering, there are G clusters denoted by g, $\hat{\mathbf{u}}_g$ is the vector of residuals for the gth cluster, and the matrix of regressors for the observations in the gth cluster is given by $\mathbf{x}_g$. "var1" refers to the variable that is used for clustering, often the primary sampling unit (PSU) such as a village. N is the number of observations, and k the number of variables in the model, including the constant

Table 2.3 Comparing estimators

Estimator used	Spending per capita	Spending squared	Motorbikes per capita
OLS			
Coefficient	0.380	−0.005	0.421
Standard error	0.020	0.001	0.177
p-value	0.000	0.000	0.018
White's robust estimator: vce(robust)			
Coefficient	0.380	−0.005	0.421
Standard error	0.035	0.002	0.321
p-value	0.000	0.031	0.195
Clustering by commune: vce(cluster comm)			
Coefficient	0.380	−0.005	0.412
Standard error	0.022	0.001	0.180
p-value	0.000	0.000	0.023
Sample weights and clustering: svy: reg			
Coefficient	0.390	−0.005	0.412
Standard error	0.022	0.001	0.180
p-value	0.000	0.000	0.023
Robust, bootstrapped s.e.: vce(bootstrap, rep(1000)			
Coefficient	0.380	−0.005	0.421
Standard error	0.042	0.003	0.330
p-value	0.000	0.095	0.202
Robust, bootstrapped s.e., clustering: vce(bootstrap, rep(1000) strata(tinh) cluster(comm))			
Coefficient	0.380	−0.005	0.421
Standard error	0.033	0.003	0.278
p-value	0.000	0.068	0.129

Notes: Dependent variable is food spending (in millions of dong per capita per year). The same variables and data are used in each of these estimates. Based on 582 observations from the Central Highlands region of Vietnam, from the Vietnam Living Standards Survey of 2006. $R^2 = 0.755$ for the OLS regression. Estimates of the constant terms are not shown here

Each triplet of rows shows the coefficients, standard errors, and p-values, for a model of food consumption based on a sample of 582 households in the Central Highlands region of Vietnam in 2006. This is a subsample of the larger Vietnam Living Standards Survey. The model shows food expenditure per capita as a function of total household expenditure per capita, expenditure per capita squared, and a proxy for household wealth given by the number of motorbikes owned per household member. In shorthand, the model is:

$$\text{Food/cap} = a + b\,\text{Exp/cap} + c(\text{Exp/cap})^2 + d\,\text{Motorbikes/cap} \qquad (2.16)$$

The model is likely incomplete, but the purpose here is to illustrate the importance of using the right estimation method.

The first set of results are estimated using plain vanilla OLS. All the coefficients are statistically significant at the 5% level or better, and the fit is solid. But White's test shows heteroscedasticity. The second group of results have been estimated using a robust Huber/White/sandwich estimator. The coefficients are unchanged, but the standard errors are larger, so the t-statistics are smaller. Now the p-values show that the motorbikes/capita variable is not statistically significant. The correction for heteroscedasticity mattered. We will return to this example below in the context of clustering, and weighted regression.

2.3.5 Clustering

Almost every household survey uses a design that involves clustering. The primary sampling unit (PSU) is typically a village or ward, and 10–20 households are chosen for sampling from within each PSU. The problem here is that there are likely to be features of a village, possibly unobserved, that influence all the households in the village together; for instance, if there is a local flood, all villagers may suffer together, or if the local school is good, all the children may achieve excellent test scores. The existence of village-specific effects means that the errors (e_i) of households in a given village will tend to be similar – perhaps they are all too high, or all too low, at the same time.

This violates the third classical assumption, of conditionally uncorrelated observations. While the OLS estimates will not be biased, the OLS standard errors will be too small and the estimates will seem to be more precise than they really are.

The solution is to use a cluster-robust estimator of the variance–covariance matrix of the estimator. In Stata (version 10 or higher), this involves appending vce(cluster clustervar) to the regress command, where clustervar defines the PSU. This estimator also corrects for heteroscedasticity, and should almost always be used with household survey data.

To illustrate the importance of taking clustering into account we return to the model of food consumption in the Central Region of Vietnam, developed above in Sect. 2.3.4. Households were surveyed in clusters at the level of individual communes, and so we allowed for the errors to be correlated within, but not across, these communes. The results are shown in the third group of numbers in Table 2.3; again, the coefficients are unchanged, but the t-statistics are lower than with OLS, as we would expect. With this adjustment, the motorbikes/cap variable is still statistically significantly different from zero, as in the OLS estimation.

An alternative approach to dealing with inference in the presence of heteroscedasticity and clustering is to bootstrap the standard errors. The results of doing this for the food consumption data are also shown in Table 2.3, in panels 5 (for a simple bootstrap) and 6 (for a bootstrap that takes the clustering into account). In both cases the motorbikes/cap variable is not statistically significant. A fuller discussion of the bootstrap is given in Chap. 12.

While clustering at the PSU level is pervasive in household survey data, it may also need to be taken into account at other levels. For instance, a study of child nutrition may have information on siblings; it is likely that they share features that are not fully captured by the model, which implies that the errors may be correlated within households. In this context the household itself is a form of cluster.

2.3.6   Outliers

When using survey data, especially data that may not have been thoroughly cleaned, it is not uncommon to encounter outliers. These are observations with an unusual value for either y and/or x. Sometimes they are simply typos – perhaps someone entered 34 instead of 3.4, or an enumerator entered values as percentages (29, 56, etc.) while another entered them as proportions (0.29, 0.56, etc.).

Box-and-whisker plots – discussed more fully in Chap. 1 – can be helpful in identifying outliers. Figure 2.5 shows such plots for data on gross domestic product (GDP) per capita for each of the (then) 53 provinces of Vietnam for 1993. The left-hand panel shows all of the observations, and it is clear that one observation lies far above any of the others; the right-hand panel excludes this outlier, and the result is a more standard-looking plot.

Outliers can have a large impact on regression estimates. Using the same Vietnamese provincial data as in Fig. 2.5, an OLS regression of tax collections per capita on GDP per capita, employing the full data set, yields

$$\text{Taxcap} = -0.806 + 0.647 \text{ gdpcap}$$

$$t = -11.4 \quad t = 21.4 \qquad\qquad \bar{R}^2 = 0.898$$

where "t" refers to the t-statistic. On the other hand, if the outlier is excluded, we get a very different equation:

$$\text{Taxcap} = -0.278 + 0.283 \text{ gdpcap}$$

$$t = -4.73 \quad t = 8.02 \qquad\qquad \bar{R}^2 = 0.554.$$

In this case, the lines corresponding to these two estimated equations are shown in Fig. 2.6 along with the underlying data.

Fig. 2.5 Box-and-Whisker
Plots, provincial GDP/capita,
Vietnam 1993

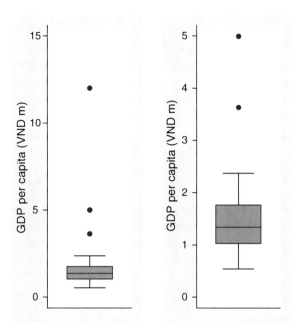

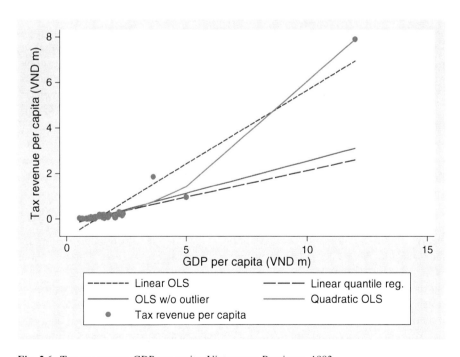

Fig. 2.6 Tax revenue vs. GDP per capita, Vietnamese Provinces, 1993

After the obvious errors have been corrected, there may still be some observations that seem somewhat extreme, and one is left with the problem of what to do. A good next step is to determine whether the outliers are influential enough to matter. There are two distinct concepts here: An *influential observation* is one that, if omitted, leads to an appreciable change in one or more of the coefficient estimates. An *observation with high leverage* is far away from the mean value of the X variable, and so potentially weighs heavily in the estimation of the coefficients.

We may illustrate this with the help of Fig. 2.7, where the top left panel presents the observations from a hypothetical dataset with homoscedastic errors. In Case 1, shown in the top right panel, there is an outlier that has a high value for both X and Y; this outlier has high leverage, but it does not affect the estimated line much, and so has low influence. Case 2, in the southwest panel, shows an outlier that has low leverage, but is somewhat influential, as it pulls the best-fit line down quite noticeably. And in Case 3, in the fourth panel, the outlier has a substantial influence on the estimated line, which makes it influential, even though it does not have a lot of leverage. Figure 2.7 also shows the p-value the Breusch–Pagan test of heteroscedasticity – a low value means that there is clear evidence of heteroskedasticity – as well as a measure of influence (the dfits number), and of leverage.

The leverage h_i of observation i is the ith diagonal entry of the hat matrix

$$H = X(X'X)^{-1}X'. \tag{2.16}$$

The predicted value of y is $\widehat{y} = Hy$, so a large value for h_i implies that observation y_i has a large influence on the predicted value. In Stata it is straightforward to get the values of leverage by typing `predict leverage` after the `regress` command.

A popular measure of influence is dfits$_i$ ("difference in fits"): obtain the predicted value $\widehat{y}_i$ using an OLS regression with, and then without, the ith observation, and take the difference. Cameron and Trivedi (2009, p. 92) suggest that if $|\text{dfits}| > 2\sqrt{K/N}$, then the observation is influential and merits closer examination. Strictly, the dfits measure is only applicable if we can assume homoscedastic errors, and such an assumption is rarely plausible with cross-section data. Nonetheless, the dfits measure can be helpful in practice.

Now we may return to our real-world example, based on data for the provinces of Vietnam in 1993. The median value of leverage 0.08, the standard deviation 1.04, the minimum -0.46, and the maximum 6.95. The relatively high maximum suggests that there is a potential problem with that observation. For this same example, the dfits threshold is 0.39; the actual values range from -1.82 to 23.10, but these are the only two values outside the threshold. Once again we appear to have at least one observation with large influence.

One commonly used solution to the problem of outliers is to truncate the dataset – by excluding the top and bottom 2% of y values, for instance – and estimating the model on the remaining observations. This is only reasonable if we believe that

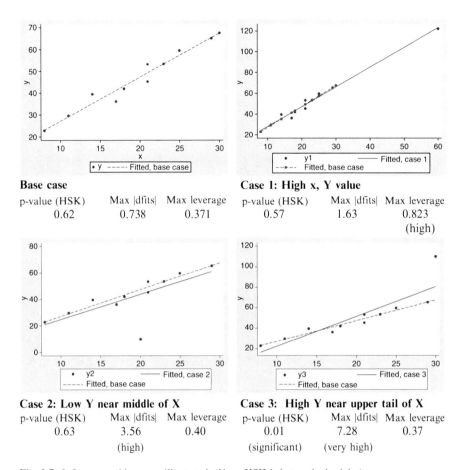

Base case

p-value (HSK)	Max |dfits|	Max leverage
0.62	0.738	0.371

Case 1: High x, Y value

p-value (HSK)	Max |dfits|	Max leverage
0.57	1.63	0.823
		(high)

Case 2: Low Y near middle of X

p-value (HSK)	Max |dfits|	Max leverage
0.63	3.56	0.40
	(high)	

Case 3: High Y near upper tail of X

p-value (HSK)	Max |dfits|	Max leverage
0.01	7.28	0.37
(significant)	(very high)	

Fig. 2.7 Influence and leverage illustrated. (*Note*: HSK is heteroskedasticity)

the observations at the extremes are uninformative, for instance because they are considered to be noisy. On the other hand, the extreme observations may often be the most informative ones, which argues against truncating the data too often.

This interpretive problem arises with the Vietnamese data. The outlier is not the result of a typo; it shows the GDP and tax revenue (per capita) for the province of Ba Ria/Vung Tau. This is where most of Vietnam's offshore oil wells are located, and their production, and the tax revenue collected from the oil producers, are included in the statistics for the province. Certainly, one can argue that the situation is anomalous, which would justify ignoring the outlier. On the other hand, the GDP and tax revenues are real, and may have policy lessons that would be missed if the outlier were excluded.

2.3.6.1 Quantile Regression

Another popular regression technique is quantile regression, which has the advantage of being robust to outliers. In a model such as

$$y = \mathbf{X}\beta + e$$

we may think of ordinary least squares as estimating the conditional mean, so $E(Y|\mathbf{X}) = \mathbf{X}\beta$. The OLS estimate, $\hat{\beta}$, of the coefficients are obtained by minimizing the sum of the squared residuals $\sum_{i=1}^{N} \hat{e}_i^2 = \sum_{i=1}^{N} \left(y_i - \mathbf{X}_i\hat{\beta}\right)^2$. Outliers typically generate large values of $\hat{e}_i$, which are exaggerated by squaring, and so have considerable influence on the $\hat{\beta}$.

In the same spirit, we may think of quantile regression as estimating the pth percentile $(Y|\mathbf{X}) = \mathbf{X}\beta$. An important special case is that of the 50th percentile (or 50th quantile); this gives us median regression, which finds the $\hat{\beta}$ by minimizing the sum of the absolute deviations $\sum_{i=1}^{N} |y_i - \mathbf{X}_i\beta|$. The estimates β in this case are less prone than in OLS estimates to being affected by outliers.

Other quantiles are possible: the qth quantile $(q \in (0, 1))$ is the value of y that divides the data so that a proportion q of values are below it and $1 - q$ values above it. When $q = 0.5$, we put the same weight on observations above the median as below it. But if $q = 0.75$, for instance, we will put more weight on observations where $y \geq \mathbf{X}\beta$ than on those for which $y < \mathbf{X}\beta$.

Quantile regression may be implemented straightforwardly in Stata using the `qreg` command; the `bsqreg` version generates bootstrap standard errors (see Chap. 11 for further details about bootstrapping) that allow the standard errors to vary across observations. This is analogous to the use of robust estimation with OLS. The use of quantile regression with panel data is more difficult; we return to this in Chap. 9.

In Fig. 2.8 we show the same data as in Fig. 2.1, where each point represents a household surveyed by the Vietnam Household Living Standards Survey in 2006; the curves show the results of regressing food expenditure per capita on expenditure per capita, and its square. The top curve is the 75th quantile regression line, the bottom curve is the 25th quantile regression line, and the median regression is shown by the solid curve in the middle. The mean regression, based on OLS, is shown by the dotted line. It is clear that all these curves have somewhat different intercepts and curvature.

If the errors are homoscedastic, then the slopes of different quantile regressions should not vary, although the intercepts will. On the other hand, if the slopes do differ, this reflects the presence of heteroskedasticity, as illustrated in Fig. 2.8. It can be helpful to estimate the coefficients of a particular model using each quantile regression – for instance, for percentiles at $10, 20, \ldots, 90\%$ – and to graph the estimates and associated standard errors, as done in Fig. 2.9. This example comes from Thailand, where Boonperm et al. (2011) use data from the 2004 Socioeconomic Survey to estimate the effect of borrowing from the Village Fund – a major, decentralized, microcredit scheme – on household incomes. The dependent variable is the log of

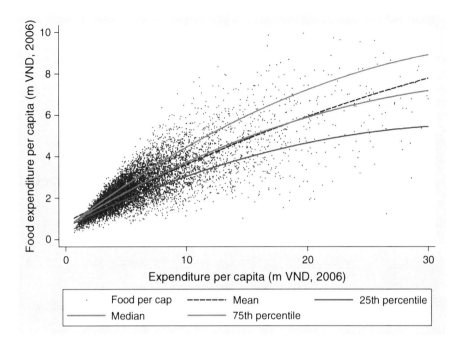

Fig. 2.8 Mean and percentile regressions of food per capita on expenditure per capita, Vietnam, 2006. (*Source*: As for Fig. 2.1)

income per capita, and the independent variable of interest is a dummy variable that equals 1 if the household borrowed from the Village Fund. The coefficient on this treatment variable should measure the impact of borrowing on income, and we are interested in knowing whether it varies across income groups.

Figure 2.9 shows that the average impact of Village Fund borrowing on incomes was a bit above 4%, and varied from 6% at the 10th percentile to just over 3% at the 90th percentile. In other words, this particular microcredit scheme appears to be relatively more influential when the borrower is poor rather than affluent.

An important use of quantile regression is to measure the differences in the marginal impact of policies across income or expenditure groups. A recent example of a distributional analysis of this nature appears in Gamper-Rabindran et al. (2010), who find that, in Brazil, the provision of piped water is particularly effective at reducing infant mortality in areas where the infant mortality rate is especially high (and, typically, incomes relatively low).

2.3.7 Simultaneity

When using regression for inference, we typically assume a direction of causality. For instance, in

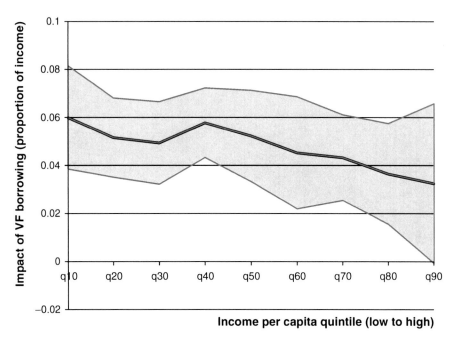

Fig. 2.9 Estimated coefficients from quantile regressions of income per capita on village fund borrowing, Thailand 2004. (*Source*: Thailand Socioeconomic Survey of 2004)

$$\text{Income} = a + b \text{ (years of education)} + c \text{ (years of experience)} + e \qquad (2.17)$$

we suppose that more education or experience causes higher income. We defer a fuller discussion of causality to Chap. 5, but two points are worth noting here. First, income, education, and experience may themselves be driven by an outside influence, such as a person's ability; in this case the model in (2.17) has been mis-specified. The second point is that to some extent income may lead to more education (such as adult training) or experience (because high-income individuals are more likely to stay in the labor force), rather than be the outcome of these inputs.

Formally, the problem is that simultaneity such as observed here violates classical assumption 2, which states that $E(e_i^2|\mathbf{X}_i) = \sigma^2$. A positive shock ($e_i > 0$) implies a higher value of y_i, but if y_i in turn influences $\mathbf{X}_i$, then e_i and $\mathbf{X}_i$ will be correlated. The $\mathbf{X}_i$ are no longer exogenous, the OLS estimator is inconsistent, and the estimated coefficients (the $\hat{\beta}$) cannot be interpreted as measuring the effect of an exogenous change in $\mathbf{X}$ on a dependent variable y.

Where simultaneity is a concern, one may want to re-think the model. The addition of plenty of other predetermined variables can also attenuate the effects of simultaneity. But probably the most common line of attack is to use instrumental variables, which can also reduce bias related to omitted variables and measurement error.

2.3.7.1 Instrumental Variables

The intuition behind instrumental variables (IV) estimation may be seen as follows. For the ith observation, let y_{1i} be the dependent variable of interest, X_i be a vector of K_1 exogenous regressors, and Y_{2i} be a vector of M other endogenous regressors – sometimes referred to as the "troublesome regressors" (Murray 2005). Following Cameron and Trivedi (2009, p. 173), we have the following structural equation:

$$y_{1i} = Y_{2i}\beta_1 + X_{1i}\beta_2 + e_i, \quad i = 1,\ldots,N. \tag{2.18}$$

The problem is that while the e_i are uncorrelated with the X_{1i}, they are correlated with the Y_{2i} (by construction, since this is the problem we are addressing).

Now suppose that we can find some additional variables X_2 that are correlated with the Y_2 but not with the error term in (2.18). Then we could regress each Y_2 variable on the X_2 (and X_1), and use the predicted values from this first stage (i.e., the $\hat{Y}_2$) in place of the Y_2 when estimating (2.18). These $\hat{Y}_2$ should be uncorrelated with the e_i – the components that were correlated with the e_i were purged in the first stage – so the second classical regression assumption now holds, and the $\hat{\beta}$ are no longer inconsistent. This is an asymptotic result, however, and IV estimation may not yield good results in small samples.

Formally, the probability limit of the OLS estimator in the case of simple regression is given by (Larcker and Rusticus 2010):

$$\text{plim}\, b_{\text{OLS}} = \beta + \frac{\text{cov}(x,e)}{\text{var}(x)} = \beta + \frac{\sigma_e}{\sigma_x}\text{corr}(x,e), \tag{2.19}$$

where σ_e and σ_x are the standard deviations of e and x respectively. When the correlation between x and the true error is zero, OLS generates a consistent estimate of β. Now if we use an instrument z for x, we will only obtain a consistent estimate of β if

$$\text{plim}\, b_{\text{IV}} = \beta + \frac{\text{cov}(z,e)}{\text{cov}(z,x)} = \beta + \frac{\sigma_e}{\sigma_x}\frac{\text{corr}(z,e)}{\text{corr}(z,x)}. \tag{2.20}$$

From (2.19) and (2.20), it follows that IV will only be less biased asymptotically than OLS if $R_{ze}^2 < R_{xz}^2 R_{xe}^2$, where the R^2 terms refer to squared population correlations; this is not a trivial requirement in practice. It is worth noting too that there is a loss in efficiency when one uses instrumental variables. The asymptotic mean square error of the IV estimate of β is given by

$$\text{asy mse}_{\text{IV}} = \left(\sigma_e^2/n\sigma_x^2\right)\left(1/R_{xz}^2\right)\left(1 + nR_{ze}^2\right) \tag{2.21}$$

(from Bartels, as in Larcker and Rusticus 2010), where n is the sample size. The first term gives the mean square error (MSE) for ordinary least squares; if there is no bias, $\text{corr}(z,e) = 0$; but if $R^2_{xz} = 0.25$, which is entirely plausible in practice, the estimate of the IV standard error will be twice as large as the one generated by ordinary least squares.

Larcker and Rusticus examine the use of IV estimation in the context of models that seek to explain the cost of capital. The problem here is that corporate disclosure of this information is voluntary, so OLS estimates risk being biased. However, they find, using relatively standard data, that the IV estimates may be just as seriously biased as the OLS ones.

The Larker and Rusticus results point to something that is increasingly recognized: Instrumental variables estimation, while mechanically straightforward – for instance, on can use the `ivregress` command in Stata – is hard to pull off successfully in practice. It can be very difficult to find variables that are instrumentally relevant – i.e., influence the Y_2 enough to be "strong" instruments – while also being valid (i.e., uncorrelated with the e_i or, put another way, have no direct influence on y_1). Instrumental relevance is testable, from the correlations between the Y_2 and X_2, but validity is not, because the true regression errors (the e_i) are unobservable.

Ultimately, IV estimation requires creativity, and the persuasiveness of IV estimates is only as strong as the case that can be made for the appropriateness of the choice of instrument.

For IV estimation to work, one needs at least as many instruments as there are endogenous right-hand variables. When there are just enough instruments, we have standard IV estimation; with extra instruments, the model is overidentified, and we get more efficiency by using two-stage least squares, or a variant of the generalized method of moments (GMM).

It is common to test whether the Y_2 variables are indeed endogenous. The underlying principle, due to Hausman, is simple: if the OLS and IV estimators vary by little, then the instrument is not needed. The Hausman test statistic for a single potentially endogenous regressor is distributed $\chi^2(1)$, and is given by

$$T_{\text{H}} = \frac{\left(\hat{\beta}_{\text{IV}} - \hat{\beta}_{\text{OLS}}\right)^2}{\hat{V}(\hat{\beta}_{\text{IV}} - \hat{\beta}_{\text{OLS}})}. \tag{2.22}$$

This test is contingent on the choice of a particular set of instruments, and in that sense does not provide an absolute measure of whether IV estimation is needed.

An interesting example of the use of instrumental variables estimation comes from an article by Narayan and Pritchett (1999), who ask whether "social capital" raises incomes or spending in rural Tanzania. The data come from a Social Capital and Poverty Survey that was undertaken in 1995 as part of a wider poverty assessment; it was merged with data from a 1993 Human Resource Development Survey that covered the same villages (but not the same individuals). Households were asked about their membership in groups and associations; the nature of these bodies; and about values and attitudes, including trust toward strangers. Narayan and Pritchett constructed an index of social capital by combining the number of groups to which a typical household belonged with characteristics of the groups (and in particularly how broad or inclusive the groups were). There was usable information on 1,376 households from 87 clusters (i.e., villages).

An OLS regression of household spending (HHE) on the index of social capital (SK), using 53 village-level averages, gave the following:

$$HHE = 0.119.SK + \text{other terms for exogenous variables}$$
$$t = 1.80; \qquad\qquad \text{Adjusted } R^2 = 0.272$$

There does seem to be an association between social capital and per capita spending, but which comes first? Can we reasonably say that social capital causes higher spending (and incomes), or does causality run in the other direction?

Narayan and Pritchett argue that the variable that measures "trust in strangers" (TIS) is unlikely to be caused by affluence, and on these grounds they use it as an instrument for social capital. In other words, they regress SK on TIS (and the other exogenous variables) and use the predicted value of SK (SKhat) instead of actual SK in the spending equation. The result is as follows:

$$HHE = 0.496 \text{ SKhat} + \text{other terms for exogenous variables}$$
$$t = 2.75$$

This is a stronger result than that of the OLS regression. They interpret it as showing that social capital causes more household spending, rather than the reverse; and argue that the smaller coefficient in the OLS regression reflects large measurement error in social capital, which biased that coefficient toward zero.

Whether the instrumental variables result is plausible is a matter of judgment. Perhaps more affluent villages are less wary of strangers, in which case the instrument is not exogenous. It was also less successful in the household-level (as opposed to village-level) estimates relating social capital to expenditure.

2.4   Conclusion

The literature on regression is vast, so in this chapter we have chosen to emphasize those aspects of the subject that, in our experience, are important, yet sometimes overlooked.

An appreciation of the power and limitations of regression comes with practice. This chapter gets one going; the rest of the book goes beyond basic regression applied to cross-sectional data, and introduces a wide variety of other techniques that are helpful in the study of living standards survey data.

References

Boonperm, Jirawan, Jonathan Haughton, and Shahidur R. Khandker. 2011. Does the village fund matter in Thailand? Suffolk University, Boston.

Breusch, T., and A. Pagan. 1979. A simple test for heteroscedasticity and random coefficient variation. *Econometrica* 47: 1287–1294.

Cameron, Colin, and Pravin Trivedi. 2009. *Microeconometrics using Stata*. College Station: Stata Press.

Deaton, Angus. 1997. *The analysis of household surveys: A microeconometric approach to development policy*. Baltimore: Johns Hopkins University Press.

Gamper-Rabindran, Shanti, Shakeep Khan, and Christopher Timmins. 2010. The impact of piped water provision on infant mortality in Brazil: A quantile panel data approach. *Journal of Development Economics* 92: 188–200.

Greene, William. 2011. *Econometric analysis*, 7th ed. Upper Saddle River: Prentice Hall.

Haughton, Dominique. 1988. On the choice of a model to fit data from an exponential family. *Annals of Statistics* 16: 342–355.

Haughton, Dominique, and Jonathan Haughton. 1997. Explaining child nutrition in Vietnam. *Economic Development and Cultural Change* 45(3): 541–556.

Haughton, Jonathan, and Shahidur Khandker. 2009. *Handbook on poverty and inequality*. Washington, DC: World Bank.

Larcker, David F., and Tjomme O. Rusticus. 2010. On the use of instrumental variables in accounting research. *Journal of Accounting and Economics* 49(3): 186–205.

Murray, Michael P. 2005. *The bad, the weak, and the ugly: Avoiding the pitfalls of instrumental variables estimation*. Lewiston: Bates College.

Narayan, Deepa, and Lant Pritchett. 1999. Cents and sociability: household income and social capital in rural Tanzania. *Economic Development and Cultural Change* 47(4): 871–897.

White, H. 1980. A heteroscedasticity-consistent covariance matrix estimator and a direct test for heteroscedasticity. *Econometrica* 48: 817–838.

Chapter 3
Sampling

3.1 Introduction

Household survey data are generated by sampling, and cannot be interpreted successfully unless the sampling has been done correctly.

Possibly the most famous case of sampling gone awry was a survey undertaken in 1936 by the *Literary Digest*, a popular general-interest weekly magazine in the USA. The Digest was interested in predicting the outcome of the 1936 general election, where the two leading candidates were Alf Landon (Republican) and Franklin Delano Roosevelt (Democrat). The magazine polled more than ten million people, getting back 2.4 million responses. Based on the poll results, it predicted that Landon would win by a large margin (55%); in fact, Roosevelt won in a landslide, with 61% of the vote.

What went wrong? One problem was the sample frame: the Digest polled its own readers, as well as registered automobile owners and households with telephones. All three groups were comparatively affluent (in the 1930s), and more likely to vote Republican. The low response rate – less than 25% – was also a concern, because it is plausible that respondents who were sufficiently wealthy or well-educated to mail in their responses also leaned toward the Republican candidate.

At the same time as the Digest poll, George Gallup correctly predicted the results of the election to within about 1 percentage point, using a sample of 50,000. A 1937 Gallup poll that asked respondents about their participation in the Digest survey confirmed the presence of response bias in the Digest poll. The Gallup Organization now employs more than 2,000 people; the Literary Digest went out of business in 1938.

Another celebrated example of results that are based on misleading sampling may be found in *Women and Love: A Cultural Revolution in Progress* (1987). The author, Shere Hite, whose books have sold over 48 million copies, based her findings on 4,500 responses to a questionnaire that was distributed to about 100,000 women. Based on the results of the survey, Hite claimed that 70% of women "are having" extramarital sex.

D. Haughton and J. Haughton, *Living Standards Analytics*, Statistics for Social and Behavioral Sciences, DOI 10.1007/978-1-4614-0385-2_3,
© Springer Science+Business Media, LLC 2011

A COMMONLY USED METHOD IS ESPECIALLY PRONE TO BIAS: IT'S CALLED AN
opportunity SAMPLE. AVOIDING ALL
THE BOTHER OF DESIGNING A
PROCEDURE, THE OPPORTUNITY
SAMPLER JUST GRABS THE
FIRST n POPULATION UNITS
TO COME ALONG.

A CLASSIC EXAMPLE IS SHERE HITE'S BOOK, *WOMEN AND LOVE*. 100,000
QUESTIONNAIRES WENT TO WOMEN'S ORGANIZATIONS (AN *OPPORTUNITY
SAMPLE*), ONLY *4.5%* WERE FILLED OUT AND RETURNED (*RESPONSE BIAS*).
SO HER "RESULTS" WERE BASED ON A SAMPLE OF WOMEN WHO WERE HIGHLY
MOTIVATED TO ANSWER THE SURVEY'S QUESTIONS, FOR WHATEVER REASON.

Fig. 3.1 Opportunity samples and response bias (d'après Gonick and Smith 1993). (Text Copyright © 1993 by Woollcott Smith. Illustrations Copyright © 1993 by Larry Gonick. Reprinted by permission of HarperCollins Publishers)

The book has been highly influential, and struck a chord with many readers. But it has been criticized for claiming to be representative of US women at large. This is in part a sampling issue: most of the questionnaires were distributed by sending them to organizations such as church societies or women's groups and asking leaders to distribute them to members; others were sent to readers of her earlier books who wrote requesting copies. Hite thus used an opportunity sample rather than a random sample, as the cartoon in Fig. 3.1 makes clear.

The questionnaire was lengthy, with more than 400 questions, many of them open-ended, frequently nonneutral, and often vague. Hite estimates that it took the typical respondent 4½ hours to complete the questionnaire, which would deter all but the most determined respondent. She also made it clear that respondents did not need to answer all of the questions, so it is possible that there was substantial item nonresponse, although information on this is lacking. Smith (1989) argues that her substantive findings "must be considered problematic and questionable because of the methodology employed." Hite's response is that she succeeded in obtaining detailed and honest responses from people who might not have spoken about such delicate matters in any other forum.

The key point here is that sampling matters for the credibility of any survey. In this chapter we address some of the issues that arise in sample design and use.

3.2 Types of Sampling

3.2.1 Simple Random Sampling

The natural place to begin our review of sampling is with a simple random sample of n items from a large population. In this case, all sets of n items are equally likely to be chosen, which implies in turn that:

1. Each unit is equally likely to be chosen
2. The selection of one unit is independent of that of other units

The great strength of simple random sampling is that the samples are automatically representative, no matter which categorization of items. For instance, if we sample people, a simple random sample will be representative of gender, race, ethnic background, income, and so on, including categorizations we might not have thought about.

Although simple random samples are very powerful, they can be hard to implement. One of the main difficulties is the problem of obtaining a complete *sampling frame*, which is a list of all items in the population from which to sample. We return to this issue when discussing respondent-driven sampling for hard-to-reach populations in Sects. 3.6 and 3.7.

3.2.2 Stratified Sampling

A stratified sampling design involves dividing the population into relatively homogenous subpopulations, called *strata*, and then taking a simple (or cluster) random sample from each stratum. The fact that the strata tend to be more homogenous than the population implies, for a given sample size, a gain in accuracy, as measured by smaller standard errors. Strata can consist of geographical areas, such as provinces or regions, but can also consist of sociodemographic groups, defined according to dimensions such as gender or education.

3.2.3   Cluster Sampling

In a cluster sample, the population is divided into a large number of small areas, referred to as clusters, or primary sampling units (PSUs). A random sample of clusters is selected, and every item (or a large number of items) in the selected cluster examined. Because items inside a cluster tend to have correlated features, standard errors when the cluster sampling design is taken into account tend to be higher than for a simple random sample with the same sample size. One virtue of cluster sampling is that it is cheaper to implement than simple random sampling: within a village, for instance, one might survey a dozen households, which cuts down on travel and other logistical costs. Clusters may also be of interest in their own right, and sometimes clusters can be used to generate variables, such as food prices, that can be too noisy at the household level.

It is common, indeed almost standard, for household surveys to use stratified cluster sampling: first one identifies strata, and then PSUs within the strata, possibly with intervening layers too (villages within communes within counties within provinces, for instance). It is essential to adjust summary statistics and regression and other results to take the survey design into account. Fortunately, this has become relatively straightforward in the main statistical packages. In Sect. 3.4 we work through an example where we adjust standard errors for a stratified cluster design.

3.3   Sample Size

The question we want to address now is this: how large does a sample need to be in order to achieve a given level of precision in the results? The issue is covered well in most statistics textbooks, so we just summarize the basic ideas here, before addressing an under-appreciated problem, which is the tradeoff between sampling and nonsampling error.

Suppose that we wish to estimate a proportion (such as a poverty rate), with a margin of error of at most e and confidence 95%. Then the minimum necessary sample size will be

$$n_{\min} = \frac{1.96^2 p(1-p)}{e^2},\qquad(3.1)$$

where p is a prior guess of what the unknown proportion might be. When no such prior guess is available, taking p to be $(1/2)$ guarantees a conservative solution, since $p(1-p)$ is maximum for $p = 1/2$.

Equation (3.1) tells us that we would need a minimum sample size of 9,604 to estimate, for instance, a poverty rate to within one percentage point – that is, a margin of error of 0.01 – with confidence 95%. This is a relatively large sample, especially if we are trying to measure poverty at the level of a province or region, so the implication is that most poverty rates are not in practice measured with this degree of precision.

When the intention is to estimate a mean rather than a proportion, the minimum sample size needed for a margin of error e and a population standard deviation S (which one needs to guess at), at confidence 95%, is

$$n_{\min} = \left(\frac{1.96S}{e}\right)^2. \tag{3.2}$$

It should be noted that these expressions are valid for simple random samples; if the sampling design is more complicated, as is common in living standard surveys, the expressions need to be adjusted accordingly. Statistical packages such as Stata can now handle this easily.

We provide an example of a Bayesian determination of sample size in the context of an uncertain poverty line in Sect. 7.6.

3.3.1 Sampling vs. Nonsampling Errors

It follows from (3.1) or (3.2) that large sample sizes yield smaller standard errors, albeit with quickly diminishing returns, since the standard errors are proportional to the inverse of the square root of the sample size.

However, it may often be more useful, when designing a survey, to pay more attention to the *total survey error* (see Biemer and Lyberg 2003; Weisberg 2005; and most recently Biemer 2011). The idea is that a discussion of survey quality has to include an evaluation not just of the sampling error, but also of other sources of measurement errors, referred to as "nonsampling" errors.

These nonsampling errors are more difficult to measure, but need to be under-stood; a classification is shown in Table 3.1. A larger sample size may yield smaller standard errors, but would end up causing a larger total error if the sample size becomes too large to maintain good-quality interviews, or rigorous quality control.

This point is at the heart of the discussion in Nguyen et al. (2010): When someone proposed that the Vietnam Household Living Standards survey cover 95,000 households, it was soon recognized that this sample would be too unwieldy, and the quality of the information collected would have been poor, for a given budget. The result was that the sample size was reduced to 45,000 households.

Table 3.1 Types of survey-related errors

Type of error	Definition and comments
Sampling error	The error that occurs when a sample of the population rather than the entire population is surveyed
Coverage error	The error that occurs when the sampling frame – i.e., the list from which the sample is taken – does not correspond to the population of interest. For instance, it might undercount migrants
Unit nonresponse error	The error when a designated respondent does not participate in the survey. A serious source of bias in the Literary Digest case
Item nonresponse error	The error when a respondent does not answer all of the questions, or answers "don't know"
Measurement error	
Respondent	Occurs when the respondent does not accurately answer the question
Interviewer	Occurs when interviewers do not pose the questions properly (or falsify the answers)
Postsurvey error	The error that occurs in processing and analyzing survey data

Source: Based on Weisberg (2005, Introduction)

3.4 Incorporating Sample Design

We now turn to the issue of how to incorporate sample design into the estimates of sample statistics, using Stata, and discuss some measures of the extent to which this makes a practical difference. For illustrative purposes we work though an example using data from the Vietnam Household Living Standards survey of 2002.

Each region, defined by reg8, is a stratum, and the primary sampling unit is the commune, defined by xa. The sampling weights are in wt30. We first define the weights, PSUs, and strata using

. svyset xa [pw=wt30],strata(reg8)

A simple tabulation, ignoring sampling design and weights, shows that 23.4% of households were in urban areas. Incorporating sample design we get

```
. svy: tab urban02
(running tabulate on estimation sample)

Number of strata    =        8      Number of obs     =      29530
Number of PSUs      =     2901      Population size   =   17276776
                                    Design df         =       2893

    urban02 | proportions
    --------+------------
          1 |     .2421
          2 |     .7579
    --------+------------
      Total |         1

  Key:  proportions  =  cell proportions
```

Here we see that a better estimate is that 24.2% of the population is urban.

If we ignore weights or the sample design, the mean household size is 4.26 (standard deviation = 1.708) in urban areas, and 4.55 (s = 1.819) in rural areas. If we take just sampling weights into account, we get:

```
. by urban02: sum hhsize[aw=wt]
```

```
-> urban02 = 1
```

Variable	Obs	Weight	Mean	Std. Dev.	Min	Max
hhsize	6909	4182442.63	4.25449	1.705642	1	15

```
-> urban02 = 2
```

Variable	Obs	Mean	Std. Dev.	Min	Max
hhsize	22621	4.491107	1.75635	1	18

In this case, the standard errors of the means are 0.0205 ($= 1.705642/\sqrt{6.909}$) for urban households, and 0.0117 ($= 1.75635/\sqrt{22.621}$) for rural households. Now, if we allow both for weights and sample design, we find that the means are the same as when we just incorporate weights, but the standard errors of the means are larger – mainly reflecting the adjustment for clustering – as we see here:

```
. svy: mean hhsize,over(urban02)
(running mean on estimation sample)

Survey: Mean estimation
```

Number of strata =	8	Number of obs	=	29530
Number of PSUs =	2901	Population size	=	17276776
		Design df	=	2893

```
              1: urban02 = 1
              2: urban02 = 2
```

	Over	Mean	Linearized Std. Err.	[95% Conf. Interval]	
hhsize					
	1	4.25449	.0338546	4.188109	4.320872
	2	4.491107	.0183805	4.455067	4.527147

It is sometimes useful to summarize the design effects, which we have done here, using the `estat` command immediately after the `svy: mean` command.

```
. estat effects, deff deft meff meft

              1: urban02 = 1
              2: urban02 = 2
```

	Over	Mean	Linearized Std. Err.	DEFF	DEFT	MEFF	MEFT
hhsize							
	1	4.25449	.0338546	2.81669	1.6783	2.714	1.64742
	2	4.491107	.0183805	2.45109	1.5656	2.3105	1.52003

We may interpret these as follows. MEFF is the variance of the estimator when the design effects (weights, stratification, clustering) are taken into account, divided by the variance of the estimator based on the assumption of simple random sampling.

MEFT is the square root of MEFF. It is clear that the sample design is associated with considerably less precision than if the same data had been drawn from a simple random sample.

The DEFF is the variance of the estimator when the design effects are taken into account, divided by the variance of the estimator that assumes weighted random sampling; and DEFT is the square root of DEFF. This shows the extent to which design effects such as clustering (but not weights) are associated with lowered precision.

In our example, 0.03385/0.02052 is approximately equal to the DEFT, and 0.03385/(1.70813/6909) approximately equals the MEFT, for urban households.

3.5 Design vs. Model-Based Sampling

Before discussing the use of sample weights, it is useful at this point to make a distinction between design-based and model-based sampling. This is a controversial issue, but survey statisticians tend to favor the design-based point of view because it makes no assumptions about the mechanism that generates the data in the survey, as we explain below. We briefly review the main points; there is a fuller discussion in the excellent book by Sharon Lohr on *Sampling: Design and Analysis* (2010), as well as in Bertolet et al. (2003).

In a design-based approach, we have at hand a sample from the population, and the randomness arises from the sampling process. "Design-based" expected values are computed as averages over all possible samples that can be drawn from the population.

On the other hand, in the model-based approach, the vector y of population values of interest is a realization of an N-dimensional random vector Y, where N is the population size, with a multivariate distribution that depends on a set of parameters summarized in a vector θ. The components of y corresponding to members of the sample are known, while the remaining components are not, and the idea is that we need to "forecast" the values of the unknown components. Expected values "under the model" are meant to be computed with respect to the distribution of Y.

3.5.1 Illustration: Design-Based vs. Model-Based Means

To help understand the concept of design- and model-based sampling, we show how one would approach the computation of the expected value of the sample mean under each approach.

We begin with the design-based approach. Assume that we have N items in the full population, $y_1, y_2, \ldots, y_N$. Define variables Z_i to equal to 1 if unit i is in the sample, 0 if not. Let S denote the sample of n items, selected with a simple random sample of the population. The sample mean is then equal to

$$\bar{y} = \sum_{i=1}^{N} Z_i y_i / n. \tag{3.3}$$

Note that the sum here is over the whole population. We can see (Lohr 2010, p. 52) that since the items were selected via a simple random sample, $P(Z_i = 1) = n/N$. Keeping in mind that the only random quantities in the expression for $\bar{y}$ are the Z_i, we have

$$E(\bar{y}) = \sum_{i=1}^{N} E(Z_i) \frac{y_i}{n} = \frac{n}{N} \frac{1}{n} \sum_{i=1}^{N} y_i = \sum_{i=1}^{N} y_i / N. \tag{3.4}$$

It follows that the expected value of the sample mean equals the population mean. In other words, the sample mean is an unbiased estimator of the population mean.

Under the model-based approach, the y_i in the population are observed values from a sequence $Y_1, Y_2, \ldots, Y_N$ of random variables that are independent and identically distributed with, for instance, mean μ and standard deviation σ. The expected value of the sample mean equals

$$E(\bar{y}) = (1/n) \sum_{i=1}^{N} E(y_i) = (1/n)n\mu = \mu. \tag{3.5}$$

The sample mean is again an unbiased estimator of the population mean, but under a slightly different meaning.

There is a very important implication: since the model-based approach supposes a single model for the whole population, then a random sample is not needed for inference! Any group of people can give insight into the whole distribution. This is presumably what Shere Hite had in mind when she claimed that the results of her surveys could be generalized to the population of US women as a whole.

Clearly the maintained assumption of the model-based approach is generally too stringent. Although in principle only those who take a design-based approach should use sampling weights, in reality, many authors recommend their use, even in the context of a model-based analysis, particularly when computing summary statistics (see Lohr 2010, pp. 287–288 and references cited, notably Pfeffermann 1993, 1996).

3.6   Weights or Not?

As a practical matter, there is little disagreement that one should take sampling weights into account when reporting summary statistics (see Lohr 2010). It is far less obvious that one should use weights in regression (see for instance Deaton 1997).

The problem is this: if we take a model-based approach, and think of our observations as random realizations from a population with a single known structure, then it should not matter whether we use regression weights or not (although by the Gauss–Markov theorem, OLS would be more efficient than weighted least squares in this case). Just because we have a rather larger number of low-income households, or female-headed households, or large households in the sample should not matter, as all the points should be arrayed along the same regression line in this homogeneous population. Cameron and Trivedi (2009, p. 108) write that the "model approach is the approach usually taken in microeconometric studies that emphasize a causal interpretation of regression."

But suppose the structure of relationships in the population is more complex. Indeed, one reason for sampling by strata is that we presumably believe that there is something inherently different between one stratum and the next. In this case both OLS and weighted least squares are inconsistent. A strong case can be made that we should be estimating a more complex model in this case – for instance, with separate regressions for each stratum – but there may not always be enough data for this to be realistic.

What is the best way to proceed? DuMouchel and Duncan (1983) suggest that it is worth comparing the weighted with the unweighted estimators and testing for differences in the coefficients. Deaton (1997, p. 72) notes that this is equivalent to applying an F-statistic to test $g = 0$ in the regression

$$y = \mathbf{X}b + \mathbf{W}\mathbf{X}g + v, \tag{3.6}$$

where y is an $n \times 1$ vector of observations on the dependent variable, $\mathbf{X}$ an $n \times k$ matrix of observations on the independent variables, $\mathbf{W}$ an $n \times n$ matrix that has the weights N_s/n_s on the leading diagonal and zeros elsewhere – where N_s is the population in the relevant stratum and n_s is the sample for that stratum – v is the usual error, and b and g are parameters. If the coefficients differ substantially between the weighted and unweighted models, then one may need to rethink the model that we are using.

Another recommendation, particularly if the weights may be related to variables that are likely predictors in the regression analysis, is to include the weights as an independent variable, possibly interacted with other predictors, and see if these independent variables are significant (DuMouchel and Duncan 1983; Winship and Radbill 1994). If these variables are significant, the model should be improved until variables including the weights become insignificant. If on the other hand the weights are not related to any likely predictors, as is common in many living standard surveys where the weights are defined on the basis of over- or undersampling of some areas, then it is better to use a weighted regression. The cost of using weights when one should not is higher standard errors.

It is agreed that if the goal of a regression is to estimate a census parameter or to summarize relationships rather than test models, then weights should generally be used.

Table 3.2 Estimates of regression of food spending (per capita) on total spending (per capita), Vietnam, 2002

	Coefficient	Standard error	*t*-statistic	*p*-value
Unweighted				
pcexp2rl	0.232	0.00096	242.9	0.00
constant	745.5	4.655	160.2	0.00
Weighted				
pcexp2rl	0.229	0.00091	251.9	0.00
constant	774.8	4.903	158.0	0.00
Auxiliary				
pcexp2rl	0.231	0.00121	191.5	0.00
pcexp2rl × wt	$0.941\ (\times 10^{-6})$	$0.892\ (\times 10^{-6})$	1.1	0.29
constant	746.2	4.698	158.8	0.00

Source: Data are from the Vietnam Household Living Standards Survey of 2002. There are 29,530 household-level observations. The weights ("wt") refer to sampling weights. The dependent variable is food consumption per capita; pcexp2rl is per capita real spending

3.6.1 Illustration: Weighting Regression

We may illustrate the practical implications of these decisions with the help of a simplified example from the Vietnam Household Living Standards Survey of 2002. We are interested in the link between food consumption per capita (foodpc) and per capita real expenditure (pcexp2rl), and so the equation that we estimate is

$$\text{foodpc} = a + b\ \text{pcexp2rl}$$

The estimates are gathered into Table 3.2, and the data are graphed in Fig. 3.2, along with the weighted and unweighted regression lines. The estimate of b is 0.232 in the unweighted regression and 0.229 in the weighted case, and visually the lines appear to be close to one another. Deaton (1987) notes that one can test for a difference in the coefficients by estimating

$$\text{foodpc} = a + b\ \text{pcexp2rl} + c\,(\text{pcexp2rl} \times \text{weights})$$

where "weights" refers to the sampling weights, and testing whether c differs from zero. This is done in the bottom part of Table 3.2., where the estimate of c is not significantly different from zero. We thus conclude that the use of weighted regression is not called for in this example. Indeed it is appropriate to surmise that the model of the relationship between spending and food consumption is not related to the way in which the sampling was done for this survey.

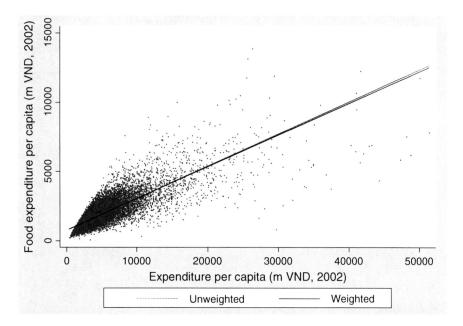

Fig. 3.2 Food consumption (per capita) graphed against expenditure (per capita), Vietnam 2002. [*Source*: As for Table 3.2. *Notes: Lines* are predicted values, based on unweighted regression (*dotted line*) and weighted regression (*lower, solid line*)]

3.7 Sampling Hard-to-Reach Groups: Vietnam

According to the Vietnam Household Living Standards Survey (VHLSS) of 2008, just 2.4% of the population of Hanoi, and 0.3% of those living in Ho Chi Minh City, had incomes below the poverty line, in contrast to a national poverty rate of 13.4%. Some believe that the urban poverty rates are understated, potentially substantially, because the sampling procedures used by the VHLSS-08 had the effect of greatly undersampling migrants, who might be assumed to be relatively poor. If indeed urban poverty is understated, then it has implications for policy, which may need to pay more attention to supporting the urban poor.

In order to address the potential underestimation of poverty in Hanoi and Ho Chi Minh City, those two cities undertook a custom-made Urban Poverty Survey in 2009 (UPS-09). The survey was explicitly designed so that it would adequately sample groups that are normally hard to reach, particularly recent migrants and house servants.

Vietnam has a system of residential permits (*ho khau*). In 2004, a mid-term census in Ho Chi Minh City found that just 71% of the population had either a KT1 or KT2 permit, which allowed the holder to reside in the city; this is in sharp contrast with the proportions of 98% found by the VHLSS-2004 and 91% in the VHLSS-2006. The living standards surveys typically selected households using lists of residents who had been in the enumeration area for 6 months or longer,

Table 3.3 Number of households and individuals interviewed in UPS-09

	Total	Hanoi	HCMC	Resident	Migrant
Total number of questionnaires	3,349	1,637	1,712	1,610	1,739
Household questionnaires	1,748	875	873	1,479	269
Individual questionnaires	1,601	762	839	131	1,470
Memo: Total number of persons	8,208	4,197	4,011	5,859	2,349

Source: Loan et al. (2011), Table ES1, based on Vietnam Urban Poverty Survey of 2009
Notes: HCMC is Ho Chi Minh City. "Resident" refers to someone who is legally allowed to live in the city, even if they were born elsewhere. "Migrant" refers to someone living in the city without legal permission, generally holding a residence permit from elsewhere

and lived as part of a family. This explains the massive underrepresentation of migrants, who are both more mobile, and more likely to live in the city as single individuals, than legal residents.

The UPS-09 was designed using a two-stage sampling method. In the first stage, enumeration areas (EAs) from the 2009 census of population were used as primary sampling units (PSUs). Entire city wards were divided into priority strata – where it was believed that poverty rates were high, the number of (illegal) migrants large, population growth rapid, and large labor-intensive factories prevalent – and other strata. Each city then chose 80 EAs, including 40 each from the priority and non-priority strata, based on probability proportional to population size.

In the second stage, households and individuals were selected using a random systematic sample. A great deal of effort went into compiling new lists of households and individuals in each of the chosen EAs; enumerators physically visited each house, rented room, or living place. Details of the protocols used are given in Loan et al. (2011). The actual surveying, in the form of a single interview, was done immediately after the compilation of the sampling frame, picking 11 households and 11 individuals from each enumeration area. The questionnaire for individuals was also administered to any domestic workers living in any of the sampled households. Students from elsewhere in Vietnam, who were studying in the two cities, were excluded from the survey.

The tally of those interviewed is shown in Table 3.3, and shows that the survey was quite successful in getting to the migrant population. The survey deliberately overweighted migrants, who constituted 17.3% of the population of the two cities in 2009, but represented 28.6% of those covered by the survey.

A comparison of legal city residents with nonlegal migrants is of interest in its own right, and some of the key variables are summarized in Table 3.4. Nonlegal migrants constitute a fifth of the population of Ho Chi Minh City, and more than a tenth of the population of Hanoi. The migrants are young, and almost half of them are still single. Mirroring the rest of the population, just over half of the migrants are women.

Compared to residents, migrants are less well-educated. They compensate for this by working harder: five out of six migrants are working, and they work for ten more hours per week (58.2 hours on average) than their resident peers.

Table 3.4 A comparison of urban residents with migrants, Hanoi and Ho Chi Minh City, 2009

	Residents	Migrants
Demographic details		
Population proportions, Hanoi	88.6	11.3
Population proportions, HCMC	79.4	20.5
% of group that is male	47.3	46.9
% of group that is single	28.9	46.5
% of group that is aged 20–29	17.1	39.2
Household size	3.9	1.7
Education and employment		
% of group with a primary education or less	24.6	32.5
% aged 10 or above who are working	59.1	84.9
% of group with manual, assembly, unskilled job	45.2	67.1
Hours worked per week for those working	48.3	58.2
% in current dwelling for 3 months or less	2.0	11.3
Material living standards		
Wage per month from main job ('000 VND)	2,225	1,987
Income per person per month ('000 VND)	2,509	2,162
% living on less than US$2 per person per day	2.6	3.0
Living area, square meters per person	20.3	8.4
% who are renting housing	7.6	63.7
Spending patterns		
Spending on food, '000 VND per person per month	1,075	858
Housing rental, '000 VND per person per month	25	190
Remittances, '000 VND per person per month	9	296

Source: Loan et al. (2011), based on Vietnam Urban Poverty Survey, 2009

The fruit of the hard work is that, despite poorer skills, migrants earn on average just 11% less than residents. The poverty rate, defined using a poverty line of US$2 per person per day, is 2.6% for residents and 3.0% for migrants, rates that are statistically indistinguishable.

Migrants spend their money very differently from residents. Since 64% of migrants rent their housing, compared to 8% of residents, they spend far more (on a per capita basis) on renting accommodation; they spend thirty times more on remittances; and they spend less on food.

The virtual omission of migrants from the VHLSS sample frames was unfortunately. But to the surprise of some, in the case of Vietnam's two great cities, it had little effect on the measurement of the poverty rate – although a properly done sample has proven to be exceptionally useful in allowing us to paint a clearer picture of the contrast between migrants and established residents.

3.8 Respondent-Driven Sampling: Hard-to-Reach Groups

Sometimes we need to gather information from individuals who, for one reason or another, are hard to reach, because they are in some sense hidden from the researcher, or the group is too small to be sampled adequately using standard sampling methods.

For example, we may be interested in understanding how HIV/AIDS is transmitted, and want to oversample groups that we believe, a priori, are important to the process, such as prostitutes or intravenous drug users. Or a business may be interested in contacting experts, such as users of, say, surgical gloves, with a view of getting feedback that would allow it to improve the product.

A technique that has gained some traction is that of *snowball sampling*, or a somewhat more rigorous version called *respondent-driven sampling*. The basic idea is that the researcher recruits an initial small number of subjects ("seeds") in the population of interest, and they in turn recruit additional subjects from among their acquaintances, and so on as the sample grows like a snowball.

One practical way of ensuring that the snowball does not stall is to provide the seeds with a small number of coupons to go and recruit other members of their network, who in turn are provided with coupons, and the process continues in a number of waves until a large enough group has been recruited and/or the group is in equilibrium vis-a-vis the characteristics of interest. After about 6–9 waves of recruitment the characteristics of the sample tend to settle down. The financial incentives provided by the coupons are modest but real, both for participating in the survey and for recruiting. It is important to keep the number of coupons small and to keep track of who recruited whom, as well as of the size of each recruiter's network, that is the number of people each recruiter knows in the population of interest. Heckathorn and Jeffri (2001, technical appendix) have a very useful description of the methods used to adjust results to correct for the nonrandomness of the sampling design; Magnani et al. (2005) also provide a useful review.

Figure 3.3 illustrates the process, is based on data from a survey by Heckathorn and Jeffri of jazz musicians in New York, and was created using the RDS Analysis Tool (RDS, Inc. 2006) and NetDraw 2.101 (Borgatti 2002). The researchers started with 13 seeds; five of these recruited nobody else, and these cases are shown at the top left corner of the graph. The other seeds recruited acquaintances who recruited acquaintances, and in some cases the process continued quite extensively; other chains came to an end relatively quickly.

Based on the 2001 survey, one may estimate the proportion of New York jazz players who are male (76%), and construct a bootstrap confidence interval around this number, as shown in Table 3.5. The ability to generalize about hard-to-reach populations rests on assumptions about the convergence properties of Markov chains, but allows one to adjust for the unavoidable biases that occur, for example, because recruiters differ in their tendencies to recruit respondents with similar characteristics to themselves.

Respondent-driven sampling is now relatively common; Goel and Salganik (2010) say that as of 2008, at least 120 studies had been undertaken that use the technique. There are some interesting examples related to developing countries, including a study of the health status of males having sex with males in Dhaka (Johnston et al. 2007), and the health status of female sex workers in Ho Chi Minh City and Haiphong in Vietnam (Johnston et al. 2006). Both of these studies are centered on issues related to HIV/AIDS. Figure 3.4 shows a sample chain of recruits that originated from a single seed in Ho Chi Minh City, and is interesting because it

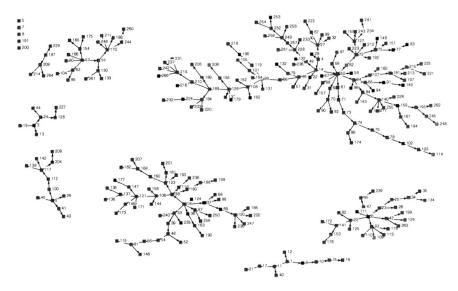

Fig. 3.3 Recruiting network of NY jazz players. [*Note*: Race is coded as follows: white (*red*), black (*blue*), other (*black*), missing (*grey*). *Source*: Data from Heckathorn and Jeffri; graph created using RDS software]

Table 3.5 Estimates of proportions of jazz players in New York who are male

	Estimated population proportions	95% bootstrapped confidence interval	
		Lower bound	Upper bound
Men	0.76	0.67	0.84
Women	0.24	0.16	0.33

Source: As for Fig. 3.3

also shows the modus operandi of those recruited – for instance, in a Karaoke parlor, on the street, or through a pimp, hotel, or guesthouse.

An important advantage of respondent-driven sampling is its proven ability to reach populations that are hard to reach, more successfully than alternatives such as location sampling (which samples areas where the population of interest is likely to be found) or institutional sampling (which might sample institutions such as jazz clubs or brothels). In addition, one obtains a representation of the social network of respondents, which is also interesting and informative.

Clever as it is, respondent-driven sampling does have limitations, as discussed by Goel and Salganik (2010a, b), and Gile and Handcock (2010). There are two main problems: first, the assumptions needed on the Markov chain that underlies the recruitment process to obtain unbiased estimators are quite strong, and typically not entirely satisfied in many applications; and second, the fact that recruiters are allowed to recruit up to (usually) three other participants can cause bottlenecks between subgroups of the network, which in turn can endanger the performance of

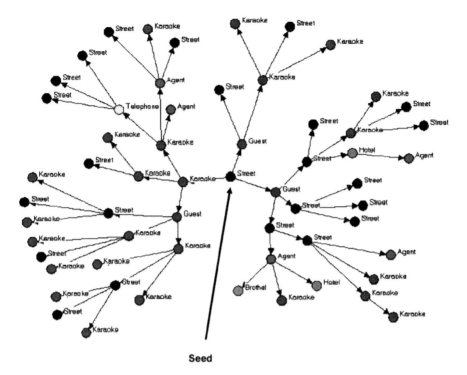

Seed

Fig. 3.4 Sample chain of recruits for a respondent-driven survey of female sex workers in Ho Chi Minh City. [*Source*: Johnston et al. (2006), p. i22. Reproduced with permission from the *Journal of Urban Health*]

the estimates. In addition, even if unbiasedness holds, Goel and Salganik find that the variances of the estimates are often quite high, and that one should plan for rather larger sample sizes than has typically been the case (Goel and Salganik 2010b).

References

Bertolet, M., H. Seltman, G. Greenhouse, and K. Kelleher. 2003. National Survey of Adolescent Well Being (NSCAW): A comparison of model and design based analyses of cognitive stimulation scores, Technical Report, Department of Statistics, Carnegie Mellon University, Pittsburgh, PA.

Biemer, P. 2011. *Latent class analysis of survey error*. New York: Wiley.

Biemer, P., and L. Lyberg. 2003. *Introduction to survey quality*. New York: Wiley.

Borgatti, S.P. 2002. *NetDraw: Graph visualization software*. Lexington: Analytic Technologies.

Cameron, Colin, and Pravin Trivedi. 2009. *Microeconometrics using Stata*. College Station: Stata Press.

Deaton, Angus. 1997. *The analysis of household surveys: A microeconometric approach to development policy*. Baltimore: Johns Hopkins University Press.

DuMouchel, W., and G. Duncan. 1983. Using sample survey weights in multiple regression analyses of stratified samples. *Journal of the American Statistical Association* 78: 535–543.

Gile, K., and M. Handcock. 2010. Respondent-driven sampling: an assessment of current methodology. *Sociological Methodology* 40(1): 285–327.

Goel, S., and M. Salganik. 2010. Respondent-driven sampling as Markov Chain Monte Carlo. *Statistics in Medicine* 28: 2202–2229.

Goel, S., and M. Salganik. 2010b. Assessing respondent-driven sampling. *Proceedings of the National Academy of Sciences USA* 107: 6743–6747. http://www.pnas.org/

Gonick, L., and W. Smith. 1993. *The cartoon guide to statistics*. New York: Harper Collins.

Heckathorn, D., and J. Jeffri. 2001. Finding the beat: Using respondent-driven sampling to study jazz musicians. *Poetics* 28: 307–329.

Johnston, L., K. Sabin, M.T. Hien, and P.T. Huong. 2006. Assessment of respondent driven sampling for recruiting female sex workers in two Vietnamese cities: Reaching the unseen sex worker. *Journal of Urban Health* 83(7): i16–i28.

Johnston, L., R. Khanam, M. Reza, S.I. Khan, S. Banu, Md S. Alam, M. Rahman, and T. Azim. 2007. The effectiveness of respondent driven sampling for recruiting males who have sex with males in Dhaka, Bangladesh. *AIDS and Behavior* 12: 294–304.

Loan, Le Thi Thanh et al. 2011. Urban poverty assessment in Hanoi and Ho Chi Minh City. Hanoi and Ho Chi Minh City: Statistics Office.

Lohr, S. 2010. *Sampling: Design and analysis*, 2nd ed. Boston: Brooks/Cole.

Magnani, R., K. Sabin, T. Saidel, and D. Heckathorn. 2005. Review of sampling hard-to-reach and hidden populations for HIV surveillance. *AIDS* 19(suppl 2): S67–S72.

Nguyen, P., D. Haughton, I. Hudson, and J. Boland. 2010. Towards data quality improvement of the Vietnam household living standard survey 2010-2020, unpublished. University of South Australia, Adelaide.

Pfeffermann, J. 1993. The role of sampling weights when modeling survey data. *International Statistical Review* 61: 317–337.

Pfeffermann, J. 1996. The use of sampling weights for survey data analysis. *Statistical Methods in Medical Research* 5: 239–261.

RDS, Inc. 2006. *RDS analysis tool v5.6: User manual*. Ithaca: RDS, Inc.

Smith, Tom. 1989. Sex counts: a methodological critique of Hite's Women and Love. In Charles Turner, Heather Miller, and Lincoln Moses (eds.), *AIDS, sexual behavior and intravenous drug use*, National Academy Press, Washington DC, pp. 537–547.

Weisberg, H. 2005. *The total error survey approach*. Chicago and London: University of Chicago Press.

Winship, C., and L. Radbill. 1994. Sampling weights and regression analysis. *Sociological Methods and Research* 23(2): 230–257.

Chapter 4
Beyond Linear Regression

4.1 Introduction

Nearly all regression analysis begins by estimating a linear model of the form:

$$y_i = \beta_0 + \beta_1 x_{i1} + \beta_2 x_{i2} + \cdots + \beta_k x_{ik} + \varepsilon_i$$
$$= \mathbf{x}'_i \beta + \varepsilon_i, \tag{4.1}$$

where $\beta = (\beta_0, \beta_1, \ldots, \beta_k)'$ is the vector of parameters to be estimated and $\mathbf{x}'_i = (1, x_{i1}, \ldots, x_{ik})$ is the vector of covariates for the ith of the n observations. For most inference, it is also assumed that the ε_i error terms are normally and independently distributed with mean zero and constant variance σ^2.

In practice, there is no reason to believe that economic or other relationships are conveniently linear, except perhaps as a first approximation. And yet theory, whether from economics or another discipline, only occasionally gives us clear guidance as to the appropriate functional form to use in statistical work. To take a well-known example: Mincer (1958) argued, based on a model of compensating differences, that an earnings regression should take the specific form

$$\ln[w(s,x)] = \alpha + \rho s + \beta x + bx^2 + \varepsilon,$$

where $w(s,x)$ is the wage rate for schooling level s and work experience x, ρ measures a rate of return to schooling, and ε is an error term with zero mean. Although widely estimated in this form, Heckman et al. (2003) suggest that Mincer's specification is too rigid and no longer serves empirical analysis well; their preferred approach is to apply nonparametric techniques when examining the relationship between schooling and wages.

This, more generally, is the subject of this chapter: how might we go about choosing an appropriate functional form to reflect relationships, including accounting for nonlinearities and interactions among variables, in regression work.

D. Haughton and J. Haughton, *Living Standards Analytics*, Statistics for Social
and Behavioral Sciences, DOI 10.1007/978-1-4614-0385-2_4,
© Springer Science+Business Media, LLC 2011

In the absence of strong prior beliefs, we have little choice but to lean on the data to guide us, so the spirit of the approach here is one of exploratory data analysis. Given that we have somehow identified which variables might appropriately be used, we turn to the data to help us determine how to use them.

We first discuss how the basic linear model may be tweaked to account for some nonlinearities and interactions. Then we turn to nonparametric regression models, including kernel regression, and smoothing splines. This is followed by a discussion of Multiple Adaptive Regression Spline (MARS) models, which provides a partially automated approach to identifying nonlinearities and interactions. The last major section of the chapter explains how to use Classification and Regression Tree (CART) models, and applies the approach to a study of child nutrition in Vietnam, where the CART model was used to help develop an appropriate (nonlinear) parametric model.

4.2   Flexibility in Linear Regression Models

Even when the relationship between x and y is nonlinear, it may be possible to transform the variables in such a way that a linear model may be applied to the transformed variables. A standard example is that of a multiplicative production function, which links inputs of capital (K) and labor (L) to output (Q) as follows:

$$Q = AK^\alpha L^\beta. \tag{4.2}$$

Here A, α, and β are parameters. A log transformation gives

$$\ln(Q) = \ln(A) + \alpha \ln(K) + \beta \ln L. \tag{4.3}$$

Equation (4.3) may be estimated straightforwardly using ordinary least squares. A standard exercise in such a case is to test whether $\beta = 1 - \alpha$, in which case we have the Cobb–Douglas production function, with constant returns to scale.

To illustrate this general approach to fitting curves, we first generate data from a hypothetical model, and then estimate a number of different functional forms. The data are generated using the following process – a spline with a single knot –

$$y_i = \begin{cases} 5.000 + 4.0 \ln(x_i) + \varepsilon_i, & \text{for } 1 \le x_i < 5 \\ 6.828 + 2.5 \ln(x_i) + \varepsilon_i, & \text{for } x_i \ge 5 \end{cases} \tag{4.4}$$

where 30 values of x_i are chosen randomly between 1 and 11 (using a uniform distribution) and the errors generated following a standard normal distribution giving $\varepsilon_i \sim N(0,1)$. The data points so generated are shown as dots in every panel in Fig. 4.1, where a variety of possible fitted forms are shown. The bottom right-hand panel shows the model estimated with the true specification.

Some of the functions fitted to the data in Fig. 4.1 clearly do not fit particularly well, but the quadratic and cubic approximations (panels on row 2) come close, as do the smoothers shown in the bottom left-hand panel. The smoothers used here are simply moving averages, using either three observations (the jagged line) or ten observations (the more regular line).

Based purely on the fitted line, the choice of appropriate functional form is not self evident, at least when models are not nested. It is tempting to pick the best-fitting model, which is the one with the highest value of R^2, but since R^2 rises as one adds more variables, this favors larger models. A popular solution is to use adjusted R^2, defined as

$$\bar{R}^2 = 1 - \frac{n-1}{n-k}(1 - R^2), \tag{4.5}$$

where n is the number of observations and k is the number of independent variables (excluding the constant). This has the effect of penalizing a model for the inclusion of additional variables, so there is a cost to the loss of degrees of freedom. However, the penalty is probably too small; adjusted R^2 rises if the (absolute value) of the t-statistic for the incremental variable exceeds 1, which is well below the level required for most conventional tests of statistical significance.

Another common approach to choosing an appropriate model is to use an information criterion. The Akaike Information Criterion (AIC) is defined as

$$\text{AIC}(k) = \ln\left(\frac{e'e}{n}\right) + \frac{2k}{n}, \tag{4.6}$$

where e refers to the vector of observed residuals. A higher-dimensional model would have a lower value of $e'e$ but a higher value of k, and so the idea here is to weigh this tradeoff by choosing a model that minimizes the AIC, as defined in (4.6). The penalty for higher dimensionality here is relatively modest, so the AIC tends to overfit; nor is the measure consistent, in the sense that as $n \to \infty$ the model chosen does not converge to the true model. As a result, many researchers prefer to use the Bayes (or Schwartz) Information Criterion, defined as

$$\text{BIC}(k) = \ln\left(\frac{e'e}{n}\right) + \frac{k\ln(n)}{n}. \tag{4.7}$$

Compared to the AIC, the BIC tends to choose more parsimonious models. When using information criteria to compare models, the dependent variable must be the

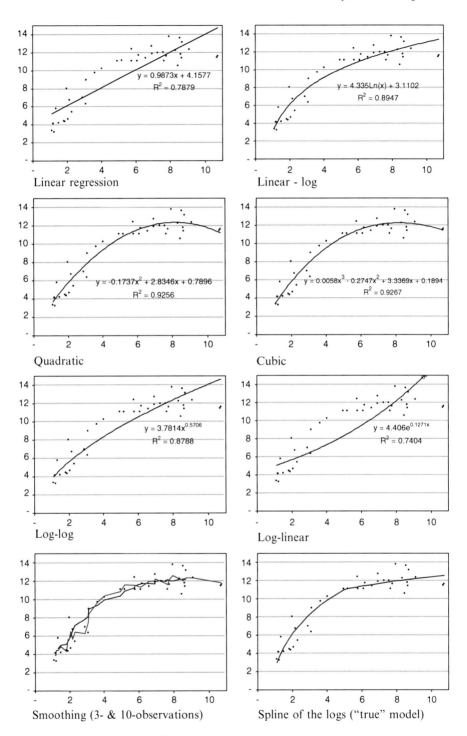

Fig. 4.1 Fitting curves to a randomized one-knot spline

Table 4.1 Applying criteria for choosing among alternative models

	R^2	$\bar{R}^2$	AIC	BIC
Models of y				
$y = a + bx$	0.787	0.782	151.4	154.7
$y = a + b \ln(x)$	0.895	0.892	123.3	126.7
$y = a + bx + cx^2$	0.926	**0.922**	**111.5**	**116.5**
$y = a + bx + cx^2 + dx^3$	0.927	0.921	112.9	119.6
Models of $\ln(y)$				
$\ln(y) = a + b \ln(x)$	0.879	0.876	−32.5	−29.2
$\ln(y) = a + bx$	0.740	0.734	−2.07	1.31
$\ln(y) = a + b \ln(x: x < 5) + c \ln(x: x \geq 5)$	0.890	**0.884**	**−34.3**	**−29.2**

Source: The underlying data are graphed in Fig. 4.1, along with the alternative models. Bold values identify the "best" models within each group

same across models; thus the technique does not allow one to choose between, for example, a log–log model and a linear–log model.

The use of these model selection criteria is illustrated in Table 4.1. Within the class models of y, all concur that the quadratic is more appropriate than the cubic; while the cubic model fits more closely, it requires an extra variable, and the improvement in fit does not justify the loss of an additional degree of freedom. And among the models of $\ln(y)$, the underlying spline model is preferred (just!) over a log–log model.

4.3 Nonlinear Models

There are occasions when we believe that a well-defined nonlinear specification is appropriate for the model under consideration. Quite generally, we have

$$y_i = h(\mathbf{x}_i, \beta) + \varepsilon_i, \tag{4.8}$$

where the linear model is a special case (Greene 2003, p. 162). For example, we might believe that a good parameterization of the Engel curve, which relates household food consumption per capita (C_F) to household income per capita (I), would be

$$C_F = \alpha + \beta I^{\gamma}, \tag{4.9}$$

where α, β, and γ are all unknown parameters. This potentially allows for curvature, but it cannot be linearized, and so the estimates of the three parameters will require the use of a technique such as nonlinear least squares. The results of such a technique tend to be sensitive to the starting values of the parameters used in seeding the iterative procedure that is used to produce the estimates.

Another popular nonlinear specification consists of the Box–Cox transformation, defined as

$$x^{(\lambda)} = \begin{cases} \dfrac{x^{\lambda} - 1}{\lambda} & \text{for } \lambda \neq 0, x > 0 \\ \log(x) & \text{for } \lambda = 0, x > 0 \end{cases} \tag{4.10}$$

One could then estimate

$$C_F = \alpha + \beta I^{(\lambda)}. \tag{4.11}$$

An attractive feature of the Box–Cox transformation is that it reduces to a linear specification if $\lambda = 1$ and to a log specification if $\lambda = 0$.[1] It is possible to use different Box–Cox parameters for each independent variable, although this is rarely done; the dependent variable may also be transformed, which is somewhat more common.

The results of estimating a food Engel curve for Vietnam are shown in Fig. 4.2, using the nonlinear specification of (4.9) in the top left panel, and using a Box–Cox specification based on (4.10) in the top right panel. The data come from a survey of 9,189 households undertaken in Vietnam in 2006 by the General Statistics Office, using a questionnaire based on the World Bank's Living Standards Survey model. The horizontal axis measures household expenditure per capita, deflated to the prices of January 2006, and also adjusted for regional price differences; the vertical axis shows (real) food consumption per person. In each panel in Fig. 4.2 the predicted values from a log–log ("constant elasticity") regression – commonly used in estimating demand elasticities – are shown (as a dashed line) in order to provide a point of reference. The actual data points are also displayed, and constitute a dense cloud from which it is difficult to infer any clear pattern on visual inspection. This is common in situations with large amounts of data, and again shows the need for techniques to summarize the information in a more intelligible form.

In this example, both nonlinear formulations of the regression flatten out at higher levels of per capita expenditure.

4.4   Nonparametric Models

At the highest level of generality, the variable y is related to the covariate x as follows:

$$y_i = g(\mathbf{x}_i) + \varepsilon_i, \tag{4.12}$$

---

[1] The constant elasticity of substitution (CES) production function may be written as $Y = (\alpha K^{\rho} + \beta L^{\rho})^{1/\rho}$, where K and L refer to inputs of capital and labor and Y denotes output. Appropriate substitution gives an estimating equation $Y^{(\rho)} = \frac{1}{\rho}(\alpha + \beta - 1) + \alpha K^{(\rho)} + \beta L^{(\rho)}$, which is a Box–Cox transformation. In the case where $\rho = 1$, this specializes to the Cobb–Douglas case.

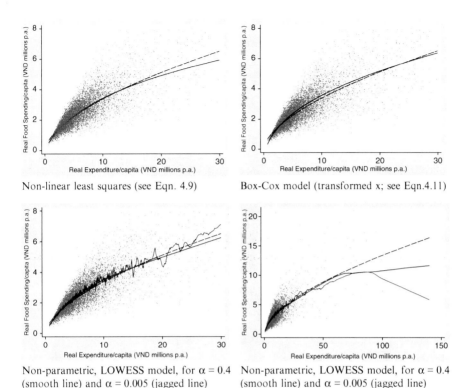

Non-linear least squares (see Eqn. 4.9)

Box-Cox model (transformed x; see Eqn.4.11)

Non-parametric, LOWESS model, for α = 0.4 (smooth line) and α = 0.005 (jagged line)

Non-parametric, LOWESS model, for α = 0.4 (smooth line) and α = 0.005 (jagged line)

Fig. 4.2 Fitting food engel curves for Vietnam. *Note*: The *bottom right panel* displays all the data; the *other panels* only show observations up to real income per capita of VND30 million p.a. and real food spending up to VND8 million p.a., in order to provide more detail of the most relevant parts of the curves. (*Source*: Author estimates based on Vietnam Household Living Standards Survey of 2006)

where g($\cdot$) is the regression function, there are n observations (indexed by i), and ε_i is a random error, usually assumed to be distributed iid $N(0, \sigma^2)$. The function g($\cdot$) may not be known a priori, and may not have an evident parametric representation.

When there is a single right-hand variable, it is possible to estimate g($\cdot$) nonparametrically, essentially allowing the data to trace the empirical regression function. The most popular method for doing this is with locally weighted scatterplot smoothing (LOESS or LOWESS), originally proposed by Cleveland (1979) and further developed by Cleveland et al. (1988). The algorithm works as follows: at each data point x_i fit a parametric weighted regression equation – typically linear, but sometimes quadratic – using neighboring data, with weights that drop off as observations are further removed from x_i. The predicted value of this equation at point x_i gives the estimate of y_i. The process is repeated for all of the n data points.

The bottom two panels in Fig. 4.2 show LOESS estimates of the food Engel curve for Vietnam in 2006. In this case each local regression is linear, and the

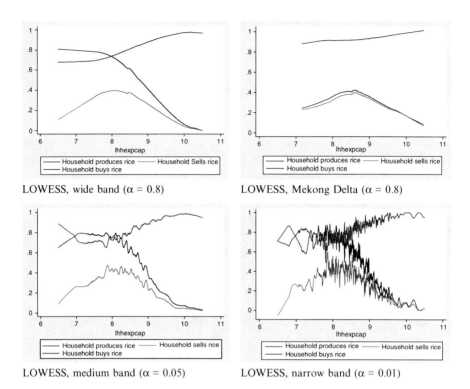

Fig. 4.3 Smoothing functions applied to rice purchases and sales, Vietnam (*Source*: Author estimates based on Vietnam Household Living Standards Survey of 2006. *Note*: α gives the proportion of observations used in estimating the regression at any given point)

weights used follow a tri-cube function, although other choices are possible.[2] The most important choice is the smoothing parameter α, which gives the proportion of data used in each fit. The smooth lower lines at the bottom of Fig. 4.2 assume α = 0.4, while the jagged line is based on a smoothing parameter of 0.005. Some researchers choose the smoothing parameter that minimizes the (bias-corrected) AIC, although for exploratory analysis such precision may not be essential.

In this example, most of the divergence between alternative nonparametric approaches occurs at the upper edge of the data, where outliers can influence the results unduly. The bottom panels of Fig. 4.2 show this, with the left-hand side truncating the x-axis at 50,000, and the right-hand side displaying the full dataset.

A nice feature of the LOESS smoother is that it handles binary values of y_i very naturally. This is evident in Fig. 4.3, which is similar in concept to an example used

---

[2] Let x be the variable under examination, scaled so that the difference between the maximum and minimum values is 1. The tri-cube weight function is given by $w(x) = (1 - |x|^3)^3 I[|x| < 1]$, where $I[\cdot]$ is an indicator function set equal to 1 if it holds and to 0 otherwise.

by Deaton (1997, p. 195); again, our data come from the Vietnam Household Living Standards Survey of 2006, and show the log of expenditure per capita on the horizontal axis. The three lines in the top left panel show, respectively, the proportion of households that buy rice (high and rising with expenditure per capita), the proportion of households that produce rice (starts high and falls), and the proportion of households that sell rice (first rises and then falls). These patterns are interesting, and suggest, at a first approximation, that a tax on rice production would disproportionally hit the poor, a tax on sales of locally produced rice would especially hurt those in the middle of the income distribution, and a tax on all rice purchases would reach almost all high-income households.

Variations on the theme are possible. The top right panel in Fig. 4.3 shows the same curves, but only for the Mekong Delta, which is Vietnam's most important rice bowl, and the source of most of its rice exports. Almost all rice-growing households in the Mekong Delta also sell rice, but a surprisingly high proportion of low-income households in the area do not produce any rice; some are landless laborers, and others may produce other crops, including fruit and shrimp.

The lower panels in Fig. 4.3 illustrate the effects of changes in the smoothing parameter; where $\alpha = 0.8$ in the top left panel, this parameter equals 0.05 in the bottom left panel and 0.01 in the bottom right panel. In this latter case this means that just 1% of the dataset is used in the regression for any given x_i, which produces a noisy and relatively uninformative set of regression functions.

The LOESS smoother, which is sometimes referred to as a locally weighted polynomial regression, is very flexible, is straightforward to use, and works well when there are large numbers of observations, as is typically the case with household survey data. On the other hand, the lack of a parametric regression function makes it difficult to convey the results economically, and forces one to rely heavily on visual methods. Although the LOESS smoother, and other similar nonparametric techniques, can work with more than one independent variable, they quickly become clumsy, and are unhelpful when there are three or more covariates.

4.5   Higher-Dimension Models

The central purpose of this chapter is to address the problem of functional form, and more specifically, how to choose an appropriate model in the absence of clear theoretical guidance. As we have seen, when there are very few independent variables, then nonparametric regression can be helpful. If, in addition, there are relatively few observations, then visual inspection is definitely useful (as in Fig. 4.1), but it is difficult to discern patterns in a swarm of thousands of observations (as in Fig. 4.2).

We are thus left with a problem of how to establish an appropriate functional form when we have a lot of data (common) and a large number of variables (also common), and we believe that the functional form is unlikely to be linear, and is likely to include interactions among the independent variables.

In the remainder of this chapter we discuss two useful approaches to the problem. The first sets up an algorithm to fit splines to the data; the second builds a regression tree. Both techniques are most helpful at an exploratory stage, and can provide guidance for model parameterization, as we will see in the example in Sect. 4.6.

4.5.1 MARS Models

Some simplification is required if one is to see patterns in a dataset with many observations and variables, and where nonlinearities and interactions are likely to be important. One useful approach, developed by Jerome Friedman (1991), is to build a multivariate adaptive regression splines (MARS) model. Friedman and Roosen (1995, p. 216) argue that the main strength of a MARS model is that it "provides a way to fit a highly general regression model without overfitting."

To see how this works, consider the simple example in Fig. 4.4, where in the left-hand panel a simple linear regression line is fitted to a scatterplot.[3] The fitted line, given by $y = 4.96 + 0.99x$, is not fully satisfactory; the residuals are negative at low and high values of x, suggesting that the underlying model is curved. An improvement would be to fit a piecewise linear regression, as shown in the right-hand panel of Fig. 4.4, with a knot (i.e., kink) at $x = 17$. This equation may be written as

$$y = 45.355 + 0.596 \max(0, x - 17) - 2.129 \max(0, 17 - x).$$

In this case y is estimated as a linear function of two *hinge functions* (aka hockey stick functions). Even with a single independent variable one can use multiple hinge functions in order to achieve greater overall nonlinearity; a three-segment line is shown fitted to the data in the bottom left panel of Fig. 4.4, and may be written as

$$y = 42.229 - 3.028 \max(0, 10 - x) + 1.022 \max(0, x - 10) - 0.593 \max(0, x - 29.2).$$

These are examples of regression splines.

---

[3] For this example, the points are generated by

$$y_i = \begin{cases} 5 + 3x, & \text{for } 0 \leq x < 10 \\ 25 + x, & \text{for } 10 \leq x < 30 \\ 43 + 0.4x, & \text{for } 30 \leq x \end{cases}$$

Onto this we added an iid error term distributed $\varepsilon \sim N(0, 2)$.

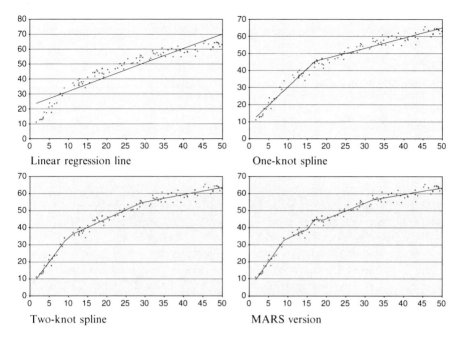

Fig. 4.4 Fitting linear and spline functions (*Note*: The data are hypothetical, and are generated following the process given in footnote 2. The knots in the *top right* and *bottom left* panels were found by searching over a grid)

The same essential idea – approximating curvature with hinge functions – can be extended to cases with many independent variables. Moreover, hinge functions can be multiplied together to create interactions. So, for instance, in examining the determinants of education on wages, one could include interactions that might allow the effect to be larger in urban than in rural areas. Such nonlinearities let one speak of multivariate regression splines.

The "adaptive" part of MARS refers to the algorithm used to fit the model, and extends a procedure used by Smith (1982; see too Friedman and Roosen 1995) for the case of a single independent variable. First the model is estimated with just an intercept. Then pairs of *basis functions* are added, starting with those that yield the maximum reduction in the residual sum of squares.[4] Each new basis function adds a variable and a knot, so at each step in this forward pass, MARS searches over all combinations of existing terms, variables, and values for each variable

---

[4] Each new pair of basis functions consists of mirrored hinge functions, $\max(0, x - c)$, $\max(0, c - x)$, times a constant or an existing term.

Table 4.2 MARS basis functions for two-knot spline model

```
BF2 = max(0, 2.000 − KID92);
BF2 = max(0, 16.880 − w);
BF3 = max(0, w − 8.949);
BF5 = max(0, w − 32.135);
BF9 = max(0, w − 15.019);
BF11 = max(0, w − 19.190);
Y = 57.935 − 3.182 × BF2 − 2.135 × BF3 − 0.526 × BF5 + 2.036 × BF9 +
    1.015 × BF11;
```

Note: Model is graphed in bottom right-hand panel of Fig. 4.4

(to select a knot). More terms are added until the change in the residual sum of squares is too small, or some preset maximum has been reached.

The forward pass creates a model that overfits. To rectify this, a backward pass procedure trims the model, removing basis functions one by one, starting with the least effective term. Typically the trimming is done using generalized cross-validation, based on a procedure introduced by Craven and Wahba (1979) that approximates the error generated by leave-one-out validation, and penalizes complexity.[5] An excellent and accessible description of the MARS algorithm is given in De Veaux et al. (1993).

The result of applying the MARS algorithm to our hypothetical data – which are generated by a two-knot spline (see footnote 3) – is shown in the bottom right panel of Fig. 4.4. The MARS model fits the data well, but there is also a hint of overfitting in this case, as it uses two additional knots. This model can be written out in terms of the basis functions shown in Table 4.2.

As tools for exploring data, MARS models have some virtues. They are straightforward to build – Salford Systems (http://www.salford-systems.com) produces well-regarded software, while Earth (implemented in *R*) has less functionality but is free – and are flexible, can handle large datasets, and may be used for forecasting (Sephton 2001). They are also more transparent, and hence easier to grasp, than "black box" techniques such as neural nets (Francis 2002). MARS models are also good at handling missing values (which can be coded, and may be selected into basis functions) without discarding potentially useful data, and at dealing with nested data (e.g., recovery from surgery, conditional on having had surgery). However, as with nonparametric regression, one cannot directly calculate confidence intervals for the parameters; and one can easily end up with a model with dozens of basis functions, which may be difficult to understand intuitively.

---

[5] For speed and tractability, MARS confines itself to hinge functions, but higher-order splines are in principle possible.

4.5.2 MARS Application: Changes in Expenditure in Vietnam, 1993–1998

Between 1993 and 1998, real GDP in Vietnam grew by an average of 8.9% annually (Haughton 2001, p. 9). But not all households saw their expenditures rise this quickly. Haughton and Loan (2005) use panel data covering 4,272 households from the Vietnam Living Standard Surveys of 1992/1993 and 1997/1998 to explore the determinants of changes in household expenditure. More specifically, their dependent variable is the log of the change in per capita household consumption between 1993 and 1998.

In a straightforward linear regression, where there are 16 independent variables, including the age and education of the household head, but the fit is poor, with $R^2 = 0.04$. In their implementation of MARS, Haughton and Loan first trim the number of variables to 9 (using a direct acyclic graph methodology implemented by the tool Tetrad, see Chap. 5), and then limit the number of basis functions to no more than 40 (although only 31 were ultimately needed). The results of applying OLS to these basis functions are shown in Table 4.3, and produced a model with $R^2 = 0.104$. The improved fit, despite fewer underlying variables, provides compelling evidence of the importance of nonlinearities in determining changes in household per capita expenditures.

To illustrate the potential usefulness of a MARS model, consider the way in which the number of children interacts with the education of the head of household in explaining proportionate changes in expenditure per capita between 1993 and 1998. Given the nonlinearities and interactions, it is helpful to present the analysis graphically, which we do in Fig. 4.5. The vertical axis represents the estimated differences in the log of per capita expenditure (DLE), while the horizontal axis shows the number of children in the household (KIDS92). Each line shows the relationship for a different level of education of the head of the households. For households where the head had no more than a primary education (solid line), or at least some high school education (dashed line), the lines initially rise steeply and then flatten. This shows that, for modestly educated households, additional children (2 or 1 vs. 0) were associated with faster growth in per capita expenditure during 1993–1998, but this effect essentially reaches its limit in two-child households. The pattern for well-educated households – of which there are 88 in the sample – is quite different. There, additional children are associated initially with a reduction in per capita expenditure growth, although the effect stabilizes once the household has two or more children.

Could such patterns have been identified without the help of MARS? In principle the answer is yes; Fig. 4.6 shows Box-plots of the dependent variable (vertical axis) broken down by the educational level of the household head and the number of children. There one may discern patterns similar to those shown in Fig. 4.5. Thus the identification of nonlinearity and interaction made by MARS is visible on an exploratory plot a posteriori. The problem is that in the presence of a large number of predictors, it may be hard for the modeler to determine which graphs to

Table 4.3 Basis functions for MARS model of growth in living standards, Vietnam 1993–1998

Basis functions	Interactions	Nonzero cases
$BF1 = \max(0, KID92 - 2.000)$;	–	1504
$BF2 = \max(0, 2.000 - KID92)$;	–	1714
$BF3 = (DISASTER = 0)$;	–	1917
$BF5 = \max(0, DISTROAD - 5.000)$;	–	190
$BF6 = \max(0, 5.000 - DISTROAD)$;	–	4004
$BF7 = \max(0, EDUCYR98 - 11.000) \times BF2$;	EDUCYR98 KID92	282
$BF8 = \max(0, 11.000 - EDUCYR98) \times BF2$;	EDUCYR98 KID92	1399
$BF9 = \max(0, HHSIZE92 - 2.000) \times BF6$;	HHSIZE92 DISTROAD	3627
$BF10 = \max(0, 2.000 - HHSIZE92) \times BF6$;	HHSIZE92 DISTROAD	93
$BF11 = \max(0, NOSICK92 - .268753E-07) \times BF6$;	NOSICK92 DISTROAD	2544
$BF12 = (MEDYR98M = 0) \times BF2$;	MEDYR98M KID92	476
$BF14 = \max(0, EDUCYR98 - 2.000)$;	–	3564
$BF15 = \max(0, 2.000 - EDUCYR98)$;	–	475
$BF16 = (DOMGIVE = 0)$;	–	3580
$BF17 = (DOMGIVE = 1)$;	–	692
$BF18 = (FAC10KML = 0) \times BF16$;	FAC10KML DOMGIVE	1753
$BF20 = (FAC10KML = 0) \times BF5$;	FAC10KML DISTROAD	72
$BF22 = \max(0, NOSICK92 - 1.000) \times BF17$;	NOSICK92 DOMGIVE	283
$BF23 = \max(0, 1.000 - NOSICK92) \times BF17$;	NOSICK92 DOMGIVE	227
$BF24 = \max(0, NOSICK92 - 4.000) \times BF15$;	NOSICK92 EDUCYR98	26
$BF25 = \max(0, 4.000 - NOSICK92) \times BF15$;	NOSICK92 EDUCYR98	425
$BF26 = \max(0, HHSIZE92 - 7.000) \times BF5$;	HHSIZE92 DISTROAD	38
$BF27 = \max(0, 7.000 - HHSIZE92) \times BF5$;	HHSIZE92 DISTROAD	135
$BF28 = \max(0, HHSIZE92 - 12.000) \times BF14$;	HHSIZE92 EDUCYR98	10
$BF29 = \max(0, 12.000 - HHSIZE92) \times BF14$;	HHSIZE92 EDUCYR98	3539
$BF30 = (MEDYR98M = 0) \times BF14$;	MEDYR98m EDUCYR98	1357
$BF32 = \max(0, HHSIZE92 - 1.000) \times BF1$;	HHSIZE92 KID92	1503
$BF33 = \max(0, EDUCYR98 - 15.000) \times BF2$;	EDUCYR98 KID92	46
$BF35 = \max(0, DISTROAD - 3.500)$;	–	342
$BF37 = \max(0, DISTROAD - 2.500)$;	–	471
$BF39 = \max(0, DISTROAD - 4.000)$;	–	268

$$
\begin{aligned}
Y = {} & -0.168 + 0.024 \times BF1 - 0.137 \times BF2 + 0.100 \times BF3 - 0.050 \times BF5 \\
& + 0.077 \times BF6 + 0.017 \times BF7 + 0.008 \times BF8 + 0.007 \times BF9 \\
& + 0.017 \times BF10 - 0.005 \times BF11 + 0.040 \times BF12 \\
& - 0.040 \times BF15 + 0.023 \times BF16 - 0.053 \times BF18 \\
& + 0.028 \times BF20 - 0.028 \times BF22 - 0.129 \times BF23 \\
& + 0.038 \times BF24 + 0.026 \times BF25 - 0.010 \times BF26 \\
& - 0.003 \times BF27 + 0.053 \times BF28 + .588324E\text{-}03 \times BF29 \\
& + 0.006 \times BF30 - 0.003 \times BF32 + 0.047 \times BF33 \\
& - 1.498 \times BF35 + 0.585 \times BF37 + 0.979 \times BF39;
\end{aligned}
$$

Variables	Description	Mean
KID92	Number of children in 1992	2.02
DISASTER	Commune received disaster relief in 1998 (Yes = 1)	0.55
DISTROAD	Distance from commune to nearest road (km)	0.88
EDUCYR98	Years of education of head in 1998	6.90
HHSIZE92	Household size in 1992	5.03
NOSICK92	Number of sick in 1992	1.39
MEDYR98M	Missing mother's education (Yes = 1)	0.66
DOMGIVE	Gave domestic remittances in 1992 (Yes = 1)	0.16
FAC10KML	Factory within 10 kms of commune in 1998 (Yes = 1)	0.52

Source: Haughton and Loan (2005)

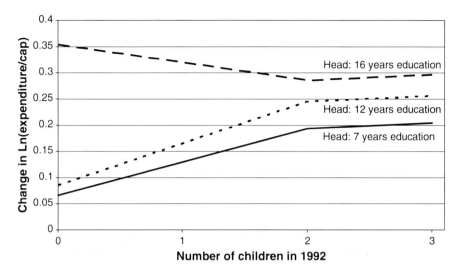

Fig. 4.5 Estimated change in log of expenditure per capita (*vertical axis*) for five-person households, for different values of education of head in 1998, and number of children, Vietnam 1993–1998. (*Source*: Haughton and Loan 2005)

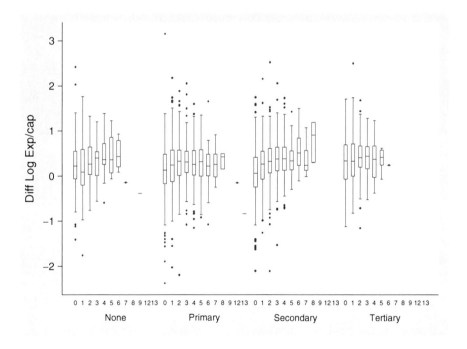

Fig. 4.6 Box-plots of estimated change in log of expenditure per capita (*vertical axis*) by number of children, and educational attainment of head of household, Vietnam 1993–1998. (*Source*: Haughton and Loan 2005)

explore a priori. This issue is at the heart of statistical research that attempts to identify interactions (and nonlinearities) automatically, an issue considered more fully in work by Friedman and Popescu (2005).

4.5.3   CART Models

Another helpful nonparametric technique for exploring nonlinearities and interactions is to split data into classification or regression tree (CART) models (Breiman et al. 1984). Such CART models are useful in their own right, but are especially valuable for preprocessing data, thereby aiding the researcher in choosing from many potentially relevant variables, and for suggesting refinements in functional form that are appropriate in subsequent parametric analysis. In what follows we begin with a simple pedagogical example that allows us to introduce the methodology, and then present two examples, one of a classification tree, and the other of a regression tree.

To see how CART works, we begin with the same scatterplot of data of Y on X as we used when introducing the MARS model (Fig. 4.4). The essential idea behind CART is that it splits the parent data into two groups (child nodes). Each of these nodes may in turn be split further, in a process of binary recursive partitioning, until a full tree structure has emerged. An algorithm is required to provide rules for splitting each node, and for deciding when a tree is complete.

At each step the goal is to partition the data into nodes that are relatively homogeneous; for continuous data, lack of homogeneity is measured by the variance of the dependent variable. Let $n(t)$ be the number of observations in the parent node, with a (population) variance of the dependent variable given by $YVAR(t)$. The idea is now to split the data into a left-hand group with $n(t_L)$ observations, and a right-hand group with $n(t_R) = n(t) - n(t_L)$ observations, so as to maximize

$$YVAR(t) - \frac{n(t_L)}{n(t)} YVAR(t_L) - \frac{n(t_R)}{n(t)} YVAR(t_R). \qquad (4.13)$$

In our example, $YVAR(t) = 14.67$. The greatest reduction in variance occurs by splitting the data at $X = 15.94$; the points below this are shown as dots in Fig 4.7, while those above are shown as circles. The new variance is now

$$\frac{n_L}{n} YVAR_L + \frac{n_R}{n} YVAR_R = \frac{30}{100} 10.107 + \frac{70}{100} 6.727 = 7.741, \qquad (4.14)$$

which represents a substantial improvement in fit. In the next round, CART splits the data at $X = 7.46$ and $X = 28.63$. As the process continues, we are in effect fitting a step function to the data; the eventual result is shown by the solid line segments in Fig. 4.7, while the final tree itself is shown in Fig. 4.8. In this simple

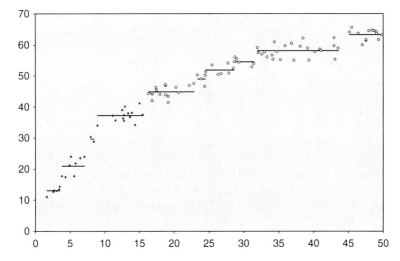

Fig. 4.7 CART model fitted to two-knot spline data. (*Note*: The data are hypothetical, and are generated following the process given in footnote 3)

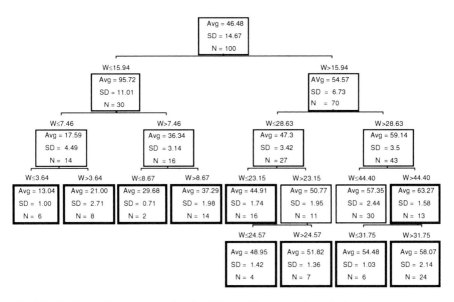

Fig. 4.8 CART tree for two-knot spline data. (*Notes*: The data are hypothetical, and are generated following the process given in footnote 3. Terminal nodes are framed in heavy lines)

example the approximation is unlikely to improve on other techniques, but as the underlying data become more complex, CART becomes relatively more useful at finding nonlinearities and interactions.

To avoid the danger of overfitting, the typical procedure first involves creating a large initial tree using a training sample consisting of a majority of the observations, and with as many nodes as observations. The tree is then pruned using the test sample (i.e., the remaining observations) and picking as the final tree the one with the lowest mean square error.

CART is probably most useful as a method of exploratory data analysis, helping the researcher identify (1) which variables to include, and (2) how to parameterize nonlinearities. It uses a stepwise procedure, so variables do not have to be selected in advance; a list of candidate variables suffices. The procedure is robust to the effects of outliers, can handle cases with missing values (using surrogates to develop splits), and generates results that are invariant with respect to monotone transformations of the independent variables (unless nodes are split using linear combinations, rather than dichotomously). Salford Systems produces software that implements the CART algorithm and is straightforward to use.

This flexibility comes at a cost. CART trees can easily become sprawling and unwieldy – testament to the complexity of the world, perhaps, but less helpful if the goal is to generate parsimonious models. We now illustrate the creation and interpretation of CART trees with two examples.

4.5.4 CART as a Preprocessor: A Nutrition Example

Haughton and Haughton (1997) use data from the Vietnam Living Standards Survey of 1992–1993 to develop a model of child malnutrition. A common problem in such studies is that some of the influences on nutritional status, including the age of the child, are known to be highly nonlinear, but parameterizing such nonlinearity is not always easy. This is where building a CART tree may be helpful.

The usual way to measure malnutrition is to use a standardized measure of height for age (for stunting, usually taken to reflect long-run malnutrition), or weight for height (for wasting, a measure of short-run malnutrition). The latter may be measured as

$$WH_{ih} = \frac{W_{ih} - W_{Mh}}{\sigma_{Mh}}, \tag{4.15}$$

where W_{ih} is the weight of individual i with height h, W_{Mh} is the median weight at a given height, relative to a reference population (typically chosen to be the US population), and σ_{Mh} is the population standard deviation.

The data come from the 4,800 households surveyed between October 1992 and October 1993 by the Vietnam Living Standards Survey, which collected information on a long list of socioeconomic variables, as well as anthropometric measurements for all household members. The usable sample consists of 4,394 children younger than 13 for which key variables are available.

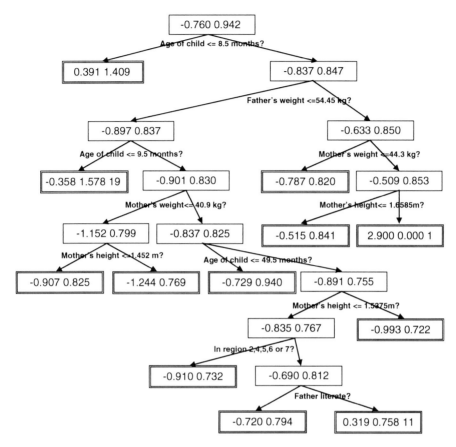

Fig. 4.9 CART tree to explore influences on standardized weight for height, Vietnam 1993. (*Source*: Haughton and Haughton 1997)

The ultimate regression tree for this analysis is shown in Fig. 4.9; the box at each node shows the mean and standard deviation, and terminal nodes are shown with double-lined boxes. The first split, determined by CART to maximize the reduction in variance, is based on the age of the child: those up to 8.5 months old are in the box on the left while all others are on the right. This is already interesting; on average, Vietnamese children in 1993 were 0.76 standard deviations below the median weight for height, but those under 8.5 months – in general, not yet fully weaned – were on average 0.39 standard deviations *above* the median weight for height. Vietnamese babies were not born thin; they became thin.

Most of the further splits in Fig. 4.9 are based on the height or weight of the mother or father, or the age of the child. Indeed, the number of relevant variables is quite limited, despite a large number of candidate variables. In Fig. 4.9, note the

Table 4.4 Parametric model of the determinants of short-term malnutrition in Vietnam in 1993

	Coefficient	p-value
Independent variable		
Standardized weight-for-height z-score		
Intercept	7.815	0.000
Variables related to the child		
Is age ≤ 8.5 months (yes $= 1$)	0.696	0.000
Is age $< =9.5$ months (yes $= 1$)	0.192	0.240
Is age $< =49.5$ months (yes $= 1$)	0.156	0.000
Was child ill in last 12 months (yes $= 1$)	−0.089	0.001
Variables related to the mother		
Log of weight (in kg)	1.335	0.001
Log of height if ≤ 1.452 m	0.021	0.023
Log of height if ≤ 1.5375 m	0.038	0.000
Age	−0.010	0.024
Age at marriage	−0.005	0.295
Variables related to father		
Log of weight (in kg)	2.041	0.000
Log of height	−4.261	0.000
Is father literate? (yes $= 1$)	−0.188	0.004
Age	0.012	0.001
Variables related to family		
Farm household? (yes $= 1$)	0.083	0.083
Variables related to community		
Water from tap? (yes $= 1$)	−0.160	0.028
Water from well? (yes $= 1$)	−0.090	0.008
Water from river, lake? (reference)		
Water from other source? (yes $= 1$)	−0.104	0.026
Flush toilet? (yes $= 1$)	0.084	0.173
Other toilet or no toilet (reference)		
Regional effects		
Remaining regions (reference)		
Central Coast, Central Highlands, Mekong Delta	−0.073	0.010
Adjusted R-squared	0.171	
Number of observations	4,394	
F-value	48.53	

Source: Haughton and Haughton (1997)

way in which the CART tree isolates an outlier (a child whose weight is 2.9 standard deviations above the median), and the very low weights (relative to height) of older children with lightweight fathers and tall, lightweight, mothers. Also of interest is the fact that the gender of the child does not enter into the tree; while Vietnamese households have a documented preference for sons (Haughton and Haughton 1995), they do not appear to discriminate in favor of sons once they are born, at least on decisions related to weight.

Based on the patterns in the CART tree, Haughton and Haughton (1997) designed and fitted a parametric model, with the results summarized in Table 4.4.

This is a relatively parsimonious model, but it now shows the nonlinear effect of age on measures of weight for height, as well as curvature in the effect of maternal height on the weight of the child. The fit of this regression is better, by about a quarter, than one that does not recognize these nonlinear effects – an improvement large enough to justify preprocessing the data using CART.

4.5.5   CART as a Classifier: An Expenditure Example

Haughton and Loan (2005) are interested in what determines whether a household in Vietnam in 1998 is poor (category 1), near-poor (category 2), or not poor (category 3). Poverty is defined using the official government poverty line, by which standard 37% of the population was poor in 1998. The near-poor, viewed as vulnerable by Haughton and Loan because they were not safely above the poverty line, are those whose expenditure per capita lies between the poverty line and 1.41 times the poverty line. One could build a multinomial logit model for this situation, but developing a CART tree is an attractive alternative. This is a classification rather than a regression problem. As usual, at each step the data are split to maximize the gain in homogeneity, but here it is defined as the greatest possible reduction in "impurity." There are a number of possible measures of impurity, including a Gini coefficient for the three output categories ($C = 3$); the measure of impurity at a node that is used here is defined as

$$I = 1 - \sum_{i=1}^{C} \left(\frac{\text{\# of cases in class } i}{\text{\# of cases in node}} \right)^2. \tag{4.16}$$

After a split, the new measure of impurity is given by $(n_L/n)I_L + (n_R/n)I_R$. The initial sample of 4,272 households consists of 1,435 poor (34%), 2,257 near-poor (53%), and 580 nonpoor households (14%), which generated an impurity measure of 0.589. CART immediately splits the sample along rural/urban lines, confirming this to be the single most important economic cleavage in Vietnam in 1998; the new value of impurity now drops to 0.551.

The urban subsample yielded a relatively simple tree, shown in Fig. 4.10a. The proximate drivers of whether one is poor, near-poor, or not poor, in urban areas include household savings – low savings are correlated with poverty – and the education of the household head. There can be no inference of causality here, but the salience of reported savings as an indicator of economic wellbeing is of interest.

The rural tree is more complex, as is apparent from Fig. 4.10b. Again, savings appear helpful in distinguishing between the poor and nonpoor, but so is the age of the household head, where younger means poorer. The effect of the number of children is more complex; having more children is associated with less poverty among low-saving and older households, but with more poverty among moderate-saving households.

4.6 Beyond Regression

Nature, or society, is rarely linear. In seeking to identify or quantify relationships between variables, a basic linear model is often inadequate, even as an approximation. But as soon as one considers nonlinear models, the choices can be overwhelming. This chapter suggests a pragmatic way to reduce these choices to a manageable level. When there are just two variables, transformations of the variables, or nonparametric smoothing, can be done easily and to good effect. For larger dimensions, techniques such as MARS or CART can be very helpful, both in identifying the most essential variables, and in suggesting the relevant form of nonlinearities. These are not the only possible techniques; neural nets, for instance, have their adherents, but they are more of a "black box" than the procedures presented here (Francis 2002).

Purists may argue that exploratory data analysis is atheoretical and leads to overfitting. The concern is valid, but does not address the increasingly pressing problem of how to make sense of growing mountains of data and a plethora of variables, many of which are close substitutes for one another.

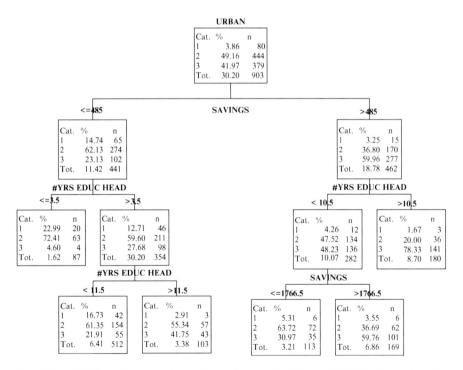

Fig. 4.10a CART tree for poverty level of urban households, Vietnam 1998. The three categories are poor (1), near-poor (2), and nonpoor (3). (*Source*: Haughton and Loan 2005)

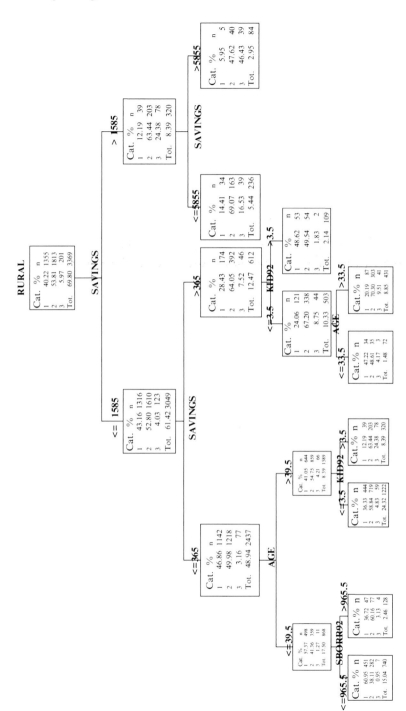

Fig. 4.10b CART tree for poverty level of rural households, Vietnam 1998. The three categories are poor (1), near-poor (2), and nonpoor (3). (*Source:* Haughton and Loan 2005)

References

Breiman, Leo, J. Friedman, R. Olshen, and C. Stone. 1984. *Classification and regression trees.* New York: Chapman & Hall.

Cleveland, W. 1979. Robust locally weighted regression and smoothing scatter plots. *Journal of the American Statistical Association* 74: 829–836.

Cleveland, W.S., S.J. Devlin, and E. Grosse. 1988. Regression by local fitting: Methods, properties, and computing. *Journal of Econometrics* 37: 87–114.

Craven, P., and G. Wahba. 1979. Smoothing noisy data with spline functions: Estimating the correct degree of smoothing by the method of generalized cross-validation. *Numerical Mathematics* 31: 317–403.

De Veaux, Richard D., D.C. Psichogios, and L.H. Ungar. 1993. A comparison of two nonparametric estimation schemes: MARS and neural networks. *Computers in Chemical Engineering* 17(8): 819–837.

Deaton, Angus. 1997. *The analysis of household surveys: A microeconometric approach to development policy.* Baltimore: Johns Hopkins University Press.

Francis, Louise. 2002. Martian chronicles: Is MARS better than neural networks? http://www.casact.org/pubs/forum/03wforum/03wf027.pdf. Accessed 3 June 2009.

Friedman, Jerome. 1991. Multivariate adaptive regression splines (with discussion). *Annals of Statistics* 19(1): 1–141.

Friedman, Jerome, and B. Popescu. 2006. Predictive learning via rule ensembles (2005), http://www-stat.stanford.edu/~jhf/ftp/RuleFit.pdf. Accessed 25 March 2006.

Friedman, Jerome H., and Charles B. Roosen. 1995. An introduction of multivariate adaptive regression splines. *Statistical Methods in Medical Research* 4: 197–217.

Greene, William. 2003. Econometric analysis, 5th edition. Upper Saddle River: Prentice Hall.

Haughton, Dominique, and Jonathan Haughton. 1995. *Son preference in Vietnam,* 325–337. November/December: Studies in Family Planning.

Haughton, Dominique, and Jonathan Haughton. 1997. Explaining child nutrition in Vietnam. *Economic Development and Cultural Change* 45: 541–556.

Haughton, Dominique, and Le Thi Thanh Loan. 2005. Shifts in living standards: The case of Vietnamese households, 1992-1998. *Philippine Journal of Development* 32(1): 79–101.

Haughton, Jonathan.J. 2001. Introduction: Extraordinary Changes. In *Living standards during an economic boom,* ed. Dominique Haughton, Jonathan Haughton, and Nguyen Phong. Hanoi: Statistical Publishing House.

Heckman, James, Lance Lochner, and Petra Todd. 2003. Fifty Years of Mincer Earnings Regressions. Working Paper 9732, National Bureau of Economic Research, Cambridge, MA.

Mincer, J. 1958. Investment in human capital and personal income distribution. *Journal of Political Economy* 66(4): 281–302.

Sephton, Peter. 2001. Forecasting recessions: can we do better on MARS? *Federal Reserve Bank of St. Louis Review* March/April: 39–49.

Smith, P.L. 1982. *Curve fitting and modeling with splines using statistical variable selection techniques, NASA Contractor Report 166034,* Old Dominion University, Norfolk, VA.

Chapter 5
Causality

5.1 Introduction

Well over 200 years ago, Adam Smith wrote his classic *An Inquiry into the Nature and Causes of the Wealth of Nations*. Of course interest in causality goes back much further: Democritus, the pre-Socratic "laughing philosopher," wrote, "I would rather discover one causal law than be King of Persia."

Why are we so interested in understanding causality? Quite apart from a desire to make sense of how the world works, the most compelling reason is that we cannot hope to change things, or offer any worthwhile policy analysis, unless we have a clear idea of what causes what. Without at least some understanding of what determines income, or causes poverty, it is difficult for anyone – academic, politician, policy analyst – to address these important issues.

There are strong, and sometimes overheated, disagreements about the best way to approach causality. For our purposes we may distinguish between three schools: the experimentalists, the economic structuralists, and the statistical school. We explain the key differences between these groups below, but note here that the debate is of some practical relevance: the experimentalist school emphasizes impact evaluation and the need for good "research design," while the structural school argues the need for theory and a proper understanding of the mechanisms that make things tick. Each side seeks to attract adherents, funding, and influence.

5.2 The Experimentalist School

The focus of the program evaluation, or experimentalist, approach is on measuring the "effects of causes." Methodologically, the emphasis is on randomized or quasi-randomized experiments – which we discuss at some length in Chap. 12 – and little attention is devoted to the mechanisms that might cause the results.

D. Haughton and J. Haughton, *Living Standards Analytics*, Statistics for Social and Behavioral Sciences, DOI 10.1007/978-1-4614-0385-2_5,
© Springer Science+Business Media, LLC 2011

Intuitively, the idea is that X causes Y if one can change X in order to modify Y. Rubin (1974) defines the causal effect of one treatment (E1) over another (E0) as the difference between what would have happened in time t_2 if the unit had been exposed to E1 (initiated in t_1) rather than E0 (initiated in t_1). This allows one to make a statement such as "because an hour ago I took two aspirins instead of just a glass of water, my headache is now gone" [Wikipedia, Rubin Causal Model (http://en.wikipedia.org/wiki/Rubin_Causal_Model)].

As a practical matter it can be difficult to measure causality. Perhaps the closest one can come is with randomized experiments, but although often touted as the "gold standard" for measuring effects, they can be quite flawed in reality, as the discussion in Chap. 12 (on Impact Evaluation) makes clear (see too Angrist et al. 1996).

The use of randomized experiments has gained traction in recent years, and is often done with flair and imagination. The Abdul Latif Jameel Poverty Action Lab at MIT (J-PAL) has become an important intellectual center of this effort; the paper by Duflo, Glennerster, and Kremer (2006), three leaders of J-PAL, summarizes the case for randomization, and considers the role of the main alternative methods. Just one policy-relevant example of a randomized experiment is the study of the effects of flip charts in schools in rural Kenya by Glewwe et al. (2000), which we discuss further in Chap. 14; they find that they had no discernible effect on test scores.

A more important study may be the one by Banerjee et al. (2010) that reports on the randomized roll-out in 2007–2008 of microcredit in Hyderabad by Spandana, a large microfinance institution. They found that the microcredit had no impact on household spending per capita, health spending per person, or school enrollment, but increased (slightly) the probability that a household would open a business. The study did not try to measure the long-run effects, because Spandana expanded its lending relatively quickly, thereby "contaminating" the households that might have served as controls. In this case the randomization helped resolve the problem, common to most other evaluations of microcredit, of endogenous placement: the borrowers are unlikely to be typical, in ways that we, as observers, may not fully understand, and so we cannot easily compare them with nonborrowers in our effort to identify the impact of taking a microloan.

Angrist and Pischke (2010) argue that the program evaluation approach has been highly productive, in part because of rigorous attention to research design including, but not confined to, the design of randomized experiments. In the words of Edward Leamer (2010, p. 33), they "offer a compelling argument that randomization is one large step in the right direction. Which it is! But like all the other large steps we have already taken, this one doesn't get us where we want to be."

Critics of the program evaluation approach are skeptical of its ability to address enough questions of real importance. Morck and Yeung (2011, p. 2) write that "econometrically useful natural experiments are few and far between," and (p. 3) "double-blind randomized trials are rare in economics." They go on to say (pp. 3–4), "the reader is invited to devise a controlled experiment to check whether or not bigger stock markets cause faster GDP growth." Sims (2010) makes a similar point, arguing that economics is not an experimental science.

Even when experiments can address issues of importance, critics worry about their low external validity, while acknowledging that they tend to have high internal validity. An inference has internal validity if it can properly demonstrate a causal relation, and this in turn generally requires that the cause precedes the effect in time, the cause and effect move together, and there are no plausible alternative explanations for the covariation (Shadish et al. 2002). There is external validity if the causal relations from a study can be applied more broadly, outside the unique settings of the experiment or test. In other words, the results of experiments may be difficult to generalize to other times and places, unless we understand *why* an intervention works (if it does). Keane (2010) worries that the experimentalist approach gives a "false sense of certainty," and that even the claim of strong internal validity often rests on shaky assumptions.

5.3   The Structuralist School

James Heckman (2008, 2010) argues that program evaluations represent "a retreat to statistics," and makes the case that unless we have a clearly formulated model, the association between inputs and outputs that is measured in a program evaluation is of very limited value. He writes (2010, p.7),

> The goal of the structural econometrics literature, like the goal of all science, is to understand the causal mechanisms producing effects so that one can use empirical versions of models to forecast the effects of interventions never previously experienced, to calculate a variety of policy counterfactuals and to use theory to guide choices of estimators to interpret evidence and to cumulate evidence across studies. These activities require models for understanding "causes of effects" in contrast to the program evaluation literature that focuses only on the "effects of causes" (Holland 1986).

This theme is echoed by Angus Deaton (2010), who stresses the need to understand the underlying causal mechanisms if we are to have any hope of deriving policy-relevant advice. As he puts it (p. 3), "finding out how people in low-income countries can and do escape from poverty is unlikely to come from the empirical evaluation of actual projects or programs, . . . unless such analysis tries to discover *why* projects work rather than *whether* they work." This is a fundamental point about how we learn. Drawing on Popper's ideas of how science progresses, Deaton argues that we learn by formulating hypotheses and testing them. Over time we discard theories that have been falsified, and formulate new ones to take their place, although in some cases there may be "acid tests" of a theory that are difficult to explain unless the theory is true.

The structural view has dominated economic thinking over the past half-century, but it is not unassailable. Structural models can be difficult to formulate. By its very nature, a model is a simplification of some aspects of reality, and can have no special claim to being "the truth." It is not always clear how some theories emerge if not from the type of evidence produced by randomized and other experiments, and the search for a complete model may be too expensive, too slow, and sometimes unnecessary.

For example, a number of recent studies of charter schools in the USA – schools that are privately run using public funding, and typically have flexibility in personnel and curricular matters – find that they are associated with higher test scores (Abdulkadiroglu et al. 2009; Hoxby et al. 2009; Haughton et al. 2011). It is not always clear *why* this is – perhaps longer school days, tighter discipline, more imaginative curricula, better-motivated teachers – but the mechanisms may not be particularly relevant if the key policy question is whether to expand the number of charter schools that are allowed. This is the spirit behind a recent article by Guido Imbens (2010) entitled "Better LATE Than Nothing."[1]

Structuralist or experimentalist? The debate has been heated, but perhaps the sides are not really so far apart. Heckman (2010) suggests that Marshak's Maxim should apply: Identify a question, and model only as much as needed. Practically, this probably calls for more use of relatively simple models. Then, writes Heckman (p. 47), "use the economics to frame the questions and statistics to help address them."

Morck and Yeung (2011) suggest that a productive way to address issues of causality is by drawing on history, where one does find many interesting natural experiments, although often these admit more than one interpretation. Leamer (2010) takes a different tack. He points out that in some cases the direction of causality is unknowable, and we need to acknowledge such limits to our understanding. He writes (p. 32), "can we economists agree that it is extremely hard work to squeeze truths from our data sets and what we understand will remain uncomfortably limited?" He is also a strong proponent of reporting the results of sensitivity analyses in econometrics, and in particular favors the use of extreme bounds analysis (p. 37).

In concluding this section, we agree with Leamer when he writes (p. 44): "ignorance is a formidable foe, and to have hope of even modest victories, we economists need to use every resource and every weapon we can muster, including thought experiments (theory), and the analysis of data from nonexperiments, accidental experiments, and designed experiments." It is of course advice that is useful well beyond the confines of economics.

5.4 The Causal Inference School

There is a third school of thought on the issue of causality that is rooted in the important work by the computer scientist Judea Pearl (2009a); see too Morgan and Winship (2007) [Wikipedia, Causality (http://en.wikipedia.org/wiki/Causality)]. This approach is not structural – there is no underlying model – and not experimentalist. Instead it uses a mixture of logic and statistical correlations to infer (where possible) the directions of causality among a set of variables.

---

[1] LATE stands for local average treatment effect; we discuss this further in Chap. 12.

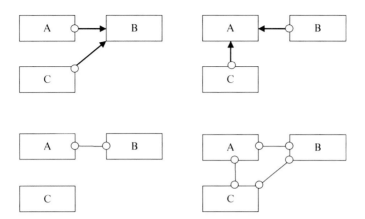

Fig. 5.1 Graphs of three variables (*A, B, C*) with varying causal structures. (*Source*: Based on Bryant et al. (2009), Fig. 2). Panels are (i) through (iv) reading clockwise from *top left*

Practically, this approach is implemented through the estimation of *directed acyclic graphs* (DAGs). In this section we explain the underpinnings of Pearl's approach, and how DAGs are created, before presenting a worked example related to the study of poverty worldwide.

5.4.1   Establishing Causality

We begin with an example, based heavily on Bryant et al. (2009), in which we illustrate how one might go about testing our null hypothesis that *A* causes *B*. Assume for now that we observe variables *A, B,* and *C,* where *C* may be correlated with *A* and/or *B.* The importance of *C* will be clear in a moment.

Now consider the causal structures illustrated in Fig. 5.1. The symbol $A \circ\!\!\rightarrow E$ represents an "edge" indicating that either A causes B, or they share a common latent cause, or both; and the edge $A \circ\!\!-\!\!\circ B$ means that either variable causes the other, or they share a common latent cause, or both.

The interesting feature of Fig. 5.1 is that we can, under certain circumstances, infer a direction of causality. If *A* and *B* are statistically independent, which we denote by $A \perp B$, then *A* cannot cause *B.* But if *A* and *B* are not independent, so $A \not\perp B$, then we need to examine the relations between *A, B,* and *C* more completely in order to discern causality. Bryant et al. distinguish between four different cases:

1. $A \perp C$ and $B \not\perp C$. This is the situation seen in panel (i) of Fig. 5.1, and *we cannot reject the hypothesis that A causes B.* This is the only logical possibility; after all, if *C* caused *B* caused *A,* then *C* and *A* would not be independent; and if *B* caused *A* and *C,* then *A* and *C* would not be independent.

2. $A \not\perp C$ and $B \perp C$. This is illustrated in panel (ii) of Fig. 5.1. If A caused B, and is not independent of C, then B would not be independent of C; yet we are told it is. So we infer that A *cannot cause* B in this case, and we reject the null hypothesis that A causes B.
3. $A \perp C$ and $B \perp C$. This is shown in the bottom left panel in Fig. 5.1. There is clearly some sort of relationship between A and B, but we cannot determine what direction it flows. Perhaps A causes B, but we cannot know this for sure.
4. $A \not\perp C$ and $B \not\perp C$. This is the case shown in panel (iv) in Fig. 5.1. We cannot reject the possibility that A causes B.

Case 2. here is interesting, because although A and B are not independent, we are able to rule out the possibility that A causes B. This was possible with the help of variable C, which serves as a test instrument. There may be nontrivial cases where this inference is useful.

Bryant et al. illustrate the logic of this situation with a persuasive example. It is well known that greater alcohol consumption is associated with higher road fatalities; but is the alcohol causing the deaths, or are the deaths inducing people to drink away their sorrows? Using data for the USA for 1947 through 1993, they examine the links between road deaths, alcohol consumption per capita, and average urban vehicle speed. They first filter the data to remove the effects of nonstationarity, and then compute the following correlation coefficients:

ρ(death, alcohol) $= 0.341^*$
ρ(death, speed) $= 0.386^*$
ρ(alcohol, speed) $= 0.136$

The correlations marked with an asterisk are statistically significantly different from zero. Following our earlier logic, there is only one way to organize this information, which is as follows:

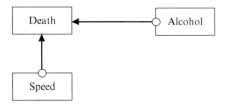

In other words, it is alcohol that causes the road deaths, and not death that leads to more drinking. We now have made a clear causal inference.

5.5   Creating Directed Acyclic Graphs

Our task is now to explain how to create a *directed acyclic graph* (DAG), which is a major contribution of the causal influence school. Much of the following discussion follows Bessler (2002) and Bessler and Loper (2001); we first review the relevant ideas from probability, relegating the most technical details to a separate box, illustrate the principles with a straightforward example, and explain how Tetrad and the partial correlation algorithm work to create a DAG. In the subsequent section we go through a worked example and show an estimated graph that tries to understand the influences that affect poverty worldwide.

5.5.1 Basic Tools: Probability

Some basic concepts are worth summarizing at this point. If A and B are two events, and the probability of A is nonzero, then the probability of B conditional on ("given") A is defined as $P(B|A) = P(B \text{ and } A)/P(A)$.

Conditional *distributions* are defined on the basis of the conditional probabilities of events involving random variables. Suppose that X and Y are two discrete random variables. The conditional distribution of X given that $Y = y$ is defined, for every y such that $P(Y = y) \neq 0$, by the expression $P_{X|Y}(x|y) = P(X = x|Y = y)$. If X and Y are continuous random variables the definition has to be modified somewhat, since for no y will we have $P(Y = y) \neq 0$. In this case, the density of X conditional on Y is defined by $f_{X|Y}(x|y) = f(x,y)/\int f(x,y)dx$. In this definition $f(x,y)$ refers to the joint density of X and Y at (x,y).

5.5.2 Directed Acyclic Graphs

A directed graph consists of a set of "vertices" (variables in our context), and a set of directed edges that link pairs of vertices. In our earlier example, the vertices were represented by A, B, and C, and the edges took a variety of forms. The graph is *acyclic* if it contains no cycle, which means that no directed path in the graph goes from one variable and back to it, either directly or indirectly.

To each such graph we will associate a set of conditional independence relations among the variables in the dataset as follows:

$$P(V_1, V_2, V_3, ..., V_n) = \prod_{i=1}^{n} P(V_i|\mathrm{pa}(V_i)), \tag{5.1}$$

where the V_i are the n variables in the dataset, $\mathrm{pa}(V_i)$ is the set of "parents" of V_i, that is the set of variables with an arrow leading directly to V_i in the graph, and P

Fig. 5.2 Three basic graphs

	Graph 1	*Graph 2*	*Graph 3*
	$A \rightarrow B \leftarrow C$		
	$\downarrow$	$K \leftarrow L \rightarrow M$	$D \rightarrow E \rightarrow F$
	D		

denotes the probability of events involving the variables. Note that if the variables are ordered from V_1 to V_n in an arbitrary fashion, it is true by the definition of conditional probability that

$$P(V_1, V_2, V_3, ..., V_n) = \prod_{i=1}^{n} P(V_i | V_1, V_2, V_3, ..., V_{i-1}). \qquad (5.2)$$

For that reason, the property in (5.1) is sometimes called the Markov property since it implies that the conditional probabilities in (5.2) depend only on the immediate parents of V_i and not on more distant ancestors of V_i.

5.5.3   d-Separation

An important concept in what follows, due to Pearl (2000), is that of *d-separation* (directional separation). The important idea here is that *d-separation* is the graphical equivalent of conditional independence; a formal definition is given in Box 5.1.

The key result (Geiger et al. 1990) that makes the concept of *d-separation* work is that there is a one-to-one correspondence between the set of conditional independence relations $(X \perp Y | Z)$ implied by (5.1) for a graph G, and the set of triplets X, Y, Z that satisfy the *d-separation* criterion for graph G.

To see how this works, consider the three basic graphs set out in Fig. 5.2. In graph 1, B is a *collider*. Intuitively, we see that A and C are unconditionally independent, because B blocks the paths from A to C. On the other hand, if we condition on B, we unblock the flows between A and C. We therefore say that A and C are *d-connected* given B. They are also d-connected given D. Formal demonstrations are given in Box 5.1.

In graph 2, we see that K and M have a common cause L, and so are not (unconditionally) independent. On the other hand, if we condition on the common cause, K and M become independent. And in graph 3 in Fig. 5.2, D and F become independent if we condition on the middle vertex E.

Box 5.1 Technical Note: *d-Separation* and Conditional Independence

In this box we gather some of the more technical material.

Definition of *d-separation*
Let X, Y and Z be three disjoint subsets of vertices [variables] in a directed acyclic graph G, and let p be any path between a vertex [variable] in X and a vertex [variable] in Y, where by "path" we mean any succession of edges, regardless of their directions. Z is said to block p if there is a vertex w on p satisfying one of the following: (*i*) w has converging arrows along p, and neither w nor any of its descendants are on Z or (ii) w does not have converging arrows along p, and w is in Z. Furthermore, Z is said to d-separate X from Y on graph G, written $(X \perp Y | Z)_G$, if and only if Z blocks every path from a vertex [variable] in X to a vertex [variable] in Y. Source: Bessler (2002), based on Pearl (2000).

d-connectedness and *d-separation* in Fig. 5.1.
Note first that if there is an edge (i.e., link) $A \to B$ in a graph, then A and B are *d-connected* (that is are not *d-separated*) given the empty set $\emptyset$ since then no vertex w can block every path from A to B.

In *graph 1* in Fig. 5.2, A and C are *d-separated* given the empty set $\emptyset$ by part (i) of the definition of *d-separation*. On the other hand, A and C are *d-connected* given B, and A and C are also *d-connected* given D. In such a graph, B is typically referred to as a *collider*. We can check that A and C are unconditionally independent $(A \perp C)$ as follows:

Equation (5.1) in the case of graph 1 yields $P(A, B, C, D) = P(A) P(C) P(B/A, C) P(D/B)$. By summing over all possible values d_i of D (assuming to simplify matters that D is a discrete random variable), we obtain

$$P(A, B, C) = \sum_{di} P(A, B, C, D = d_i)$$

$$= \sum_{d_i} P(A) P(C) P(B/A, C) P(D = d_i/B)$$

$$= P(A) P(C) P(B/A, C) \sum_{d_i} P(D = d_i/B) = P(A)P(C)P(B/A, C)$$

On the other hand by definition of conditional probability we have $P(A, B, C) = P(B|A, C)P(A, C)$. It follows that $P(A,C) = P(A) P(C)$.

In the case of *graph 2* in Fig. 5.2, K and M are *d-connected* (given the empty set), but K and M are *d-separated* given L by part (ii) of the definition of *d-separation*. We can check that indeed $K \perp M | L$.
We have $P(K, L, M) = P(K/L)P(M/L)P(L) = P(K/L)P(M, L)$
We also have $P(K, L, M) = P(K|L, M)P(M, L)$ so

$$P(K/L, M) = P(K/L).$$

(continued)

Box 5.1. (continued)

In the case of *graph 3* in Fig. 5.2, by part (ii) of the definition of *d-separation*, D and F are *d-connected* given the empty set, but are *d-separated* given E. We can indeed check that $D \perp F | E$.

We have $P(D,E,F) = P(D)P(E|D)P(F|E)$. We also have $P(D,E,F) = P(D/F,E)P(F/E)P(E)$. So $P(D)P(E|D) = P(D|F,E)P(E)$ and therefore since $P(E,D) = P(D|E)P(E)$ we have $P(D|F,E) = P(D|E)$. Conditioning on the middle vertex E makes D and F be independent.

5.5.4   Illustrative Example of Measuring Causality

Before discussing a full study using directed acyclic graphs, it is helpful to consider an illustrative example. The essential information in set out in Fig. 5.3, and is again largely drawn from Bessler (2002).

In situation 1, assume that the distribution of X and U is thus: $X = \{100, 200\}$ each with probability 1/2; $U = \{-50, -40, -30\}$ each with probability 1/3. The joint distribution of *(X,U)* is then as follows:

Value	$(100, -50)$	$(100, -40)$	$(100, -30)$	$(200, -50)$	$(200, -40)$	$(200, -30)$
Probability	1/6	1/6	1/6	1/6	1/6	1/6

In this case (situation 1), the distribution of *Y, given that X equals 200*, is $\{30, 40, 50\}$ with probabilities of 1/3 each. Now assume that X actually does equal 200 with probability 1; this would correspond, for instance, to a policy that would set X to be 200.

Situation 1	Situation 2
$X \rightarrow Y \leftarrow U$	V $\swarrow \quad \searrow$ $X \rightarrow Y \leftarrow U$
Assume: Y=100-.1X+U	Assume Y=100-.1X+U, X=600-100V, and U=-5V
Implications: X and Y are not independent U and Y are not independent X and U *are* independent	Implications: X and Y are not independent U and Y are not independent X and U are independent *given V* X and U are not independent
Notes: Y is poverty, X is GDP per person, U refers to omitted variables, and V is an index of freedom.	

Fig. 5.3 Two illustrative situations

The distribution of Y is the same, $\{30, 40, 50\}$ with probabilities of 1/3 each. So in this case, the distribution of Y conditional on $X = 200$ that we observe on the dataset is the same as the one that we would get if we imposed a value of 200 for X.

By way of contrast, in situation 2, suppose that $V = \{4, 5\}$ with probabilities of 1/2 each; then $U = \{-20, -25\}$ with probabilities of 1/2 each. The joint distribution of (Y, X, U, V) is then as follows:

Value	(60, 200, −20, 4)	(65, 100, −25, 5)
Probability	1/2	1/2

Here Y equals $\{60, 65\}$ with probability 1/2 each. Suppose now that X is 200 with probability 1. The joint distribution of (Y, X, U, V) now becomes

Value	(60, 200, −20, 4)	(55, 200, −25, 5)
Probability	1/2	1/2

Moreover, if X is now 100 with probability 1, the joint distribution of (Y, X, U, V) now becomes

Value	(70, 100, −20, 4)	(65, 100, −25, 5)
Probability	1/2	1/2

The interesting point of this example is this: It is now clear that if we attempt to evaluate the effect on Y of raising X from 100 to 200 on the basis of the observational data, we will underestimate this effect: we see a decrease of five percentage points (from 65 to 60) from the observational data, while the mean of the distribution of Y when X is forced to be 100 is 67.5 and the mean of the distribution of Y when X is forced to be 200 is 57.5, implying a ten-percentage-point decrease. It is in conundrums such as these that the whole problem lies in trying to measure the strength of causality from observational data.

The problem is due to the fact that if we try to estimate the influence of X on Y from observational data, we risk ignoring an unblocked "backdoor" path from X to Y through another variable V.

5.5.5 Tetrad, and the Partial Correlation Algorithm

We now explain how the *partial correlation (PC) algorithm*, due to Scheines et al. (1994) works. It is available under the name Tetrad (Version IV, The Tetrad Project 2010). We confine our discussion to the essential logic of the algorithm; Tetrad IV includes a number of further refinements that users can pursue – see Soremekun and Malgwi (2011) for an application.

The PC algorithm works as follows. First, a complete undirected graph is created, where each variable corresponds to a vertex. Then edges (i.e., links between vertices) are removed from pairs of variables that are independent, either unconditionally, or conditionally on a subset of the remaining variables. Continuous variables are assumed to be multivariate normal – and may need to be transformed initially to achieve this – so that independence may then be tested with standard correlation tests.[2]

In order to orient the surviving links, the PC algorithm proceeds as follows: For each triplet (X, Y, Z) such that both pairs (X, Y) and (Y, Z) are linked, but the pair (X, Z) is not linked, if Y does not appear in any set of variables which, when conditioned upon, makes X and Z independent, then the triplet (X, Y, Z) is oriented $X \rightarrow Y \leftarrow Z$, in effect making Y a collider. This makes sense, since such an orientation implies that X and Z are dependent, given Y.

Once all such colliders have been identified, the algorithm continues like this: If $X \rightarrow Y$, Y and Z are linked, and X and Z are not linked, and if there is no arrowhead at Y from Z, then (Y, Z) is oriented as $P(D, E, F) = P(D/F, E)P(F/E)P(E)$. Such an orientation implies that X and Z are independent, given Y. Appendix B of the Tetrad user manual (The Tetrad project 2010) explains how the algorithm unfolds for a particular example.

The question is now whether, and under which assumptions, a graph obtained from the PC algorithm would imply causality in its directed links. A result due to Spirtes et al. (2000) finds that causality can be inferred, but under three strong assumptions.

The first assumption is that the set of variables can be a *causally sufficient* set. That means that there are no omitted variables that cause any two of the variables included in the set. The second condition is that the joint distribution of all the variables in the set satisfy a *causal Markov condition*. That means that one only needs to condition on parents, and not on grand-parents, uncles or aunts or siblings, to fully capture the probability distribution for any variable. The third assumption is that of *faithfulness*, which means that for any pair X, Y, X and Y are dependent if and only if there is an edge (i.e., a link) between X and Y.

These assumptions, particularly the first one, are quite hard to guarantee. For that reason, causality relations from graphs obtained via the PC algorithm are difficult to infer. Nevertheless, as we will see in the worked example in the next section, the graphs typically generate some very useful insights.

5.6   A DAG to Explain World Poverty

To illustrate the practical workings of a directed acyclic graph, and the uses to which it could be put, we discuss here a study by Bessler (2002), which we have replicated. His interest is in understanding why poverty rates differ from one country to the next, and in disentangling the variables that might be considered to cause poverty from those that may be related to poverty in some other way.

---

[2] Tetrad allows one to use either continuous data, or categorical data, but not a mixture of both, unless the user provides a priori information on which pairs of variables are independent conditionally on other variables. When categorical data are used, Tetrad tests for independence using contingency tables. For further details see Haughton et al. (2006).

Table 5.1 Summary statistics for Bessler (2002) study of the causes of poverty

Variable [variable label]	Min	Max	Mean	SD
% of population with <$2/day [$2/day]	0.0	90.8	43.2	28.9
Gini Index of inequality [Glx]	19.5	63.4	40.6	10.0
Un-Freedom Index [Free]	2.2	4.8	3.3	0.5
ln(Agricultural Value Added/worker) [Ag.Inc]	121	29,860	2,226	3,623
ln(Life Expectancy) [L.Exp]	35.2	76.5	63.3	9.9
Percent of population rural [%Rur]	10.0	94.3	51.5	20.0
ln(Child Mortality rate) [CldMor]	6.3	286.0	74.5	68.5
ln(GDP per Capita) [GDP/Per]	110	11,467	1,916	2,264
ln(Illiteracy Rate) [Illt.]	0.1	87.1	26.0	24.4
ln(Foreign Aid) [ForAid]	−2.6	118.4	31.5	29.7
ln(Undernourishment) [Und.Nour]	0.0	58.0	17.5	15.1
Birth Rate [BR]	8.6	52.3	27.1	12.1
International Trade [Trade]	16.3	150.0	72.2	30.8

Note: Summary statistics show underlying values, not logs. Where ln(·) is shown, the log of the variable was used in the subsequent Tetrad analysis

To fix ideas, we report, in Table 5.1, summary statistics for the variables used in his study. They cover 80 countries, and refer to about the year 2000.

A number of these variables are right-skewed, and violate the assumption of multivariate normality. Our solution was to take the logarithm of these variables before pursuing the Tetrad analysis. These variables are marked "ln" on the list in Table 5.1 and their variable names are preceded with an "l" in the Tetrad output discussed below.

Figure 5.4 displays the directed acyclic graph (DAG) obtained with Tetrad IV using the PC algorithm, and applying a significance level of 0.10 for testing whether correlations are zero or not. Tetrad produces not one but in general a collection of graphs, all of which are compatible with the dataset. In Fig. 5.4, the presence of a directed arrow indicates that all graphs agreed on the direction for that arrow. So, for instance, all of the graphs show that the poverty rate – defined as the proportion of people living on less than $2 a day – leads to (the log of) undernourishment, and not vice versa.

The presence of an undirected arrow, as for example between the birth rate and (the log of) the child mortality rate indicates that the direction for this edge is ambiguous: some of the Tetrad graphs oriented it one way, and some graphs the other way. A double arrow indicates that a probable common cause exists that would link into both variables if the link were included in the dataset; this is the case of (the log of) illiteracy and (the log of) life expectancy. Interestingly, the variables on international trade, and the Gini index, did not connect to other variables in the dataset.

Some of the directions of causality mapped in the directed acyclic graph in Fig. 5.4 do appear reasonable, although one has to wonder about a finding that higher per capita GDP does not affect the poverty rate. The relations shown in the DAG do not constitute a theory of the causes of poverty, or a test of hypotheses related to poverty, or a measure of how a policy or program affects poverty. The exercise is also limited by the assumptions that the vertices (variables) are normally

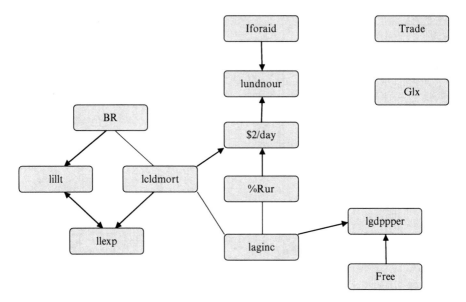

Fig. 5.4 Tetrad graph obtained using the PC algorithm (significance level = 0.10) on Bessler poverty data

distributed, that we have a tolerably complete list of relevant variables, and that the relationships apply everywhere (so there is homogeneity in the units). This particular exercise is also static, in the sense of relying on a cross-section of data at a single point in time. And each of the countries included in the sample gets equal weight, regardless of population or total GDP.

Despite such limitations, the DAG is at least suggestive, and may perhaps be useful in guiding an agenda for further research. The absence of any apparent relationship between the headcount poverty rate and inequality (as measured by the Gini coefficient), suggests that research on this nexus may be unproductive; the more surprising link that runs from child mortality to poverty (rather than vice versa) challenges us to ask why this might occur.

5.6.1   DAGs and Theory: Publishing Productivity

The strongest advocates of DAGs and other "discovery algorithms" argue that "the necessity of theory is badly exaggerated," and that common sense, coupled with attention to the underlying statistical assumptions, suffices in much of the social sciences (Spirtes et al. 2000). To back up this contention, Spirtes and his collaborators examine a study by Rodgers and Maranto (1989) that seeks to explain the determinants of publishing productivity, as measured by the rate at which one's publications are cited. The data come from 162 responses to a survey of academic psychologists who obtained doctoral degrees between 1966 and 1976; the variables

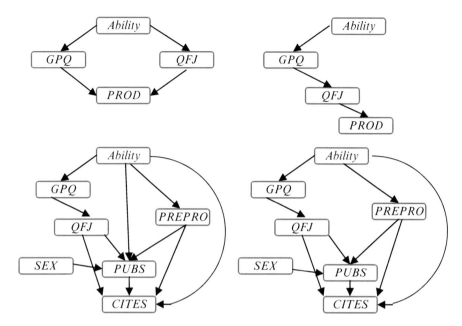

Fig. 5.5 Graphs showing causes of research productivity in psychology. *Notes: Top left panel* shows human capital model; *top right panel* shows "screening" model; *bottom left panel* shows Rodgers and Maranto (1989) graph; *bottom right panel* has DAG from Spirtes et al. (2000). GPQ is quality of graduate program attended; QFJ is quality of first job; PREPRO is pre-doctoral publications; PUBS measures publication rate; CITES measures citation rate

include measures of "ability" (based on undergraduate performance), the quality of the graduate program, the number of early publications, the quality of the first job, gender, and publication rate.

There are several possible theories that seek to explain labor productivity. A standard human capital model would have ability (ABILITY) influencing both the quality of the graduate program (GPQ) and quality of the first job (QFJ), and through these channels to the publication rate (PROD), as shown in the top left panel of Fig. 5.5. A version of the "screening" hypothesis supposes that individuals with ability need to signal their capability by attending a high-quality graduate program, and this in turn propels them into a high-quality first job, which provides the setting for scholarly productivity, as shown in the top right panel of Fig. 5.5. There are a number of other possible models, and after reviewing the literature and trying several models, Rodgers and Maranto eventually settle on the pathways shown in the bottom left panel of Fig. 5.5.

Using the same data, Spirtes et al. use TETRAD to create a very similar graph – as shown in the bottom right panel of Fig. 5.5 – a process that they say "takes a few minutes." Their conclusion is bold: "Any claim that social scientific theory – other than common sense – is required to find the essentials of the Rodgers and Maranto model is clearly false" (p. 102).

The challenge posed here goes well beyond the specifics of this particular case – it is odd, for instance, that in this example "ability" has no apparent direct effect on PUBS – to the issue of how to divide time and effort between theory and numbers, and even to the nature of what constitutes useful knowledge.

5.7 Conclusion

Most social scientists do not believe in predestination. There is room for free will, for advice to influence policy, for research to matter in the practical world.

Yet the disagreements run deep. The structural school sees a need for at least some theoretical structure to anchor ideas, help formulate hypotheses, and provide an understanding that can be applied usefully in new contexts. Its adherents are leery of data mining, skeptical about the usefulness or relevance of many controlled or natural experiments, and shy away from mechanistic approaches such as DAGs. At the same time, they make the case for some exploration of the data, and for a clear understanding of where the information comes from and what its limitations are (Deaton 1997).

The experimentalists argue that the measurement of effects can be useful for policy even if the underlying mechanisms are not fully understood. They take their cue from Gustav Papanek, who has argued that economic development theory is an "earnest search for a mirage." To wait for a model, which will necessarily be a simplification of reality, may be misplaced effort. So if one finds that microcredit does not work, this is worth knowing, even if we may not know why it does not work. On the other hand, there are very many important questions that cannot be answered with experiments or quasi-experiments; Martin Ravallion (2009) is concerned that the "randomistas" write off such knowledge gaps as "lost causes for scientific inquiry," which would seriously diminish the questions about economic development that one can hope to address.

The causal influence school may have formal logic on its side, but is the least compelling for most social scientists. Some of the causal links it unearths in DAGs seem silly, and the underlying assumptions are often violated. But this approach challenges the theoreticians to justify their intellectual edifices, rather than assume that without theory there can be no understanding.

The very best practitioners make it look easy – moving with seemingly effortless ease from theory to data and back. That is a model worth aspiring to, and our book is written in the desire to make it easier to do – casting our net over a wide variety of techniques, and encouraging readers to try the offerings on the menu when they seem tasty enough.

References

Abdulkadiroglu, A., J. Angrist, S. Dynarski, J. Fullerton, T. Kane, and P. Pathak. 2009. Accountability and flexibility in public schools: Evidence from Boston's charters and pilots. NBER Working Paper 14459, Cambridge, MA.

Angrist, J., G. Imbens, and D. Rubin. 1996. Identification of causal effects using instrumental variables. *Journal of Econometrics* 71(1): 145–160.

Angrist, Joshua, and Jörn-Steffen Pischke. 2010. The credibility revolution in empirical economics: How better research design is taking the con out of econometrics. *Journal of Economic Perspectives* 24(2): 3–30.

Banerjee, Abhijit, Esther Duflo, Rachel Glennerster, and Cynthia Kinnan. 2010. The miracle of microfinance? Evidence from a randomized evaluation. Department of Economics, MIT.

Bessler, D.A., and N. Loper. 2001. Economic development: Evidence from directed acyclic graphs. *The Manchester School* 69: 457–76.

Bessler D.A. 2002. On world poverty: Its causes and effects. http://agecon2.tamu.edu/people/faculty/bessler-david/WebPage/Bessler%20Poverty.pdf. Accessed July 30, 2011.

Bryant, Henry, David Bessler, and Michael Haigh. 2009. Disproving causal relationships using observational data. *Oxford Bulletin of Economics and Statistics* 71(3): 357–374.

Deaton, A. 1997. *The analysis of household surveys: A microeconometric approach to development policy*. Baltimore: John Hopkins University Press.

Deaton, Angus. 2010. Understanding the mechanisms of economic development. *Journal of Economic Perspectives* 24(2): 3–16.

Duflo, Esther, Glennerster, Rachel, and Kremer. Michael, Using Randomization in Development Economics Research: A Toolkit (December 12, 2006). MIT Department of Economics Working Paper No. 06-36. Available at SSRN: http://papers.ssrn.com/sol3/papers.cfm?abstract_id=951841##. Accessed July 30, 2011.

Geiger, D., T. Verma, and J. Pearl. 1990. Identifying independencies in Bayesian networks. *Networks* 20: 507–534.

Glewwe, Paul, Michael Kremer, Sylvie Moulin, and Eric Zitzewitz. 2000. Flip charts in Kenya. NBER Working Paper 8018, Cambridge, MA.

Haughton, D., A. Kamis, and P. Scholten. 2006. A Review of three directed acyclic graphs software packages: MIM, Tetrad, and WinMine. *The American Statistician* 60(3): 272–286.

Haughton, Jonathan, Paul Bachman, David Tuerck, and Eli Cutler. 2011. Why Massachusetts should double the number of charter schools. Beacon Hill Institute at Suffolk University, Boston, MA.

Heckman, J.J. 2008. Econometric causality. *International Statistical Review* 76: 1–27.

Heckman, James. 2010. Building bridges between structural and program evaluation approaches to evaluating policy. NBER Working Paper 16110, Cambridge, MA.

Holland, Paul. 1986. Statistics and causal inference. *Journal of the American Statistical Association* 81: 945–960.

Hoxby, Caroline, Sonali Murarka, and Jenny Kang. 2009. How New York City's charter schools affect achievement. New York City Charter Schools Evaluation Project, Stanford, CA.

Imbens, Guido. 2010. Better LATE than nothing: Some comments on Deaton (2009) and Heckman and Urzua (2009). *Journal of Economic Literature* 48: 399–423.

Keane, Michael. 2010. A structural perspective on the experimentalist school. *Journal of Economic Perspectives* 24(2): 47–58.

Leamer, Edward. 2010. Tantalus on the road to asymptotia. *Journal of Economic Perspectives* 24 (2): 31–46.

Morck, Randall, and Bernard Yeung. 2011. Economics, history, and causation. NBER Working Paper 16678, Cambridge MA.

Morgan, S., and C. Winship. 2007. *Counterfactuals and causal inference: Methods and principles for social research*. Cambridge: Cambridge University Press.

Pearl, Judea. 2000. *Causality: Models, reasoning, and inference*. Cambridge: Cambridge University Press.

Pearl, Judea. 2009. Causal inference in statistics: An overview. *Statistics Surveys* 3: 96–146.

Ravallion, Martin. 2009. Should the randomistas rule?" *Economists' Voice*, 6(2): Article 6. http://www.bepress.com/ev/vol6/iss2/art6/. Accessed March 30, 2011.

Rodgers, Robert, and Cheryl Maranto. 1989. Causal models of publishing productivity in psychology. *Journal of Applied Psychology* 74(4): 636–649.

Rubin, Donald. 1974. Estimating causal effects of treatments in randomized and nonrandomized studies. *Journal of Educational Psychology* 66(5): 688–701.

Scheines, R., P. Spirtes, C. Glymour, and C. Meek. 1994. *TETRAD II: Tools for discovery*. Hillsdale: Lawrence Erlbaum Associates.

Shadish, W., T. Cook, and D. Campbell. 2002. *Experimental and quasi-experimental designs for generalized causal inference*. Boston: Houghton Mifflin.

Sims, Christopher. 2010. But economics is not an experimental science. *Journal of Economic Perspectives* 24(2): 59–68.

Soremekun, Olumayokun, and Charles Malgwi. 2011. Exploring the relationship between foreign direct investment and mobile technology in Africa: An application of directed acyclic graphs. *Case Studies in Business, Industrial, and Government Statistics*, forthcoming.

Spirtes, Peter, Clark Glymour, and Richard Scheines. 2000. *Causation, prediction, and search*, 2nd ed. Cambridge, MA: MIT Press.

The Tetrad Project. Tetrad IV. http://www.phil.cmu.edu/projects/tetrad/tetrad4.html, 2010. Accessed July 30, 2011.

Chapter 6
Grouping Methods

6.1 Introduction

We are often interested in grouping observations. Whenever we report statistics broken down by expenditure quintile, or by region, or by household size, we are gathering observations into clusters. The purpose is to help make more sense of the data, to create more order out of a potentially chaotic mass of information.

In this chapter we pursue this idea further, and explore some of the many methods that statisticians and others have used to cluster their data. Cluster analysis is one of the most common techniques in applied statistics, with applications in essentially every branch of science: for instance, market researchers try to create clusters of potential clients, the better to target them for marketing purposes; economists try to create groupings of the poor; and biologists create groupings of organisms. It appears that the term "cluster analysis" was used first by Tryon (1939), and is typically defined as the classification of similar objects into groups (Vermunt and Magidson 2002, citing Kaufman and Rousseeuw 1990). Another classic reference is Hartigan (1975); the StatSoft (2011) provides a sound implementation of clustering.

A cluster analysis is exploratory in nature, in that the discovery of groups of similar objects may or may not be inspired by any a priori theory. Each object, which could be a person, a household, or an inanimate item, is described by a set of variables, generally on a standardized numerical scale. The distance between two items is usually computed as the Euclidean distance based on the vectors of numerical variables.[1] Items that are, by this measure, close together are assigned to a common cluster, using one of the methods that we discuss below.

---

[1] Let there be k variables, $x_1, \ldots, x_k$, which we observe for individuals 1 and 2. Thus x_{11} is the observed value of variable x_1 for individual 1, x_{31} is the observed value of variable x_3 for individual 1, and so on. Then the Euclidian distance $d(x_{.1}, x_{.2})$ between the two individual observations is given by $\sqrt{\sum_{i=1}^{k}(x_{i1} - x_{i2})^2}$.

D. Haughton and J. Haughton, *Living Standards Analytics*, Statistics for Social and Behavioral Sciences, DOI 10.1007/978-1-4614-0385-2_6,
© Springer Science+Business Media, LLC 2011

Recent extensions allow the variables to be categorical, or form a mix of continuous and categorical variables, and distances other than Euclidean distances are sometimes used, notably with categorical variables. However, by far the most common situation is that of a clustering of objects on the basis of vectors of continuous variables, so we will focus on this particular case.

The two most standard methods for clustering are *hierarchical* and *nonhierarchical* (or *k-means*) cluster analysis. In this chapter, we summarize how these methods work, point out some of the strengths and limitations, and illustrate their application with a number of examples. We then turn to a discussion of latent class models, and Kohonen maps.

6.2   Hierarchical Cluster Analysis

It is useful to think of hierarchical clustering by analogy with a tree in winter: twigs are joined into branches, which are grouped into limbs, which attach to the trunk. Broadly, the idea is that observations that are somehow close to one another should be clustered together, using a metric such as Euclidean distance. The process of creating such clusters is mirrored in a tree-like dendrogram, for which we present an example below. The algorithms for clustering may be top down ("divisive") or bottom up ("agglomerative"); in the first case we assume all observations are in a single cluster at the start – the trunk of the tree – and then we divide the observations into successively smaller groups.

Agglomerative clustering works in the other direction, starting by supposing that each observation is itself a cluster, and then combining them step by step, and is the approach we consider first. We thus begin with as many initial clusters as there are objects in the data set. Now, assuming for the purposes of illustration that we have 60 observations in the dataset and 10 variables describing them, we construct a 60 by 60 matrix of Euclidean distances between any pair of observations. The matrix is symmetric, since the distance between object 1 and object 2 is the same of between object 2 and object 1, and the diagonal elements are all zeros. Pick the pair of observations for which the observed distance is the smallest, and join them to form a cluster. We now have 59 new objects, consisting of one cluster and 58 observations alone in their clusters.

At this point, it becomes necessary to define not only the distance between two objects, but also the distance between two clusters, or between one cluster and one object. One simple (and common) option is to compute the means of the ten variables for all cluster members, yielding what is called a *centroid* for that cluster. The distance between two clusters is then the Euclidean distance between the two 10-dimensional *centroid* vectors. This particular way of defining the distance between two clusters gives rise to the *Centroid method* for hierarchical cluster analysis. Once this choice of distance is settled, the hierarchical clustering algorithm proceeds by repeating the first step to the set of 59 objects, merging into a cluster the two items for which the distance is smallest.

At the end of the process, all objects are clustered into one group, and most statistical packages report the list of all "agglomerations" – i.e., merges – typically with one measure for each merge, most commonly the distance between the two clusters merged at that stage. On the basis of this "agglomeration schedule," one decides on a suitable number of clusters by stopping merges when a "large" jump occurs in the measure; we consider an example in Sect. 6.5 below. The decision about how many clusters to retain is of course rather arbitrary, and most analysts in fact try several solutions, with different numbers of clusters, until a sensible solution is obtained.

Once a clustering has been established, the variable that defines cluster membership is used to compute summaries, not only of the variables that were used in the cluster analysis, but often of other variables such as geographical location. This process of analyzing cluster summaries, frequently accompanied by graphs – for instance, box-plots of variable by cluster, or pie charts to indicate the geographical distribution of each cluster – is often referred to as "profiling the clusters." Clusters are typically given a catchy name at this stage, such as "poor rural households" or "families keen on video games and consumer durables."

One can think of hierarchical cluster analysis as a process which is similar to that of individuals arriving by themselves at a cocktail party, and then merging into groups by affinities.

The centroid method is not the only approach to computing distances among clusters. Among the other options, one of the most common is Ward's method, which at each stage merges clusters in such a way that the resulting current clusters are as homogeneous within themselves, and as different from each other, as possible. Ward's method tends to produce clusters that are better balanced in terms of number of members, but also tends to be sensitive to outliers.

One limitation of hierarchical cluster analysis is that an object, once in a cluster, cannot move out of that cluster – the "no divorce" rule. Another issue is that the algorithm is greedy in computing resources, calculating a matrix of distances at each step, so that it will often run out of memory when attempted on large datasets (say 30,000 cases on most laptops).

6.3   Nonhierarchical Clustering

The drawbacks of hierarchical clustering help explain the popularity of nonhierarchical (or k-means) cluster analysis. It assumes that we know in advance, for example from a preliminary hierarchical cluster analysis, the number of clusters to be built. The method then works as follows:

1. Begin with k (the number of clusters) well-separated cases from the data set as initial seeds, defined by their ten-dimensional vectors of variables. How well-separated cases are defined varies somewhat across statistical packages, but the

essential idea is to use as initial seeds cases that are far apart, as measured by the Euclidean distance.

2. For each case in the dataset, find the seed that is the closest to it (according to the Euclidean distance), and join that case to that seed to form a cluster.
3. When all cases are assigned to their closest seed, compute the cluster means, yielding k new ten-dimensional vectors, which become the new seeds.
4. Repeat the process of assigning cases to seeds, computing cluster means, and so on, until little or no further change occurs in the cluster means, at which point the cluster analysis has converged.

It is useful to note that nonhierarchical analyses, unlike hierarchical analyses, can run on large datasets. On the other hand, the analyst needs to know in advance how many clusters to construct. A sensible way to proceed is first to run a hierarchical analysis, if necessary on a random subsample of the dataset if the latter is too large, to give an idea of the number of clusters. The cluster means from that analysis can then be used as seeds in a nonhierarchical analysis applied to the whole dataset.

The reader may have noticed that no mention is made so far of p-values or statistical significance. Indeed a cluster analysis is an exploratory rather than inferential procedure. Some statistical packages present an analysis of variance test to decide whether means of some variables are statistically significantly different across clusters. While the F-test from these analyses can be used to help detect which variables tend to be better separated by the clusters, the p-value cannot be taken at face value, since the clusters were themselves constructed with the objective of yielding means that are as different as possible. Most statistical packages post a warning to that effect on the output.

6.4 Examples of Cluster Analysis

6.4.1 Regions of Slovakia

Our first example of a cluster analysis is based on a tiny dataset covering the eight regions of Slovakia (Matejková et al. 2008). The goal of their study is to cluster the Slovakian regions, using information for 2005 on four macroeconomic variables: regional GDP per capita, the unemployment rate, value added per worker (labor productivity), and foreign direct investment flows. They use the furthest linkage method, which defines the distance between two clusters as the distance between the two members that are furthest apart.

Their study uses a hierarchical cluster analysis, and the process by which the regions were clustered may be followed with the aid of the *dendrogram* in Fig. 6.1. At the bottom, each region is in its own cluster. At an early stage, Trnava (TT) was paired with Trenčín (TN), Nitra (NR) with Žilina (ZA), and Banská Bystrica (BB) with Košice (KE). Continuing upward, we see that at the next step Prešov (PO) was joined to the BB-KE cluster; and the TT-TN and NR-ZA clusters were combined.

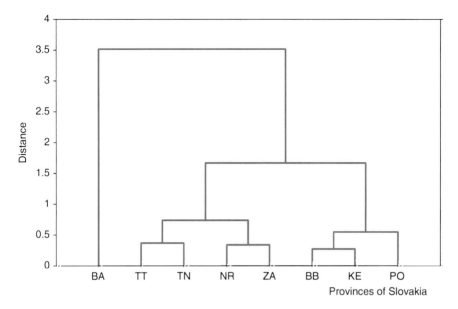

Fig. 6.1 Dendrogram of regional clusters for Slovakia. *Source*: Matejková et al. 2008. Regions are Bratislava (BA), Trnava (TT), Trenčín (TN), Nitra (NR), Žilina (ZA), Banská Bystrica (BB), Prešov (PO), and Košice (KE)

One could go further, but at this point it made sense to stop; the capital Bratislava (BA) is in a cluster on its own; cluster 2 includes TT-TN-NR-ZA; and the third cluster has three regions, BB-KE-PO.

Do these clusters make sense? One way to judge this is with the help of Fig. 6.2, which shows a scatterplot of the regional observations arrayed by GDP per capita and the unemployment rate. Bratislava stands out, with high levels of per capita GDP and low unemployment; cluster 2 is characterized by moderate unemployment and low GDP; and cluster 3 has high unemployment and the lowest GDP. The centroids of each cluster are marked on the scatterplot as boxes.

6.4.2   Households in South Africa

Vella and Vichi (1997) undertake a cluster analysis using information on 5,464 households from the 1993 South Africa Living Standards and Development Survey, where their interest is in grouping households according to their living standards. Instead of measuring living standards using per capita income or expenditure, they seek to develop a metric for living standards that could be constructed using information from a set of easy-to-collect indicators, such as a household's province, language, source of water, dependency ratio, and so on.

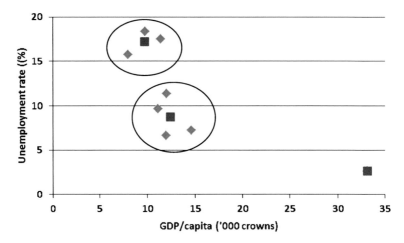

Fig. 6.2 Cluster scatterplot for the eight regions of Slovakia, 2005. [*Source*: Matejková et al. (2008). GDP is in tens of thousands of Slovak crowns per person. Based on a hierarchical cluster analysis using furthest linkage to measure proximity]

They have 25 initial variables, which they are able to winnow down to just 13 as they group them into ten "factors" – i.e., linear combinations of the initial variables – that explain 99% of the variance in the data.[2] The most important factor, which they refer to as a "socioeconomic index," reflects the household's ownership of durable goods and educational level: higher values are associated with *lower* socioeconomic status. The second important factor is described as "a composite index of vulnerability of the household" (p. 10), although it mainly reflects the dependency ratio, and age of the head of the household; higher values appear to imply greater vulnerability.

Having created the factors, Vella and Vichi use them to group the households in their sample into five clusters, using a nonhierarchical cluster analysis. They seed their clusters using the mean values of the factors for each income per capita quintile, and interpret the clusters as gathering together households that are ultra-poor (7% of the sample), poor (10%), semi-poor (16%), have medium living standards (20%), and have the highest living standards (47%).

In Fig. 6.3a, b we show their scatterplots of the clustered observations, for rural and urban areas, respectively, against the two main indexes, socioeconomics and vulnerability. A household's socioeconomic position improves as one goes from right to left, and "vulnerability" is lower at the bottom than at the top of the graph.

---

[2] The initial variables are race; residence; province; language; type of house; *type of toilet*; sources of *water*, lighting, cooking; ownership of a *motor vehicle*, bicycle, *TV, telephone*, radio, *fridge*, electric kettle, and electric stove; *whether there are debts; dependency ratio; head's gender, age, education, travel for work, illness in the last two weeks*, and expressed needs. The items in italics were retained in the factor analysis.

a

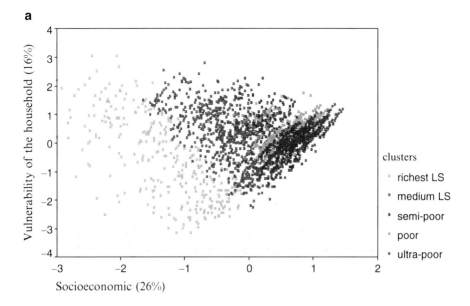

b

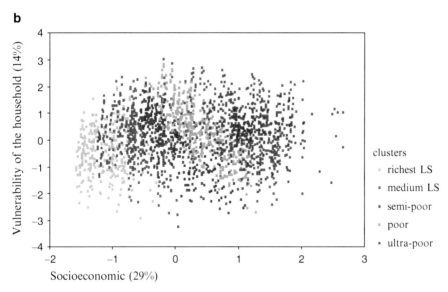

Fig. 6.3 (a) Location of clustered households on the socioeconomic-vulnerability plane, rural South Africa. [*Source*: Vella and Vichi (1997); reproduced with permission]. (**b**) Location of clustered households on the socioeconomic-vulnerability plane, urban South Africa. [*Source*: Vella and Vichi (1997); reproduced with permission]

The richest rural households are indeed clustered near the left and bottom of the picture. In urban areas, the clusters are essentially sorted along the socioeconomic dimension, with "vulnerability" playing little role, as Fig. 6.3b shows. For a comparable analysis in the context of South Africa, see Kironji (2008).

There is a long history of trying to measure poverty using cheaper and simpler instruments than a classical living standards survey, and the study by Vella and Vichi is in this tradition. It has proven difficult to find alternative indicators that are sufficiently reliable. Ravallion (1996) reports on one such effort, and is skeptical about the prospects for substituting method for data.

6.5 Model-Based Clustering: Latent Class Models

Recent advances in computing, and notably the possibility of fitting finite mixtures of distributions to data, have made it possible to conduct cluster analyses that are based on a statistical model, and not purely exploratory as are traditional cluster analysis techniques.

The advantages of this approach to cluster analysis are that a number of diagnostic tools are available to help determine the appropriate number of clusters, and that the clustering is model-based in that it relies on a statistical model. In that, it is reminiscent of structural equations models (SEMs) and, as a special case, factor analysis.

To see how latent class models work, consider the following relatively simple example. Suppose that we have information from n individuals on a variable $y_1, \ldots, y_n$ that measures, on a continuous scale, their attitudes toward gay marriage. We are interested in clustering individuals into two groups – let us call them liberals and conservatives, but these are "latent" categories that cannot be observed directly – and believe that the responses y_i were generated by a mixture of two normal distributions with means μ_1 and μ_2, and standard deviations σ_1 and σ_2, respectively. Thus the density of y_i is given by:

$$f(y_i|\mu_1, \sigma_1, \mu_2, \sigma_2) = \pi_1 N(y_i, \mu_1, \sigma_1^2) + \pi_2 N(y_i, \mu_2, \sigma_2^2), \quad \text{with } \pi_1 + \pi_2 = 1$$

$$= \pi_1 \frac{1}{\sigma_1\sqrt{2\pi}} e^{\frac{-(y_i-\mu_1)^2}{2\sigma_1^2}} + \pi_2 \frac{1}{\sigma_2\sqrt{2\pi}} e^{\frac{-(y_i-\mu_2)^2}{2\sigma_2^2}}, \tag{6.1}$$

where π_1 and π_2 are probabilities attached to each distribution, and the likelihood is given by

$$\text{likelihood}(\mu_1, \sigma_1, \mu_2, \sigma_2) = \prod_{i=1}^{n} f(y_i|\mu_1, \sigma_1, \mu_2, \sigma_2). \tag{6.2}$$

The problem here is to estimate the parameters μ_1, μ_2, σ_1, σ_2, and π_1, given the observations y_i. Once that has been done, we may assign any given observation y_i to the cluster k such that $\hat{\pi}_k N(y_i, \hat{\mu}_k, \hat{\sigma}_k)$ is as large as possible, thereby creating our pools of "liberals" and "conservatives."

A slightly more complicated model is discussed by Magidson and Vermunt (2003), who describe a latent class clustering exercise done by McCutcheon in the course of their excellent expository paper. That study had survey information on four variables that measured respondents' attitudes toward surveys, and it was hoped that the responses would allow one to cluster respondents into broad groups – the latent, or unobserved, classes – on the basis of these observed responses (the manifest variables). They were able to test formally for the appropriate number of clusters, ultimately classifying respondents into three groups, labeled "ideal respondents" (who believed surveys tend to be right and serve a good purpose), "believers," and "skeptics."

More generally, we suppose that there is an underlying model that implies that a cluster is generated with a certain probability π_j, and that the data are then generated given this cluster via a distribution with parameters θ_j that depend on the cluster. Given the observed values of the y_n, the unknown parameters θ_j as well as the probabilities π_j are estimated via maximum likelihood.

For a situation where a latent variable defines the unknown cluster membership, a latent cluster analysis can be used to estimate a likelihood function of the form

$$P(y_n|\theta) = \sum_1^S \pi_j P_j(y_n|\theta_j), \tag{6.3}$$

where y_n is the nth observed (possibly vector) value, S is the number of clusters, and π_j is the prior probability of membership in cluster j. Here P_j is the cluster-specific probability of y_n given the unknown parameter vector θ_j, which may differ across clusters. This can then be employed to cluster the observations into the latent classes. Note that (6.3) defines what is commonly referred to as a finite statistical mixture of the distributions that describe the observed vector in each cluster.

6.5.1 Applications

Zhang et al. (2009) provide a very interesting application of latent class models to diagnoses in traditional Chinese medicine (TCM). They collected data from 2,600 people above the age of 60 who were asked whether they experienced, at each of four levels of severity, 67 different symptoms related to kidney function (although ultimately the authors were only able to use 35 of the variables, given limitations on computing power).

The authors consider not one, but several, latent variables, which can be linked to each other, yielding what is referred to as a Latent Tree Model; this is a Bayesian Network, and is similar to a Directed Acyclic Graph (see Chap. 5). Each latent variable is categorical, with three, four, or five states, and thus generates a clustering of the data set with as many clusters as there are states in the latent variable. The clusters can then be profiled with the occurrence of the four severity levels for each of the symptoms linked to the latent variable.

For example, a latent variable X_1 with five states is linked directly to three symptoms – intolerance to cold, cold limbs, and cold lumbus and back – and indirectly via another latent variable X_2 with three states to two symptoms, loose stool, and undigested grain in stool. The five clusters differ in the level of severity of the five symptoms linked (directly or indirectly) to X_1.

The estimation of the model is complex, and the results tend to confirm known theories in Chinese traditional medicine. This is a significant advance, since the scientific bases for these theories are not known, and the model proposed by the authors provides at least a statistical justification for them.

Another useful example of a latent class analysis is provided by Eshghi et al. (2011), who set out to cluster 160 countries based on a set of variables on socioeconomic wealth, and digital development. The analysis generated solutions ranging from 1 to 13 clusters and found the solution with seven clusters to be optimal.

This study used the software package Latent GOLD 4.0 to implement the analysis. Haughton et al. (2009) review a number of software packages that perform latent cluster analysis, including Latent GOLD 4.0, and R packages poLCA and MCLUS.

6.6   Case Study: Vietnamese Households, 2002

The 2002 round of the Vietnamese Household Living Standards Survey collected information on 29,530 households. In this exercise, we seek to group these households into clusters, based on eight variables. The file was too large to run a hierarchical cluster analysis, so we began by extracting a 10% random subsample of households and used hierarchical clustering on this group. Table 6.1 lists the variables used in the analysis, and provides descriptive statistics both for the full sample and for the 10% subsample; the subsample closely tracks the full sample.

Table 6.1 Summary statistics for variables used in cluster analysis, Vietnam 2002

	Full sample		10% subsample	
	Mean	SD	Mean	SD
Cost of education per person (educpc)	181.98	373.9	189.03	391.2
Cost of water per person (waterpc)	13.73	41.86	13.88	42.21
Cost of electricity per person (elecpc)	87.20	124.30	85.04	115.79
Garbage collection cost per cap (garbpc)	2.82	8.85	2.75	8.08
Rent spending per capita (rentpc)	424.90	1,047.22	472.16	1,783.34
Household size (hhsize)	4.48	1.80	4.49	1.78
Food consumption per capita (foodpc)	1,596.33	912.31	1,597.24	872.14
Real expenditure per capita (pcexp2rl)	3,667.37	3,210.44	3,726.27	3,623.80
Valid sample size	29,452		2,951	

Source: Vietnam Household Living Standard Survey of 2002. Monetary values are in thousands of Vietnamese dong

Table 6.2 Agglomeration schedule for hierarchical cluster analysis

Stage	Cluster 1	Cluster 2	Coefficients
. . .	. . .	. . .	. . .
2936	8	56	6,933.4
2937	36	38	7,190.5
2938	1	37	7,571.9
2939	2	73	7,974.9
2940	4	21	8,381.5
2941	99	177	8,810.9
2942	1	36	9,253.7
2943	9	1506	9,723.8
2944	2	80	10,295.0
2945	4	8	11,198.1
2946	4	999	12,707.0
2947	4	99	14,494.8
2948	1	2	16,485.9
2949	1	4	23,592.0

Source: Based on data summarized in Table 6.1

Table 6.2 displays the last several lines of the *agglomeration schedule* generated by the hierarchical clustering on the 10% sample. The first column lists the stage in the analysis; by the end of the table all the observations have been aggregated into a single cluster. Columns 2 and 3 indicate which of the clusters were joined at each stage; for instance, in stage 2947, cluster 99 was added to cluster 4; and in the last stage, cluster 4 was merged with cluster 1.

The most important column in Table 6.2 is the last one, which shows the "coefficients." In this example we used Ward's method to join together clusters, and so the coefficient column shows the within-cluster sum of squares at that stage. As more clusters are agglomerated, the within-cluster sum of squares rises, at the expense of the between-cluster sum of squares (not shown here).

A sensible way to choose how main clusters to retain is by looking for a large jump in the column of coefficients: if there are too few clusters there will be too much variation within clusters, but if there are too many clusters it is difficult to make any generalizations, and to interpret the results. In our example we see a substantial jump in the coefficient between stages 2944 and 2945, and so we choose to retain five clusters for the next stage of our analysis.

We then undertake a nonhierarchical cluster analysis using the full dataset. We use the cluster means for the five-cluster solution as initial seeds, and then begin the iterative process that leads to the final clustering. Table 6.3 shows the seeds in the top panel, and the final means and standard deviations in the bottom half of the table. It is interesting to note that the proportion of observations allocated to cluster 2 at the initial stage (169 out of 2,950 observations, or 5.7%) is substantially smaller than the proportion in the final allocation (9.6%).

The final cluster means of standardized variables, along with the inter-quartile range and other information, are shown in the box-and-whisker plots in Fig. 6.4. Cluster 1 represents an affluent group, with especially high levels of spending on

Table 6.3 Cluster means sizes, for seed values and final clusters, Vietnam 2002

Variable	Cluster 1	Cluster 2	Cluster 3	Cluster 4	Cluster 5	Overall
	Mean values					
Seed values						
educpc	1,056.5	277.3	103.0	1,240.9	88.2	189.3
waterpc	139.3	81.5	10.5	14.6	1.4	13.8
elecpc	615.8	259.3	78.1	112.7	36.5	85.0
garbpc	27.1	21.3	1.5	4.3	0.1	2.8
rentpc	6,791.6	1,726.9	316.5	479.7	121.5	446.8
foodpc	4,603.1	3,091.3	1,575.4	1,892.8	1,161.2	1,587.6
pcexp2rl	21,022.6	8,910.8	3,354.3	5,665.3	2,207.7	3,702.8
hhsize	3.31	3.38	3.52	4.85	6.15	4.49
N	49	169	1,542	170	1,020	2,950
Final cluster means						
educpc	870.4	279.7	94.1	1,405.1	112.5	182.3
waterpc	164.5	73.3	4.0	23.4	3.1	13.7
elecpc	654.0	223.1	71.6	143.1	39.6	87.3
garbpc	33.2	16.3	0.7	5.4	0.4	2.8
rentpc	5,467.5	1,312.1	269.4	662.2	136.4	424.8
foodpc	4,924.0	2,778.3	1,535.4	2,131.6	1,149.1	1,596.8
pcexp2rl	19,447.6	7,716.5	3,166.0	6,626.1	2,212.5	3,670.3
hhsize	3.2	3.8	3.4	4.5	6.2	4.5
N	498	2,818	14,487	1,339	10,510	29,452

Source: As for Table 6.1, where the variables are also described

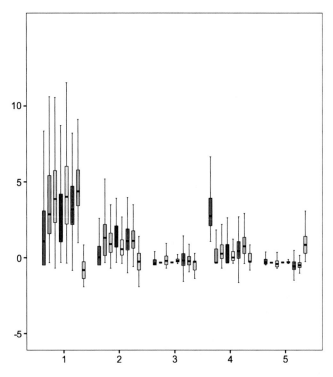

Fig. 6.4 Box-and-Whisker plot of variables, by five clusters, Vietnam 2002. (*Source*: As for Table 6.1. *Vertical axis* shows standardized values; clusters are shown from *left* (cluster 1) to *right* (cluster 5); within each cluster, variables are educpc, waterpc, elecpc, garbpc, rentpc, foodpc, pcexp1rl, and hhsize

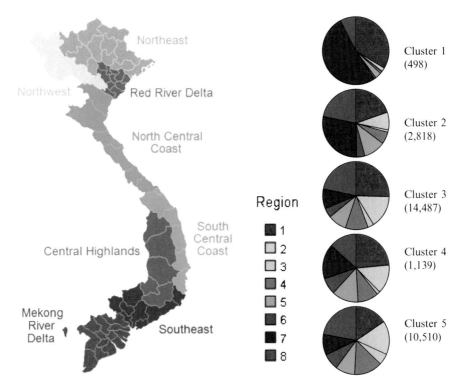

Fig. 6.5 Geographic breakdown of five clusters for Vietnam, 2002. (*Source*: As for Table 7.1; map from http://en.wikipedia.org/wiki/File:VietnameseRegions.png and reproduced under Wikimedia Commons)

rent, suggesting that the group includes a lot of urban residents. Clusters 3 and 5 are both poor, but cluster 5 is distinctive for its large households, and the very low spending levels, including on food.

In Fig. 6.5 we graph the geographic representation in each of the clusters. For instance, residents of the Southeast Region (which includes Ho Chi Minh City, and is shown on the map in purple) and of the Red River Delta (which includes Hanoi, and is shown on the map in red) dominate cluster 1, confirming our intuition that it is mainly a cluster of relatively affluent urban residents.

6.7 Kohonen Maps

Kohonen maps, which create a sophisticated (and colorful) form of clustering, represent a special case of a competitive neural network. They are also referred to as *self-organizing maps* (SOMs). A useful introduction to the methodology for constructing the maps is given in Larose (2005), and a Matlab 6.0 toolbox

Table 6.4 Variables used to construct Kohonen map for Vietnam, c.2000

Wealth of household	
GDPindex99	GDP index normalized between 0 and 1
Hpiindex99	UN composite poverty index, 1999
Gdppc99vnd	GDP per capita in 1999 dong
Mincpccurpric	Average income per capita in current prices
Percexpfood	% of spending allocated to food
Valdurgoods	Average value of durable goods owned
Percpermhouse	% of residents with permanent houses
Povrate	Poverty rate
Education of household	
Eduindex99	Literacy rate (2/3) + combined enrollment rates (1/3)
Adlircy	Adult literacy rate
Percunivcoll	% of population with university of college diplomas
Percmsphd	% of population with masters or PhD degrees
Schlen3to5	School enrolment rate, ages 3–5
Schlenlowsec	Lower secondary school enrolment rate
Schlenupse	Upper secondary school enrolment rate
Health of household	
Lifexpindex99	Life expectancy (normalized between 0 and 1), 1999
Malnuunder598	Under-5 malnutrition rate
Lifexpmale	Male life expectancy (years)
Lifexpfem	Female life expectancy (years)
Wgtforht	Weight for height malnutrition
Htforage	Height for age malnutrition
Wgtforage	Weight for age malnutrition
Matdeathp1000	Number of pregnancy-related deaths per 1,000
Infmort	Infant mortality rate
Other	
Hhsize	Number of members of household

Sources: National Human Development Report 2001, National Political Publishing House (2001). Figures on Social Development: Doi Moi in Vietnam (Statistical Publishing House 2000)

(which was used for the example below) can be found at the Kohonen map site at http://www.cis.hut.fi/projects/somtoolbox/ . Deichmann et al. (2007) provide a detailed description of the methodology, as do Kaski and Kohonen (1996). Their reliability is discussed by De Bodt et al. (2005); a nice example is presented in Ponthieux and Cottrell (2001).

In this section we work backwards, first presenting an example of a Kohonen map, then interpreting the results, and finally explaining the algorithm by which the maps are generated.

Our example is adapted from Nguyen et al. (2009), and uses provincial-level data on 25 variables for 61 provinces in Vietnam. Details for the variables are shown in Table 6.4, and are more or less equally divided among measures of household wealth, education, and health.

The goal is to create a "map" that shows how close the provinces are to one another. In part this represents clustering, especially when several provinces find

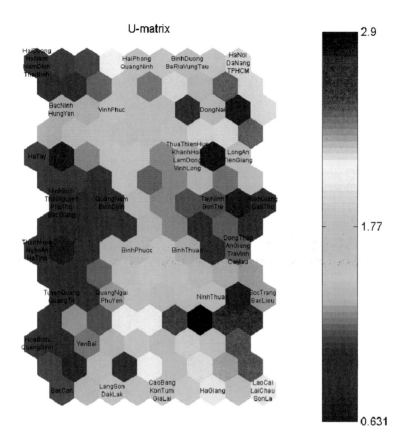

Fig. 6.6 Kohonen map of 61 Vietnamese provinces, c.2000. (*Source*: Data sources as in Table 6.4; analysis from Phong et al. 2009)

themselves on the same cell of the map, but it also allows one to gain an appreciation of the "distance" between the provinces, as described more fully below.

Mechanically, the Kohonen map was created with the following Matlab code:

```
cd C:\MATLAB6p1\toolbox\Kohonen\somtoolbox
dn=som_read_data ('C:\provincekohonen_p25.txt')
dn=som_normalize (dn,'var',[1:25])
dnmap=som_make (dn)
dnmaplab=som_autolabel (dnmap,dn)
som_show (dnmaplab,'umat','all')
som_show_add ('label',dnmaplab,'Textsize', 8)
som_show (dnmap,'comp','all')
```

The resulting map is shown in Fig. 6.6. It is two-dimensional, with 8 rows and 5 columns, the default values of the Kohonen Matlab toolkit software. Each of the 40 positions is associated with a 25-dimensional estimated component vector, obtained at the convergence of the Kohonen algorithm (and explained more fully below).

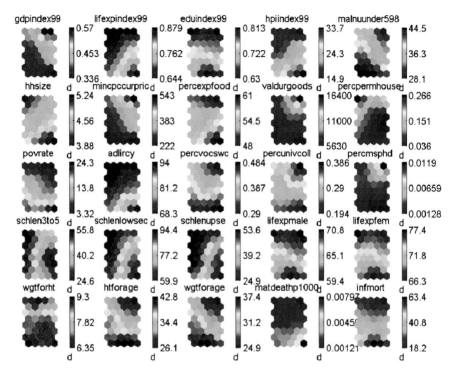

Fig. 6.7 Component map associated with Kohonen map of Vietnam. (*Source*: As for Fig. 6.6; this is a companion figure)

The 40 positions in Fig. 6.6, referred to as the U-matrix, are each represented by a hexagon, with additional hexagons on each side of the positional hexagons. The color of these surrounding hexagons varies depending on the average "distance" to the estimated vectors for the positions on either side. For instance, the top right hexagon (Hanoi, Danang, and Ho Chi Minh City) has an estimated vector that is moderately different from that of the hexagon with Binh Duong and Ba Ria-Vung Tau (pale blue intervening hexagon). The color of the positional hexagon itself represents the average distance between the estimated vector at that position and that of all its neighbors; thus the pale green color of the Hanoi/Danang/Ho Chi Minh City hexagon indicates that it is somewhat different from that of all its neighbors.

The map, and specifically the U-matrix, shows that Ba Ria-Vung Tau, which would be ranked first by the United Nations human development index (HDI), (see Nguyen et al. 2009), now is clustered by the two-dimensional Kohonen Map with Binh Duong, which is ranked sixth by HDI; this is a more credible result if one takes into account area knowledge about these provinces. Note that a one-dimensional Kohonen map (not shown here), with the same 25 variables, would place Ba Ria-Vung Tau in the third position.

Figure 6.7 shows the *component map* that is associated with the Kohonen map in Fig. 6.6. Each panel in Fig. 6.7 shows the estimated value at convergence of one of the variables for each of the 40 positions in the map. High values of the variables are displayed in browns and dark reds, low values in blues. So, for example, the top left panel in Fig. 6.7 shows the values of the GDP index, which are high in the north-east part of the graph, and fall as one moves toward the south-west. Surprisingly, and this is one of the remarkable features of Kohonen maps, the patterns on these component graphs vary monotonically, which makes them relatively easy to interpret.

Consider, for example, the provinces of Lao Cai, Lai Chau, and Son La. On the main map in Fig. 6.6 they are clustered together in the very bottom right-hand position. The blue/green hexagon next to this position tells us that they are somewhat similar to the "nearest" province, which is Ha Giang. From the component graphs, we see by looking at the bottom right-hand corners that the three provinces have low GDP, low life expectancy, low educational enrolments, low adult literacy, high poverty rates, and high levels of infant mortality. By any measure they are very poor. This is hardly surprising: all three provinces are found in the remote mountainous northwest region of Vietnam.

6.7.1 Building Kohonen Maps

In this section, we explain briefly how Kohonen maps are constructed. The basic algorithm proceeds as follows:

1. Begin with a grid, which is typically two-dimensional, and a set of k variables that we propose to use to construct the map. In our earlier example the grid was 8×5, and there were 25 variables.
2. For each position on the grid, indexed by i, generate a vector $m_i(t)$ of "weights" of dimension k. Note that t indexes the step, so $t = 0$ at this point. These initial vectors may be chosen arbitrarily.
3. The competition step: Take the vector $x(t)$ that contains data on the k variables for the first observation, and compare it to each of the $m_i(0)$ vectors of weights. Find the index c, referred to as the Best Matching Unit (BMU), such that for every i, $\|m_c(t) - x(t)\| \leq \|m_i(t) - x(t)\|$. In other words, find the position whose weight vector is closest to the data vector, and assign the observation to this position.
4. The adaptation step: Update the weight vector $m_c(t)$ as follows: $m_c(t + 1) = m_c(t) + h_c(t)(x(t) - m_c(t))$, where $h_c(t)$ is often taken to be a constant, and may be thought of as a "learning rate" because it determines the speed at which the vectors in each position react when new observations are added.
5. Repeat steps 3 and 4 for all the remaining variables. There will now be a new set of vectors that may be labeled $m_i(1)$.
6. Repeat steps 3, 4, and 5 for the data once again. Some of the observations may now be allocated to different positions, and the vectors $m_i(t)$ will continue to change.
7. Continue the process until little further change is observed in the $m_i(t)$.

Fig. 6.8 Initial weight
vectors for a sample 2×2
Kohonen map

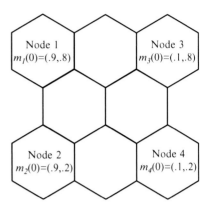

The resulting map tends to organize the components of the estimated vectors, the
$m_i(t)$, in a monotonic way (increasing or decreasing) as one moves on the map,
hence the appellation self-organizing maps.

6.7.2   An Illustration

Since the way in which a Kohonen map is constructed is not self-evident, we
illustrate the key steps here with a simple numerical example, modified from the
one developed by Larose (2005, pp. 166–169).

Suppose we have just four observations, and for each observation we have
information on two (normalized) variables, age and income. Our interest is in
constructing a 2×2 Kohonen map to reveal hidden clusters in the data. The dataset
is as follows:

Observation	Age	Income	Characteristics of individual
1	0.8	0.8	Old, high-income
2	0.8	0.1	Old, low-income
3	0.2	0.9	Young, high-income
4	0.6	0.6	Middle-aged, moderate income

We first choose a set of arbitrary initial weight vectors $m_i(0)$ that are shown in
Fig. 6.8. Now take the first observation from the data set, and compute the
Euclidean distance between this observation and each of the weight vectors. So,
for example, when we compare $(0.8, 0.8)$ with the weight vector in Node 1, which is
$(0.9, 0.8)$, we get the Euclidean distance

$$d(x_1, m_1(0)) = \sqrt{(0.8 - 0.9)^2 + (0.8 - 0.8)^2} = 0.1.$$

We find that the distance of observation 1 from nodes 2, 3, and 4 are, respectively, 0.61, 0.70, and 0.92. Clearly, observation 1 is closest to node 1, and so we assign it to that node. This makes sense: the first observation represents an old, high-income person, and the arbitrary weight vector in node 1 happens to represent an old, high-income person too, unlike the initial weights in the other nodes.

We now adjust the weight in node 1, which "won" the competition in the previous step. Let us assume that the learning rate, h, is set to 0.5. Then we have

$$m_{1,\text{new}} = m_{1,\text{current}} + h(x_1 - m_{1,\text{current}}). \qquad (6.4)$$

and in this case:

$$\begin{pmatrix} 0.85 \\ 0.80 \end{pmatrix} = \begin{pmatrix} 0.90 \\ 0.80 \end{pmatrix} + 0.5 \begin{pmatrix} 0.80 - 0.90 \\ 0.80 - 0.80 \end{pmatrix}. \qquad (6.5)$$

The addition of the new observation tugs the old weight toward the value of the observation.

We now repeat the process for the other three observations. One can verify that observation 2 will be assigned to node 2, and observation 3 to node 3, and the weights will need to be modified somewhat. Note however that the fourth observation will be assigned to node 1. This will require a further revision of the weights in node 1, as follows:

$$\begin{pmatrix} 0.725 \\ 0.700 \end{pmatrix} = \begin{pmatrix} 0.85 \\ 0.80 \end{pmatrix} + 0.5 \begin{pmatrix} 0.60 - 0.85 \\ 0.60 - 0.80 \end{pmatrix}. \qquad (6.6)$$

Now we label the new sets of weights as $m_i(1)$, and start again, comparing each observation with the weights at each node, allocating the observations to nodes, revising the weights, and so on. Eventually the process will converge, and we will have our final self-organized map.

6.8   Conclusion

When we cluster observations we are not trying to test a theory. We are, however, trying to get a better feel for the patterns into which our observations fall. This can be done by assigning observations into predefined bins, such as quintiles of per capita income, but such assignment is not so obvious when we have several variables for each observation. The techniques of cluster analysis help us mine the data for patterns that we might not otherwise have noticed, and that is often a useful prelude to framing good questions and developing more rigorous models.

References

Albert, Jose R., L. Elloso, E. Suan, and M.A. Magtulis. 2003. Visualizing regional and provincial poverty structures via the self-organizing map. *The Philippine Statistician* 52(1–4): 39–57.

De Bodt, Eric, M. Cottrell, and M. Verleysen. 2005. Statistical tools to assess the reliability of self-organizing maps. *Neural Networks* 15: 967–978.

Deichmann, J., D. Haughton, A. Eshghi, S. Sayek, and S. Woolford. 2007. Measuring the international digital divide: An application of Kohonen self-organizing maps. *Journal of International Knowledge and Learning* 3(6): 552–575.

Hartigan, J.A. 1975. *Clustering algorithms*. New York: Wiley.

Haughton, D., P. Legrand, and S. Woolford. 2009. Review of three latent class cluster analysis packages: Latent GOLD, poLCA, and MCLUST. *The American Statistician* 63(1): 81–91.

Eshghi, A., D. Haughton, P. Legrand, M. Skaletsky, and S. Woolford. 2011. Identifying groups: A comparison of methodologies. *Journal of Data Science* 9: 271–291.

Kaufman, L., and P.J. Rousseeuw. 1990. *Finding groups in data: An introduction to Cluster Analysis*. New York: Wiley.

Kaski, S., and T. Kohonen. 1996. Exploratory data analysis by the self-organizing map: Structures of welfare and poverty in the world. In *Neural networks in financial engineering*, Proceedings of the third international conference on neural networks in the capital markets, London, England, October 1–3, 1995, ed. Refenes Apostolos-Paul, Abu-Mostafa Yaser, Moody John, and Weigend Andreas, 498–507. Singapore: World Scientific.

Kironji, E. 2008. Measuring quality of life in South Africa: A household-based development index approach. PhD diss., University of Pretoria. http://upetd.up.ac.za/thesis/available/etd-01252008-090610/unrestricted/00front.pdf.

Larose, Daniel. 2005. *Discovering knowledge in data: An introduction to data mining*. New York: Wiley.

Magidson, Jay, and Jeroen Vermunt. 2003. *Latent class models*. Belmont: Statistical Innovations.

Matejková, E., A. Qineti, and R. Serenčéš. 2008. Macroeconomic aspects of the development of Slovak regions in the post-accession period. *Agricultural Economics* 54: 367–375.

National Political Publishing House. 2001. Doi Moi and human development in Vietnam. http://planipolis.iiep.unesco.org/upload/Viet%20Nam/Viet%20Nam%20HDR%202001.pdf. Accessed July 30, 2011.

Nguyen, Phong, D. Haughton, and I. Hudson. 2009. Living standards of Vietnamese provinces: A Kohonen map. *Case Studies in Business, Industry and Government Statistics* 2(2): 109–113.

Ponthieux, S., and M. Cottrell. 2001. Living conditions: Classification of households using the Kohonen algorithm. *European Journal of Economic and Social Systems* 15(2): 69–84.

Ravallion, Martin. 1996. How well can method substitute for data? Five experiments in poverty analysis. *The World Bank Research Observer* 11(2): 199–221.

Statistical Publishing House. 2000. *Figures on social development; Doi Moi period in Vietnam*. Hanoi: Statistical Publishing House.

StatSoft. 2011. Cluster analysis. In *Electronic statistics textbook*. http://www.statsoft.com/textbook/cluster-analysis/. Accessed March 2011.

Tryon, R.C. 1939. *Cluster analysis*. New York: McGraw-Hill.

Vella, V., and M. Vichi. 1997. Identification of standards of living and poverty in South Africa. *Consultant Report*. Washington, DC: World Bank.

Vermunt, J.K., and J. Magidson. 2002. Latent class cluster analysis. In *Applied latent class analysis*, ed. J. Hagenaars and A. McCutcheon, 89–106. Cambridge, UK: Cambridge University Press. http://spitswww.uvt.nl/~vermunt/hagenaars2002b. Accessed March 2011.

Zhang, N.L., S. Yuan, T. Chen, and Y. Wang. 2009. Latent tree models and diagnosis in traditional Chinese medicine. *Artificial Intelligence in Medicine* 42(3): 229–245.

Chapter 7
Bayesian Analysis

7.1 Introduction

In the classical (or *frequentist*) approach to statistical methods, the analyst uses a sample of data to make inferences about the value of fixed but unknown population parameters. Among other things, this allows one to construct confidence intervals. Suppose, for example, we wish to estimate a proportion p, say a poverty rate, from a simple random sample in the population. The classical formula for a 95% confidence interval for p is $\left(\hat{p} - 1.96\sqrt{\hat{p}(1 - \hat{p})/n}, \hat{p} + 1.96\sqrt{\hat{p}(1 - \hat{p})/n}\right)$. The interpretation is that if we draw 100 random samples from the population and each time compute such an interval, the interval will include the population proportion about 95 times out of 100. The wording is important: we are not making a probability statement about the population parameter, because it is assumed to be fixed, a "truth" that has to be revealed by the data.

There is a curious inconsistency in most applications of the classical approach: we have a "fixed and immutable" specification of the underlying statistical model (Greene 2003, p. 429), yet so little information about the population parameters that we rely entirely on the data sample to estimate them!

An alternative approach, referred to as *Bayesian*, is to treat population parameters as random variables about which we have some "degree of belief." When new data become available we are able to update and sharpen these (subjective) beliefs.

In the language of Bayesian analysis, we begin with an initial probability distribution for parameters θ given by $\pi(\theta)$, known as the *prior*. With observed data $\mathbf{y} = \{y_1, \ldots, y_n\}$ we select a statistical model with density $p(\mathbf{y}|\theta)$ that describes the distribution of the data, given θ. In the third step we combine our prior beliefs about θ with the data $\mathbf{y}$ to create the *posterior distribution* $p(\theta|\mathbf{y})$.

The posterior distribution reflects our updated beliefs, and may be summarized in the form of posterior statistics such as the (posterior) mean and standard deviation, and through the creation of *credible intervals*. Such intervals have a natural

D. Haughton and J. Haughton, *Living Standards Analytics*, Statistics for Social
and Behavioral Sciences, DOI 10.1007/978-1-4614-0385-2_7,
© Springer Science+Business Media, LLC 2011

interpretation; we may say, for instance, that "the true parameter θ has a 95% probability" of falling within the relevant credible interval. Some researchers construct symmetric credible intervals around the mode or mean; others prefer to use highest posterior density intervals, which are the smallest intervals that contain 95% of the posterior values.

It makes sense to use Bayesian methods if one has substantial prior information about the parameters that should be incorporated into the analysis. Such information may come from expert opinion or previous research; in principle, as knowledge accumulates, the case for taking a Bayesian approach becomes stronger.

As shown below, Bayesian methods allow one to incorporate prior information in a disciplined way, and to update one's beliefs whenever new information becomes available. Bayesian analysis provides exact inferences (conditional on the data), yields results that have a natural interpretation, and typically uses numerical methods that allow one to estimate a very wide range of parametric models.

The Bayesian approach has some drawbacks too. The most problematic step is selecting a prior. There is a leap between accepting in principle the value of incorporating prior information, and actually doing so in a satisfactory manner. Priors are typically highly parameterized, and must be chosen with caution, a process that is as much art as science. Even when done well, either a prior influences the posterior, in which case it becomes a lightning rod for controversy, or it does not, in which case one could question how much is added by taking a Bayesian approach.

Until recently, the computation of posterior distributions was difficult, and it can still be time consuming for models with many parameters. But recent advances, including the widely used WinBugs software (WinBugs 2007), have brought Bayesian analysis within reach of all data analysts, and the routine use of Bayesian methods can no longer be dismissed on the grounds of being impractical.

This chapter first covers in detail a worked example of an estimation of a poverty rate, first assuming that a simple random sample is available (Sect. 7.2.1), and then that the sample arose from a more complicated design (Sect. 7.2.2). The choice of priors is discussed in Sect. 7.3, and is followed in Sect. 7.4 by a presentation of the main ideas involved in the comparison of Bayesian models, such as Bayes factors and posterior predictive checking, in the context of applications to living standards, with examples related to wage mobility in the USA for those who have and have not been in prison, and to diagnostic tests for a disease in East Africa. Section 7.5 introduces the reader to the ideas behind Bayesian model averaging in the context of a study of determinants of poverty rates in the 61 provinces of Vietnam. A short introduction to the Bayesian approach to sample size determination is given in Sect. 7.6, in the context of estimating poverty rates when poverty lines are not known with certainty and thus an error occurs in the poor/nonpoor classification.

7.2 A Worked Example

In this section, we apply the steps required to obtain a Bayesian estimate of the distribution of the poverty rate in the rural areas of Nghe An province in Vietnam. Nghe An is one of the poorest provinces in Vietnam, located as it is in the typhoon-prone North Central Coastal region, about 320 km south of Hanoi.

Before providing further specifics, it is helpful first to set out in somewhat more detail how one combines the prior information in $\pi(\theta)$ with the data **y**, in order to generate a posterior distribution.

From Bayes' theorem, we have that the probability of event A, conditional on event B, is given by

$$p(A|B) = \frac{p(B|A)\,p(A)}{p(B)}. \tag{7.1}$$

Interpreting A as the parameters and B as the sample data, we have

$$p(\theta|\mathbf{y}) = \frac{p(\mathbf{y}|\theta)\,\pi(\theta)}{p(\mathbf{y})}, \tag{7.2}$$

which we may interpret as

$$p(\text{parameters}|\text{data}) = \frac{p(\text{data}|\text{parameters})\,p(\text{parameters})}{p(\text{data})}. \tag{7.3}$$

Note that the posterior density of the parameter θ is simply the density of θ conditional on the data **y**, and is thus given by the left hand side of (7.2) and (7.3), while $p(\mathbf{y}|\theta)$ denotes the likelihood function of θ, representing the density of the data **y** for each value of θ. The denominator, which is given by $\int p(\mathbf{y}|\theta)\,\pi(\theta)\,d\theta$, is the marginal distribution of the data and is in effect a normalizing constant. It is helpful to simplify (7.2) to

$$p(\theta|\mathbf{y}) \propto p(\mathbf{y}|\theta)\,\pi(\theta), \tag{7.4}$$

where $\propto$ denotes proportionality or, equivalently,

posterior density $\propto$ likelihood function of θ × prior density.

The problem is that in a number of cases the posterior density cannot be computed in closed form, so special techniques are needed to simulate it. In the next section we illustrate the case where the posterior density is available in closed form, and then move to a case where we need to simulate from the posterior density.

Table 7.1 Frequentist and Bayesian measures of poverty in rural Nghe An Province, Vietnam, 1998

	Prior			Posterior		
	Distribution	Mode	95% Interval	Distribution	Mode	95% Interval
Bayesian, informative prior	$\beta(48, 50)$	0.49	(0.40, 0.60)	$\beta(158, 165)$	0.49	$(0.43, 0.54)^a$
Bayesian, noninformative prior	$\beta(1, 1)$	None	(0.025, 0.975)	$\beta(111, 116)$	0.49	$(0.42, 0.55)^a$
Frequentist	None	n/a	n/a	None	n/a	$(0.42, 0.55)^b$

[a]Credible interval [b]Confidence interval

7.2.1 Assuming i.i.d. Observations

In this example, we use data from the 1998 Vietnam Living Standards Survey (VLSS98), which interviewed 225 households from rural areas of Nghe An province, out of a total national sample of 5,999. For illustrative purposes, let us assume for the moment that these 225 households represent a simple random sample of households from rural Nghe An; and we defer to the next section a discussion of how to take the actual survey design into account. Among these 225 households, 110 were identified as poor.

The province-level sample is so small that accurate inference at this level becomes rather difficult. Under our assumption of a simple random sample, the standard deviation of the poverty rate is of about 3.3%, yielding a confidence interval for the poverty rate of (42%, 55%), see Table 7.1. However, if prior information on poverty rates were available, this would potentially be useful in sharpening our beliefs about the poverty rate in Nghe An.

Suppose that prior to the 1998 survey, a poverty expert expressed his belief that he was 95% certain that the headcount poverty rate – i.e., the proportion of people falling below a poverty line based on the cost of providing basic needs such as food and shelter – in Nghe An was between 0.4 and 0.6, with the most likely rate being 0.49.

One of the commonest ways to summarize prior beliefs about proportions (such as the headcount poverty rate, for instance) is with the Beta distribution, which has just two parameters, α_1 and α_2 and a density given by the following expression, for x between 0 and 1:

$$x^{\alpha_1}(1 - x)^{\alpha_2}/B(\alpha_1, \alpha_2),   \tag{7.5}$$

where $B(\alpha_1, \alpha_2)$ is a normalizing constant. The mean value of $\beta(\alpha_1, \alpha_2)$ is given by $\alpha_1/(\alpha_1 + \alpha_2)$ and the variance by

$$\text{var}(\beta(\alpha_1, \alpha_2)) = \frac{\alpha_1 \alpha_2}{(\alpha_1 + \alpha_2)^2(\alpha_1 + \alpha_2 + 1)}.   \tag{7.6}$$

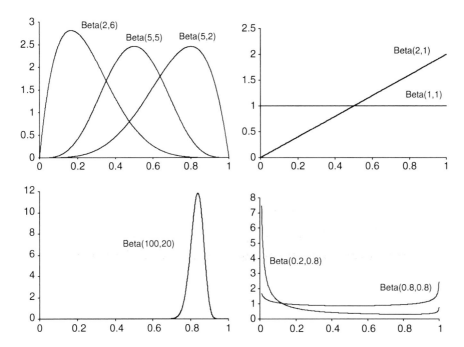

Fig. 7.1   A selection of beta distributions

The Beta distribution owes its popularity to its remarkable flexibility, as the graphs in Fig. 7.1 illustrate. Vose (1996) argues that the Beta distribution is also very useful when one wants to summarize expert opinion, and notes that it can be rescaled to run from a to b (instead of 0 to 1) using $a + \beta(\alpha_1, \alpha_2) \times (b - a)$.

The mode of the Beta distribution (for $\alpha_1, \alpha_2 > 1$) is given by

$$\frac{\alpha_1 - 1}{\alpha_1 + \alpha_2 - 2}, \tag{7.7}$$

which is equal to 0.49 in this case. We can use this equation to solve for α_2 in terms of α_1. It is then straightforward (using for example a spreadsheet) to search over values of α_1 such that we are 95% certain that the poverty rate is between 0.40 and 0.60. This gives the $\beta(48, 50)$ distribution shown in the left panel of Fig. 7.2.

If the prior follows a Beta distribution, as assumed here, and the number of poor follows a binomial distribution – in this case the prior is proportional to $\pi^{47}(1 - \pi)^{49}$ and the likelihood function to $\pi^{110}(1 - \pi)^{225-110}$ – then the posterior will also follow a Beta distribution, namely $\beta(158, 165)$. This posterior distribution is shown in the left panel of Fig. 7.2; it has a 95% credible interval (0.43, 0.54) centered at the mode of 0.49.

This result may be compared with the case of a diffuse prior (as shown by the horizontal line in the right panel of Fig. 7.2), which yields the relatively broader posterior shown in the right panel of Fig 7.2 and gives a 95% credible interval of

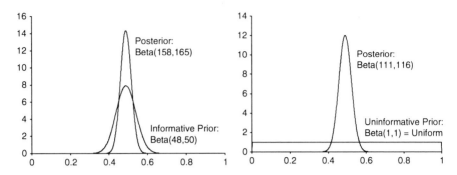

Fig. 7.2 Prior and posterior distributions of the headcount poverty rate in rural Nghe An province, Vietnam, 1998, under informative and uninformative priors

(0.42, 0.55). The prior information has brought (slightly) greater precision to our estimate of poverty rates in rural Nghe An. Under the frequentist approach only the data are informative, and they yield a 95% confidence interval of (0.42, 0.55). These results are summarized in Table 7.1.

7.2.2   Taking Survey Sampling into Account

Only in relatively special cases – such as when the prior follows a Beta distribution and the data are generated by a single binomial distribution – can one obtain closed-form expressions for the posterior distribution, such as that shown in Sect. 7.2.1. Until the 1990s this was a serious practical constraint on the use of Bayesian estimation. Since then, however, advances in computing have made it relatively straightforward to estimate posterior distributions using simulation. The development of these techniques, which for the most part rely on MCMC (Monte Carlo Markov Chain) methods, constitutes a major part of current Bayesian research activity. The idea behind the MCMC algorithm is to simulate a Markov chain whose stationary limit distribution is the posterior distribution of interest.

Although some researchers write their own programs to implement MCMC or other methods, software is now available to perform these simulations. Among the best-known tools is WinBugs (WinBugs 2007), but SAS also includes procedures for Bayesian analysis (SAS 2007). The researcher needs to provide the prior distribution(s) for the parameters, and the model that generates the data from the unknown parameters. WinBugs can then decide which variant of the MCMC simulation arsenal to use, and can provide output for the posterior distribution of each parameter, including summary posterior statistics and graphs of kernel densities.

Table 7.2 Snapshot of data from district 1 in Ho Chi Minh City

Ward	M_k	VLSS code	m_k	m_k'
Tan Dinh	7,522			
Da Kao	5,180	8	25	0
Ben Nghe	4,982			
Ben Thanh	5,040			
Nguyen Thai Binh	4,602			
Pham Ngu Lao	4,894	7	21	1
Cao Ong Lanh	3,475			
Co Giang	4,487			
Nguyen Cu Trinh	5,524			
Cau Kho	4,500			

Notes: M_k is number of households in ward, from census; m_k is number of households sampled by VLSS98 in ward; m_k' is number of poor households in sample

7.2.3   An Illustration

We may illustrate some of these points using data from Ho Chi Minh City, where the 1998 Vietnam Living Standards Survey (VLSS98) interviewed 433 households, just 2 of whom were poor (for a raw household poverty rate of 0.00462). The data are of the form illustrated in Table 7.2, where the first column gives the name of the ward, the second the number of households in the ward, and the third column gives the Vietnam Living Standards Survey (VLSS) code, for those wards that were part of the survey. The final two columns contain the number of interviewed households and the number of poor household among those surveyed.

The VLSS98 survey, which covered 5,999 households, attempted to re-interview households interviewed in 1993 by VLSS93 (which interviewed 4,800 households nationwide). The urban areas of the cities of Hanoi and Ho Chi Minh City (taken together) formed one stratum of VLSS98. The urban wards from VLSS93 were surveyed again and some were added, with a procedure that essentially amounted to ward selection with probability proportional to size. Then households were selected from chosen wards with equal probabilities. Further details of the sampling design may be found at the World Bank Living Standards Measurement Survey site.[1] Because of the use of cluster sampling, we need to assume that the data *in any given ward* are generated by a binomial distribution. With many such distributions, it is no longer possible to generate the full posterior distribution analytically, and so simulation methods are needed.

The cluster sampling affects the estimation of the standard deviation of the poverty rate, but not the estimated poverty rate, which, we recall, is 0.00462 (equal to 2 divided by 433). The standard deviation (0.00334) is computed with a standard formula for an approximation to the standard deviation of a ratio under

---

[1] http://www.worldbank.org/html/prdph/lsms/country/vn98/VIE14.pdf

Table 7.3 Prior densities and posterior density statistics, Ho Chi Minh City, Vietnam, 1998

Weight, ω_i	x	Mean	Std. dev.	β
0.07	1st component	0.00875	0.010	(0.7, 79.3)[a]
0.43	2nd component	0.01625	0.014	(1.3, 78.7)
0.43	3rd component	0.02375	0.017	(1.9, 78.1)
0.07	4th component	0.03125	0.019	(2.5, 77.5)
	Overall	0.02	0.017	
		Posterior mean	Posterior SD	
Computed by	Closed form[b]	0.0137	0.0046	
	MCMC[c]	0.0135	0.0045	

[a] A mean of 0.00875 and $\alpha_1 + \alpha_2 = 80$ implies a $\beta(0.7, 79.3)$ distribution, and so on
[b] Based on a formula from Nandram and Sedransk (1993)
[c] Computed using WinBugs. *Source*: Haughton and Phong (2003)

cluster sampling, such as given for instance in Stata (1999), page 69, equation (7), which yields in our case:

$$\text{Est. Var. of pov. rate} = \frac{14}{13} \sum_{\text{allwards}} \left(\frac{\#\text{poorinward} - .00462\#\text{hholdsinward}}{433} \right)^2$$

Note that when poverty rates are very low, as in this case, it could well happen that a survey finds no poor people in the sample. But it is hardly reasonable to conclude that there is no poverty!

Could we use Bayesian methods to get a more realistic (posterior) distribution of poverty rates in Ho Chi Minh City? Suppose that an expert at the Government Statistics Office ventures, prior to the 1998 VLSS survey, that he is 95% certain that the poverty rate in Ho Chi Minh City is 2% (μ), plus or minus 1 percentage point; this would imply an approximate standard deviation (σ) of 0.005 (the length 0.02 of the expert's prior probability interval, divided by 4). Haughton and Phong (2003), noting that, under some reasonable assumptions, mixtures of Beta distributions can approximate any prior on proportions (Nandram and Sedransk 1993), capture the prior information in the form of a mixture of four Beta distributions. They center their Beta distributions in the middle of four bins whose limits are ($\mu - 3\sigma$, $\mu - 1.5\sigma$, μ, $\mu + 1.5\sigma$, $\mu + 3\sigma$), and use a tightness parameter (i.e., $\alpha_1 + \alpha_2$, from the Beta distribution) of 80; a higher value of this parameter implies a tighter distribution. Further details are given in Table 7.3. The prior distribution that results from the mixture of Beta distributions is shown in the left panel of Fig. 7.3.

The prior was then combined using data from the 1998 VLSS to generate information on the posterior distribution, using MCMC simulation. The kernel density of the posterior distribution is graphed in the right hand panel of Fig. 7.3, and shows a trimodal outcome. The mean of the posterior distribution was 0.014, with a standard deviation of 0.0046; this represents a higher poverty rate and a wider credible interval that would be implied by reliance on the survey data alone. However, the posterior mean is located in a low posterior density region, so it is more informative to look at the graph of the kernel density estimate of the posterior

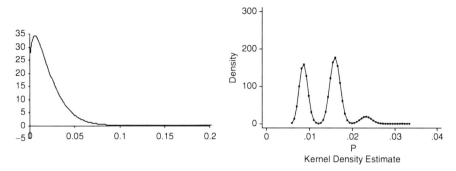

Fig. 7.3 Prior densities and posterior kernel densities, Ho Chi Minh City, Vietnam, 1998

density in Fig. 7.3, which shows that – a posteriori – the poverty rate is likely to be either very small (about half a percent), or larger than 1% (about 1.6 or 1.7%).

The MCMC simulation was performed with Winbugs (Winbugs 2007); the code is given in Appendix, and follows the structure provided in Congdon (2001, Program 5.18).

In passing it is worth noting that in this particular case, although the density of the posterior distribution cannot be computed in closed form, formulae for the posterior mean and standard deviation are in fact available (Nandram and Sedransk 1993) and the results are also reported in Table 7.2. They are very close to the values computed using MCMC simulation with WinBugs, which gives one considerable confidence in the simulation approach.

7.3   Prior Distributions and Implications of Their Choice

7.3.1   Eliciting Priors

It is not enough to assert that one has prior beliefs about the distribution of a parameter (such as a poverty rate, or the effectiveness of a drug). That information has to be summarized mathematically before it can be updated with new data. This raises the thorny issue of how to formulate an appropriate prior.

There are a number of possible sources of prior information, including the researcher's own beliefs, expert opinion, and the results of previous research. Since they measure degrees of belief, priors are necessarily subjective in nature.

Sooner or later almost every analyst needs to consult experts when constructing a prior, and needs to convert their opinions into probability distributions. Vose (1996) makes a strong case that this process is "harder than it looks." He cautions analysts to recognize their own limitations and not assume that they are the best sources for expert advice. He then notes the potentially serious biases to which expert opinion is subject, most notably availability (the overemphasis on a recent or dramatic event that is readily "available" in one's memory) and anchoring (the construction of overly narrow confidence intervals around a most likely, or "anchor," value).

A further problem, when having recourse to experts, is that they are human too. Some may not in fact be expert, but try to come up with estimates in order to be helpful; others may come from a culture of optimism (sales personnel, for instance) or pessimism (production personnel), which would affect their advice; at times, the experts may have a vested interest in the result; in some cases, they may be too busy to provide serious estimates, or may try to second guess what they believe the analyst wants.

In establishing a prior based on expert opinion, it is often difficult to ask the expert to specify an entire distribution, but it is quite feasible to ask for a minimum value, most likely value, and maximum value. These can then form the basis of a triangular distribution, or a Beta distribution. When experts disagree on the appropriate prior distribution, it may be because they differ in their appreciation of the problem at hand. In this case it is frequently productive to follow a two-step procedure – similar to the Delphi technique pioneered by the RAND corporation – which begins with a brainstorming session and follows with individual interviews. Different opinions may be aggregated using a mixture – essentially by drawing from the distributions proposed by each expert, using probability weights to reflect the confidence we have in each.

7.3.2 Noninformative Priors

A noninformative prior may be thought of as a flat distribution, and it brings little or no information to bear on the analysis: the resulting posterior distribution is essentially based on the data sample, and differs from classical results in the way it is interpreted. Noninformative priors are often improper: for example, a uniform prior on the real line, where $\pi(\theta) \propto 1$, integrates to infinity (i.e., $\int \pi(\theta)\,d\theta = \infty$) rather than to 1. However, this does not necessarily yield an improper posterior distribution – fortunately, since the latter would render inference invalid.

7.3.3 Priors in a Linear Regression Context

As we saw in Sect. 7.2.1, it is sometimes possible to parameterize the likelihood function, $L(\theta) = p(\mathbf{y}|\theta)$, and prior in such a way as to generate the posterior analytically. For instance, consider a linear regression model of the standard form

$$\mathbf{y} = \mathbf{X}\beta + \mathbf{e},$$

where our prior beliefs about the K coefficients β follow a K-variate normal distribution with mean β_0 and variance matrix Σ_0. Assume further that $\Sigma_0 = \sigma^2 I$, where σ^2 is known. Then the posterior density of β, conditional on σ and the data, is itself normal, and one can show that (Greene 2003, p. 435)

$$E(\beta|\sigma^2, \mathbf{y}, \mathbf{X}) = \mathbf{F} \cdot \beta_0 + (\mathbf{I} - \mathbf{F}) \cdot \mathbf{b} \tag{7.8}$$

where $\mathbf{b}$ is the vector of coefficients estimated by OLS, and

$$\mathbf{F} = \left\{ \Sigma_0^{-1} + [\sigma^2(\mathbf{X'X})^{-1}]^{-1} \right\}^{-1} \Sigma_0^{-1}$$

$$= \left\{ [\text{prior variance}]^{-1} + [\text{conditional variance}]^{-1} \right\}^{-1} [\text{prior variance}]^{-1} \tag{7.9}$$

In other words, the posterior mean values of the coefficients are weighted averages of the prior means (β_0) and least squares estimates based on the data ($\mathbf{b}$). As the size of the data sample rises, the conditional variance of the estimated parameters shrinks and $\mathbf{F}$ becomes smaller, putting more weight on the estimated coefficients ($\mathbf{b}$) and therefore less weight on the priors.

Sometimes we do not have strong prior beliefs; in the limit we might have an entirely uninformative (or diffuse) prior. We may think of this as driving the elements of Σ_0 to infinity, in which case $\mathbf{F} \rightarrow 0$ and

$$E(\beta|\sigma^2, \mathbf{y}, \mathbf{X}) \rightarrow \mathbf{b}. \tag{7.10}$$

This simply means that in the case of no worthwhile prior information, our posterior mean is based entirely on the data – i.e., on the ordinary least squares estimates in this case. On the other hand, the stronger our prior beliefs, the smaller the value of Σ_0, the larger $\mathbf{F}$ is, and the greater the weight on the prior (β_0) relative to the data-based parameter estimates ($\mathbf{b}$).

In this particular regression example, we also have

$$\text{Var}(\beta|\sigma^2, \mathbf{y}, \mathbf{X}) = \left\{ \Sigma_0^{-1} + [\sigma^2(\mathbf{X'X})^{-1}]^{-1} \right\}^{-1}, \tag{7.11}$$

an estimator that was first proposed by Theil and Goldberger in 1961. The addition of prior information reduces the variance of the posterior mean, and so allows greater precision when making inferences. This can be especially useful in cases where there may be insufficient data to allow for accurate inferences as we saw in the poverty rate example in Sect. 7.2.

7.4 Bayes Factors and Posterior Predictive Checking

7.4.1 Bayes Factors

When testing hypotheses, the frequentist approach seeks to reject, or not reject, a null hypothesis in favor of an alternative. Bayesians find this dichotomy to be too austere; after all, in practice we put great store on our intuition and can be slow to jettison these prior beliefs, even if classical results indicate that we should. A more nuanced approach would therefore be to revise, but not necessarily overturn, our prior beliefs in the light of new evidence.

So rather than testing hypotheses, the Bayesian approach is one of comparing hypotheses, with a view to assessing which has the higher probability of being correct. Let $P(H_0)$ be our prior probability that hypothesis H_0 is correct and $P(H_1)$ be our prior probability that hypothesis H_1 (which need not be the complement of H_0) is correct. Then we may define the prior odds ratio as

$$\text{Odds}_{\text{prior}} = P(H_0)/P(H_1). \tag{7.12}$$

Now suppose, in the context of a standard linear regression model with parameters β and unknown error variance σ^2, that data on the dependent variable (y) and independent variables (X) become available. This allows us to construct the posterior odds ratio, given by

$$\text{Odds}_{\text{posterior}} = \frac{P(H_0|\mathbf{y}, \mathbf{X})}{P(H_1|\mathbf{y}, \mathbf{X})} = B_{01}\text{Odds}_{\text{prior}}. \tag{7.13}$$

The B_{01} term here is referred to as the *Bayes factor*; it measures the effect of the sample data on the prior odds. It can be shown in our case that the Bayes factor equals

$$B_{01} = \frac{f(\mathbf{y}|\mathbf{X}, H_0)}{f(\mathbf{y}|\mathbf{X}, H_1)}. \tag{7.14}$$

where $f(\mathbf{y}|\mathbf{X}, H_j) = \iint_{(\beta,\sigma^2)\in H_j} f(\mathbf{y}|\mathbf{X}, \beta, \sigma^2, H_j) g(\beta, \sigma^2) d\beta \, d\sigma^2$.

To illustrate, suppose that we have two possible simple regression models of the form

$$\begin{aligned} H_0 : \quad & y = \mathbf{X}'_0\beta_0 + e_0, \\ H_1 : \quad & y = \mathbf{X}'_1\beta_1 + e_1, \end{aligned} \tag{7.15}$$

where the sample sizes are n and m respectively, and we believe that $P(H_0) = 0.8$ and $P(H_1) = 0.2$. Zellner showed in 1971 (Greene 2003, p. 439) that under certain reasonable assumptions

$$B_{01} \approx \left(\frac{1 - R_0^2}{1 - R_1^2}\right)^{-(n+m)/2} \tag{7.16}$$

Here R_i^2 measures the relevant coefficient of determination. Thus, new data cause us to tilt toward the model with the better fit, especially if there are many new observations. But, and this is the interesting point, we do not necessarily find the new information compelling enough to make us change our mind. If $R_1^2 = 0.32$ and $R_0^2 = 0.30$, and $n=m=40$, then the Bayes factor is 0.314, the prior odds ratio is 4, and the posterior odds ratio is 1.25. The new data have weakened our relatively strong preference for H_0, but we still believe that, on balance, it is more probably correct than H_1. For a useful discussion of Bayes factors, including an example where Bayes factors are helpful and one where Bayes factors are a distraction, we refer the reader to Gelman et al. (2003), p. 185.

7.4.2   Posterior Predictive Checking

We are often faced with the challenge of choosing the model that is most appropriate for the research question we wish to address. Standard goodness-of-fit statistics may not help us much in choosing between models if our main interest is in predicting rare events, or if the models are nonnested. In such circumstances, Bayesian posterior predictive checks may be helpful as diagnostic tools, even though they are not statistics for model selection per se.

Posterior predictive checking functions essentially as follows. Suppose we have a model that generates a data set, given a value of a parameter (which may be vector-valued) – we provide an example below. Draw a parameter from the posterior distribution, and use it to generate another dataset, typically of the same size as the initial dataset. Repeat the process many times, in order to create histograms of chosen summaries of the datasets (such as the median, or a decile, for instance), which may then be compared with summary statistics based on the original data. If the model fits the data, the original value should fall comfortably within the range of the histogram, not in any extreme positions.

More formally, the posterior predictive distribution is given by

$$p(\mathbf{y}^{\text{rep}}|\mathbf{y}) = \int p(\mathbf{y}^{\text{rep}}|\theta) \cdot p(\theta|\mathbf{y}) \cdot d\theta, \tag{7.17}$$

where $\mathbf{y}^{\text{rep}}$ gives the replicated (hypothetical) values of $\mathbf{y}$, and shows the values that "might have been observed if the conditions generating $\mathbf{y}$ were reproduced" (Lynch and Western 2004, p. 306). The $p(\mathbf{y}^{\text{rep}}|\theta)$ term gives the probability density of $\mathbf{y}^{\text{rep}}$, for given values of θ, and reflects sampling uncertainty, since it is based on the sampling distribution of $\mathbf{y}$. The second term, $p(\theta|\mathbf{y})$, gives the posterior distribution for θ, and is proportional to $L(\theta|\mathbf{y}) \cdot p(\theta)$, where $L(\cdot)$ is the likelihood and $p(\theta)$ the prior. This term picks up parametric uncertainty about θ. Thus the posterior predictive distribution in (7.17) is obtained by picking a parameter using $p(\theta|\mathbf{y})$, using it to generate replicated values of $\mathbf{y}$ (as in $p(\mathbf{y}^{\text{rep}}|\theta)$), and repeating the process enough times to obtain a full distribution $p(\mathbf{y}^{\text{rep}}|\mathbf{y})$, against which the actual data ($\mathbf{y}$) may be compared.

For example, consider the regression case where

$$\mathbf{y} = \mathbf{X}\beta + e, \quad e \sim N(0, \sigma^2), \tag{7.18}$$

and σ is assumed to be known. With a diffuse prior, the posterior distribution of the vector of regression coefficients can be shown to be

$$\beta \sim N(\hat{\beta}, \sigma^2(\mathbf{X}'\mathbf{X})^{-1}), \tag{7.19}$$

where $\hat{\beta}$ is the OLS estimate (see for example, Box and Tiao 1973, p. 47). A random draw from (7.19) will yield $\beta^*_{(j)}$, and using this we take random draws to generate a set of replicates

$$\mathbf{y}^{\text{rep}}_{(j)} \sim N(\mathbf{X}\beta^*_{(j)}, \sigma^2). \tag{7.20}$$

Taking, say, 1,000 random draws from the posterior distribution for the coefficients, we are able to construct histograms for *each* value of the $\mathbf{y}$ variable. This generates posterior predictive intervals for each value of $\mathbf{y}$; these are wider than the classical intervals (given by $\hat{\mathbf{y}} \pm 2s$, where s is the standard error of the residuals), because they reflect parametric uncertainty in addition to the usual sampling uncertainty.

The real value of posterior predictive checks comes from examining *discrepancy statistics*, $T(\mathbf{y})$, such as the first decile ($T(\mathbf{y}) = \mathbf{y}_{0.1}$) or 90th percentile ($T(\mathbf{y}) = \mathbf{y}_{0.9}$). One may then assess model fit, for a given discrepancy statistic, by comparing the observed value, $T(\mathbf{y})$, with the distribution of the replicated value, $T(\mathbf{y}^{\text{rep}})$. A Bayesian p value, defined as

$$p = P(T(\mathbf{y}^{\text{rep}}) \geq T(\mathbf{y})|\mathbf{y}) \tag{7.21}$$

gives the probability, conditional on the model, of observing data at least as extreme as those actually observed (Lynch and Western 2004, p. 307).

7.4.3 Example: Fixed vs. Random Effects

Bayesian posterior predictive checking can be useful when we have panel data and are trying to choose between using fixed and random effects. A basic panel data model, with information on units i (such as households) for times t may be written as

$$y_{it} = \alpha_i + \mathbf{X}'_{it}\beta + e_{it}. \tag{7.22}$$

With fixed effects the intercept, α_i, is estimated for each unit i, and 7.22 can be fitted using OLS. It yields unbiased estimates of β even with some types of omitted variables. But it is relatively inefficient at estimating the β coefficients, because the data have to generate a potentially large number of α_i parameters too. The use of fixed effects also makes it impossible to include many of the most interesting variables (which we denote with $\mathbf{Z}$), such as a person's ethnicity or gender, since these are "swept away" by the individual intercepts.

The random effects model assumes that α_i is a random variable, independently drawn from some distribution (typically assumed to be normal). The estimates of β have smaller variance, but are more prone to omitted variable bias, than the fixed effects estimates. There is no standard way to compare a fixed effects model using independent variables $\mathbf{X}$ with a random effects model using independent variables $\mathbf{X}$ and $\mathbf{Z}$, since the two are nonnested.

But the fit of such models can be compared using posterior predictive checking. Lynch and Western (2004) make such a comparison using data from the US National Longitudinal Survey of Youth, which first surveyed men and women aged 14–21 in 1979 and followed them annually for 15 years. They are interested in measuring the difference in wage mobility between those who have been to prison and those who have not. Both fixed and random effects models fit median wages adequately; this may be seen from the left panel in Fig. 7.4, which shows a smoothed histogram of the median for the models, and the median for their data (shown as a vertical line): the observed median is near the middle of the posterior predictive distribution of the median.

On the other hand, all three models have a harder time fitting the 90th percentile of the distribution, since as seen in Figure 7.4 (bottom panel), the observed 90th percentile is far to the right of the posterior predictive distribution of the 90th percentile. Figure 7.4 (bottom panel) reveals that the random effects model does a slightly better job of modeling the difference in wage mobility at the 90th percentile of the wage distribution than the fixed effects model, and that the model with random slopes and intercepts does better. This does not imply that the random effects model is generally preferable to the fixed effects model in this case, but it does show that it does a better job for this particular discrepancy statistic.

7.4.4   Example: Modeling Diagnostic Tests

Another useful example of Bayesian posterior predictive checking comes from a recent study by Menten et al. (2006) that examines the diagnostic success of four tests for visceral leishmaniasis. This protozoal disease is carried by sand flies, and occurs in poor rural areas of eastern Africa, Southern Asia, and Latin America. It is fatal if untreated, but the treatment is painful and expensive. Thus it is important to identify those, and only those, who have the disease.

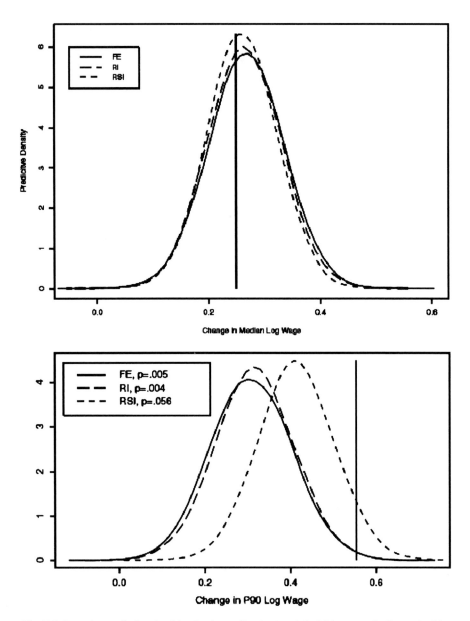

Fig. 7.4 Posterior predictive densities for the median (*top*) and the 90th percentile (*bottom*) of the change in log wages from ages 22 to 35, using fixed effects (FE), random intercept (RI), and random slope and intercept (RSI) models. (*Source*: Lynch and Western 2004)

A total of about 300 subjects in Sudan were subjected to four tests for the disease, referred to as DAT, RK39, Katex, and MEA, respectively, with the latter test being considered the gold standard, with sensitivity (the probability that the test shows positive if the patient is ill) and specificity (the probability that the test shows

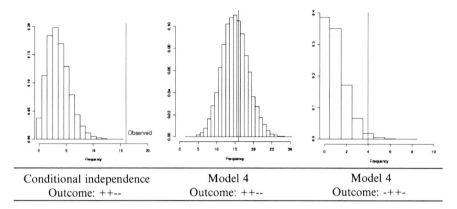

Conditional independence	Model 4	Model 4
Outcome: ++--	Outcome: ++--	Outcome: -++-

Fig. 7.5 Posterior predictive histograms for selected outcomes of tests for visceral leishmaniasis in East Africa. (*Source*: Menten et al. 2006)

negative if the patient is not ill) both equal to 1. The result for each test is either positive (+) or negative (−). For each subject, the outcome consists of a 4-tuple of test results; for instance, −−++ would represent a negative result on the two first, and a positive result on the two last, tests. There are 16 possible patterns, for which Menten et al. specify a number of alternative models. For example, their Model 4 assumes correlated outcomes for tests 1 and 2, and for tests 3 and 4; and their conditional independence model assumes (implausibly) that the outcomes of the four tests are independent.

Figure 7.5 shows three posterior predictive check histograms; in each case a vertical line indicates where the observed frequency lies. The left panel shows that the observed frequency of ++−− patterns is far higher than the conditional independence model would lead one to expect, while the center panel shows that it is in line with what Model 4 would predict. On the other hand, the right panel in Fig. 7.5 shows that Model 4 does a relatively poor job of predicting the −++− pattern. If it is important to use a model that gets the ++−− pattern right, then the diagnostic results in Fig. 7.5. suggest that Model 4 would be appropriate, or at least certainly a lot better than the conditional independence model.

The examples in this section involve the use of posterior predictive checking in the context of data related to living standards. For a further discussion of this method, and examples in other areas of application, we refer the reader to Gelman et al. (2003), Sect. 6.3.

7.5 Combining Models: Bayesian Model Averaging

Suppose we are interested in finding the determinants of poverty, and we have at hand a long list of K plausible explanatory variables. The classical econometric approach assumes that we know the fundamental structure of the model that generates this poverty; the main task is then to use the data to measure the strength of the effects of the different variables.

In contrast, the Bayesian Model Averaging approach treats the models themselves (within a set $\mathcal{M}$ of possible models) as random variables: we do not necessarily know which variables to include in the analysis, and furthermore, we often do not know how to combine these variables in an appropriate model M_j. We therefore need to use the data to help resolve some of the ambiguity about model selection; this will reduce the precision with which the size of effects are measured, but this also implies that the classical approach, by ignoring model uncertainty, generates statistically significant results too often.

Bayesian Model Averaging is a method for dealing with model uncertainty that generates a posterior distribution for the effects or parameters of interest (θ) given data $\mathbf{y}$ – the left hand side of (7.22) – as a weighted average of the posterior distributions of the parameters under each model M_j. More formally, if we have a total of K covariates that could be used in linear combinations, we have

$$P(\theta|\mathbf{y}) = \sum_{j=1}^{2^K} P(\theta|\mathbf{y}, M_j) \cdot P(M_j|\mathbf{y}), \qquad (7.23)$$

since there are 2^K potential models, corresponding to the inclusion or not of a covariate. The weights here are the *posterior model probabilities*, which equal the posterior probabilities of the models, given the data, and are given by

$$P(M_j|\mathbf{y}) = \frac{P(\mathbf{y}|M_j) \cdot P(M_j)}{\sum_{i=1}^{2^K} P(\mathbf{y}|M_i) \cdot P(M_i)}. \qquad (7.24)$$

Here the $P(M_i)$ terms are the prior probabilities of the models M_i belonging to $\mathcal{M}$; and $P(\mathbf{y}|M_i)$ is the marginal likelihood of model M_i, that is, the likelihood of the data given the parameters and the model M_i, integrated with respect to the priors of the parameters.

It appears, both in theory and in practice, that Bayesian averaging over all the models has greater predictive ability than using any single model M^* (Hoeting et al. 1999), even a single model that has been chosen using, for instance, the Bayesian Information Criterion (BIC). This provides a powerful argument for using this technique, at least in principle.

7.5.1   Practical Issues

If the number of variables under consideration is small, then Bayesian Model Averaging (BMA) is relatively straightforward: for each of the 2^K models, find the posterior model probabilities (7.24), and then use these to weight the posterior distributions of the parameters (as in (7.23)) to get the posterior probabilities of all the possible explanatory variables.

The main practical problem is that this is a formidable task as soon as the number of possible models is large, which is almost always the case. The commonest solution is to use a simulation approach, typically the Markov Chain Monte Carlo Model Composition (MC^3) algorithm, which avoids the need to evaluate every possible model. The MC^3 algorithm draws an initial model from the model space, constructs the posterior, picks the next candidate model from regions in the model space in the neighborhood of the current model, constructs its posterior, and accepts the new model with a certain probability. The process is iterated many times; the outcomes of the early iterations are discarded, because they represent the "burn in" replications where the results are likely to be sensitive to the choice of initial model.

It is also worth noting that BMA, like all Bayesian techniques, requires one to specify priors for the model parameters. For BMA, the priors are typically relatively noninformative, but priors can rarely be entirely neutral. For instance, it is typically assumed that each model in the set $\mathcal{M}$ is equally likely; this is convenient, if $\mathcal{M}$ has 2^K models, but probably does not reflect the true prior beliefs of most researchers.

Klump and Prüfer (2006) have applied Bayesian Model Averaging to an analysis of the determinants of the poverty rate in the 61 provinces of Vietnam in 2002. They identify 36 possible variables that influence the headcount poverty rate at the provincial level, and assume that these variables may influence poverty linearly. But they are agnostic as to which particular model – i.e., which particular combination of covariates – is most appropriate.

In implementing their BMA analysis, Klump and Prüfer take 2,500,000 draws, discarding the first 500,000. They test for convergence – Fernández et al. (2001b) provide further details – and they find that their ten best models only explain 8% of the total posterior mass. In other words, no single model is dominant, which suggests that BMA is highly appropriate; Fernández et al. (2001a) reached a similar conclusion in the context of cross-country growth regressions.

The BMA analysis typically yields three types of output: a posterior probability that a variable is relevant, a posterior mean (of the regression coefficient) for each variable, and forecasts of the dependent variable. Table 7.4 reproduces a small sample of the output reported by Klump and Prüfer: it shows that there is a 98% posterior probability that the "expenditure Gini" (a measure of the inequality of expenditure per capita) should be included in models of the determinants of provincial-level poverty rates in Vietnam. The posterior mean effect of this variable on poverty is +147, which is averaged over the models in which this variable is included. Another important explanatory variable is the share of population living in urban areas, with a BMA posterior probability of 0.65, but a negative posterior mean (-0.36); this says that when the urban share rises, the proportion of people living in poverty is lower, which is certainly what one would expect.

Table 7.4 Comparison of regressor posterior probabilities, from models of determinants of provincial-level poverty rates in Vietnam in 2002

Regressors		BMA posterior probability	Posterior mean
1	Expenditure Gini	0.9757	146.934
2	Land holding Gini	0.6605	−26.697
3	Share of population that is urban	0.6532	−0.356
4	Crude birth rate	0.5700	0.546
5	Program 135 present (poverty alleviation program)	0.4732	0.0002
. . .			
25	Quality of roads	0.0513	−0.028
26	Infant mortality rate	0.0509	0.0002
. . .			
36	Government consumption spending	0.0304	−0.007

Source: Klump and Prüfer (2006)

7.6 Bayesian Approach to Sample Size Determination

A common applied problem is determining how large a sample is needed in order to generate statistics with a given degree of precision. Suppose that we want to determine the sample size required such that a 95% interval for a binomial parameter will have width w – for instance, such that the headcount poverty rate can be estimated to within 2 percentage points (so $w = 0.04$). Provided that there are no errors in the poor/nonpoor classification, then one can use a sample size formula based on the normal approximation to the binomial distribution:

$$n = \left(\frac{2Z_{\alpha/2}}{w}\right)^2 \theta(1 - \theta), \qquad (7.25)$$

where θ is the population poverty rate, $Z_{\alpha/2}$ the upper $100(1 - \alpha/2)\%$ percentile of the normal distribution, and n the required sample size. Typically θ is not (yet) known, in which case one can use the conservative value of $\theta = 0.5$.

Now suppose, more realistically, that there are errors in classification, so that the probability that a household is classified as poor if it is in fact poor (the sensitivity, s) is not necessarily 1; and the probability that a household is classified as nonpoor if it is not poor (the specificity, c) is not necessarily 1 either. Let p be the probability that a household is classified as poor, in which case

$$p = \theta s + (1 - \theta)(1 - c), \qquad (7.26)$$

which is the sum of the true positive and false positive outcomes. If s and c are known, then the required sample size is given by (Rahme et al. 2000, p. 2):

$$n_{\text{adj}} = \left(\frac{2Z_{\alpha/2}}{w(s+c-1)}\right)^2 p(1-p). \tag{7.27}$$

For a 95% interval, $Z_{\alpha/2} = 1.96$; if $w = 0.04$, and the classification of the poor is perfect, then $n = 2,401$, which is already a large sample. If, furthermore, $s = c = 0.95$, then $n = 2,964$, which tells us that if there are even modest errors in determining who is poor and who is not, the increase in required sample size can be quite substantial – over five hundred, in this case. In passing we note that if $c = 0.95$ but now $s = 0.9$, the required sample size is 3,323; if we can improve the accuracy with which we identify the poor, the payoff is that we do not need as large a sample.

In practice, the values of sensitivity (s) and specificity (c) are not known with certainty, and are not known in advance. The methodological challenge then becomes one of computing the appropriate sample size while taking this uncertainty into account. Rahme et al. (2000) suggest a Bayesian solution to this problem, as follows.

First, specify prior distributions for the parameters of concern, here the poverty rate (θ), sensitivity (s), and specificity (c). Beta distributions are typically used, since these are proportions: let them be given by $\beta(\alpha_{1\theta}, \alpha_{2\theta})$, $\beta(\alpha_{1S}, \alpha_{2S})$, and $\beta(\alpha_{1C}, \alpha_{2C})$. Second, draw a random sample of size k (typically $k \geq 1,000$) from the joint density of (θ, S, C), generating points (θ_i, S_i, C_i). Third, attach weights $\omega_i(x)$ to each sampled point. These weights are proportional to the marginal posterior density for θ, which can be shown, given x poor in a sample of n, to be

$$f(\theta|x) \propto [\theta s + (1-\theta)(1-c)]^x [\theta(1-s) + (1-\theta)c]^{n-x} \\ \times \theta^{\alpha_{1\theta}}(1-\theta)^{\alpha_{2\theta}} s^{\alpha_{1S}}(1-s)^{\alpha_{2S}} c^{\alpha_{1C}}(1-c)^{\alpha_{2C}}. \tag{7.28}$$

The posterior mean, given x, is then

$$\hat{\theta}(x) \approx \frac{\sum_{i=1}^{k} \theta_i.\omega_i}{\sum_{i=1}^{k} \omega_i}. \tag{7.29}$$

For each x, the coverage probability is given as the sum of the weights associated with $\theta \in (\hat{\theta}(x) \pm (w/2))$. This coverage probability depends of course, on the data x, which are not yet available. One can, however, compute an average of this coverage probability, averaged over the likelihood of the data integrated with respect to the priors (see Rahme et al. 2000 for details and S-plus code for its implementation for a given w and n).

Haughton and Phong (2003) use this approach to determine the sample size that would be required to estimate the poverty rate in Nghe An province in Vietnam to the nearest 2 percentage points. They assume:

Table 7.5 Average coverage of probability intervals for poverty rates, rural Nghe An Province, Vietnam, 1998

Width of interval	Sample size	Prob. coverage
0.04	1,000	0.6439
0.04	2,000	0.6924
0.04	3,000	0.6995
0.08	1,000	0.9261
0.08	2,000	0.9471
0.08	3,000	0.9587
0.08	801[a]	0.9587

[a] Sample size required if there is no uncertainty about model sensitivity or specificity. For assumptions used to generate this table, see accompanying text
Source: Haughton and Phong (2003)

- For θ (the poverty rate), a mean of 0.477 and standard deviation of 0.041 (Baulch and Minot 2002), which implies a $\beta(70.3, 77.1)$ distribution
- For s (sensitivity) and c (specificity), a mean of 0.95 and standard deviation of 0.025, which yields a $\beta(71.25, 3.75)$ distribution

This yields the results shown in Table 7.5. For an interval width of 0.04, which would allow one to estimate the poverty rate to within 2 percentage points, one could only get a 70% credible interval even with a sample size of 3,000.

The clearest lesson from Table 7.5 is that even with sample sizes as large as 3,000, it is unrealistic to expect to be able to detect differences in poverty of, say 2 percentage points. This result depends heavily on the uncertainty about sensitivity and specificity; if they equal 0.95 with certainty, then a sample of 801 (rather than 3,000) would suffice to ensure that the poverty rate is measured with an 8 percentage-point-wide credible interval with 95.87% probability.

There are two useful practical implications. If one can take steps to ensure that the poor are identified accurately – for instance, using a questionnaire that minimizes measurement errors – then the consequent reduction in sensitivity and specificity (and their uncertainty) can greatly enhance the precision of poverty measurement. The other implication is less optimistic: the sample sizes required for the precise measurement of poverty are quite large, which suggests that it is probably not worth the trouble to measure poverty too frequently, especially in slow-growing economies, because it may be difficult statistically to pick up any movement in the poverty rate.

7.7 Conclusion

There is a large, and rapidly growing, literature on Bayesian analysis, but relatively few of the applications have concerned less-developed countries. An interesting exception is the recent study by Kandala et al. (2001) that presents a Bayesian semiparametric analysis of the influence of a child's age and mother's body mass index on chronic malnutrition in Zambia and Tanzania. This article combines the use of splines to capture nonlinear effects – which are common in malnutrition studies – with Bayesian techniques.

When samples sizes are large, as is typically the case with household surveys, then the data tend to overwhelm all but the most tightly specified priors, and the case for using Bayesian analysis in some such situations is not compelling. On the other hand there are situations when the techniques are potentially very useful, as with Bayesian Model Averaging, or when trying to determine the appropriate sample size for a survey when one has uncertainty about the precision with which poverty rates (or other variables) are measured. Another important area of application is that of small area estimation, discussed in Chap. 13.

There are also a number of situations where models are sufficiently complicated that a Bayesian analysis may be the only feasible solution. This arises, for example, in the analysis of multilevel models, which are considered in more detail in Chap. 13.

Finally, we refer to work by Gelman et al. (2003, Chap. 7) in which a general framework is presented for the inclusion of information about data collection into a Bayesian analysis, along with examples, notably an analysis of the proportion of children in the Melbourne area who walk to school (Gelman et al. 2003, p. 214).

Appendix A   Winbugs Code for the Ho Chi Minh City Urban Example

A.1   Program hcmcurban

```
Model A {tau <- 80
tau.beta <- tau-beta
# discrete prior on first beta parameter
beta <- a[rval]
rval ~ dcat(prior[]);
for (r in 1:R) { a[r] <- b[r]*tau;
                 prior[r] <- w[r]; }
# model for observed data
for (k in 1:n) {m.t[k] ~ dbin(theta[k],m[k]);
# sample population prediction by cluster
            poor.s[k] <- theta[k]*m[k];
# non-surveyed population in sampled cluster
            V[k] <- M[k]-m[k]}
# non-surveyed population in non-sampled cluster
for (k in n+1:N) { V[k] <- M[k]}
# sample cluster proportions
for (k in 1:N) {theta[k] ~ dbeta(beta,tau.beta)}
# predicted poor among non-surveyed population
for (k in 1:N) { poor.v[k] ~ dbin(theta[k],V[k])}
```

predicted population proportion
P <− (sum(poor.s[])+sum(poor.v[]))/sum(M[])}

A.2   Model A Data

list(M=c(5180.00,4894.00,1981.00,3494.00,3188.00,3684.00,
1897.00,2762.00,2325.00,3426.00,11482.00,5760.00,2783.00,
2553.00,7522.00,4982.00,5040.00,4602.00,3475.00,4487.00,5524.00, 4500.00,1516.00,
1818.00,3136.00,1418.00,2005.00,2110.00,1459.00,2380.00,1799.00, 1286.00,1849.00,3859.00,
2473.00,2963.00,4589.00,3491.00,3621.00,3684.00,4273.00,4666.00, 2267.00,4708.00,2139.00,
1965.00,3773.00,1968.00,2523.00,2214.00,3288.00,1677.00,1968.00, 2598.00,2173.00,
1966.00,2372.00,2871.00,2150.00,3053.00,2155.00,4536.00,3661.00, 1450.00,2424.00,3677.00,
3113.00,3309.00,2048.00,3061.00,2905.00,3320.00,1507.00,3567.00, 2952.00,
2460.00,2509.00,2544.00,3021.00,3253.00,4313.00,2685.00,3286.00, 3927.00,5474.00,
4108.00,3970.00,1649.00,1418.00,1898.00,3445.00,3195.00,3055.00, 2772.00,726.00,
3538.00,4472.00,5197.00,4749.00,6159.00,6242.00,3983.00,3017.00, 2341.00,4367.00,3847.00,
2470.00,3525.00,1876.00,3764.00,5438.00,1435.00,3214.00,3436.00, 3463.00,1789.00,1185.00,
1180.00,3093.00,3007.00,3609.00,2497.00,3022.00,1295.00,945.00, 2549.00,3623.00,2206.00,
2325.00,1878.00,2079.00,2719.00,3738.00,2155.00,
2820.00,4918.00,4929.00,4400.00,5227.00,2641.00,2840.00,4489.00, 2468.00,5135.00,2463.00,
3429.00,3003.00,2085.00,2042.00,2721.00,2142.00,2692.00,3302.00, 3556.00,2963.00,
4549.00,7826.00,2627.00,3384.00,3325.00,2755.00,2632.00,3522.00, 2035.00,3058.00,
6262.00,2631.00,3923.00,3430.00,6587.00,6067.00,10922.00,2630.00, 3138.00,4467.00,10518.00,
3056.00,5961.00,2874.00,4371.00,4101.00,4626.00,3194.00,3855.00, 5620.00,7144.00,4119.00,
4558.00,11314.00,3757.00,8469.00,8121.00,4121.00,9000.00,2831.00, 2817.00,
4471.00,2103.00,2740.00,5416.00,7216.00,3627.00,2342.00,3915.00, 4215.00,3163.00,
4434.00,4519.00,4154.00,6444.00,4766.00,5541.00,1401.00,2401.00, 3181.00,1704.00,
3057.00,4081.00,1833.00,3811.00,1947.00,2131.00,1415.00,1748.00, 1648.00,2384.00,1829.00,
4158.00,6080.00,4202.00,2833.00,3876.00,2744.00,4197.00,4627.00, 2932.00,2178.00,2811.00,
4509.00,2414.00,3319.00,7459.00,3118.00),
R=4,n=14,N=242,b=c(0.00875,0.01625,0.02375,0.03125),
w=c(0.07,0.43,0.43,0.07),
m=c(25,21,29,29,23,33,20,19,32,41,34,40,36,51),
    m.t=c(0,1,0,0,0,0,0,1,0,0,0,0,0,0))

References

Baulch, Robert, and Nicholas Minot. 2002. The spatial distribution of poverty in Vietnam and the
    potential for targeting. Policy Research Working Paper 2829. Washington, DC: World Bank.
Box, George, and George Tiao. 1973. *Bayesian inference in statistical analysis*, Wiley Classics
    Edition. New York: Wiley.
Congdon, Peter. 2001. *Bayesian statistical modelling*. New York: Wiley.
Fernández, Carmen, Eduardo Ley, and Mark F.J. Steel. 2001a. Model uncertainty in cross-country
    growth regressions. *Journal of Applied Econometrics* 16: 563–576.

Fernández, Carmen, Eduardo Ley, and Mark F.J. Steel. 2001b. Benchmark priors for Bayesian model averaging. *Journal of Econometrics* 100: 381–427.

Gelman, Andrew, John B. Carlin, Hal S. Stern, and Donald B. Rubin. 2003. *Bayesian data analysis*, 2nd ed. Boca Raton: Chapman and Hall/CRC.

Greene, William H. 2003. *Econometric analysis*, 5th ed. Upper Saddle River: Prentice Hall.

Haughton, Dominique, and Nguyen Phong. 2003. Bayesian analysis of poverty rates: The case of Vietnamese provinces. *Journal of Modern Applied Statistical Methods* 2(1): 189–194.

Hoeting, Jennifer A., David Madigan, Adrian E. Raftery, and Chris T. Volinsky. 1999. Bayesian model averaging: A tutorial. *Statistical Science* 14(4): 382–417.

Kandala, N.D., S. Lang, S. Klasen, and L. Fahrmeir. 2001. Semiparametric analysis of the sociodemographic and spatial determinants of undernutrition in two African countries. *Research in Official Statistics* 1: 81–100.

Klump, Rainer, and Patricia Prüfer. 2006. How to prioritize policies for pro-poor growth: Applying Bayesian model averaging to Vietnam. CentER Discussion Paper 2006-117, Tilburg University.

Lynch, Scott, and Bruce Western. 2004. Bayesian posterior predictive checks for complex models. *Sociological Methods and Research* 32(3): 301–335.

Menten, J, A. Hailu, M. Wasunna, S. El-Safi, and M. Boelaert. 2006. Bayesian modelling of a multi-country diagnostic study. Institute of Tropical Medicine, Antwerp, Belgium.

Nandram, B., and J. Sedransk. 1993. Bayesian predictive inference for a finite population proportion: Two-stage cluster sampling. *Journal of the Royal Statistical Society Series B (Methodological)* 55(2): 399–408.

Rahme, E., L. Joseph, and T. Gyorkos. 2000. Bayesian sample size determination for estimating binomial parameters from data subject to misclassification. *Applied Sttatistics* 49: 119–128.

SAS. 2007. Introduction to Bayesian analysis procedures. http://support.sas.com/documentation/cdl/en/statug/63962/HTML/default/viewer.htm#introbayes_toc.htm. Accessed July 30, 2011.

Stata Corporation. 2009. *Stata 11.0 manual*. College Station: Stata Press.

Theil, H., and A. Goldberger. 1961. On pure and mixed estimation in economics. *International Economic Review* 2: 65–78.

Vose, David. 1996. *Quantitative risk analysis: A guide to Monte Carlo simulation modelling.* Chichester: Wiley.

WinBugs. 2007. http://www.mrc-bsu.cam.ac.uk/bugs/winbugs/contents.shtml. Accessed July 30, 2011.

Chapter 8
Spatial Models

8.1 Introduction

Economists and statisticians are rediscovering geography. Until relatively recently, most economic models essentially ignored spatial variations in data and in relationships; these were not at the heart of the issues that were considered to be interesting.

In practice, geography is important. Programs aimed at tackling poverty may find it useful to target their interventions by region or district; this requires *poverty mapping*, which we discuss more fully in Chap. 13. The patterns of demand, or household behavior, may vary from area to area, in which case policy measures may need to be calibrated to take this into account. The simple measurement of poverty will itself depend heavily on the accurate estimation of price differences across time and space.

More generally, our understanding of economic processes often requires an appreciation of the spatial dimension. For instance, why do unemployment rates, or wages, vary systematically from one district to another? What role do spatial differences play in explanations of agricultural productivity? What are the determinants of deforestation, and can we model the likelihood that a given area of forest will be cut down in the foreseeable future?

In this chapter, we explain why spatial information needs to be incorporated into many models, and how this may be done. Only a handful of studies in less-developed countries have used these techniques with household survey data, but the number is growing rapidly, and we refer to this literature at the appropriate points in the chapter.

The chapter is constructed around an example based on a study of the determinants of unemployment rates in the communities of the Midi-Pyrenées region in France, which serves to illustrate the essential methods and conclusions of spatial econometrics.

Every spatial analysis has to begin with a map, so a good place to start is with Fig. 8.1, which graphs the residuals from an ordinary least squares regression of the unemployment rate on a number of explanatory variables, for hinterlands in the

D. Haughton and J. Haughton, *Living Standards Analytics*, Statistics for Social
and Behavioral Sciences, DOI 10.1007/978-1-4614-0385-2_8,
© Springer Science+Business Media, LLC 2011

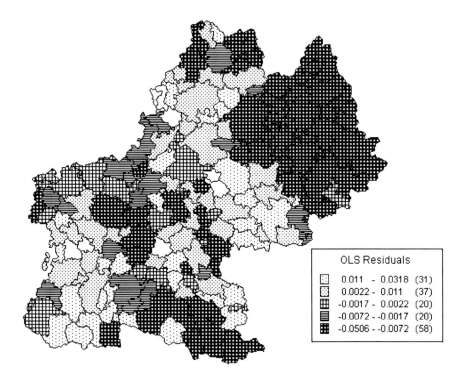

OLS Residuals

⬚	0.011 - 0.0318	(31)
⬚	0.0022 - 0.011	(37)
⊞	-0.0017 - 0.0022	(20)
▤	-0.0072 - -0.0017	(20)
⊞	-0.0506 - -0.0072	(58)

Fig. 8.1 Residuals from OLS regression of the determinants of the unemployment rate for hinterlands in the Midi-Pyrénées region of France, 1990. (*Source*: Aragon et al. 2003)

Midi-Pyrénées region of France in 1990. The interesting point is that the residuals show some spatial clumping – with negative values in the northeast, and positive values in the southwest. In other words, the unemployment rate in a given area appears to be correlated with the unemployment rate in neighboring areas, even after controlling for observable variables. Unfortunately, the use of OLS in this context will generate estimates that are inefficient and, depending on the form of the spatial links, may be biased and inconsistent. Much of this chapter is devoted to dealing with this problem.

8.2   The Starting Point: Including Spatial Variables

8.2.1   *Exploratory Spatial Data Analysis*

Even before introducing statistical techniques, it is helpful to examine a few basic maps in some detail, to get a "feel" for the spatial structure of the data. One useful tool is the GeoXp package developed at Université Toulouse I (Thomas-Agnan, Aragon, Ruiz-Gazen, Laurent, and Robidou, 2006) and implemented in R.

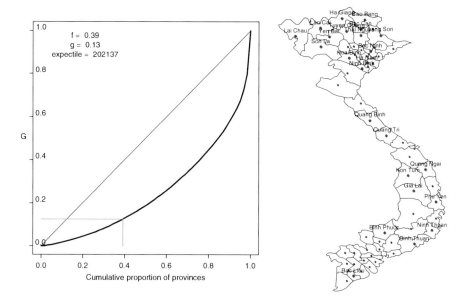

Fig. 8.2 Lorenz curve and map of GDP/capita for Vietnamese provinces, 1998

To illustrate how GeoXp works, consider Fig. 8.2, which shows on the right-hand side a map of the provinces of Vietnam, and on the left-hand side a Lorenz curve that graphs the cumulative proportion of the provinces (from poorest to richest) on the horizontal axis and the cumulative proportion of GDP/capita on the vertical axis. This is thus a measure of inequality in per capita GDP between the provinces. As the user moves a cursor along the Lorenz curve, more and more provinces are named and highlighted on the map. The snapshot in Fig. 8.2 shows the poorest two-fifths of the provinces in Vietnam, as of 1998.

Another way to use GeoXp is to create a map and an associated histogram, as done in Fig. 8.3. In this case, the variable in question is the human development index (HDI), which varies between 0 and 1 and is a weighted average of normalized measure of life expectancy at birth (1/3 weight), adult literacy (2/9 weight), gross school enrollment rates (1/9 weight), and GDP per capita (1/3 weight). By moving a cursor along the horizontal axis, it is possible to select the poorest seven provinces, which are then highlighted on the accompanying map. As one moves the cursor, the map adjusts immediately, allowing one to form a clear impression of the spatial effects.

Other commands in GeoXp help one to visualize which areas – provinces in the Vietnamese context – are most closely correlated with their neighbors.

8.2.2   Including Spatial Variables

One of the most straightforward ways to handle geographic effects is to include spatial variables directly as explanatory variables in a model. Consider, for example,

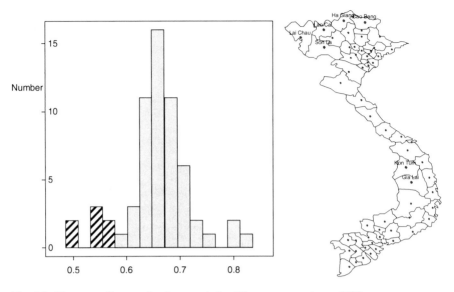

Fig. 8.3 Histomap of human development index, Vietnamese provinces, 1998

the recent study by Kaimowitz et al. (2002) of the determinants of deforestation in the province of Santa Cruz, a well-watered and relatively heavily forested area located on the eastern side of Bolivia. Based on satellite data, the researchers divided the province (other than protected areas and indigenous territories) into 24,208 relatively homogeneous polygons, representing areas that were forested in 1989. The dependent variable ("forest") is set equal to 1 if an area was still forested in 1994, and to zero otherwise. The goal is thus to identify the variables that were associated with deforestation during the 5 years up to 1994.

Forest is more likely to be felled or burned if it is accessible – closer to towns and roads – and if it is unprotected. Kaimowitz et al. also hypothesize that the most vulnerable areas are forest that are not those in areas of high rainfall (too wet) or low rainfall (not enough wood), but areas in between. They fit a logistic model, where each observation is weighted by the area of the polygon. The results of one of their more parsimonious models, including a variety of geographic variables, are shown in Table 8.1. The estimates show that areas designated for settlement, and close to the regional capital (Santa Cruz) and to trails, were more likely to lose forest cover. Curiously, areas located closer to roads were more likely to remain forested. Moreover, whether an area was designated as protected or indigenous was unrelated to deforestation (results not shown here).

Although regression estimates that include spatial variables are common enough, they typically suffer from the problem that the observations may not be independent of one another. A hilly district is likely to be close to another hilly district. Or again, shocks such as floods that hit one area are likely to affect nearby areas. These are but two examples of spatial correlation, but when they occur we need to use some additional statistical tricks.

Table 8.1 Logistic regression of the correlates of deforestation in Santa Cruz province, Bolivia, 1989–1994

	Coefficient	t-value
Dependent variable: =1 if area forested in 1989 and 1994, =0 if forested in 1989 but not in 1994		
Independent variables		
Intercept	0.833	3.72
Area is a forest concession (yes = 1)	1.771	5.99
Area is zoned for colonization (yes = 1)	−0.600	4.23
Soil quality (USDA soil group, from 1 through 8)	0.150	4.53
Rainfall (in millimeters p.a.)	−0.001	4.61
Distance to nearest classified road (km)	−0.051	9.61
Distance to nearest trail outside a forest concession (km)	0.008	6.04
Distance to nearest trail inside a forest concession (km)	0.003	2.21
Distance to Santa Cruz (km)	0.008	12.33

Source: Kaimowitz et al. (2002)
Note: Pseudo $R^2 = 0.23$. Number of observations: 24,208

8.3 Spatial Models

Following LeSage (1998, p. 2), we may distinguish two problems that arise when working with data that have a locational component: spatial dependence, and spatial heterogeneity. When either is present, the method of ordinary least squares is inappropriate (as we explain below), and alternative estimation methods are required.

8.3.1 Spatial Dependence

Spatial dependence occurs when the value of an observation in location i depends on observations in locations $j \neq i$. For instance, if unemployment is high in location i, then it is also likely to be high in the neighboring area j. Formally, we have

$$y_i = f(y_j), \quad i = 1, \ldots, n, \quad j \neq i, \tag{8.1}$$

where y_i is the variable of interest, such as the unemployment rate.

Such dependence may occur because it is inherently important to the problem at hand, and reflects the fundamental theorem of regional science, which states that "distance matters." Thus the price of a house may be related to the neighboring house, perhaps because they were built at the same era, or because they are equally close to the beach, or because one well-kept house begets another. To model this spatial dependence, we need to determine an appropriate form for the function $f(\cdot)$.

Spatial dependence can also arise as a consequence of measurement error, particularly if the spatial units (e.g., zip-code area, census tract, state) are not congruent

Table 8.2 Illustrative example of spatial dependence due to measurement error

District	A	B	C
Labor force	2,000	2,000	2,000
Employment in district	1,350	1,800	1,350
True unemployment in district	500	500	500
True unemployment rate in district (%)	25	25	25
Observed unemployment rate in district (%)	32.5	10	32.5

with the underlying process. We may illustrate this with a simplified version of a (semirealistic) example used by LeSage (1998, p. 4), using the numbers set out in Table 8.2. Let there be three districts, each with a labor force of 2,000 adults. Assume that the truth (which we cannot observe) is that a quarter of the residents in each district are unemployed. Of the total of 4,500 jobs, assume that a 1,800 are in the central district, while each of the other districts has 1,350 jobs. It follows that 150 people who live in districts A and C travel to the central district B in order to work. If the unemployment rate is defined as 1 − (number employed/number in the labor force) *in each district*, then the observed rate will be 10% in district B and 32.5% in each of districts A and C. The spatial pattern of unemployment observed in this case is an artifact of the geographic units employed for measurement.

The problem that arises in this case is that if we try to estimate an equation of the form

$$y_i = \mathbf{X}_i \beta + \varepsilon_i, \tag{8.2}$$

then the errors will be spatially correlated, so that $E(\varepsilon_i \varepsilon_j) \neq 0$. In this case, ordinary least squares estimation of (8.2) will not be best linear unbiased ("BLUE"), and the values of R^2 and the t-statistics may be overestimated. These issues must be addressed if one is serious about the validity of the statistical inference behind the OLS model.

8.3.2   Spatial Heterogeneity

Spatial heterogeneity refers to variation over space in the relationships themselves (LeSage 1998, p. 6). So, for instance, we might believe that the relationship between fertilizer inputs and the output of maize differs from place to place. Formally, in the case of a linear relationship, we have

$$y_i = \mathbf{X}_i \beta_i + \varepsilon_i, \tag{8.3}$$

where the i refers to observations at $1, \ldots, n$ locations, X_i is a $1 \times k$ vector of explanatory variables, y_i is the dependent variable at location i, and ε_i is a stochastic disturbance with zero mean and constant variance.

If we had enough multiple observations *at each geographic point*, we could estimate (8.2). However, this is rarely possible in practice, given data limitations. Yet if we simply assume that $\beta_i = \beta$, $\forall i$, then we are not resolving the problem that the relationships may vary from place to place.

It is sometimes reasonable to assume that the location that matters is relatively broad – for instance, urban vs. rural areas. This is acceptable if we can assume that the errors are independent of one another *within each given geographic unit.*

This assumption underpins the approach taken by Ravallion and Wodon (1997) in a recent study based on household survey data from Bangladesh. The question they ask is this: "Should poverty programs target households with personal attributes that foster poverty, no matter where they live?" Their answer is "possibly not." In an economy with no apparent constraints on mobility, there may still be sizeable geographic effects on living standards, even after controlling for a wide range of observable variables.

Ravallion and Wodon divide their data into two geographically based groups, urban and rural, and estimate separate models of the determinants of consumption for each. A selection of their regression results, based on data from the 1991/92 Household Expenditure Survey of the Bangladesh Bureau of Statistics, are shown in Table 8.3. They reject the null hypothesis that all coefficients are the same in rural and urban areas – the F-value for a test restricting all 57 coefficients to be equal is 5.63, which rejects equality at the 1% level – and so conclude that "different models are determining consumption in urban and rural areas." This suggests a possible role for geographic targeting.

Their estimates show most of the expected effects: households whose members have more education, or more land, or who work in business or industry, are better off, but these effects are more pronounced in urban areas. Their study includes an extended discussion of the potential for selection bias that might arise because a household's place of residence may not be exogenous; they do not find evidence of such bias, but grant that the available test procedures have their limitations (Ravallion and Wodon 1997, Sect. 3).

8.4 Classifying Spatial Models

It is often the case that geographic variation is more fine-grained than the use of standard regression with spatial variables (as in Kaimowitz et al. 2002) would allow, or than a broad division into a few distinct categories would permit (as in Ravallion and Wodon 1997). In this case, it is necessary to specify the spatial dimensions of our models in more detail.

The most general possible model has the form

$$\mathbf{y} = \xi \mathbf{W}_1 \mathbf{y} + \mathbf{X}\beta + \mathbf{W}_2 \mathbf{X}^* \rho + (\mathbf{I} - \lambda \mathbf{W}_3)^{-1} \varepsilon, \tag{8.4}$$

Table 8.3 Estimates of influences on log real consumption, Bangladesh, 1991–1992

	Urban		Rural	
	Coefficient	SE	Coefficient	SE
Intercept	0.33	0.12	0.19	0.06
Number of children	−0.16	0.02	−0.17	0.01
Number of children squared	0.02	0.00	0.02	0.00
Number of adults	−0.10	0.02	−0.11	0.01
Number of adults squared	0.01	0.00	0.01	0.00
Education of head				
Below class 5	0.15	0.03	0.07	0.01
Class 5	0.16	0.03	0.10	0.02
Classes 6–9	0.28	0.03	0.15	0.02
Higher level	0.42	0.04	0.22	0.03
Land ownership				
0.05 to 0.49 acres	0.08	0.02	0.08	0.02
0.50 to 1.49 acres	0.07	0.03	0.17	0.02
1.50 to 2.49 acres	0.13	0.05	0.17	0.03
2.50 acres or more	0.37	0.08	0.12	0.04
Main occupation				
Factory worker, artisan	0.30	0.06	0.15	0.03
Petty trader, small businessman	0.36	0.05	0.25	0.02
Memo items				
Number of observations	1,908		3,817	
R^2	0.55		0.50	

Source: Ravallion and Wodon (1997), Table 1
Notes: The full regressions include 56 variables. The dependent variable is (the log of) consumption, normalized by a poverty line that reflects the estimated cost of living in the area where the household lives. The standard errors reflect the Huber–White correction for heteroskedasticity. All the coefficients shown are significant at the 5% level of confidence. The excluded categories for the dummy variables are illiterate (for education of head), no land (for land ownership), and landless agricultural worker (for main occupation)

where $\mathbf{y}$ is an $n \times 1$ vector of observations on the dependent variable (e.g., the unemployment rate in an area) and $\mathbf{X}$ is an $n \times k$ matrix of observations on the k independent variables; $\mathbf{X}^*$ is $\mathbf{X}$ without the column of ones corresponding to the constant term; and $E(\varepsilon) = 0$ and $\mathrm{var}(\varepsilon) = \Omega$, where Ω is a diagonal matrix. The $\mathbf{W}_i$ are $n \times n$ spatial weights matrices that measure the strength of contiguity; we discuss their construction in more detail in the next section.

The first term on the right-hand side of (8.4) is the spatially lagged dependent variable; the third term on the right-hand side reflects the spatially lagged independent variables; and the error terms here are also spatially lagged. The model in (8.4) could also be written as

$$\mathbf{y} = \zeta \mathbf{W}_1 \mathbf{y} + \mathbf{X}\beta + \mathbf{W}_2 \mathbf{X}^* \rho + u, \qquad (8.5)$$

Fig. 8.4 Five regions, to illustrate concepts of contiguity

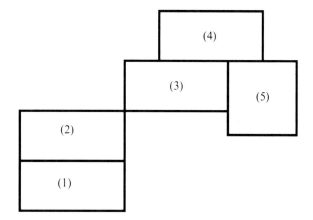

where $u = \lambda \mathbf{W}_3 u + \varepsilon$, and ε is a zero-mean random error with diagonal covariance matrix. This simply serves to define the nature of the spatial correlation in the error terms, analogous to first-order autocorrelation in a time-series model.

8.4.1 Measuring Spatial Contiguity

Before proceeding further, we need to ask how one might measure the degree of connectedness between one area and another, with a weights matrix $\mathbf{W}$. In this, we follow the presentation in LeSage (1998, Sect. 1.4.1). Suppose that we are studying unemployment in five regions, marked (1) through (5) in Fig. 8.4. Our interest is in creating a 5×5 matrix that measures the likely strength of the spillovers from one region to the next.

The key idea in a *contiguity matrix* is to set element $W_{ij} = 1$ if areas i and j are contiguous, and to 0 otherwise. A popular choice is *rook contiguity*, where $W_{ij} = 1$ if the regions share a common side. In the case of Fig. 8.4 this would generate the following matrix:

$$W = \begin{pmatrix} 0 & 1 & 0 & 0 & 0 \\ 1 & 0 & 0 & 0 & 0 \\ 0 & 0 & 0 & 1 & 1 \\ 0 & 0 & 1 & 0 & 1 \\ 0 & 0 & 1 & 1 & 0 \end{pmatrix}. \tag{8.6}$$

Note that although regions (2) and (3) touch, they do not have a common side. By convention, the diagonal elements of W are zero.

An alternative would be *queen contiguity*, where $W_{ij} = 1$ if regions i and j share a common side or vertex. There are of course other possibilities; for instance, the entries in the W matrix could be in proportion to the length of shared borders; or the time that it takes to travel between the main towns in the areas.

In practice, it is common to normalize the W matrix so that the rows sum to unity. This creates a standardized, first-order contiguity matrix, and would transform (8.6) into the following:

$$
C = \begin{pmatrix}
0 & 1 & 0 & 0 & 0 \\
1 & 0 & 0 & 0 & 0 \\
0 & 0 & 0 & \frac{1}{2} & \frac{1}{2} \\
0 & 0 & \frac{1}{2} & 0 & \frac{1}{2} \\
0 & 0 & \frac{1}{2} & \frac{1}{2} & 0
\end{pmatrix}.
\tag{8.7}
$$

If z is a vector of observations on some variable associated with these regions, then the matrix product $z^* = Cz$ creates a variable equal to the mean of observations from the contiguous regions, so

$$
\begin{pmatrix} z_1^* \\ z_2^* \\ z_3^* \\ z_4^* \\ z_5^* \end{pmatrix} = \begin{pmatrix}
0 & 1 & 0 & 0 & 0 \\
1 & 0 & 0 & 0 & 0 \\
0 & 0 & 0 & \frac{1}{2} & \frac{1}{2} \\
0 & 0 & \frac{1}{2} & 0 & \frac{1}{2} \\
0 & 0 & \frac{1}{2} & \frac{1}{2} & 0
\end{pmatrix} \begin{pmatrix} z_1 \\ z_2 \\ z_3 \\ z_4 \\ z_5 \end{pmatrix} = \begin{pmatrix} z_2 \\ z_1 \\ 0.5(z_4 + z_5) \\ 0.5(z_3 + z_5) \\ 0.5(z_3 + z_4) \end{pmatrix}
\tag{8.8}
$$

As LeSage points out, this is one approach to specifying a relationship of the form $y_i = f(y_j), j \neq i$, as set out in (8.1).

8.4.2 Types of Spatial Model

The parameters of the fully general model in (8.4) are not fully identified, but there are a number of special cases that merit further comment.

A good starting point is the relatively simple *first-order spatial autoregressive model*. In this case we assume $\beta = \rho = \lambda = 0$, and we simply have

$$
y = \xi \mathbf{W}y + \varepsilon, \quad \text{with } \varepsilon \sim N(0, \sigma^2 I_n).
\tag{8.9}
$$

In this case the only variable that drives y is the value of the same variable in contiguous areas, appropriately weighted. The least-squares estimate of ξ is biased and inconsistent, but maximum likelihood estimators are available that solve this problem (see LeSage 1998, Chap. 2).

The first-order spatial autoregressive model is rather basic, and is typically augmented with other independent variables, giving rise to the *mixed autoregressive-regressive model*, also known as a *spatial lag model*, or simply the *spatial autoregressive model*, of the form

$$
y = \xi \mathbf{W}y + \mathbf{X}\beta + \varepsilon, \quad \text{with } \varepsilon \sim N(0, \sigma^2 I_n).
\tag{8.10}
$$

The analog in time-series analysis would be a regression model with a lagged dependent variable; here, the dependent variable is lagged spatially rather than temporally, but otherwise the concept is the same. If OLS is applied without the spatially lagged dependent variable, the estimates of the β coefficients will be biased and inconsistent. One can test whether a spatial lag is warranted using a Lagrange multiplier test to determine whether $\xi = 0$; the LM statistic is distributed χ^2 with one degree of freedom.

With a spatially lagged dependent variable on the right-hand side, the interpretation of β changes: it only shows the immediate, but not the total, effect of a change in an explanatory variable on y. Suppose that the value of the kth explanatory variable changes; this affects y in that district – the effect that is captured by β_k – but the change in y in turn influences the value of y in neighboring districts (through the $\xi \mathbf{W} y$ term), which feeds back to affect y in the home district. The eventual effect is that y will change by $C^{ii}\beta_k$, where C^{ii} is the (i,i) element of $(\mathbf{I} - \xi \mathbf{W})^{-1}$.

One of the most popular models that take spatial effects into account is the *spatial errors model*. In this case we have

$$y = \mathbf{X}\beta + (\mathbf{I} - \lambda \mathbf{W})^{-1}\varepsilon, \quad \text{with } \varepsilon \sim N(0, \sigma^2 I_n). \tag{8.11}$$

The structure of this model is analogous to a time-series model with first-order autocorrelation in the errors. A shock in one area propagates to neighboring areas; Anselin and Florax (1995) refer to this as "nuisance spatial dependence."

Traditionally, the test of whether the error structure is of the form shown in (8.11) was based on Moran's I. If $\mathbf{W}$ is a standardized contiguity matrix, then $I \equiv \varepsilon'\mathbf{W}\varepsilon/\varepsilon'\varepsilon$ should be distributed as asymptotically normal. This is of course a test for the presence of spatial effects as captured by the particular weights matrix $\mathbf{W}$; a different choice of weights matrix might generate a different value of Moran's I.

Rather than using Moran's I, it has become increasingly common to use a Lagrange multiplier test first proposed by Burridge (see Anselin 1992, p. 179; also Anselin 1998) the LM statistic is distributed χ^2 with one degree of freedom, and a large value of the statistic would suggest that a spatial error model would be appropriate.

If the spatial errors model is the correct one, but one uses least squares to estimate (8.11) on the assumption that $\lambda = 0$ (i.e., without spatially correlated errors), then the estimates of the β coefficients will be inefficient.

The spatial errors model can also be written as

$$y = \lambda \mathbf{W} y + \mathbf{X}\beta - \lambda \mathbf{W}\mathbf{X}\beta + \varepsilon, \quad \text{with } \varepsilon \sim N(0, \sigma^2 I_n). \tag{8.12}$$

which in turn is a special case, sometimes referred to as the common factor hypothesis model, of the more general model

$$y = \lambda \mathbf{W} y + \mathbf{X}\beta + \mathbf{W}\mathbf{X}\rho + \varepsilon, \quad \text{with } \varepsilon \sim N(0, \sigma^2 I_n). \tag{8.13}$$

One can test whether the common factor hypothesis is an acceptable simplification by applying a Lagrange multiplier test to check whether $\rho = -\lambda\beta$.

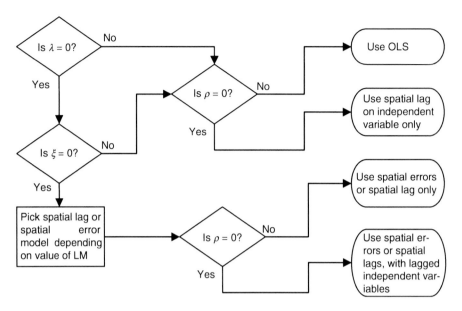

Fig. 8.5 Decision diagram for choosing the most appropriate spatial model

A more *general spatial model* would allow spatial lags both in the dependent variable and in the error, and would take the form

$$y = \zeta \mathbf{W}_1 y + \mathbf{X}\beta + (\mathbf{I} - \lambda \mathbf{W}_3)^{-1}\varepsilon, \quad \text{with } \varepsilon \sim N(0, \sigma^2 I_n). \qquad (8.14)$$

It is possible to have $\mathbf{W}_1 = \mathbf{W}_3$, but this sometimes leads to identification problems.

It is natural to ask when the general spatial model would be preferable to a simpler model. At the intuitive level, it would make sense to use, or at least consider, such a model if there is evidence of spatial dependence in the error structure of the spatial autoregressive model; or if the contiguity differences can reasonably be assumed to differ – for instance, if one is a first-order, and the other a second-order, contiguity matrix; or if one is a contiguity matrix and the other is a matrix that shows, for instance, the distance between the central cities in the regions.

Given the abundance of choices of model, it would be valuable to have an algorithm for choosing the "best" model. Florax and Folmer (1992) suggest that one should first test whether it is appropriate to include autoregressive disturbances (i.e., is $\lambda = 0$?) or a spatially lagged dependent variable (i.e., is $\zeta = 0$?). If neither should be included, one may then test whether spatially lagged *independent* variables should be included (i.e., is $\rho = 0$?).

On the other hand, if the initial test strongly suggests autoregressive errors, then this is the model to use. And if the initial test favors a lagged dependent variable, then one should test whether spatially lagged independent variables should be included as well. Anselin (1992, p. 180) proposes that as a practical matter, one could choose between a spatial error, and a spatial lag model, on the basis of which LM statistic is larger. The relevant decision diagram is set out in Fig. 8.5.

8.4.3 Illustrating the Choice of Spatial Model

We illustrate the process by which one might choose an appropriate spatial model using the study by Aragon et al. (2003) of the determinants of local unemployment rates in the Midi-Pyrénées region of France. The key results are set out in Table 8.4, where column 1 shows the estimates based on ordinary least squares estimation.

The dependent variable is the unemployment rate, which is measured in each area; these hinterlands, called "bassins de vie quotidienne" in French, are typically centered on a town. The results show that unemployment is higher if the labor force in an area has a high proportion of young workers or old people, if incomes are higher, and if an area is more densely populated. Aragon et al. argue that unemployment rates are higher in more-urbanized and richer areas as a result of the better amenities and jobs offered in these areas, which attract job-seekers who are willing to tolerate longer unemployment in the hope of obtaining higher-paying jobs in interesting locations.

The residuals from the equation whose estimates are shown in column 1 of Table 8.4 are mapped in Fig. 8.1, and are spatially clustered. This visual evidence of spatial interaction is confirmed by the Lagrange multiplier (LM) statistics reported at the bottom of column 1. Specifically, a test of $\lambda = 0$ is rejected (LM $= 70.4$, p-value $= 0.00$), which would argue in favor of a spatial errors model. The results of estimating such a model are displayed in column 2 of Table 8.4. A formal test shows that there is no remaining spatial lag dependence (LM $= 0.14$, p-value $= 0.71$). This also shows in the map of residuals from this equation, which is displayed in Fig. 8.6, and where the errors now appears to be distributed randomly across the region, in contrast to the clumping of the OLS residuals that is evident in Fig. 8.1. It is worth noting that the index of "enclavement" – essentially a measure of remoteness – is statistically significant in the OLS model, but not when one allows for spatially autocorrelated errors. This suggests that spatial autocorrelation is picking up the effects of remoteness satisfactorily.

The high value of λ, at 0.79, indicates that shocks in one area propagate outward to the neighboring areas to a very substantial degree. The pain of a local shock is thus spread widely, illustrating the strong degree of connectedness across hinterlands in the Midi-Pyrénées region.

It is worth exploring further whether the common factors model with autocorrelated errors is indeed the best choice. First one might ask whether a more general model, as in (8.13), would be preferable; however, a formal test (LR $= 9.4$, p-value $= 0.23$) does not allow us to reject the common factors specification, as in (8.12).

It is also clear from column 1 in Table 8.4 that a test of $\xi = 0$ is also rejected (LM $= 55.2$, p-value $= 0.00$), which suggests that a spatial lag model might be appropriate, even though the lower LM statistic in this case establishes a presumption in favor of a spatial error model. The results of estimating a spatial lag model are shown in column 3 of Table 8.4. Unfortunately, this model does not remove spatial autocorrelation in the errors. Moreover, it performs less well than the spatial error model as measured by the values of the AIC (Akaike information criterion)

Table 8.4 Regression results of models of the determinants of unemployment in the Midi-Pyrénées region of France, 1990

	Column 1	Column 2 Auto-correlated errors	Column 3 Lagged dependent variable	Column 4 Lagged independent vars	
	OLS	MLE	MLE	Unlagged terms	Lagged terms
				MLE	
% Lab force 20–39	0.171 (0.00)	0.224 (0.00)	0.194 (0.00)	0.206 (0.00)	‥
% Pop 60–64	0.430 (0.00)	0.394 (0.00)	0.580 (0.00)	0.424 (0.00)	‥
% Employment secondary sector	0.032 (0.01)	0.029 (0.00)	0.026 (0.01)	0.27 (0.00)	−0.048 (0.03)
SE monthly unemployment rates	1.228 (0.00)	0.921 (0.00)	1.345 (0.00)	0.925 (0.00)	‥
Ln(population/ha)	0.010 (0.00)	0.008 (0.00)	0.010 (0.00)	0.010 (0.00)	‥
Index of "enclavement"	0.074 (0.00)	0.015 (0.38)	0.056 (0.00)	0.041 (0.02)	0.078 (0.01)
Taxable income/wkr ('000)	0.568 (0.00)	0.579 (0.00)	0.487 (0.00)	0.563 (0.00)	−0.645 (0.00)
Constant	−0.087 (0.00)	−0.110 (0.00)	−0.137 (0.00)	−0.102 (0.00)	‥
Memo items					
Number of observations	174	174	174	174	
Log likelihood	454.4	489.8	478.3	493.2	
LM ($\lambda = 0$?) [test of spatial errors]	70.40 (0.00)		13.09 (0.00)	0.11 (0.73)	
$\hat{\lambda}$		0.790 (0.00)			
$\hat{\xi}$			0.456 (0.00)	0.679 (0.00)	
LM ($\hat{\xi} = 0$?) [test of spatial lags]	55.16 (0.00)	0.14 (0.71)	62.41 (0.00)	62.41 (0.00)	
LR ($\rho = -\lambda\beta$?) [test of common factors]		9.4 (0.23)			
AIC	−890.7	−959.6	−936.5	−960.4	
BIC	−862.5	−928.3	−905.2	−919.7	

Source: Aragon et al. (2003). *Notes*: Bracketed values are *p*-values from *t*(*z*) tests. Data source is the FIDEL database, INSEE 1996. Dependent variable is the unemployment rate. *OLS* ordinary least squares, *MLE* maximum likelihood estimation, *LM* Lagrange multiplier, *LR* likelihood ratio, *AIC* Akaike information criterion, *BIC* Bayes information criterion. "‥" denotes not significant at the 10% level. The index of "enclavement" is 0 if all services are found locally; a higher number means that the hinterland is more economically remote

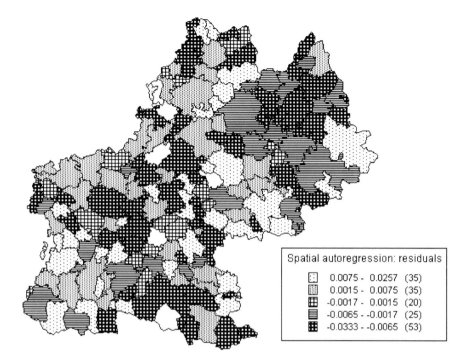

Fig. 8.6 Residuals from regression, with autocorrelated errors, of the determinants of the unemployment rate for hinterlands in the Midi-Pyrénées region of France, 1990. (*Source*: Aragon et al. 2003)

and BIC (Bayes information criterion), where lower values generally denote a more satisfactory model.

The last two columns of Table 8.4 show the results of estimating an augmented version of the spatial lag model, where not only is a lagged version of the unemployment rate included on the right-hand side, but also spatially lagged values of the independent variables. This model has virtues: there is no remaining spatial autocorrelation in the errors, and it has the highest log likelihood and lowest AIC of the models considered here. On the other hand, it is a less parsimonious model than the spatial error model, and this is reflected in lower (and hence better) value of the BIC for the latter model. When trying to choose between competing models, the BIC is typically a better guide than the AIC, because the AIC tests to favor larger and potentially overfitted models (see Haughton et al. 1990).

8.5   Other Spatial Models

There are a number of other possible approaches to modeling spatial effects; in this section we briefly summarize two of these – the spatial expansion model and geographically weighed regression. LeSage (1998) provides further details.

8.5.1   *Spatial Expansion Models*

When we believe that there is spatial heterogeneity, so that the relationships between variables differ from place to place, we argued in Sect. 8.3 that one might want to estimate a model of the form

$$y_i = \mathbf{X}_i\beta_i + \varepsilon_i. \tag{8.3}$$

The problem is that we rarely have enough observations at each location to allow us to estimate the β_i. However, if we could impose some structure on the β_i, then estimation might be feasible. This is the approach taken by Casetti (1972) in the spatial expansion model, where the maintained assumption is that the parameters of the model vary systematically with latitude and longitude. Each observation has coordinates of latitude and longitude, represented by $(Z_{d,i}, Z_{g,i})$, $i = 1, ..., n$.

To see how this model works, consider the case in which there are three independent variables (including a constant), so we have

$$y_i = \beta_{0,i} + \beta_{1,i}X_{1,i} + \beta_{2,i}X_{2,i} + \varepsilon_i, \tag{8.15}$$

where the i observations refer to the n households. The coefficients are themselves influenced by the measures of latitude and longitude, so we have

$$\beta_{0,i} = \gamma_{0,d}Z_{d,i} + \gamma_{0,g}Z_{g,i},$$
$$\beta_{1,i} = \gamma_{1,d}Z_{d,i} + \gamma_{1,g}Z_{g,i},$$
$$\beta_{2,i} = \gamma_{2,d}Z_{d,i} + \gamma_{2,g}Z_{g,i}. \tag{8.16}$$

After substituting (8.16) into (8.15), the model can be estimated using ordinary least squares, which yields estimates of the $2k$ parameters $\gamma_{k,d}$ and $\gamma_{k,g}$; since $k = 3$ in our example, there are six such parameters. From these one can use (8.16) to generate estimates of the $\beta_{k,I}$ coefficients for each observation. LeSage (1998) discusses the general case for k variables.

The model ensures that areas that are close neighbors will have similar coefficients, and so it does not allow for sharp discontinuities, for instance when a rich neighborhood abuts a poor area.

It is reasonable to imagine that there might be some error – captured by a stochastic term u_i – in the expansion relationship in (8.16), giving terms such as

$$\beta_{0,i} = \gamma_{0,d}Z_{d,i} + \gamma_{0,g}Z_{g,i} + u_{0,i}. \tag{8.17}$$

Substituting these into (8.15) gives a model with a composite error term that will in general be heteroscedastic. LeSage (1998, Chap. 4) discusses how to correct for this in estimating the parameters of this model.

8.5.2   Geographically Weighted Regression

If geography matters, then the relationships between the **X** and y variables may vary over space. These may be approximated by a series of locally linear regressions, much as is done in standard nonparametric regression. The key idea behind these *geographically weighted regressions* is to use distance-weighted subsamples of the data in order to estimate locally linear regression estimates at every point in space.

Each observation i has a vector-valued distance-based weight W_i. For instance, one popular method for constructing the weight function (Brunsdon et al. 1996) is to set

$$W_i^2 = \exp(-d_i/\theta), \tag{8.18}$$

where each element of the vector d_i is the geographic distance between location i and each other location in the dataset, and θ is a decay parameter. The distance vector is typically measured as

$$d_i = \sqrt{\left(Z_{d,i} - Z_{d,j}\right)^2 + \left(Z_{g,i} - Z_{g,j}\right)^2}, \tag{8.19}$$

where the $Z_{d,j}$ and $Z_{g,j}$ measure the latitude and longitude of the observations $j = 1,\ldots,n$. The decay parameter θ determines how quickly the influence of location tails off with greater distance. Other methods of constructing the weighting function are of course possible.

The geographically weighted regression model may be written as

$$\mathbf{W}_i^{1/2} y = \mathbf{W}_i^{1/2} X \beta_i + \varepsilon_i. \tag{8.20}$$

Here, $\mathbf{W}_i$ is an $n \times n$ diagonal matrix with the distance-based weights for observations i on its diagonal, y is an $n \times 1$ vector of observations on the dependent variable collected at n points in space, X is an $n \times k$ matrix of data on the k explanatory variables, and ε is an $n \times 1$ vector of normally distributed disturbances with constant variances (LeSage 1998, p. 155). The interesting point here is that there is a vector of parameter estimates for each of the i observations.

The estimates of β_i differ for each location, but they are based on the same sample of data, and so are not independent. This lack of independence means that one cannot draw inferences from the regression parameters. LeSage also points out that the results are highly sensitive to outliers, and to sparse data; he argues that these problems can be largely overcome by taking a Bayesian approach to estimation.

8.5.3   Spatial Effects as Random Effects

In her study of the demand for rice in Indonesia, Anne Case (1991) has survey information on 2,089 households in 141 districts in Indonesia, where each district is included only if it abuts at least one other district in the sample. She specifies a model with both spatial errors and spatial lags, of the form

$$\mathbf{y} = \xi \mathbf{W} \mathbf{y} + \mathbf{X}\beta + u, \tag{8.21a}$$

$$u = \lambda \mathbf{W} u + \varphi + \varepsilon. \tag{8.21b}$$

There are T districts with N households per district, so ε is a $TN \times 1$ vector of random errors with zero mean and constant variance. There is also a district-specific random error term φ, where we have $E(\varphi_k) = 0$ for household k in district i, and $E(\varphi_k\varphi_j) = \sigma_\varphi^2$ if $j \in i$ but is 0 otherwise. Note that we could rewrite (8.21a) and (8.21b) as

$$\mathbf{y} = \mathbf{X}\beta + \varepsilon + [\xi \mathbf{W} \mathbf{y} + \lambda \mathbf{W} u + \varphi]. \tag{8.22}$$

The bracketed expression in (8.22) is the same for every observation in a given district and is in effect a vector of "constrained random effects." This random effect is composed of ξ times the average value of $\mathbf{y}$ in abutting districts, plus λ times the average error in abutting districts, plus a nonspatial district-specific error (Case 1991, p. 958).

We may also think of (8.22) as a special case of a model that incorporates fixed effects for every district, and that takes the form

$$\mathbf{y} = \mathbf{X}\beta + \mathbf{D}\theta + \varepsilon, \tag{8.23}$$

where $\mathbf{D}$ is a $TN \times (T-1)$ matrix of district dummy variables. One may test formally whether the model in (8.22) represents an appropriately constrained version of the fixed effects model in (8.23) using a Hausman test, although there are also times when it is more helpful to work with the spatial effects structure – for instance, if the question of interest is whether households mimic their neighbors.

It is also possible to use multilevel models, with random effects that capture geographic disparities that are unexplained by the available predictors; we return to this topic in Chap. 12 (see too Haughton and Phong 2010).

8.6   Conclusion

Data from living standards surveys always have a spatial dimension, and a growing number of studies explicitly take this into account. For instance, in his study of the impact of the Impres Desa Tertingal program in Indonesia – a program of block grants to poor areas – Daimon (2001) finds that a spatial lag model is called for. And Druska and Horrace (2004) use spatial techniques to improve their measures of the efficiency of rice farmers in Indonesia, estimating a stochastic frontier using panel data. In this case productivity shocks, which could be related to weather or unobserved influences, spill over from one area to the next.

As the technology for estimating spatial models becomes more accessible, and geographic data become more easily available, it will become increasingly standard to consider spatial models. The use of spatial models does not always change the standard coefficient estimates by much, but it changes the way in which we think about the spread of economic effects. This is how economists and statisticians are rediscovering geography.

8.6.1 Estimating Spatial Models

To estimate spatial models, a relatively straightforward solution is to draw on the Matlab routines that have been developed and well-documented by Jim LeSage (LeSage 1998). Luc Anselin's *SpaceStat* (Anselin 1992) is still used by some. For users of Stata, Maurizio Pisati has written a routine for spatial regression called `spatreg`, and Mark Pearce has developed a routine called `gwr` that fits geographically weighted regression. There is now a large library of relevant routines in R, most notably the `spdep` package maintained by Roger Bivand, and the `spgwr` package that does geographically weighted regression.

References

Anselin, Luc. 1992. *SpaceStat tutorial*. Urbana-Champaign: University of Illinois.

Anselin, Luc. 1998. *Spatial econometrics: Methods and models*. Dordrecht: Kluwer Academic.

Anselin, Luc, and R. Florax. 1995. Introduction. In *Net directions in spatial econometrics*, ed. L. Anselin and R. Florax. Berlin: Springer.

Aragon, Yves, Dominique Haughton, Jonathan Haughton, Eve Leconte, Eric Malin, Anne Ruiz-Gazen, and Christine Thomas-Agnan. 2003. Explaining the pattern of regional unemployment: The case of the Midi-Pyrénées region. *Papers in Regional Science* 82: 155–174.

Brunsdon, C., A.S. Fotheringham, and M.E. Charlton. 1996. Geographically weighted regression: A method for exploring spatial non-stationarity. *Geographical Analysis* 28: 281–298.

Case, Anne. 1991. Spatial patterns in household demand. *Econometrica* 59(4): 953–965.

Casetti, E. 1972. Generating models by the expansion method: Applications to geographic research. *Geographical Analysis* 4: 81–91.

Daimon, Takeshi. 2001. The spatial dimension of welfare and poverty: Lessons from a regional targeting programme in Indonesia. *Asian Economic Journal* 15(4): 345–367.

Druska, Viliam, and William Horrace. 2004. Generalized moments estimation for spatial panel data: Indonesia rice farming. *American Journal of Agricultural Economics* 86(1): 185–198.

Florax, R., and H. Folmer. 1992. Specification and estimation of spatial linear regression models: Monte Carlo evaluation and pre-test estimators. *Regional Science and Urban Economics* 22: 405–432.

Haughton, D., J. Haughton, and A. Izenman. 1990. Information criteria and harmonic models in time-series analysis. *Journal of Statistical Computation and Simulation* 35: 187–207.

Haughton, Dominique, and Nguyen, Phong. 2010. Multilevel models and inequality in Vietnam. *Journal of Data Science* 8: 289–306.

INSEE. 1996. *FIDEL Base de Données – 1996: Guide de L'Utilisateur*. Paris: Institut National de la Statistique et des Études Économiques.

Kaimowitz, David, Patricia Mendez, Atie Puntodewo, and Jerry Vanclay. 2002. Spatial regression analysis of deforestation in Santa Cruz, Bolivia. In *Land use and deforestation in the Amazon*, ed. C.H. Wood and R. Porro. Gainesville: University Press of Florida.

LeSage, James. 1998. *Spatial econometrics*. Toledo: Department of Economics, University of Toledo.

Ravallion, Martin, and Quentin Wodon. 1997. Poor areas, or only poor people? Policy Research Working Paper 1798. Washington, DC: World Bank.

Chapter 9
Panel Data

9.1 Introduction

Most household survey data come from a single cross-section of households surveyed at a single point in time. This is useful if the purpose is to get a snapshot of income or poverty, and it does allow for a detailed analysis – for instance, of the proximate determinants of health or malnutrition or income. However, it is rarely possible to get an adequate appreciation of dynamic effects – how incomes in a household rise and fall, how households form and re-form – without panel data.

When a survey is repeated over time, so we have multiple observations for the same person (or household, or firm, or village), we have panel data. In this chapter we first summarize the types of panel data, and review their strengths and weaknesses. We then look at what can be learned from transition matrices, review an application to the growth of household enterprises, and discuss the econometric issues that arise when working with panels. The last example in the chapter uses panel data to measure the effects of microcredit in Thailand.

9.2 Types of Panel Data

The commonest form of panel is based on interviewing households over more than one round of a sample survey. For instance, the 1993 Vietnam Living Standards Survey interviewed 4,800 households. The 1998 round tried to contact 4,704 of these, and succeeded in interviewing 4,305 of the original households. It also added 1,694 new households, so that a total of 5,999 were surveyed in 1998.

This case illustrates several of the features of panels. Some of the initial households were not contacted again, in a bid to improve the efficiency of the sampling. This in turn required some adjustments in the sample weights. Of the 4,704 households to be resurveyed in 1998, 399 could not be contacted, representing an annual attrition rate of 1.8%. And the addition of new households to the sample in 1998 was, in part, due to a desire to maintain the representativeness of the sample.

D. Haughton and J. Haughton, *Living Standards Analytics*, Statistics for Social and Behavioral Sciences, DOI 10.1007/978-1-4614-0385-2_9, © Springer Science+Business Media, LLC 2011

Occasionally, a sample of households is surveyed several times. The most famous example, in developing countries at least, may be the 240 households that were surveyed by the Institute for Crop Research in the Semi-Arid Tropics (ICRISAT) in southwest India annually from 1975 to 1985. A more recent important multi-year panel is that collected by Robert Townsend and his collaborators in central Thailand: the initial survey of households was undertaken in 1997, on the eve of the Asian financial crisis, and there have been annual rounds of surveys since then (see http://cier.uchicago.edu/data/ for details, and access to much of the data).

It is much more common to find rotating panels, where some fraction of the households are surveyed for two rounds, and then rotate off. For instance, the first living standards survey in the Côte d'Ivoire covered 1,600 households in 1985; the following year, about 800 of these households were resurveyed, and 800 new households were added to the roster of those interviewed. The use of rotating panels helps reduce respondent fatigue, and limits the loss of representativeness.

Although the household is nearly always the unit that is (re-) sampled, there have been some exceptions. The Peru Living Standards Survey of 1990 returned to the 1,280 *dwellings*, rather than households, that had been surveyed in Lima in 1985–1986. Of the 1,052 interviews, 745 were for the same households. And the much-used Panel Survey on Income Dynamics in the USA began with a sample of 4,800 *individuals* in 1968, and has resurveyed them regularly ever since.

9.3   Why Panel Data?

The most important reason for collecting panel data is to be able to measure transitions over time (Haughton and Khandker 2009). Only with panel data could we, for example, accurately determine how many people move into and out of poverty between one year and the next. Thus panel data are essential for the understanding of poverty dynamics.

Table 9.1 illustrates this nicely (Haughton et al. 2001). It is based on the panel data component of the Vietnam Living Standards Surveys of 1993 and 1998. Households are sorted into expenditure per capita quintiles for each year, and

Table 9.1 Expenditure quintile transition matrix, Vietnam, 1993–1998

	No. of households, by expenditure/capita quintile, 1998					
	Poor	Poor-mid	Middle	Mid-upper	Upper	Total
Quintile 1993						
Poor	**384**	216	127	54	9	**791**
Poor-mid	193	**264**	223	120	32	**832**
Middle	100	183	**234**	254	85	**856**
Mid-upper	38	127	217	**301**	205	**888**
Upper	12	35	100	209	**550**	**906**
Total	**727**	**825**	**901**	**938**	**881**	**4,272**

Source: Vietnam Living Standards Surveys of 1993 and 1998
Note: Totals in each quintile are unequal because of differential attrition in the sample between 1993 and 1998. Bold values give totals (bottom row) and diagonal elements

Table 9.2 Chronic, persistent, and transient poverty, Chinese Provinces, 1985–1990

| | Chronically poor | | | | |
	Persistently poor $c_t \leq z, \forall t$	Not persistently poor $\bar{c} \leq z, c_t > z$ for some t	Transient poor (and not chronically poor) $\bar{c} > z, c_t < z$ for some t	Never poor $c_t > z, \forall t$	Percentage of poverty (measured by P_2) that is transient
Total sample	6.2	14.4	33.4	46.0	49
Guangdong	0.4	1.0	18.3	80.3	84
Guangxi	7.1	16.1	37.4	39.4	49
Guizhou	11.9	21.2	40.2	26.7	43
Yunnan	4.9	18.0	35.6	41.5	57

Source: Jalan and Ravallion (1998)
Notes: c_t is the consumption by a person in time t, z is the poverty line, and $\bar{c}$ is mean consumption of the person over the time period under study. P_2 is the squared poverty gap measure of poverty (see Chap. 10 for details)

these are then cross-tabulated to create a *transition matrix*. For this we may see, for instance, that 550 of the 4,272 households were in the top quintile in both years.

Taken at face value, this matrix shows considerable economic mobility. Of the 790 households that were in the poorest quintile in 1993, more than half (406) had moved a higher quintile by 1998, and 200 of these had jumped two quintiles or more.

Another interesting example comes from Jalan and Ravallion (1998), who have information on a sample of households in four large provinces in China for each year from 1985 to 1990. From these data, one may classify households into:

• The *persistently poor*, who are poor every year, so consumption (c_t) is always below the poverty line (z)
• The *chronically but not persistently poor*, who are poor on average ("chronically"), a but occasionally rise above the poverty line
• The *transient poor*, who are not poor on average, but who dip into poverty from time to time
• The *never poor*

Table 9.2 summarizes the main findings. A striking feature of these numbers is that many people are only poor from time to time. These households may need insurance more urgently than income support, unlike the persistently poor.

If economic mobility is high, it becomes more difficult to target just the chronically poor. It also paints a picture of income distribution that is highly dynamic. However, these measures almost certainly overstate the extent of economic mobility, possibly quite seriously. The problem arises because of measurement error. We know (see Chap. 10) that income and expenditure are measured imperfectly, and the ratio of noise to signal is only amplified when we look at changes in these magnitudes.

By definition, we cannot know the precise extent of measurement error. Nonetheless, there is some evidence that it is important. Breen and Moisio (2004), using data from the European Community Household Panel for ten countries, estimate a latent class model that tries to correct for measurement error. They find that more people are persistently poor, and fewer people move into and out of poverty, than the survey data suggest. The effects can be large: using a poverty rate that is 60% of median net income, they find, for example, that 7.3% of the Danish population is persistently poor, and not 3.7% (as a straightforward reading of the survey data would imply). Similarly, Lee et al. (2010), using a simulation approach, estimate that the rate at which people move out of poverty from 1 year to the next in South Korea is only three-quarters as large as the raw survey data would indicate.

Panel data have some other advantages. Econometrically, they help us reduce the effects of unobserved heterogeneity, an issue we return to below. They may allow for more powerful measures of impact evaluation when they permit double differencing.

Panel data also allow one to compare the means of variables more precisely. Let X_1 be a vector of observations on a variable, such as income per capita, from a first sample, and X_2 be the observations from a second sample. We want to see whether $\bar{X}_1$ and $\bar{X}_2$ are statistically significantly different, and for this we need $\text{var}(\bar{X}_1 - \bar{X}_2)$. Ignoring other complications, such as clustering, we have $\text{var}(\bar{X}_1 - \bar{X}_2) = \text{var}(\bar{X}_1) + \text{var}(\bar{X}_2) - 2\text{cov}(\bar{X}_1, \bar{X}_2)$. If the samples are independent – for example, from two unrelated surveys – then $\text{cov}(\bar{X}_1, \bar{X}_2) = 0$. However, if the data are drawn from a panel, it is likely that $\text{cov}(\bar{X}_1, \bar{X}_2) > 0$, which reduces $\text{var}(\bar{X}_1 - \bar{X}_2)$, and makes the test of differences more powerful.

9.4 Why Not Panel Data?

Helpful as panel data can be, there are some drawbacks. The two biggest problems are attrition, and nonrepresentativeness.

Attrition occurs when some of those who were interviewed in the first round drop out of the panel in the second or subsequent rounds. There are a number of possible reasons: the household may have dissolved, members may have died, the family may have moved, the household is no longer willing to respond to the survey, and so on. The trouble is that those who drop out are unlikely to be representative of the initial sample; older households are more likely to die off, for instance. The 1998 Vietnam Living Standards Survey was able to interview only 4,305 out of the 4,704 they wanted to resample from 1993; this represents an attrition rate of 1.8% per year, which is actually rather modest. It requires good record keeping, and some persistence, to keep attrition low.

The second problem with a panel is that as it ages, it becomes less representative of the sampling frame, even if there is no attrition. The reason is that a panel does not, by definition, add newly formed households, and so gradually reflects only older, and more stable, households. This is not an insuperable problem, provided that one is willing to "top up" the panel from time to time, or use rotating panels.

9.5   Application: The Birth and Growth of NFHEs

During the 1990s the Vietnamese economy grew rapidly, with GDP rising by about 7% per year. Yet some observers (e.g., Perkins 1994) worried about the potential lack of private enterprises, and particularly of non-farm household enterprises (NFHEs). Vijverberg and Haughton (2004) address the issues of whether NFHEs in this period were up to the task of spawning enough firms with promise, of creating jobs in their own right, and of fostering upward income mobility.

The analysis is based on the Vietnam Living Standards Surveys (VLSS) of 1993 and 1998. A good place to start is by noting that the proportion of adults working in an NFHE fell from 25.7% in 1993 to 23.7% in 1998, although the proportion of those for whom this was the sole source of income rose from 9.5% to 10.4% over the same period.

An affluent household is more likely to participate in an NFHE than a poor one. This shows clearly in Table 9.3, where we see that about one in three chronically poor households, but more than one in two affluent ones, had someone working in an NFHE. Here, the chronically poor are those who were in the bottom 60% of the expenditure per capita distribution in 1993 and the bottom 40% in 1998; affluent households are those who were in the top two quintiles in both years. The computations are based on the panel of 4,304 households surveyed in both 1993 and 1998.

An interesting feature of this study is the way in which the authors created a panel *of non-farm household enterprises*. Both VLSS surveys asked households about the NFHEs in which they participated, including the age of the enterprise, the sector in which it operated, turnover, and so on. In principle, by matching households and their associated enterprises it should be straightforward to construct a panel of enterprises. In practice it was much more difficult; the authors write (p. 103), "the 1997–98 round uses a different set of industrial codes. The respondents are decidedly imprecise about the enterprise's age. There are changes in the identity of the person who is most knowledgeable ... a household could list up to three enterprises in 1992–93 and up to four in 1997–98." Enterprises are matched over time based on the survey information on enterprise age, industry

Table 9.3 Reliance on non-farm household enterprises, Vietnam

	% of households with a non-farm household enterprise	
	in 1993	in 1998
Chronically poor households	35.6	35.0
Affluent households	58.0	54.9

Source: Vijverberg and Haughton (2004), based on Vietnam Living Standards Surveys of 1993 and 1998

Table 9.4 Accounting for the panel enterprises

	1993	1998	Type of ent.
Total enterprises surveyed	2,795	3,493	
− not included in the 1998 sample	47		
− not included in the 1993 sample		1,042	
− dropped out of the sample in 1997 (attrition)	267		Attrited
= **Enterprises potentially matchable**	2,481	2,397	
− household had no enterprise in 1998	764		Terminated
− household had no enterprise in 1993		701	Startup
= **Enterprises potentially in panel**	1,717	1,696	
− household has another enterprise in 1993 but not in 1998	83		Terminated
− household has another enterprise in 1998 but not in 1993		96	Startup
− no match at all among industry code, entrepreneur, age	321		
−		306	Startup
− manual inspection found no possible match	345		Terminated
−		326	Startup
= **Matched**	968	968	Panel
of which: automatic match between 1993 and 1998 enterprises	514	514	
manual match between 1993 and 1998 enterprises	454	454	

Source: Vijverberg and Haughton (2004), Table 6

code, and the identity of the entrepreneur, but many of the matches had to be made by hand, given the imprecision in the data.

Of the 2,795 NFHEs reported in the 1993 survey, and 3,439 in the 1998 survey, only 968 could be matched to form a panel. Table 9.4 accounts for the problem. Thus attrition bias is a potential concern, although it does not appear to have been too damaging for the analysis in practice.

Vijverberg and Haughton first ask what predicts whether a firm survived between 1993 and 1998, using a logistic regression model (where the dependent variable is 1 if an enterprise survives) to tease out the effects. Overall, 39% of the enterprises surveyed in 1993 survived, in that they were identified as still operating in 1998. An NFHE was more likely to survive if it was larger and older in 1993, run by a woman, or operated by a prime-age entrepreneur.

The performance of NFHEs over time may be summarized with the help of Table 9.5, where the firms are divided into quintiles by enterprise income ("net revenue"). About half of the top-quintile firms in 1993 were still operating in 1998, and over half of these survivors were still in the top net-income quintile. Nothing succeeds like success! Firms with low net income in 1993 – in the bottom two quintiles – were only half as likely to be operating still in 1998.

The analysis suggests that NFHEs play a role during the transition from an agrarian to an urban society. NFHEs are relatively unimportant in poor rural areas, where there is a shortage of credit, weak infrastructure, low levels of education, and a limited amount of local demand for goods and services. NFHEs are also relatively unimportant in the most affluent urban areas, where wage labor may offer a better alternative to the family business. In between these extremes, NFHEs are important. Vijverberg and Haughton conclude (p. 94) that, "between 1993 and 1998 ... the

Table 9.5 Dynamics of enterprise income in Vietnam: what happened to the 1993 enterprises by 1998?

Quintile of 1998 enterprise net income	Quintile of 1993 enterprise net income				
	Low	Low-mid	Middle	Mid-upper	Upper
Low	5.90	6.80	6.80	3.04	1.25
Low-mid	5.19	7.51	8.59	7.33	3.40
Middle	4.65	6.26	10.20	10.02	6.98
Mid-upper	2.50	3.76	7.69	12.88	10.91
Upper	0.89	1.97	4.65	8.41	25.58
Enterprise terminated	69.23	64.22	52.59	45.26	39.36
Household attrited	8.05	8.41	8.23	11.09	11.99
Household dropped	3.58	1.07	1.25	1.97	0.54
Total (%)	100.00	100.00	100.00	100.00	100.00
No. of observations	559	559	559	559	559

Source: Vijverberg and Haughton (2004), Table 12

proportion of adults working in NFHEs fell, as did the proportion of households with such an enterprise. The growth in NFHE sales, expenditures, and income lagged behind GDP growth ... based on the experience of recent history, non-farm household enterprises [can be expected to] play only a modest supporting role in fostering rapid economic growth in Vietnam."

9.6 Statistical Analysis of Panel Data

Suppose we are interested in measuring the determinants of rice production. We have some measure of output for the ith farmer in time t, given by y_{it}, and observations on a set of regressors $\mathbf{x}_{it}$ that might include the area sown, fertilizer and water use, and the like. Based on data for year $t = 1$ we might estimate

$$y_{i1} = \alpha + \mathbf{x}_{i1}'\beta + \varepsilon_{i1}. \qquad (9.1)$$

Among the problems that we are likely to face here is omitted variable bias, which arises because we are unable to observe farmers' abilities (A_i), which prevents us from estimating a truer model like

$$y_{i1} = \alpha + \mathbf{x}_{i1}'\beta + \gamma A_i + \varepsilon_{i1}. \qquad (9.2)$$

Now suppose that we have a panel with data for 2 (or more) years. Then we may difference (9.2) and estimate

$$\Delta y_i = \Delta \mathbf{x}_i'\beta + \Delta \varepsilon_i. \qquad (9.3)$$

We have now swept away the effects of ability, and presumably removed much of the omitted variable bias from our estimate of β.

Quite generally we have

$$y_{it} = \alpha_i + \mathbf{x}'_{it}\beta + \varepsilon_{it}, \quad t = 1, 2, \ldots \quad (9.4)$$

We could simply pool the data and apply ordinary least squares (OLS), as in

$$y_{it} = \alpha + \mathbf{x}'_{it}\beta + (\varepsilon_{it} + \alpha_i - \alpha). \quad (9.5)$$

Note, however, that the errors are now likely to be correlated over time, because they include a component (the α_i) that recurs for a given farmer year after year.

A *fixed effects* model would allow for a different intercept (i.e., α_i) for each individual. We may think of the error term as being $\varepsilon_{i1} + \alpha_i$, consisting of a time-invariant component (α_i) and an idiosyncratic part (ε_{it}). For unbiasedness, we require that the $\mathbf{x}_{it}$ be uncorrelated with ε_{it}, but one can allow $\mathbf{x}_{it}$ to be correlated with α_i. Cameron and Trivedi (2009, p. 231) view this as a limited form of endogeneity.

The fixed effects model produces a "within" estimator. The estimate of the coefficients β is identified on the basis of variation in the $\mathbf{x}_i$ variables over time; if these variables do not change over time, $\hat{\beta}$ cannot be computed. This is problematic if the variable of interest is time invariant, or nearly so. For instance, suppose we want to estimate the effect of education on earnings, and we have a panel data of adults. In most cases, the level of education of an adult does not change over time, in which case the influence of education will be subsumed into the individual fixed effects, and cannot be identified separately.

In a *random effects* model we assume that the α_i from (9.4) are independently and identically distributed (iid), in addition to the usual assumption that the idiosyncratic error ε_{it} is iid. Given

$$y_{it} = \mathbf{x}'_{it}\beta + (\varepsilon_{i1} + \alpha_i), \quad (9.6)$$

this means we are assuming $\alpha_i \sim (\alpha, \sigma_\alpha^2)$ and $\varepsilon_{it} \sim (0, \sigma_u^2)$. This is a stronger assumption than with fixed effects, where we allowed α_i to be correlated with the $\mathbf{x}_{it}$ regressors. Put another way, for consistency:

- Fixed effects requires the assumption $E(\varepsilon_{it}|\alpha_i, \mathbf{x}_{it}) = 0$
- Random effects requires the assumption $E(\varepsilon_{it}|\mathbf{x}_{it}) = 0$.

In choosing between the two models, the key question is whether the individual effects (α_i) are correlated with the regressors ($\mathbf{x}_{it}$); if they are, we cannot use random effects.

The standard way to determine whether we should use a fixed effects (FE) or random effects (RE) estimator is using a Hausman test. If the FE estimates $\hat{\beta}_{FE}$ are close to the RE estimates $\hat{\beta}_{RE}$, then the RE specification is acceptable. Unfortunately, the test requires the RE estimator to be efficient, which will not be the case if, for instance, the survey data are clustered. One can handle this problem using bootstrapped standard errors; Cameron and Trivedi (2009, p. 262) provide Stata code, and we discuss bootstrapping more completely in Chap. 11.

It is much more difficult to apply panel data to nonlinear models. In the fixed effects case we cannot usually avoid estimating every α_i – whereas in the linear regression case these could be differenced out – and this is problematic in short panels, which are the norm when working with household survey data. The choice in such cases is typically between a RE and a pooled model. This is a relatively specialized field, nicely handled in Chap. 18 of Cameron and Trivedi (2009), and the references therein.

9.7 Illustration: Thai Microcredit

In order to illustrate the power of panel data, we return to the case of the Thailand Village Fund, which is discussed in the context of impact evaluation in Chap. 12.

Starting in 2001, the Thaksin government in Thailand began to provide a million baht (almost US$25,000) to every village in the country, to be used as working capital for locally run rotating credit associations. By 2004 the funds were operating in most villages, extending short-term (up to 1 year) loans that averaged US$402 each. In the same year, the Thailand Village Fund was easily the largest microcredit scheme in the world, with a gross loan portfolio of $3.00 billion, and 7.5 million active borrowers, 48% of whom were women.

Naturally, we would like to know what effect the introduction of the Village Fund had on measures such as household income or expenditure.

Because the Village Fund was put in place so quickly, there are almost no villages that could serve as controls (because they lack a local fund), and even if there were, such villages are likely to be atypical. Thus, if one is to measure the impact of Village Fund loans, there is no choice but to make comparisons between borrowers and nonborrowers within Village Fund villages, or between periods of time when a given person does, and does not, borrow.

Our interest is in the effect of T_{it}, a binary "treatment" variable that is equal to 1 if household i borrows from the Village Fund in time t, and to 0 otherwise. We would like to know whether, and to what extent, Village Fund borrowing affected household per capita spending (y_{it}).

One could estimate a cross-sectional regression, or use propensity score matching – as done in Chap. 12 – but this does not fully resolve the problem of bias due to unobserved heterogeneity: those who borrow may be more dynamic than, or somehow different from, their peers, possibly in ways that we cannot effectively measure. Hence the attraction of panel data, which would allow us to remove at least some of these effects.

It turns out that the 2004 round of the Thailand Socio-Economic Survey included 5,755 rural households that were also surveyed in 2002. This is the panel that we use in all the estimations described below. But before performing any regressions, it is helpful to generate some summary statistics that show the extent to which variables

Table 9.6 "Within" and "between" variances for Thailand data, 2002 and 2004

Variable		Mean	Std. Dev.	Min	Max	Observations
vfborrow	overall	.4130392	.4924041	0	1	N = 10108
	between		.4190994	0	1	n = 5054
	within		.2585244	−.0869608	.9130392	T = 2
malehead	overall	.7189355	.4495411	0	1	N = 10108
	between		.4262321	0	1	n = 5054
	within		.1429384	.2189355	1.218935	T = 2
nadultm	overall	1.147111	.7150896	0	6	N = 10108
	between		.648015	0	5.5	n = 5054
	within		.3024422	−1.352889	3.647111	T = 2

Notes: Output generated by the xtsum command in Stata. Data are from the panel component of the 2002 and 2004 Thailand Socio-Economic Surveys. Each observation represents one adult. "vfborrow" is equal to 1 if the person borrows from the Village Fund, and to 0 otherwise. "malehead" is equal to 1 for a male head of household, 0 otherwise. "nadultm" is the number of adult males in the household

show variation over time ("within" variation) and across observations at a point in time ("between" variation).

The overall variance of observations on a variable x in the dataset is given by

$$s_{\text{overall}}^2 = \frac{1}{NT - 1} \sum_{i=1}^{N} \sum_{t=1}^{T} (x_{it} - \bar{x})^2, \tag{9.7}$$

where N is the number of observations in a given year, T is the number of years (here just 2002 and 2004), $\bar{x}$ is the grand mean of all the observations, and x_{it} is the value of variable x for individual i at time t. The between variance measures how much an individual's value, averaged over the time periods – i.e., $\bar{x}_i = (1/T) \sum_{t=1}^{T} x_{it}$– varies from the overall mean, so

$$s_{\text{between}}^2 = \frac{1}{N - 1} \sum_{i=1}^{N} (\bar{x}_i - \bar{x})^2. \tag{9.8}$$

The within variance measures how much the values for an individual vary from the temporal mean – in other words, how much the values for a single individual vary over time. We note that

$$s_{\text{overall}}^2 \simeq s_{\text{within}}^2 + s_{\text{between}}^2. \tag{9.9}$$

The xtsum command in Stata computes these variances, and a few lines of output are shown in Table 9.6. Note how the mean value of vfborrow (i.e., T_{it}) is 0.41, so 41% of those sampled borrowed from the Village Fund. The within variance is 0.259, which implies that a considerable number of people borrowed in one, but not both, of 2002 and 2004. This is important, because without such variation we

Table 9.7 Panel estimates of the effect on (the log of) spending per capita of Village Fund borrowing ($\hat{\gamma}$) and earners per household ($\hat{\beta}$)

	Village Fund borrowing			Earners per household		
	$\hat{\gamma}$	SE	t-stat	$\hat{\beta}$	SE	t-stat
Pooled	0.016	0.014	1.17	0.119	0.063	1.89
Random effects	0.017	0.012	1.36	0.134	0.050	2.66
Fixed effects	0.035	0.015	2.26	0.110	0.035	3.15
IV (differenced)	0.142	0.064	2.20	0.106	0.034	3.10

Source: Boonperm et al. (2011), based on Thailand Socio-Economic Surveys of 2002 and 2004. Based on 5,054 usable observations from the (rural) panel component of these surveys. "SE" is standard error; "t-stat" refers to the t-statistic. Other variables included in the equations, but not shown here, include age, education, gender of head of household; number of adults, women, in household; number of men, women, working in agriculture, industry, trading, services; one-adult, two-parent, one-parent households; number of earners in the household; whether head is self-employed. Instruments for the IV ("instrumental variables") model include inverse of number of households in the village interacted with education of head; number of adult men, women, in household; age of head; and number of men, women, working the agricultural sector

would not be able to identify the effects of Village Fund Borrowing on income using the fixed effects ("within") estimator.

The model we wish to estimate looks like this:

$$y_{it} = \alpha_i + \mathbf{x}'_{it}\beta + \gamma T_{it} + \varepsilon_{it}. \qquad (9.10)$$

We are particularly interested in the sign and magnitude of γ, which would give us the average treatment effect of Village Fund borrowing.

In Table 9.7 we report a selection of the results of estimating a variety of specifications of (9.10); similar results appear in Boonperm et al. (2011). In each case we adjust for the clustering of observations at the village level, which increases the size of the standard errors relative to the unadjusted case.

The first row in Table 9.7 shows the coefficient estimates and standard errors for the pooled regression, where $\alpha_i = \alpha$. We have $\hat{\gamma} = 0.016$ (and $t = 1.17$); the estimate is not statistically significant, but if it were, it would tell us that Village Fund borrowing is associated with about 1.6% more spending, other things being equal. The random effects results, shown in the second row, tell a similar story, with $\hat{\gamma} = 0.017$ and $t = 1.36$.

We get somewhat different results when we employ fixed effects or, equivalently, estimate a differenced equation [as in (9.3)]. Now $\hat{\gamma} = 0.035$ and $t = 2.26$ (with a p-value of 0.024). It appears that Village Fund borrowing is associated with a 3.5% increase in spending. This is not implausible; for Village Fund borrowers the loans represented, on average, 11.6% of income in 2004.

At this point, it is worth emphasizing again that our estimate of the effect of Village Fund borrowing on household spending is based on *changes in borrowing* by individuals between 2002 and 2004. Some households borrowed in 2002 but not in 2004, others in 2004 but not 2002. In effect, our estimates hinge on the behavior of these individuals, and not on a comparison between borrowing adults and different nonborrowing adults.

Which results are more plausible, fixed or random effects? Using a Hausman test, we reject the null hypothesis of no differences between the estimated random effects and fixed effects coefficients; it follows that the fixed effects specification is more appropriate.[1]

The use of fixed effects goes a long way toward addressing concerns about the endogeneity of borrowing. However, it is worth asking whether it would be better to use instrumental variables estimation. For this to be credible, we would need to find at least one instrument that plausibly affects whether one borrows, but is not correlated with the errors ε_{it}. One possibility is the size of the village; each village got an initial million baht in funds, irrespective of size. So households in larger villages are likely to have a smaller probability of getting a loan. On the other hand, we have no reason to believe that the size of the village would influence how a loan affects household spending.

We only have a measure of village size for 2004, so this is a time-invariant variable, and cannot serve directly as an instrument for T_{it}. However, we can interact village size (or its inverse) with time-varying variables, and use these hybrids in the first-stage regression.

The results are shown in the final row of Table 9.7. They show a much larger effect of Village Fund borrowing on household spending per capita, at a statistically significant 14% (with a p-value of 0.028). But is this a more plausible estimator than the basic fixed effects specification? We note first that our chosen instruments are relevant, in that they have a statistically significant influence on whether someone borrows from the Village Fund ($F(8,674) = 33.5$; p-value $= 0.00$). The GMM C-statistic tests whether the treatment variable (T_{ij}) should be considered endogenous, and provides only weak support for the endogeneity of Village Fund borrowing, given the instruments available.

In short, one can make a plausible case that the best specification here is fixed effects. We thus conclude that, until more information suggests otherwise, our best estimate is that Village Fund borrowing raised spending by about 3.5% in 2004.

References

Boonperm, Jirawan, Jonathan Haughton, and Shahidur R. Khandker. 2011. Does the Village Fund matter in Thailand? Suffolk University, Boston.

Breen, Richard, and Pasi Moisio. 2004. Poverty dynamics corrected for measurement error. *Journal of Economic Inequality* 2: 171–191.

---

[1] We used a robust version of the Hausman test, which allows for clustering in the design. Cameron and Trivedi (2009, p. 262) provide details.

Cameron, Colin, and Pravin Trivedi. 2009. *Microeconometrics using Stata*. College Station: Stata Press.

Haughton, Dominique, Jonathan Haughton, Le Thi Thanh Loan, and Nguyen Phong. 2001. Shooting stars and sinking stones. In *Living standards during an economic boom: The case of Vietnam*, ed. Dominique Haughton, Jonathan Haughton, and Nguyen Phong. Hanoi: Statistical Publishing House.

Haughton, Jonathan, and Shahidur Khandker. 2009. *Handbook on poverty and inequality*. Washington, DC: World Bank.

Jalan, Jyotsna, and Martin Ravallion. 1998. Transient poverty in Postreform rural China. *Journal of Comparative Economics* 26: 338–357.

Lee, Nayoung, Geert Rider, and John Strauss. 2010. *Estimation of poverty transition matrices with noisy data*. Shatin: Chinese University of Hong Kong.

Perkins, Dwight. 1994. Industrialization. *In Search of the dragons' trail: Economic reform in Vietnam [Viet Nam cai cach kinh te cheo huong rong bay]*, ed. Dapice David, Haughton Jonathan, and Perkins Dwight. Hanoi: Political Publishing House [Nha Xuat Ban Chinh Tri Quoc Gia]. 89–101.

Vijverberg, Wim, and Jonathan Haughton. 2004. Household enterprises in Vietnam: Survival, growth, and living standards. In *Economic growth, poverty, and household welfare in Vietnam*, ed. Paul Glewwe, Nisha Agrawal, and David Dollar. Washington, DC: World Bank.

Chapter 10
Measuring Poverty and Vulnerability

10.1 Introduction

The measurement of poverty and inequality is surprisingly intricate. The purpose of this chapter is to provide a self-contained overview of the issues that arise when trying to measure poverty. The virtue of this chapter is concision; for more extensive treatments, one might start with the *Handbook* by Haughton and Khandker (2009), or the classic exposition by Ravallion (1992). A more formal treatment may be found in Duclos and Araar (2006), and a sophisticated treatment of issues related to the measurement of multidimensional poverty in Kakwani and Silber (2008).

We start by asking why one might even want to measure poverty, and then review the three key steps – defining a measure of welfare, establishing a poverty line, and generating useful summary statistics. Since it is expensive to measure poverty (and inequality) using lengthy household surveys, we also ask whether there might be short cuts that would do the job adequately.

Once poverty has been measured, it is possible to contemplate making poverty comparisons over time and space, but this in turn raises further difficulties: Have differences in prices been accounted for? Were the data collection methods sufficiently comparable? Have sampling issues been adequately resolved? Are the differences statistically significant?

10.2 What and Why?

The World Bank (2000) defines poverty as "a pronounced deprivation in well-being." Operationally, poverty is usually measured in monetary terms, using income or expenditure to reflect command over resources. In this "welfarist" approach, the household is assumed to be able to manage its resources effectively, and the central problem is seen as a simple lack of material wherewithal.

D. Haughton and J. Haughton, *Living Standards Analytics*, Statistics for Social and Behavioral Sciences, DOI 10.1007/978-1-4614-0385-2_10,
© Springer Science+Business Media, LLC 2011

Sometimes poverty is viewed as a lack of something specific, so a person might be food poor, or house poor, or health poor. This reflects a more paternalistic approach, and its proponents would generally prefer to give food stamps or health care to those who need it, rather than cash.

Amartya Sen (1987) takes a broader view, seeing poverty as a lack of capability to function in society. This includes a lack of material resources, but might include poor health, low self-esteem, and limited rights and freedoms. Philosophically, this broad view is satisfying, but it is more problematic in practice, because it leaves open the issue of how one might trade off different capabilities. For instance, is someone with low self-confidence, but adequate income, poor? Or is she poorer than someone with inadequate income but more political rights?

As we will see, poverty is expensive to measure – it invariably requires the use of household surveys – which raises the issue of whether it is worth the trouble. Perhaps the strongest case for measuring poverty is that it keeps the poor on the agenda (Ravallion 1998). Measurement is also essential in targeting pro-poor interventions, in monitoring projects designed to help the poor, and in evaluating the effectiveness of those who presume to help.

10.3   Basic Measurement

In order to measure poverty, one must first define a suitable measure of welfare, then establish a poverty line, and ultimately generate useful summary statistics. Let us consider each step in more detail.

10.3.1   Measuring Well-Being

Ideally, we would like to measure well-being ("utility") directly, but in practice one has to find an appropriate proxy. By far the most commonly used measures are expenditure per capita and income per capita. There are two distinct issues here: is income or expenditure a better indicator of well-being? And is it satisfactory to express these in per capita terms?

Most less-developed countries (LDCs) use consumption to reflect well-being, while affluent countries typically use income. A plausible explanation is that income is relatively straightforward to measure in a rich society where most people earn wages and salaries, but is difficult to measure in poorer countries where income is largely derived from agriculture or from self-employment. Conversely, consumption may be easier to measure when people are poor, and spend on a limited range of goods and services, but increasingly difficult as people become more prosperous.

Another reasonable explanation is that for most households in LDCs, income may vary considerably more than consumption, making the latter a better guide to "lifetime" well-being (or "permanent income," to use Milton Friedman's phrase). If the goal of measuring poverty is to identify those who have long-term needs, then the use of consumption makes more sense. By way of contrast, income tends to be more stable from year to year in developed countries, and so is a more adequate measure of "command over resources" there; and a shortfall in income is of interest to policy makers if the concern is with making up temporary gaps – for instance, in a recession.

There will always be some inaccuracy in the measurement of consumption and income, partly due to underreporting, but also because the operational definitions often vary from country to country. The Haig-Simons definition of income has

$$\text{Income} \equiv \text{Consumption} \; + \; \text{Change in Net Worth.} \qquad (10.1)$$

If the change in net worth were straightforward to measure, then one could move easily between income and consumption, but this is rarely the case. For instance, if the value of one's home rises by $10,000 between 1 year and the next, this should in principle be included as part of income; in practice it almost never is.

Some components of income, most notably wages and salaries, are relatively straightforward to measure in surveys. But agricultural and self-employment income are very difficult to quantify accurately, and this is also true of income from assets. To take one simple, if important, example: income should include the services provided by a home that one owns and occupies, but in practice it can be difficult to put a value of housing services of this kind (it is usually done based on a hedonic price equation applied to rental properties). Or again, if the number of sheep in one's flock rises during the year, this represents income, yet most household surveys do not collect information at this level of detail.

The net effect is that reported income is invariably understated – partly because of incomplete questions, but also because people forget, or do not want to reveal the true extent of their income to anyone (let alone an official enumerator), or have illegal income. The Vietnam Living Standards Survey of 1992–1993 found that average income per capita was VND1.105 million, while average expenditure per capita was 1.227 million. For a society where consumers had almost no access to bank credit, and where income was growing rapidly, these numbers are not credible, and income was clearly understated quite substantially.

The measurement of consumption has its own problems. The problem of recall still arises. Some surveys ask respondents to keep a diary of spending; others ask respondents to remember their routine spending over the past few weeks, and less-frequent spending over a longer period. In LDCs, almost all surveys make a point of asking about the amount of home-production that is consumed by the household. But problems in the measurement of the value of housing services consumed, and in quantifying the value of services provided by durable goods such as cars or fridges, are commonplace. In principle the value of the services provided by such goods should be measured as the rental rate that one would have to pay to use them; this is given (approximately) by $i + \delta$,

Table 10.1 Income vs. consumption as a measure of welfare

Pro:	Cons
Income ("potential")	
Measures household "command over resources"	Likely to be underreported
	Subject to short-term, including seasonal, fluctuations
Can be measured with fewer questions than consumption, so cheaper to collect	Some components hard to observe (e.g., informal sector income, home production, self-employment income)
	Tenuous link between income and welfare
	Reporting period might not capture the long-term average income of the household
Consumption ("achievement)	
Shows current actual material standard of living	Households may have difficulty smoothing consumption
Smoothed, so reflects long-term well-being	Consumption choices may mislead (e.g., if a rich household chooses to live simply)
Less understated than income	Some expenses are irregular, so data may be noisy
	Some components are hard to measure (e.g., durable goods, housing services)

Source: Adapted from Albert (2004)

where i is the interest rate and δ is the depreciation rate. Very often this rental rate has to be estimated, based on relatively imperfect data.

As with income, consumption is always understated. The US consumer expenditure survey of 1972–1973 measured spending on alcohol that was only half of the value of alcohol sales as reported by the producers (Carlson 1974). It is generally accepted that the more detailed the questions are, the higher the reported level of consumption spending; It follows that when the number of questions is relatively limited – as is generally the case – then reported consumption will also be understated. There are further problematic issues: should spending on weddings and funerals, or rare events in general, be included when measuring consumption? And where does one draw the line between spending on a durable good (which is an investment that is "consumed" over a number of years) and a current good? The purchases of an encyclopedia or a DVD are usually treated as current expenditures, but could legitimately be classified as investments. The main points in a comparison of income relative to consumption as measures of welfare are summarized in Table 10.1.

The value of publicly provided or freely provided goods and services, such as schooling or health care, should in principle be included in income and consumption, but in practice such items are usually omitted. It is not easy to value these services; for instance, if it costs $300 p.a. to school a child, and the family values this service at $250, what price should be used?

There are two clear conclusions from this discussion. First, both income and consumption tend to be understated at the household level, which implies that poverty is overstated. Second, comparisons between surveys, whether over space or time, can easily be misleading if there are variations in the questions asked or the protocols followed. This means that poverty comparisons are difficult to make, and the first step in any comparative analysis has to be to find out, in detail, how the survey was administered.

10.3.2   Adult Equivalents

Most measures of well-being use consumption or income *per capita*. This has virtues: it is easy to compute and to explain, and feels roughly right. But there are at least three problems. First, there are some economies of scale in consumption, particularly for items such as housing, so it is cheaper to provide a given material standard of living to two people living together than the same people living separately. Second, not everyone in a household has the same needs, especially for food; a household with two adult farmers is likely to require more food than a household with a white-collar adult living with a young child. The third difficulty is that the use of a per capita measure implicitly assumes that consumption or income is equally distributed within the household, yet in practice we know that there can be substantial intra-household inequality.

One popular solution is to measure consumption or income *per adult equivalent*, although this of course begs the question of how to define or construct adult equivalents. A common approach is simply to define a scale that seems reasonable. The widely used OECD scale defines an adult equivalent (AE) as

$$AE = 1 + 0.7(N_a - 1) + 0.5N_c, \tag{10.2}$$

where N_a is the number of adults and N_c the number of children. An elegant formulation of adult equivalence has

$$AE = (N_a + \alpha N_c)^\theta. \tag{10.3}$$

In this case θ, the economy of scale parameter, is taken to be a number smaller than 1 (for instance, 0.8), and α, the parameter that creates an equivalence between children and adults, is also less than 1 (for instance, 0.7). The central difficulty with such formulations is that there is no consensus about which is most appropriate, which makes them little more satisfying than using per capita values.

This has led some researchers to try to estimate adult equivalence scales directly. If households allocate their internal resources in line with needs then one could, for instance, look at the costs incurred by households where the prime-age males consume (say) 2,100 kcal per day, but have different numbers of other adults and children.

The maintained assumption here – that households allocate resources internally in proportion to needs – is definitely not trivial, and indeed there is clear evidence that the intra-household allocation of resources to some extent reflects the distribution of power within the household. If this is common – and given the difficulty of obtaining good information on the intra-household distribution of resources – it is no longer possible to arrive at a satisfactory measure of adult equivalents empirically. This is also the conclusion reached by Deaton and Zaidi (1998), who argue that "there are so far no satisfactory methods for estimating economies of scale. There is also a good discussion in Deaton (1997)."

There is also a deeper philosophical problem, which applies to any measure of material well-being, whether per capita or per adult equivalent: if a household, currently just at the poverty line, has another child, it will now fall into poverty. But is it really worse off than it was before?

10.3.3 Choosing a Poverty Line

10.3.3.1 Theoretical Considerations

The second step in measuring poverty is to define a poverty line. One approach is to define the line in a relative way. Thus the poor might be those whose income or consumption per capita falls into the lowest quintile. Then, by definition, the poor are always with us. This approach can be useful in identifying poor areas or poor subgroups in a society – perhaps with a view to targeting interventions to alleviate poverty – but it does not serve if the purpose is to measure the effectiveness of these interventions.

A related approach, used by the European Union for instance, is to define the poor as those with an income that is less than half the industrial wage. This comes closer to being a rough measure of income distribution than of poverty, and could generate anomalous results. For instance, a recession that pushes down the real industrial wage and compresses the lower end of the income distribution could lead to less poverty, by this measure.

An absolute poverty line for the ith household, z_i, sets a fixed boundary below which one is considered poor. Ravallion (1998) defines it as the minimum spending or income required to achieve some minimum utility level u_z, given the demographic characteristics of the household (x) and the prices it faces (p), so

$$z_i = e(p, x, u_z). \tag{10.4}$$

The poverty line is expressed in monetary terms, and so needs to be adjusted for differences in prices across time (e.g., for inflation) and across space (e.g., urban vs. rural households). We return to the thorny issue of making price adjustments in a later section of this chapter. Meanwhile, one still needs to find a practical way to arrive at a poverty line; to use Ravallion's terminology, one has both a referencing problem (what is the appropriate level of u_z?) and an identification problem (given u_z, what is the appropriate level of z_i?).

The distinction between an absolute and a relative poverty line can become blurred if, as many believe, utility depends not just on one's own income but also on one's income relative to everyone else, so

$$u = g\left(y, \frac{y}{\bar{y}}\right).$$ (10.5)

Here, y refers to income, and $\bar{y}$ is the mean income in society. Replacing y with the poverty line z, and inverting, we get an expression for the poverty line as

$$z = g^{-1}(\bar{y}, u_z).$$ (10.6)

In this case, the poverty line, measured in terms of income, is not solely a function of some arbitrary level of utility – as would be the case with a absolute (monetary) poverty line – but also of the level of income in society as a whole, as would occur with a relative (monetary) poverty line. In Sen's words, "an absolute approach in the space of capabilities translates into a relative approach in the space of commodities."

10.3.3.2   Practical Considerations

The first principle in establishing a poverty line is that it should be useful, and this in turn depends on what purpose it has to serve. A poverty line of a dollar a day in the USA would be unhelpful, because essentially nobody would fall below such a line; but in Ethiopia such a line might be too high, identifying too many people for the purposes of targeting the least fortunate. In practice, most middle- and upper-income countries adjust their poverty lines from time to time as they develop; when the dollar-a-day poverty line identifies only a handful of poor, it gives way to a two-dollars-a-day standard, and so on. Using data from a sample of 36 countries, Ravallion et al. (1991) estimated the following relationship between the official poverty line and per capita consumption:

$$\ln(z_i) = 6.704 - 1.7732 \ln(C/\mathrm{cap}) + 0.228[\ln(C/\mathrm{cap})]^2$$
$$t = 5.1 \quad t = -3.6 \qquad\qquad t = 5.1 \quad R^2 = 0.89 \qquad (10.7)$$

In other words, at low levels of per capita consumption (C/cap) the poverty line changes little – the elasticity of the poverty line with respect to C/cap is close to zero – but for high income countries the poverty line tracks average per capita consumption quite closely, with an elasticity close to 1.

In their review of 40 poverty assessments in Africa, Hanmer et al. (1999) found that relative poverty lines were used in 23 cases; almost half of these were specified in terms of a percentage of the income distribution (e.g., the poorest 20 or 25%), and

Table 10.2 Typology of poverty lines in World Bank assessments in Africa

Absolute (17 cases)	
Calorie requirement (12)	Calories only
	Calorie cost/food share (1)
	Calories + basket of goods (5)
Basket of goods (including food) (5)	
Relative (23 cases)	
Relative to income base	Multiple of wage
	Share of mean income or expenditure (11)
Specified percentage of income distribution (11)	

Source: Hanmer et al. (1999)

almost half in terms of a proportion of mean income or expenditure (see Table 10.2). The remaining 17 assessments used absolute poverty lines, and most of these sought to measure a "cost of basic needs."

In determining the *cost of basic needs*, the commonest approach is first to stipulate a consumption bundle, including both food and nonfood, and to estimate the cost required to acquire this bundle. Practically, one typically begins by choosing a nutritional requirement for good health, estimates the cost of meeting this food energy requirement, and adds a nonfood component on top.

Practice varies somewhat in the choice of food energy requirement – Pakistan uses 2,550 kcal while Vietnam and Indonesia use 2,100 kcal and Thailand applies different requirements that vary by age and gender.

Affluent households often spend twice as much as poor households in order to buy a calorie of food, so the choice of "price per calorie" matters; typical practice is to try to mimic the per-calorie cost of a diet that is plausibly used by those close to the poverty line. There is a circularity here, which underlies the suggestion by Pradhan et al. (2000) that one use an interactive procedure: pick a reference group that is relatively poor and compute their cost per calorie consumed; use this to compute the poverty line; now take as a reference group those close to this poverty line, and calculate the calorie cost of their diet. Recompute the poverty line, and so on, until the poverty line stabilizes. A simpler approach is to use the cost per calorie for those who consume between, say, 2,000 and 2,200 kcal per person per day, and who are, essentially by construction, close to the poverty line.

The measurement of the nonfood component of the poverty line is more problematic. It is included because households cannot live by food alone; we observe that even those who cannot afford to buy enough food still spend some money on items such as shelter and clothing. A pragmatic solution is to use the level of nonfood spending observed among households whose food consumption is close to the 2,100 kcal per person per day threshold. In Vietnam in 1992–1993, households in the poorest three quintiles (of expenditure per capita) spent on average 65% of their income on food; the total poverty line was created by grossing up the food spending by 1.54 (=100/65). The poverty line used in the USA was created by Mollie Orshansky in 1963–1964 by computing the cost of an "adequate" amount of food

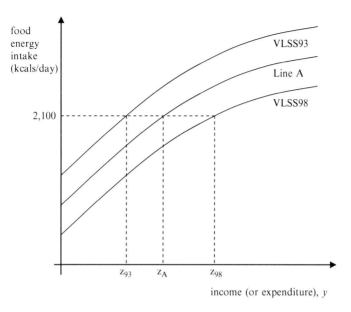

Fig. 10.1 The determination of poverty lines for Vietnam, 1993 and 1998

intake and multiplying this by 3, on the grounds that a third of US consumption went to food spending at that time. The same poverty line is still in use, and is updated annually to reflect price changes.

Indeed once an absolute poverty line has been established to measure the cost of basic needs, it is typically simply updated over time to reflect inflation. This is not a trivial job, since it requires information on changes over time in the prices of food and nonfood items. The latter can be particularly problematic, and price indexes of nonfood items, especially services, may be unreliable, or use weights that do not reflect the consumption patterns of the poor.

The food energy intake method provides a tempting short cut to this problem. It is generally agreed that a household's intake of food, measured in kcal/capita/day, is a monotonically increasing function of income (or expenditure) per capita, as shown by line VLSS93 in Fig. 10.1, drawn from the Vietnam Living Standards Survey of 1992–1993. One could use household survey data to estimate this curve, and find the level of income that corresponds to buying just enough food, such as point z_{93} in Fig. 10.1. With each new set of survey data one could repeat the exercise; the line VLSS98 shows the relationship between income and calories in Vietnam in 1998, with the new (nominal) poverty line z_{98}.

The temptation to use this approach should be resisted. The difficulty is that the calorie income function, shown in Fig. 10.1, shifts for reasons other than inflation alone. For instance, between 1993 and 1998 the price of food rose by 70% while the price of nonfood increased by 25%. The higher *relative* price of food led consumers to substitute away from food; in the absence of this shift, line VLSS98 would have been line A, and the poverty line would have risen (in nominal terms) from z_{93} to z_A. This represents a more modest rise in the poverty line, and a more substantial reduction in poverty, than if one had compared z_{93} with z_{98}. The application of the food energy intake method was tried, and abandoned, in the case of Vietnam in 1998, because it implied a rise in the poverty line that was so large that the poverty rate would have been shown to rise between 1993 and 1998 – a wholly implausible conclusion, given the 9% annual growth in GDP during this period.

Ravallion and Bidani (1994) had a similar experience; the food energy intake method appeared to imply that the poverty rate was higher in urban than in rural Indonesia – again an implausible result, in this case largely because urban residents appear to have a taste for a more refined (and hence expensive) diet.

10.3.3.3 Subjective Poverty Lines

The measurement of poverty is expensive, mainly because it requires the administration of elaborate questionnaires by well-trained enumerators. The high unit cost limits the sample size, and makes it difficult to produce a fine-grained geographic breakdown of poverty rates – an issue that has been addressed through small area estimation, as discussed in Chap. 14.

The expense of household surveys also leads one to ask whether there might be cheaper alternatives. One possibility would be to use "quick and dirty" surveys that ask a small number of simple questions, an issue to which we return below; another would be to ask people to rate their own poverty.

There is a long tradition in political polling of asking people about their well-being. One of the most ambitious, and consistent, efforts in a developing country is that undertaken by Mahar Mangahas and the Social Weather Station Project in the Philippines. Every month, about 1,200 households are shown a card with a line running across it; the space below the line is marked *mahirap* ("poor") and the space above it is marked *hindi mahirap* ("not poor"), and they are asked to mark their position on the card with an X. In addition, respondents are asked to define a poverty line. Figure 10.2 shows the evolution of the subjectively determined poverty rate since 1983, along with the official poverty headcount rate, which is based on relatively standard living standards surveys.

In assessing poverty trends in the Philippines, should we give more credence to the self-rated poverty rate, or to the official rate? In his assessment of the Filipino data, Gaurav Datt (2002) notes that the self-rated poverty lines are relatively high – typically close to 60% of the population – and essentially trendless. It does not fall much when material conditions improve, or rise much when there is a slowdown; for instance, it rose from just 59 to 61% between the boom year of 1996–1997 and the crisis year of 1998.

One interesting feature of the Social Weather Station results is that urban households define a poverty line that is essentially twice as high as that defined by rural households. While the cost of living in the Philippines is certainly higher in urban than in rural areas, few would argue that it differs by two to one. It is possible

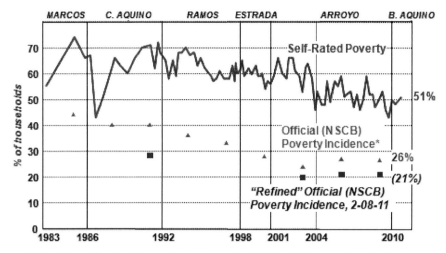

Fig. 10.2 Self-rated poverty in the Philippines: Percentage of poor households, 1983 to March 2011 (*Source*: Social Weather Stations, http://www.sws.org.ph/. Reproduced with permission)

that urban households have higher expectations than their rural counterparts. A policy implication is that efforts designed to reduce poverty may, by focusing on objective measures of material deprivation, be putting too little weight on the felt burden of urban poverty.

Self-rated measures of satisfaction can be informative. In 2006, the Gallup organization collected self-rated measures of "life satisfaction" in 123 countries. Rated on a scale of 0 (dissatisfied) through 10 (satisfied), the question asked "all things considered, how satisfied are you with your life as a whole these days?" Angus Deaton (2008) regressed this measure against GDP per capita (in 2000 international PPP dollars), and found the following:

$$\text{Average life satisfaction} = \text{Constant} + 0.845 \ln(\text{GDP}/\text{capita})$$
$$\text{SE} = 0.050$$
$$-3.25 \text{ GDP growth rate}, 2003 - 2005$$
$$\text{SE} = 1.46 \tag{10.8}$$

This cross-section regression has an R^2 of 0.71, and it shows clearly that greater material affluence is quite closely associated with higher life satisfaction. More unexpected is the negative coefficient on the growth rate; it is possible that faster GDP growth creates psychological and other adjustment costs that accompany change.

Table 10.3 Summary of answers to the subjective welfare questions for Jamaica (%)

Answer	All respondents	Poorest quintile	Richest quintile
Food is inadequate	44.2	67.1	19.1
Housing is inadequate	48.7	71.7	16.2
Clothing is inadequate	40.6	64.1	16.3
Transportation is inadequate	51.5	65.4	34.0
Health care is inadequate	45.0	62.3	23.0
Schooling is inadequate	51.8	58.2	52.1

Source: Ravallion (1996, p. 209)
Notes: Quintiles are based on expenditure per capita. Data are from the 1993 Jamaica Survey of Living Conditions

While Deaton concludes that "reports of life satisfaction … may provide a useful summary of different components of people's capabilities," he still believes that more-objective measures of poverty are needed, because people may have merely adapted to hardship. Philosophically, this is slippery terrain; if some people are objectively poor but say they are not miserable, should public policy make it a priority to help them?

10.3.3.4   Shortcuts to Measuring Poverty

Complete living standards surveys are expensive to undertake, mainly because of the complexity of the questions related to consumption and income. It is reasonable to wonder whether one might be able to measure poverty adequately using a cheaper method, such as a rapid-appraisal technique that relies on short interviews and direct observations to gather a set of relatively simple variables (Kumar 1993).

Ravallion (1996) tests this proposition in an interesting study using data from the 1993 Jamaica Survey of Living Conditions (JSLC). In addition to standard questions on consumption and income, and several straightforward objective questions (for instance, about housing, and family demographics) of the type that feature in rapid-appraisal surveys, the JSLC included a number of easy-to-answer subjective questions. These asked respondents whether they considered that the level of household consumption of food (or housing, clothing, health care, etc.) was "less than adequate," "just adequate," or "more than adequate." Some summary results are reproduced in Table 10.3.

Although households in the poorest quintile (as defined by expenditure per capita) are more likely than others to report inadequacies in food and housing, it is noteworthy that a third of them did not say that they had inadequate food, while a fifth of those in the top quintile did say that their food consumption was inadequate.

A regression of the log of consumption per capita on these responses showed a poor fit, with an R^2 of 0.20. In other words, taken alone, answers to simple subjective questions do not substitute for detailed information on per capita consumption levels.

Ravallion then expanded the regression model to include, as covariates, the answers to 25 short questions – such as the location of the household, the number of rooms in the dwelling, the size of the household, and the like. The inclusion of these variables raised the fit of the regression equation, yielding an R^2 of 0.77. Despite the better fit, the out-of-sample performance of the model is weak; Ravallion estimated the model using a quarter of the observations, used the model to predict consumption per capita for the remaining cases, and compared these predictions with the objectively measured consumption per capita. He found that 60% of those in the poorest decile were predicted, by the model, to be in other deciles.

Even this exercise likely overstates the potential performance of a rapid-appraisal approach to measuring poverty, because Ravallion was able to use an optimal set of (regression-based) weights to apply to the variables used to predict consumption per capita; in the absence of detailed survey data one would have to generate weights in some other way. The Jamaica survey also applied rigorous standards to sampling households; similar rigor is not a hallmark of many rapid-appraisal exercises. Ravallion's conclusion (p. 212) is worth repeating:

> a rapid-appraisal survey lasting, say, twenty minutes on a relatively small sample can yield some significant predictors of the more expensive objective surveys. A significant share of the variance of consumption will almost certainly be left unexplained, however, and the predictions from such methods are unlikely to be highly correlated with actual standards of living.

More recent evidence has not fundamentally changed this conclusion. For instance, in a study of a major rural development in south-west China, Chen et al. (2006) note that rapid-appraisal methods using subjective-qualitative questions have a severe bias in giving too much weight to current circumstances.

10.3.4 Summarizing Poverty Information

Once we have established a measure of welfare, and set a poverty line, we can summarize the information on poverty in a number of ways. It is widely accepted that a good measure of poverty should satisfy three axioms (Ravallion and Chen 2001): the *focus axiom* says that the measure should not vary if the income of the nonpoor varies; the *monotonicity axiom* states that any income gain for the poor should reduce poverty; and the *transfer axiom*, first articulated by Dalton (1920), asserts that inequality-reducing transfers among the poor should reduce the measure of poverty.

The most widely used measure is the *headcount index* (P_0), defined as the proportion of those in the sample who fall below the poverty line. The measure is straightforward to calculate and easy to understand. On the other hand, it does not measure the intensity of poverty; if a poor person becomes yet poorer, the headcount index does not change, thereby violating the monotonicity axiom. And like all measures of poverty that are based on data collected at the household

level, it relies on the assumption that all members of a given household enjoy the
same level of welfare.

The *poverty gap index* (P_1) does a better job of taking the depth of poverty into
account. Define the poverty gap (G_i) for individual i as the difference between
the poverty line (z) and actual income or expenditure (y_i) for the poor, so

$$G_i = (z - y_i) \times I(y_i < z), \tag{10.9}$$

where $I(\cdot)$ is an indicator function that equals 1 if the condition is true and
0 otherwise. The poverty gap index may then be written, for a sample of
N individuals, as

$$P_1 \equiv \frac{1}{N} \sum_{i=1}^{N} \frac{G_i}{z}. \tag{10.10}$$

One intriguing interpretation of this measure runs as follows: An expensive way
to ensure that nobody is poor would be to make a universal transfer of z to each
person. The cheapest possible way to eliminate poverty would be to transfer G_i
to the poor, to top up their income in order to raise it to the poverty line. The poverty
gap index is thus the ratio of the least-expensive to the most-expensive cost of
eliminating poverty or, put another way, a measure of the potential cost savings
from targeting support successfully to the poor.

The poverty gap index does have the drawback that it violates the transfer
axiom: if a somewhat poor person were to transfer income to an extremely poor
person, the poverty gap index would not change.

The squared poverty gap index (P_2), sometimes referred to as the poverty
severity index, does satisfy the Dalton transfer principle. It is defined as

$$P_2 \equiv \frac{1}{N} \sum_{i=1}^{N} \left(\frac{G_i}{z} \right)^2. \tag{10.11}$$

This index is not very widely used, partly because it typically provides similar
rankings to the poverty gap index, but also because it lacks intuitive appeal. It is one
of a class of measures proposed by Foster et al. (1984) that may be written as

$$P_\alpha \equiv \frac{1}{N} \sum_{i=1}^{N} \left(\frac{G_i}{z} \right)^\alpha. \tag{10.12}$$

A strength of these FGT measures is that they may be disaggregated for
population subgroups; for instance, if the urban poverty rate is 12% and the rural
poverty rate is 28%, and a quarter of the population is urban, then the national
poverty rate is 24% ($=12\% \times 25\% + 28\% \times 75\%$), and 87.5% of all the poor live in
rural areas. On the other hand, one is still left with the vexing issue of what measure
of α is most appropriate.

There are other measures of poverty that have found favor from time to time. The index proposed by Sen (1976) is given by

$$P_S = P_0 \left(1 - (1 - G^P) \frac{\mu^P}{z} \right),$$ (10.13)

where μ^P is the mean expenditure (or income) of the poor and G^P is the Gini coefficient of inequality among the poor – ranging from 0 if expenditure among the poor is equally distributed, to 1 if it is fully unequally distributed. While the index thus takes the distribution among the poor into account, it lacks intuitive appeal, and, unlike the FGT measures, cannot easily be decomposed into the contributions to poverty from different subgroups.

A variant on the Sen index is the *Sen–Shorrocks–Thon index*, given by

$$P_{SST} = P_0 P_1^P \left(1 + \hat{G}^P \right),$$ (10.14)

where the poverty gap index here is applied to the poor only, and the Gini index $(\hat{G}^P)$ refers to the poverty gap ratios. Osberg and Xu (1999) used this index to compare poverty in Canada and the USA over time, using bootstrapping (see Chap. 12) to compute confidence intervals, as well as to examine trends in poverty within Canada. For instance, the SST index in the province of Newfoundland fell from 0.125 in 1995 to 0.092 in 1996, a drop of 31%. This occurred because the headcount poverty rate fell from 0.21 to 0.16 (-25%), the poverty gap index for the poor declined from 0.32 to 0.29 (by 7%), but the third term rose from 1.86 to 1.90 (+2%). In other words, between 1995 and 1996 the number of poor in Newfoundland fell, and on average the poor were better off than before, but inequality among the poor widened.

The Watts index is also sensitive to the distribution of income (or expenditure) among the poor. It takes the form

$$W = \frac{1}{N} \sum_{i=1}^{q} [\ln(z) - \ln(y_i)] = \frac{1}{N} \sum_{i=1}^{q} \ln\left(\frac{z}{y_i} \right),$$ (10.15)

where the N individuals are indexed in ascending order of income, and the ratio of the poverty rate to income is summed over the q individuals who are poor. This measure does satisfy the three axioms that underpin any good measure of poverty.

An extension of the Watts index is the *time taken to exit* measure, which measures the average time that it will take a poor person to exit poverty, assuming that the consumption (or income) of every poor person grows by g (Morduch 1998). It may be computed as

$$\text{Time taken to exit} = W/g.$$ (10.16)

For example, Morduch shows that if the incomes of the poor in Cambodia were to grow by just 1% per year, it would take over 20 years for the average poor

Table 10.4 Measures of poverty for selected countries (US$2/day poverty line)

Country	Year	Mean per month	P_0 (%)	P_1 (%)	$P_2 \times 100$	Watts	Gini
Nigeria	2003	39	83.9	46.9	30.8	0.838	42.9
India – rural	2004	50	75.6	30.9	14.7	0.429	30.5
Uganda	2005	53	75.6	36.4	21.1	0.581	42.6
India – urban	2004	62	65.8	26.0	12.9	0.378	37.6
Haiti	2001	64	72.1	41.8	29.0	0.812	59.5
Senegal	2005	67	60.3	24.6	13.0	0.374	39.2
China – rural	2005	71	55.6	19.5	8.9	0.274	35.9
Vietnam	2006	83	48.4	16.2	7.0	0.223	37.8
Armenia	2003	84	43.4	11.3	4.1	0.143	33.8
South Africa	2000	153	42.9	18.3	9.7	0.273	57.8
Morocco	2007	161	14.0	3.1	1.1	0.040	40.9
China – urban	2005	162	9.4	2.1	0.8	0.029	34.8
Thailand	2004	190	11.5	2.0	0.5	0.021	42.5
Guatemala	2006	192	25.7	9.6	4.8	0.137	53.7

Source: World Bank, PovcalNet, accessed October 12, 2009
Note: P_0 is the headcount poverty rate; P_1 is the poverty gap index; and P_2 is the poverty severity index. The poverty line is set at US$2 per day (US$60.8 per month) in 2005 prices. Gini index measures inequality, ranging from 0 (equality) to 1 (complete inequality). The "Mean per month" figures refer to mean expenditure per capita per month, in US dollars at purchasing power parity

person to exit poverty. Where the time taken to exit is long, there is a case for interventions that target the poor directly, rather than wait for the slowly flowing tide to raise all boats.

Given the large number of choices of summary measures of poverty, which ones should one favor? And how much does this choice even matter?

We may address this issue with the help of Table 10.4, which presents some measures of poverty for a selection of countries and regions. The measures are based on the data in the World Bank's PovcalNet database, which fits a Lorenz curve to available data on the distribution of per capita expenditure (or income), and interpolates the poverty rate. Cross-country comparisons are somewhat problematic – a point we return to below – but our concern here is with whether different measures of poverty tell a consistent story.

As a general proposition, poorer countries have higher poverty rates, however measured. And the FGT measures of poverty, as well as the Watts index, are highly correlated with one another, as Table 10.3 shows; note the particularly high correlation between the Watts index and P_2. This suggests that the precise choice of poverty measure may be of secondary importance, in which case one might as well use the headcount rate, given its simplicity and directness.

On the other hand, there are outliers: Haiti has unexpectedly high poverty as measured by the poverty gap index, a reflection of high levels of inequality there. At the other end of the spectrum, India has comparatively modest numbers of deeply poor people (given the high headcount rates), which suggests that continued economic growth has the potential to lower headcount poverty there relatively rapidly.

10.4   Robustness

If the headcount poverty rate falls from 18% to 15% between one year and the next, how confident can we be that poverty really has fallen? More generally, how robust are our measures of poverty?

The problem arises because there are at least four main sources of error: sampling error, measurement error, differences in needs, and uncertainty about the appropriate poverty line.

10.4.1   Sampling Error

Our measures of poverty are based on a sample of households; had we, by chance, chosen a different sample, we might have found a somewhat different measure of poverty. In short, our estimates of poverty are random variables, and come from a distribution.

Given a sample of n individuals with observed expenditure levels x_i, the sample mean is given by $\bar{x} = \sum_{i=1}^{n} x_i/n$, and the sample variance by $s^2 = \sum_{i=i}^{n} (x_i - \bar{x})^2/(n-1)$. Then the standard error of the sample mean is

$$\widehat{v}(\bar{x}) = \sqrt{s^2/n}. \tag{10.17}$$

Invoking the Central Limit Theorem, we may suppose that the sample mean is distributed normally, at least with large enough samples, and so there is an approximately 95% probability that the interval $\bar{x} \pm 1.96 \times \widehat{v}(\bar{x})$ contains the population mean. Thus a survey of 500 persons with a mean income of $850 and sample standard error of $200 would imply that there is a 95% probability that the population mean is in the interval ($833, $868).

Constructing a confidence interval for the headcount poverty rate, which is estimated as a proportion $\widehat{p}$, is also relatively straightforward, because the variance of the sample proportion takes the form $\widehat{v}(\widehat{p}) = \widehat{p}(1 - \widehat{p})/(n-1)$, and the sample proportion is asymptotically normally distributed. Given an estimated poverty rate of 0.28 and sample size of 500, we are 95% confident that the population poverty rate is in the interval (0.24, 0.32). Rather than baldly stating that "the poverty rate is 28%," it would be more appropriate to report this interval, so that users are reminded that the estimated poverty rate is not a single number graven in stone.

We note in passing that in order to halve the confidence interval it is necessary to quadruple the sample size; there are diminishing marginal returns from sampling additional households. On the other hand if we want, for instance, to be able to measure the poverty rate within a band of ±2 percentage points (with 95% confidence), then we need a sample of about 1,000 (if the poverty rate is about 0.12; more if it is above this). With a typical survey size of perhaps 6,000 households, this only allows one to disaggregate the results into about six to eight regions.

The combination of stratification and clustering makes the computation of the standard error of the estimated poverty rate more complex (see Chap. 4), although certainly manageable with a good statistical package. But it is important to take these into account properly. To illustrate, consider the case of the headcount poverty rate in Vietnam in 2006, estimated at 16.6%. If clustering is ignored, one obtains a value of 0.45% for the standard error of the poverty rate, yielding a 95% confidence interval of (15.7%, 16.6%). However, when clustering is taken into account, the standard error of the poverty rate rises to 0.69%, producing a substantially wider confidence interval of (15.2%, 18.0%).

For more complex measures of poverty, the computation of the standard errors of the estimates is now typically performed by bootstrapping. First one computes the poverty rate many times by sampling, with replacement, from the survey data. With clustering, one samples a cluster (rather than a single observation) at a time. From the distribution of the computed poverty rates one may measure the standard error of the estimate directly.

A quite different form of sampling error occurs if we fail to survey some households that should in fact be included. For instance, poor migrants might not be surveyed if they do not appear on the list of registered villagers from which the final cluster of households to be surveyed is drawn, or if they do not have a permanent address. The extent of such omissions will depend on the particular context of the survey – the 2000 census in the USA missed three million people or about 1.2% of the total population – but it is widely presumed that this group includes a disproportionately large number of poor people.

As countries become more affluent, it is increasingly difficult for survey teams to persuade everyone to respond to questionnaires. High-wage individuals in particular may be reluctant to spend the time required to answer a hundred pages of questions. But this creates a *response bias*, which is likely to lead to an overestimate of the headcount poverty rate. To see this, suppose that a in a 12-person society, 6 people (i.e., 50%) are poor; and suppose that all of the poor people, and two-thirds of the nonpoor, respond to the survey. Since we do not observe whether the nonrespondents are poor or not, we have to leave them out of our calculation, but this yields a headcount poverty rate of 60%.

10.4.2 Measurement Error

Inevitably, we are unable to measure well-being with complete accuracy. We argued above that surveyed households routinely underestimate both expenditure and income, due to incomplete recall and deliberate omissions. A corollary of this *underreporting bias* is that we overestimate poverty rates for any given poverty line. Potentially the effect could be large. Ravallion (1998) argues that the elasticity of the headcount index to errors in mean income (holding the income distribution constant) is about 2; in other words, if income is understated by, say, 5%, the poverty rate may be overstated by 10%. The effect is likely to be even stronger for higher-order Foster–Greer–Thorbecke measures of poverty.

Even if the measurement error in the underlying welfare measure has zero mean, under plausible conditions it is likely to lead to an overstatement of the poverty rate (Ravallion 1998).

One of the areas most prone to measurement problems is in computing the price deflators that are needed in order to compare poverty across different regions of a country, or over time. There are two distinct issues here: the first is what prices to use, and the second is how to construct an appropriate price index.

Consider the following problem: prices are typically higher in urban than in rural areas, so we cannot compare rural and urban incomes (per capita) directly. The solution is to deflate incomes with a price index. The principle is straightforward: measure the basket of goods and services that households consume using household survey data, and then compute the cost of this basket using rural, and then urban, prices.

In practice, things are not so simple. The quantities in the basket may be measured accurately enough, but the real problem is with the prices. Living standards surveys typically ask households to report the value and volume of consumption – for instance, they might have spent $100 to buy 250 kg of rice during the year. This yields a unit value of $0.40 per kilo of rice. This is not quite the same as an independent measure of the price of rice, for two reasons: first, since rice varies in quality, we do not really know what quality of rice is referred to. If urban households consume higher quality rice, the price they pay may be higher than in rural areas, but this does not necessarily measure the price differential between the two areas. The second difference is that unit values are noisy, because it is a ratio of two variables that are themselves measured with some error. In practice, there are also aggregation problems, and many categories of spending may not be homogeneous enough to yield meaningful unit values (e.g., the price of "fish"), or may not report quantities (e.g., spending on "transportation" is not usually accompanied by information on how many miles were travelled).

In some cases, it may be possible to obtain prices from elsewhere. Some surveys include community questionnaires that ask for local information on prices, and are undertaken at the same time as the household survey, but these rarely pay enough attention to assuring comparability in the quality of goods from place to place. In a few cases, price data collected to support the consumer price index may be usable, but this information has its own limitations: the number of commodities whose prices are collected may be relatively limited, and price data may only be collected in some parts of the country (as in the USA, where the consumer price index is based on urban prices only).

Even with good price information, there is still the task of aggregating this information into an index. Most price indexes designed to track inflation over time are base-weighted ("Laspeyres"), where each price is weighted by the quantity consumed in the base period. More formally,

$$L_P = \sum_i p_{it} q_{i0} \Big/ \sum_i p_{i0} q_{i0}, \qquad (10.18)$$

where the p_{it} refers to the ith commodity in time t, p_{i0} is the price of the ith commodity in the base period, and q_{i0} is the base-period (or location) quantity. The Laspeyres index generally overstates the true rise in the cost of living, mainly because it does not adjust for the way in which, over time, consumers shift from items whose prices rise relatively quickly to items whose prices rise relatively slowly (or fall). Its main virtue is that one does not need to re-measure the quantities in every time period; for an index of inflation that has to be published monthly, this is important, but when comparing two household surveys, both of which have information on quantities, it is far less compelling.

Other price indexes are available. The end-weighted ("Paasche") index weights price changes using the end-of-period quantities, and so tends to understate inflation. Fisher's "ideal" index splits the difference, by taking the geometric mean of the Laspeyres and Paasche indexes, and measures the cost of living correctly if households have quadratic utility functions.

A number of researchers favor using the Törnqvst index, which weights the price increases of each good by the average budget share of the good during the period in question. It is given by

$$T_P = \prod_i \left\{ \left(\frac{p_{it}}{p_{i0}} \right)^{0.5(S_{i0}+S_{it})} \right\}, \quad \text{where} \quad S_{it} \equiv \frac{v_{it}}{\sum_i v_{it}}. \qquad (10.19)$$

Here, $v_{it} = p_{it} q_{it}$ represents spending in time t on the ith good. The Törnqvst index gives the true cost of living index if the underlying utility function is logarithmic.

The choice of appropriate price index is at the heart of Angus Deaton's re-examination of the trend in the poverty rate in India in the 1980s and 1990s (Deaton 2001). Between 1987–1988 and 1993–1994, the official numbers show a modest reduction in rural poverty in India, from 39 to 37%; by Deaton's estimates, the reduction was from 39 to 33%. The difference – which is not trivial, because it represents over 30 million people! – is essentially because the official measure uses a Laspeyres price index to inflate the poverty line, while Deaton used a Törnqvst index. The Laspeyres price index, by overstating the increase in the true cost of living, led to an overestimate of the poverty rate in 1993–1994.

The Indian National Sample Surveys have not been entirely consistent, over time, in the way they posed some of the questions on expenditure. By stripping out the noncomparable components, Deaton (2001) was able to construct a more consistent picture of the evolution of Indian poverty over time. He also estimated a rural–urban price differential that turned out to be far smaller than in the official figures. The net result of these various adjustments was that for 1999–2000, while the official poverty rates were 27% in rural areas and 24% in urban areas, Deaton estimated these poverty rates at 25 and 13%, respectively.

10.4.3 Equivalence Scales

We argued above that, in principle at least, well-being would be measured better as expenditure (or income) per adult equivalent, rather than expenditure per capita. One might reasonably ask whether this choice matters, for instance in measuring the depth of poverty, or its evolution over time.

The evidence suggests that measures of poverty are not particularly sensitive to the choice of adult equivalence scale. Short et al. (1999) examined the sensitivity of the headcount poverty rate in the USA for a variety of OECD adult equivalence scales; the poverty rate was 13.3% based on per capita income, and varied from 12.3 to 13.8% depending on what equivalence scale was used.

Using data from the Vietnam Household Living Standards Survey of 2006, we tried to identify the poorest 20% of the population using one of three scales: expenditure per capita, the OECD scale (given by $1 + 0.7(N_a - 1) + 0.5N_c$), and an "economies of scale in expenditure" schedule (given by $(N_a + N_c)^{0.7}$). The correlation between expenditure per capita and expenditure per OECD scale was 0.986, and between expenditure per capita and the third scale was 0.967. About a tenth of those identified as poor by the expenditure per capita measure would not be so classified by the other scales – a relatively modest level of disagreement.

10.4.4 Choice of Poverty Line

Although the choice of a poverty line has to be reasonable, it is also essentially arbitrary. That is why it is usually desirable to check for the sensitivity of the poverty rate to different assumptions about the poverty line. For instance, for Vietnam in 2006, the headcount poverty rate was 16.6%; if the poverty line were 10% higher, the poverty rate would be 21.2%; if it were 10% lower, the rate would have fallen to 12.6%. These show that the poverty rate in Vietnam at that time was highly sensitive to the choice of poverty line. Sensitivity tests such as these are worth doing routinely; the World Bank's ADePT 2.0 program, which helps automate the production of tables for the construction of poverty profiles, computes such results automatically.

In comparing poverty across two regions, or for a country at two points in time, we would like to know whether the choice of poverty line matters. It would matter if, for instance, poverty appears to have fallen if a low poverty line is used, but appears to have risen if a higher poverty line is used.

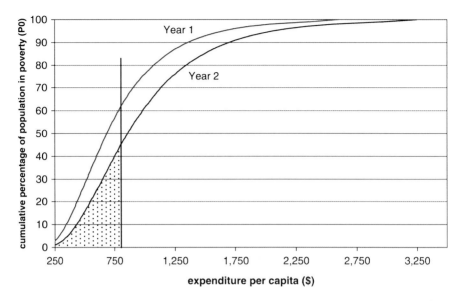

Fig. 10.3 Poverty incidence curves with first-order stochastic dominance

An elegant way to check this is by graphing the cumulative distribution functions for the welfare measure – referred to in this context as the *poverty incidence curves, F(z)* – as is done, for a hypothetical example, in Fig. 10.3. For any given poverty line, we may read off the curve the proportion of people who are in poverty. If the poverty incidence curves for 2 years do not intersect – the case in Fig. 10.3 – we have first-order stochastic dominance, and may conclude that the choice of poverty line is essentially unimportant when determining whether the poverty rate has risen or fallen over time. Formally, first-order stochastic dominance holds if, for two income distributions y_1 and y_2 with associated cumulative distribution functions $F(y_1)$ and $F(y_2)$ we have $F(y_1) \leq F(y_2)$ for all y.

If the ranking of the poverty incidence curves is ambiguous, so that they intersect, it is still possible to check for second-order stochastic dominance. For every level of expenditure per capita one may compute the area under the poverty incidence curve – such as the shaded area in Fig. 10.3. This is the poverty deficit, and when graphed against the poverty line, as done in Fig. 10.4, it traces out the *poverty deficit curve* $D(z)$. Each point on this curve is the total value of the poverty gap (which is the poverty gap index multiplied by the poverty line).

In our example, the poverty deficit curve for year 2 is below that for year 1 in the relevant range – i.e., at least up to the maximum reasonable level for the poverty line. Suppose, for instance, that in year 2 the measured poverty rate has fallen if we use a low poverty line, and has risen if we use a high poverty line. We do not have first-order stochastic dominance. But the poverty gaps in year 2 are lower for those at the bottom of the expenditure distribution; if these gains outweigh the wider poverty gaps experienced by those further up the income distribution, then we may

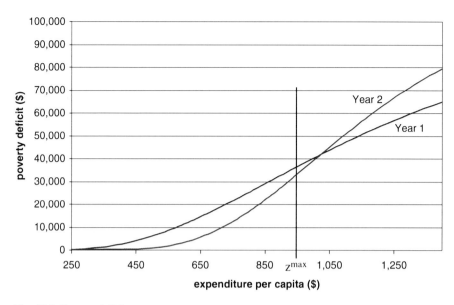

Fig. 10.4   Poverty deficit curves

say that there has been an reduction in poverty (at least if we use a poverty measure such as P_1 or higher).

Even when the poverty incidence curve for year 2 is everywhere below that for year 1 – as in Fig. 10.3 – it is possible that this may reflect sampling error, and that if we had happened to choose another sample, the curves might have intersected. So it would be useful to be able to test whether the difference between two poverty incidence curves – more generally, two cumulative density functions (cdfs) – is statistically significant.

A first pass at this problem would be to use the Kolmogorov–Smirnov test, which focuses on the largest vertical distance between the two cdfs. Stata has a built-in `ksmirnov` function; most statistics textbooks provide tabulations of critical values.

Tse and Zhang (2003) make the case for an approach that would divide the horizontal axis, up to a maximum plausible poverty line, into ten or a dozen segments; for each segment one could then test whether there is a statistically significant difference between the two cdfs at the edge of each interval. Further details are set out by Davidson and Duclos (2000).

10.5   International Poverty Comparisons

The key target of the Millennium Development Goals is to halve the number of people living in poverty in the developing world between 1990 and 2015. In order to determine whether we are on track to meet this target it is necessary to create a measure of poverty worldwide, by aggregating poverty rates from different

Table 10.5 Percentage of population in LDCs living below US$1.25/person/day

Region	1981	1984	1987	1990	1993	1996	1999	2002	2005
East Asia and Pacific	77.7	65.5	54.2	54.7	50.8	36.0	35.5	27.6	16.8
China	*84.0*	*69.4*	*54.0*	*60.2*	*53.7*	*36.4*	*35.6*	*28.4*	*15.9*
Europe and Central Asia	1.7	1.3	1.1	2.0	4.6	4.6	5.1	4.6	3.7
Latin America and Caribbean	11.5	13.4	12.6	9.8	9.1	10.8	10.8	11.0	8.4
Middle East and N. Africa	7.9	6.1	5.7	4.3	4.1	4.1	4.2	3.6	3.6
South Asia	59.4	55.6	54.2	51.7	46.9	47.1	44.1	43.8	40.3
India	*59.8*	*55.5*	*53.6*	*51.3*	*49.4*	*46.6*	*44.8*	*43.9*	*41.6*
Sub-Saharan Africa	53.7	56.2	54.8	57.9	57.1	58.7	58.2	55.1	51.2
All LDCs	**51.8**	**46.6**	**41.8**	**41.6**	**39.1**	**34.4**	**33.7**	**30.6**	**25.2**
Memo:									
LDC, $1.00/day	41.4	34.4	29.8	29.5	27.0	23.1	22.8	20.3	16.1
LDC, $2.00/day	69.2	67.4	64.2	63.2	61.5	58.2	57.1	53.3	47.0
LDC, $2.50/day	74.6	73.7	71.6	70.4	69.2	67.2	65.9	62.4	56.6

Source: Chen and Ravallion (2008); also available on World Bank's PovcalNet
Note: US$1.25 refers to prices in 2005. LDC = Less-developed country. Bold figures refer to average for all LDCs

countries. International agencies are also interested in comparing poverty rates across countries, as an input into their decisions about where to allocate their scarce resources.

All discussions of international poverty comparisons begin with the work that Chen and Ravallion (2004, 2008) have undertaken for the World Bank. The necessary steps are as follows:

1. Pick a poverty line, usually specified in US dollars.
2. Convert this poverty line into its equivalent in foreign currency, using a purchasing power parity (PPP) exchange rate for some specified year.
3. Use a domestic consumer price index to create a (nominal) local-currency poverty line for each year from 1981 to the present.
4. Use data from local living standards surveys – often only available in the form of published summary tables – to estimate Lorenz curves that show the distribution of consumption (or income) per capita.
5. Apply the local poverty line to the Lorenz curve to get the poverty rate in any given year.
6. For years between household surveys, interpolate the poverty rate.
7. For every third year, beginning in 1981, aggregate the poverty rates in all countries to get a world poverty rate.

The underlying distributional data come from 675 household surveys in 116 developing countries. The computations have been automated, and it is straightforward to use PovcalNet – a Web-based application – to calculate poverty rates using different poverty lines, and for individual countries or regions.

Some typical output from this exercise is shown in Table 10.5, using a poverty line of $1.25 per person per day. It shows that the poverty rate in less-developed countries fell from 52% in 1981 to 25% by 2005, with a particularly spectacular reduction in China (from 84 to 16%) and minimal change in Sub-Saharan Africa (from 54 to 51%). Worldwide, the number of people living on less than US$1.25 a day fell from 1.9 billion in 1981 to 1.4 billion by 2005. On the other hand, if the poverty line is set at $2.50 per day, there were 2.7 billion poor in 1981 and 3.1 billion in 2005.

The approach taken by Chen and Ravallion is cost-effective and pragmatic, but inevitably has its critics. It is worth saying a bit more about each step in the process.

Chen and Ravallion pick a poverty line of US$1.25 per person per day in 2005 prices; this corresponds to an earlier line that was loosely referred to as the "dollar a day" poverty line, but actually stood at US$1.08 per person per day in 1993. The official poverty line in the poorest 15 countries in the Chen and Ravallion sample averaged about $1.25 per day, and this has become the de facto new benchmark.

The poverty line is converted to local currencies using a PPP exchange rate rather than an official or market exchange rate. This is done because it is widely recognized that market exchange rates do not do a good job of reflecting differences in the cost of living in different countries; a haircut that might cost $15 in Boston costs about 100 baht (about $3, at the exchange rate of 2009) in Bangkok. A PPP exchange rate tries to compensate for such differences; Chen and Ravallion use the rates developed by the 2005 round of the International Comparison Project.

While this is certainly an improvement over using market exchange rates, it is worth noting that PPP exchange rates are not particularly calibrated to the goods and services consumed by the poor (although in principle they could be; see Deaton 2003). They can also vary sharply when recomputed after a gap of several years; the 2005 revision of PPP exchange rates effectively reduced China's GDP per capita from $6,750 to $4,091. Some also wonder, for example, whether one could even survive on $1.25 a day in a country like the US or Japan (Pogge and Reddy 2003).

Once the poverty line has been converted to local prices for 2005, it is adjusted to other years using a consumer price index. This is designed to track the cost of a "standard" basket of goods, and may not always be a very accurate guide to the evolution of the prices facing the poor.

Bhalla (2002) argues that poverty is lower, and has fallen faster, than the Chen and Ravallion numbers show. The essence of his argument is that survey data understate income and consumption – due to high and rising nonresponse bias and underreporting bias. Deaton (2003) writes that consumption worldwide, as measured by household-based surveys, averages 86% of consumption as measured by national accounts, and grows about half as rapidly. If the underreporting is evenly spread across poor and rich, then Bhalla's argument is indeed correct. This is, however, a strong assumption, and it is quite plausible that much of the growing underreporting of consumption occurs at the upper end of the distribution, which would have a minimal impact on measures of poverty.

Is there a practical alternative to the approach taken by Chen and Ravallion to measuring world poverty? Pogge and Reddy (2003) favor asking every country to measure poverty using a cost-of-basic-needs approach, based on the expenditure required to provide sufficient food energy, plus a nonfood component of spending. This would be labor-intensive – it can only be done using the original survey data – and it would be difficult to achieve methodological consistency across countries, although as the capacity to undertake poverty analysis has increased, it may now be feasible, if expensive.

10.6 Vulnerability to Poverty

Measures of poverty are essentially backward-looking, since they measure who was poor in the recent past, *ex post*. But, in principle, policy makers are more interested in identifying who is likely to be poor in the future, so that they may be helped. These households are poor *ex ante*, and are the people who may be considered to be vulnerable to poverty. Vulnerability thus measures "exposure to poverty rather than the poverty outcome itself" (Dercon 2001, p. 27).

Only if people are persistently poor will a measure of poverty be a good guide to vulnerability to poverty. In practice, however, people move into and out of poverty quite regularly. Table 10.6 shows that in Vietnam, 29% of the population was poor in both 1993 and 1998, and 39% of the population was not poor in either year. The remaining 32% of the population was poor in only one of these 2 years. Movements of this magnitude are routinely found in developing countries (see, for instance, Baulch and Hoddinott 2000). This provides a justification for a measure of vulnerability, distinct from a measure of poverty.

A much-cited definition of vulnerability to poverty is "the propensity to suffer a significant welfare shock, bringing the household below a socially defined minimum level" (Alwang, Siegel, and Jorgensen 2001). The welfare shock is typically taken to mean a blow to income or expenditure per capita; the socially defined minimum level may be equated with the poverty line; and the propensity to suffer a significant shock may be measured as the probability of being poor in the next year (Chaudhuri et al. 2002) or within the next few years (Pritchett et al. 2000).

Conventionally, if arbitrarily, someone with more than an even chance of being poor next year is considered to be "highly vulnerable"; if someone has a probability of being poor between P_0 and 0.5, they are referred to as "vulnerable"; and everyone else has "low vulnerability." Someone classified as having low

Table 10.6 Transition matrix for poverty, Vietnam, 1993 and 1998

	Poor in 1998	Not poor in 1998	Poverty rate, 1993
Poor in 1993	0.287	0.274	0.561
Not poor in 1993	0.048	0.391	
Poverty rate, 1998	0.335		

Source: Glewwe et al. 2002
Note: Based on Vietnam Living Standards Surveys of 1993 and 1998. Size of panel is 4,281 households

vulnerability may well turn out to be poor next year, but they are less likely than the average person to find themselves in such a situation.

A household h is poor if its per capita consumption (or income, denoted here by c_{ht}) falls below the poverty line, so $c_{h,t} \leq z$. This may be contrasted with the definition of the vulnerability to poverty of household h in time t, which is the probability that the household will be poor in time $t + 1$ or, more formally,

$$v_{h,t} = \Pr(c_{h,t+1} \leq z). \tag{10.20}$$

The key problem here is that $c_{h,\,t+1}$ is not observable. Whether a household will be poor next year will depend, in principle, on the resources they can draw on (including human and capital assets), the risks they face, the extent of insurance (including family support networks), and access to credit.

The information ideally needed to model vulnerability is overwhelming, so one is obliged to simplify. In the most basic case, just four pieces of information are needed:

-   $E(c_{t+1})$, which is the household's expected level of per capita consumption in the next period
-   The variance of $E(c_{t+1})$, given by σ^2
-   The poverty line, z
-   An assumption that $E(c_{t+1})$ follows a known distribution, usually taken to be normal (Gaussian)

To illustrate, suppose we expect household consumption per capita to be 120 next year, normally distributed with a variance of 900. We are interested in measuring the probability that consumption per capita will be below the poverty line (of 100) next year. The answer in this case is 25.2%, represented by the shaded area in Fig. 10.5.

To make the concept of vulnerability operational, we still need a practical way to measure $E(c_{t+1})$ and σ^2. If longitudinal data on households were available, then one could use past experience to generate estimates, but such data are almost nonexistent in less-developed countries.

An alternative is to infer information on consumption levels and variability from cross-section data. First, build a model of the determinants of per capita consumption, based if possible on observable household characteristics (X_h), economy-wide shocks (β_t), household time-invariant fixed effects to pick up unobservables (α_h), and idiosyncratic errors (e_{ht}), of the form

$$c_{h,t} = c(X_h, \beta_t, \alpha_h, e_{h,t}). \tag{10.21}$$

With a measure of this relationship, as well as the variance of expected consumption, then we could measure vulnerability as

$$v_{h,t} = \Pr(c_{h,t+1} = c(X_h, \beta_{t+1}, \alpha_h, e_{h,t+1}) < z | X_h, \beta_t, \alpha_h, e_{h,t}). \tag{10.22}$$

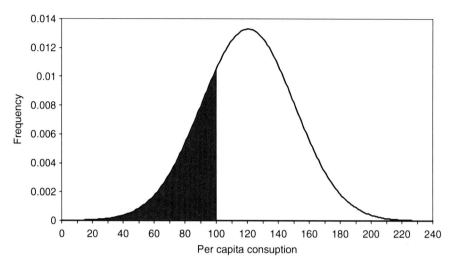

Fig. 10.5 Illustrating the measurement of vulnerability. (*Note*: Poverty line is 100, expected income per capita is 120, and standard deviation of expected income is 30)

Chaudhuri et al. (2002) estimate a simplified model of 10.22 using data on Indonesia for 1998–1999, which takes the form

$$\ln c_h = X_h \cdot b + e_h, \tag{10.23}$$

where

$$e_h \sim N(0, X_h\theta). \tag{10.24}$$

They first regress the log of per capita consumption on the X_h covariates, and then regress the squared residuals from this equation on the same covariates to obtain an estimate of θ. On the assumption that the X_h variables do not change from one year to the next, Chaudhuri et al. generate a value of expected log consumption (using 10.23) and its variance. Note that the variance will differ from household to household; for a given expected consumption level, a higher variance will be associated with greater vulnerability.

The final step is to use these estimates to estimate vulnerability for each household, using

$$\widehat{v}_h = \Pr(\ln c_h < \ln z | X_h) = \Phi\left(\frac{\ln z - X_h b}{\sqrt{X_h\widehat{\theta}}}\right), \tag{10.25}$$

where Φ is the cdf of the standard normal distribution. The results of this exercise are shown in Table 10.7, and are revealing. The headcount poverty rate in Indonesia

Table 10.7 Poverty and vulnerability in Indonesia, 1998–1999

	Criterion	Proportion of total population		
		Poor	Nonpoor	Poor and nonpoor
High vulnerability	$\bar{v}_h \geq 0.50$	0.05	0.03	0.08
Low vulnerability	$0.50 > \bar{v}_h \geq 0.22$	0.12	0.25	0.37
Not vulnerable	$\bar{v}_h < 0.22$	0.05	0.50	0.55
All groups		0.22	0.78	1.00

Source: Dercon (2001), based on Chaudhuri et al. (2002)

at the time was 22%, but 8% of the population were highly vulnerable and a further 37% somewhat vulnerable to being poor next year. Indeed, more than half of the vulnerable population was not currently poor.

There are some policy implications here. Efforts that aim to help only those who are poor now are likely to miss a substantial number of households who are at significant risk of being poor in the future. Conversely, not every poor person is highly vulnerable; a significant proportion can be expected to move back out of poverty after a temporary drop below the poverty line. More broadly, the focus on vulnerability makes efforts at targeting the (future) poor much harder.

Measurements of vulnerability are less compelling than measures of poverty, because of the chain of assumptions and that estimates are required. Errors in the measurement of consumption imply that the estimate of σ^2 is overstated; Pritchett et al. (2000) argue that between a third and a half of this variance is attributable to measurement error alone. As noted above, the measurement of σ^2 is usually based on cross-section data, which is less than ideal; in particular it does not allow one to pick up the effects of rare but important shocks, such as a recession or drought. The assumption that expected consumption is normally distributed may also be too strong, but can be relaxed by bootstrapping to construct an empirical distribution. And the regression estimates generally need to be computed using generalized (rather than ordinary) least squares (see Chaudhuri et al. 2002).

Measures of vulnerability will not supplant measures of poverty, but they are useful in drawing attention to the role of risk and uncertainty. Those who are persistently poor need more income; but those who risk poverty from time to time may need insurance mechanisms. The World Bank now encourages the use of Risk and Vulnerability Assessments, which are viewed as diagnostic tools to understand the sources of vulnerability to poverty, catalog the public interventions aimed at managing social risks, and identify potentially prod-uctive and feasible policy actions (Holzmann et al. 2003). Such assessments look at ways in which the vulnerable can reduce risk (e.g., by building flood dikes), mitigate risk (e.g., by diversifying course of income), or cope with shocks (e.g., by selling assets).

In sum, it is possible to measure vulnerability, however imperfectly. The results show that vulnerability to poverty is more widespread than poverty; for instance, 8% of urban Indonesians were poor in 1998–1999, but 30% were vulnerable to poverty (Pritchett et al. 2000). This increases our estimates of the number of people who are in an economically precarious position. The focus on vulnerability also expands the policy menu, beyond the traditional concern of antipoverty measures, which is to raise consumption, to greater attention to social protection.

References

Albert, Jose Ramon. 2004. Measuring Poverty. PowerPoint notes, Statistical Research and Training Center, Philippines.

Alwang, Jeffrey, Paul Siegel, and Steen Jorgensen. 2001. Vulnerability: A view from different disciplines. Social Protection Discussion Paper No. 0115, Social Protection Unit, Human Development Network. Washington, DC: World Bank.

Baulch, Bob, and John Hoddinott. 2000. Economic mobility and poverty dynamics in developing countries. *Journal of Development Economics* Special Issue: 1–24.

Bhalla, Surjit. 2002. *Imagine there is no country: Poverty, inequality, and growth in the era of globalization*. Washington, DC: Institute for International Economics.

Carlson, Michael D. 1974. *The 1972-73 consumer expenditure survey*, 16–23. December: Monthly Labor Review.

Chaudhuri, Shubham, Jyotsna Jalan, and Asep Suryahadi. 2002. Assessing household vulnerability to poverty from cross-sectional data: A methodology and estimates for Indonesia. Discussion Paper Series No. 0102-52, Department of Economics, Columbia University, New York.

Chen, Shaohua, and Martin Ravallion. 2008. The developing world is poorer than we thought, but no less successful in the fight against poverty. Policy Research Working Paper No. 4703. Washington, DC: World Bank.

Chen, Shaohua, and Martin Ravallion. 2004. How have the world's poorest fared since the early 1980s? Development Economics Working Paper No. 3341. Washington, DC: World Bank.

Chen, Shaohua, Ren Mu, and Martin Ravallion. 2006. Are there lasting impacts of aid to poor areas? Evidence from rural China. Research Brief. Washington, DC: World Bank.

Dalton, Hugh. 1920. The Measurement of the inequality of incomes. *Economic Journal* 30: 384–361.

Datt, Gaurav. 2002. *Implementation completion report. Philippines: enhanced poverty monitoring – studies component*. Washington, DC: World Bank.

Davidson, Russell, and Jean-Yves Duclos. 2000. Statistical inference for stochastic dominance and for the measurement of poverty and inequality. *Econometrica* 68(6): 1435–1464.

Deaton, Angus. 1997. *The analysis of household surveys: A microeconometric approach to development policy*. Baltimore: Johns Hopkins University Press.

Deaton, Angus. 2001. Computing prices and poverty rates in India, 1999-2000. Research Program in Development Studies Working Paper, Princeton University, Princeton, NJ.

Deaton, Angus. 2003. Measuring poverty in a growing world (or measuring growth in a poor world). NBER Working Paper No. 9822, National Bureau of Economic Research, Cambridge MA.

Deaton, Angus. 2008. Income, health, and well-being around the world: Evidence from the Gallup World Poll. *Journal of Economic Perspectives* 22(2): 53–72.

Deaton, Angus, and Salman Zaidi., 1998. Guidelines for constructing consumption aggregates for welfare analysis. Woodrow Wilson School of Public and International Affairs, Princeton University, Princeton NJ.

Dercon, Stefan. 2001. Assessing vulnerability to poverty. Paper prepared for the UK Department for International Development. Department of Economics, Oxford University.

Duclos, Jean-Yves, and Abdelkrim Araar. 2006. *Poverty and equity: Measurement, policy and estimation with DAD*. New York: Springer; Ottawa: International Development Research Centre.

Foster, James, J. Greer, and Eric Thorbecke. 1984. A class of decomposable poverty measures. *Econometrica* 52(3): 761–765.

Glewwe, Paul, Michele Gragnolati, and Hassan Zaman. 2002. Who gained from Vietnam's boom in the 1990s? *Economic Development and Cultural Change* 50(4): 773–792.

Haughton, Jonathan, and Shahidur Khandker. 2009. *Handbook on poverty and inequality*. Washington, DC: World Bank.

Kakwani, Nanak, and Jacques Silber (eds.). 2008. *Quantitative approaches to multidimensional poverty measurement*. New York: Palgrave Macmillan.

Hanmer, Lucia, Graham Pyatt, and Howard White. 1999. What do the World Bank's Poverty Assessments teach us about poverty in Africa? *Development and Change* 30: 795–823.

Holzmann, Robert, Lynne Sherburne-Benz, and Emil Tesliuc. 2003. *Social risk management: The World Bank's approach to social protection in a globalizing world*. Washington, DC: World Bank.

Kumar, Krishna. 1993. An overview of rapid appraisal methods in development settings. In *Rapid appraisal methods*, ed. Krishna Kumar. Washington, DC: World Bank.

Morduch, Jonathan. 1998. Poverty, economic growth, and average exit time. *Economics Letters* 59: 385–390.

Osberg, Lars, and Kuan Xu. 1999. Poverty intensity: How well do Canadian provinces compare? *Canadian Public Policy-Analyse de Politiques* 25(2): 179–195.

Pogge, Thomas, and Sanjay Reddy. 2003. Unknown: The extent, distribution, and trend of global income poverty. Columbia University, New York.

Pradhan, Menno, Asep Suryahadi, Sudarno Sumarto, and Lant Pritchett. 2000. Measurements of poverty in Indonesia, 1996, 1999, and beyond. Policy Research Working Paper Series No. 2438. Washington, DC: World Bank.

Pritchett, Lant, Asep Shryahadi, and Sudarno Sumarto. 2000. Quantifying vulnerability to poverty: A proposed measure, applied to Indonesia. Social Monitoring and Early Response Unit, Jakarta.

Ravallion, Martin. 1992. Poverty comparisons: A guide to concepts and methods. LSMS Working Paper No. 88. Washington, DC: World Bank.

Ravallion, Martin. 1996. How well can method substitute for data? Five experiments in poverty analysis. *The World Bank Research Observer* 11(2): 199–221.

Ravallion, Martin. 1998. Poverty lines in theory and practice. LSMS Working Paper No. 133. Washington, DC: World Bank.

Ravallion, Martin, and Benu Bidani. 1994. How robust is a poverty profile? *World Bank Economic Review* 8(1): 75–102.

Ravallion, Martin, and Shaohua Chen. 2001. Measuring pro-poor growth. Policy Research Working Paper No. 2666. Washington, DC: World Bank.

Ravallion, Martin, Gaurav Datt, and Dominique van de Walle. 1991. Quantifying absolute poverty in the developing world. *Review of Income and Wealth* 37(4): 345–361.

Sen, Amartya. 1976. Poverty: An ordinal approach to measurement. *Econometrica* 44 (2): 219–231.

Sen, Amartya. 1987. *Commodities and capabilities*. Amsterdam: North-Holland.

Short, Kathleen, Thesia Garner, David Johnson, and Patricia Doyle. 1999. Experimental poverty measures: 1990 to 1997. US Census Bureau, Current Population Reports, Consumer Income, 60–205, US Government Printing Office, Washington, DC.

Tse, Y. K., and Xibin Zhang. 2003. A Monte Carlo investigation of some tests for stochastic dominance. Department of Econometrics and Business Statistics, Monash University, Clayton, Victoria, Australia.

World Bank. 2000. *World development report 2000/2001: Attacking poverty*. Washington, DC: World Bank.

Chapter 11
Bootstrapping

11.1 Introduction

It is rarely sufficient simply to present estimates of means, coefficients, or poverty rates that have been calculated based on survey data. We also need measures of the variability of these measures, so that we may judge how much confidence to have in them.

In many useful cases we have analytical expressions for the standard errors. For example, given sample observations x_1, ..., x_n, we have that the sample mean is $\bar{x} = \sum_{i=1}^{n} x_i/n$, and the standard error of the sample mean is $s/\sqrt{n} \equiv \sqrt{\frac{1}{n-1} \sum_{i=1}^{n} (x_i - \bar{x})^2}/\sqrt{n}$. In the classical regression case the variable y_i depends linearly on a vector of variables x_i, so

$$y_i = \mathbf{x}_i'\beta + e_i, \tag{11.1}$$

and we have, in matrix form (see Chap. 2),

$$\hat{\beta} = (\mathbf{X}'\mathbf{X})^{-1}\mathbf{X}'\mathbf{y}. \tag{11.2}$$

Here the variance–covariance matrix of the estimated coefficients is given by

$$\mathrm{var}\hat{\beta} = s^2(\mathbf{X}'\mathbf{X})^{-1}, \tag{11.3}$$

where s^2 is $(1/n)\sum_{i=1}^{n} u_i^2$, and the residuals are defined as $u_i \equiv y_i - \mathbf{x}_i\hat{\beta}$. In large samples, we may invoke the Central Limit Theorem to note that $\hat{\beta}$ is approximately normally distributed.

However, it is not always possible to compute the standard error, or other measure of variation, using a straightforward analytical formula. For instance, there is no easy way to measure the standard error of the median, or of the coefficient of variation (i.e., of σ/μ).

D. Haughton and J. Haughton, *Living Standards Analytics*, Statistics for Social and Behavioral Sciences, DOI 10.1007/978-1-4614-0385-2_11, © Springer Science+Business Media, LLC 2011

11.2   Bootstrap: Mechanics

The bootstrap represents a clever solution to this problem that is both simple and intuitive. The foundation of the bootstrap is the idea that the empirical cumulative density function F_n, based on our data sample, gives us a good sense of what the true unknown (population) distribution is. The empirical distribution is defined as the discrete distribution that gives a weight of $1/n$ to each observation x_i.

Given a dataset $x_1, \ldots, x_n$, of independent and identically distributed (iid) sample observations, we randomly draw m of the observations (with replacement), and calculate the statistic of interest, such as the median. The size of the drawing, m, is typically taken to be the same as the sample size. We then repeat this process many times, thereby generating a distribution of the statistic, which gives us the measure of variability that we were seeking, and more generally a glimpse of what the unknown distribution looks like.

It helps to illustrate the process with a straightforward example. The Stata code in Table 11.1 first generates 10,000 iid observations of variable x that is distributed $N(0,1)$. This is our sample dataset. We then:

1. Pick a sample of 10,000 observations from the dataset, with replacement. This means that some of the observations will likely be chosen more than once.
2. Compute the mean, and also the median ("p50") and 75th percentile ("p75").
3. Repeat the process 1,000 times.
4. Report the mean values from the sample, along with the bootstrap standard errors.

Theoretically, in this example, $\mu = 0$ and $\sigma_\mu = \sigma/\sqrt{n} = 1/\sqrt{10,000} = 0.01$. The bootstrap value for s that we obtain is 0.0099, which is very close to the theoretical value (0.01), and to the analytically computed value (0.010007). We note in passing that the standard error of the median is estimated to be 0.0113.

How does a bootstrap analysis work? The main idea is quite simple and intuitive, and yet when the bootstrap was introduced by Efron (1979), most researchers found it hard at first to believe that it worked. Essentially the idea is as follows.

The success of the enterprise depends on just how close to the true distribution F the empirical distribution F_n is, and that in turns depends on the sample size and other assumptions. Moreover, how good a job we do at simulating the empirical distribution F_n depends on the number of bootstrap samples we generate. Another issue to keep in mind is that we have assumed that the data are iid; bootstrapping non-iid data is somewhat harder, although simple cluster structures can be accommodated, as discussed below.

The bootstrap methodology was introduced by Bradley Efron at the 1977 Rietz lecture, and subsequently published in the *Annals of Statistics* in 1979 (Efron 1979). The context of application of this new methodology was, and still is, a situation where we cannot readily compute the standard deviation of an estimator, as is the case for as seemingly a simple statistics like the sample median.

Table 11.1 Bootstrapping the mean, median, and 75th percentile

Stata code for generating bootstraps for simulated dataset

```
drawnorm x, n(10000) seed(12345)
sum x, detail
sum x
set seed 54321
bootstrap r(mean), reps(1000) : summarize x, detail
estat bootstrap
bootstrap r(p50),  reps(1000) saving(p50file) : summarize x,
detail
estat bootstrap
bootstrap r(p75),  reps(1000) saving(p75file) : summarize x,
detail
estat bootstrap
```

Classical results for the mean

```
    Variable |        Obs        Mean    Std. Dev.        Min        Max
-------------+--------------------------------------------------------
           x |      10000     .0000318    1.000722   -3.586378   3.632756
```

Bootstrap results for the mean

```
-----------------------------------------------------------------------
             |   Observed   Bootstrap                       Normal-based
             |      Coef.   Std. Err.      z    P>|z|    [95% Conf. Interval]
-------------+---------------------------------------------------------------
       _bs_1 |   .0000318   .0098987    0.00    0.997    -.0193693    .019433
-----------------------------------------------------------------------

             |   Observed               Bootstrap
             |      Coef.       Bias   Std. Err.   [95% Conf. Interval]
-------------+---------------------------------------------------------------
       _bs_1 |   .00003183  -.0002194  .00989873   -.0179543   .0213362  (BC)
-----------------------------------------------------------------------
```

Bootstrap results for the median

```
-----------------------------------------------------------------------
             |   Observed   Bootstrap                       Normal-based
             |      Coef.   Std. Err.      z    P>|z|    [95% Conf. Interval]
-------------+---------------------------------------------------------------
       _bs_1 |   .0064932   .0113056    0.57    0.566    -.0156653    .0286517
-----------------------------------------------------------------------

             |   Observed               Bootstrap
             |      Coef.       Bias   Std. Err.   [95% Conf. Interval]
-------------+---------------------------------------------------------------
       _bs_1 |   .0064932   .0011407  .01130558   -.0131823   .0290252  (BC)
-----------------------------------------------------------------------
```

Bootstrap results for the 75th percentile

```
-----------------------------------------------------------------------
             |   Observed   Bootstrap                       Normal-based
             |      Coef.   Std. Err.      z    P>|z|    [95% Conf. Interval]
-------------+---------------------------------------------------------------
       _bs_1 |   .6785049    .014283   47.50    0.000     .6505107    .7064991
-----------------------------------------------------------------------

             |   Observed               Bootstrap
             |      Coef.       Bias   Std. Err.   [95% Conf. Interval]
-------------+---------------------------------------------------------------
       _bs_1 |   .67850491  -.002995  .01428302    .6486374   .7039045  (BC)
-----------------------------------------------------------------------
```

When the bootstrap was introduced, it generated considerable attention, and some surprise and incredulity: how could one sample give access to the whole population? This was quickly addressed in a series of talks by Efron, who argued that the bootstrap is an application of what he referred to as "the plug-in principle," which consists in plugging in an estimate for a population parameter, as is commonly done when computing standard errors of a sample mean (replacing the population standard deviation by its estimate). The analogy is that the bootstrap consists of plugging in the empirical distribution F_n for the true distribution F. Many publications discuss the bootstrap; useful references include the book by Efron and Tibshirani (1993), the Stata manual (Stata Corporation 2009), Efron's "second thoughts" on the bootstrap (2003), and a very practical chapter in Cameron and Trivedi (2009).

11.2.1   Further Considerations

When using the bootstrap to estimate the standard deviation of a statistic, one might think that the mean value of the statistic itself *over the bootstrap samples* might be a better estimator of the population value. However, it is known that if the estimator is biased, the mean value of these bootstrap estimators will be even more biased (see Stata 2011 and references listed there). This is why, in the output above, when bootstrapping the mean or median of a normal sample, the estimate of the mean and median based on the original sample are given (labeled "Observed Coefficient" in Table 11.1) in that case the sample mean and medians, rather than the average values of the mean and median for all bootstrap samples.

The bias, for example, in the sample median as an estimator of the population median, can be estimated by the difference between the average of sample medians over all bootstrap samples and the observed value on the initial sample. The command estat bootstrap executed immediately after a bootstrap run in Stata yields this bias, along with a bias-corrected confidence interval, as shown in Table 11.1.

The option to save the bootstrap sample is implemented by the code saving (filename) where in our example the 1000 values of the medians are stored. Summary statistics and a histogram of these values can then be obtained, yielding the results graphed in Fig. 11.1.

Having obtained a bootstrapped standard error for the statistic of interest (se_b), we may construct a 95% confidence interval in one of two ways. The first approach is to compute

$$\bar{x} \pm (1.96 \times se_b) \tag{11.4}$$

as shown in the Stata output displayed in Table 11.1 under the label "Normal-based" confidence intervals. An alternative, which in principle is preferable, is to compute the 2.5% and 97.5% quantiles of the (bootstrapped) distribution of the statistic.

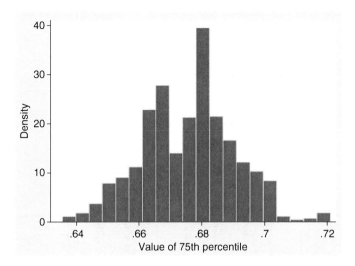

Fig. 11.1 Histogram of estimates of the 75th percentile. (*Source*: Based on the hypothetical dataset used in Table 11.1)

These need to be adjusted for the bias that occurs when using the bootstrap estimate of the statistic rather than the direct estimate. These "bias-corrected" 95% confidence intervals are labeled "(BC)" in Table 11.1.

11.3   Applications to Living Standards

One of the most useful exercises in the analysis of poverty is to make comparisons across countries or over time. Such comparisons should include measures of variability, such as 95% confidence intervals or standard errors. However, it is not always possible to compute the standard errors of poverty measures analytically, in which case we need to use bootstrapping.

An example of this appears in the work of Osberg and Xu (1999, 2000), who compare poverty across a number of developed countries using the Sen–Shorrocks–Thon (SST) index. This index is defined as

$$P_{SST} \equiv P_0 \times P_1^{poor} \times (1 + G_g). \tag{11.5}$$

This measure is a composite of three terms:

- The headcount poverty index (P_0), which measures the proportion of people whose income falls below the poverty line z.
- The poverty gap index, for the poor only (P_1^{poor}). Given income y_i, the poverty gap is defined as

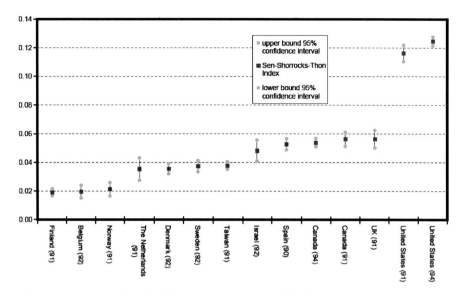

Fig. 11.2 Country rankings by SST poverty index in the 1990s. [*Source*: Osberg and Xu (1999). Reproduced with kind permission. The Poverty line is based on half the median income]

$$g_i = z - y_i, \quad z > y_i,$$
$$= 0, \quad z \leq y_i. \tag{11.6}$$

The index measures the average shortfall in income relative to the poverty line, for the poor. Thus if $z = 120$, and we have two poor people with incomes $y_1 = 110$ and $y_2 = 106$, we obtain $P_1^{poor} = (1/2)\{10/120 + 14/120\} = 10\%$. On average, these poor people have consumption levels that fall short of the poverty line by 10%.

• G_g measures the Gini coefficient for the poverty gaps. A Gini coefficient is a measure of inequality that varies from 0 (perfect equality) to 1 (complete inequality), and in the current context picks up inequality among the poor. Since the poverty gaps are rather unevenly distributed, G_g will be close to 1 in practice.

For example, based on numbers used by Osberg and Xu (1999), 12.4% of the population of Quebec province (Canada) lived in poverty in 1996; the poverty gap index for the poor was 0.272; and the Gini coefficient of the poverty gap ratios was 0.924. This yielded an SST index of 0.065.

The Sen–Shorrocks–Thon index is a complex statistic, and there is no way to calculate its standard error or distribution analytically. So Osberg and Xu (2000) generated confidence intervals using a bootstrap with 300 replications. An example of one of their charts is reproduced in Fig. 11.2, which compares the SST index in the USA with those of several European countries. The poverty line used here is half the median income, so the SST measures shown here give relative, rather than absolute poverty (and so come closer to tracking inequality than poverty).

We see immediately from Fig. 11.2 that poverty, as measured in this way, is much higher in the USA than in any of the other countries shown. The confidence intervals do not overlap, so we may conclude that this gap between the USA and its peers is real, and not a mere artifact of the samples used to compute the indexes.

11.3.1 SST Index for Vietnam

We have computed the Sen–Shorrocks–Thon index for real per capita expenditure, and associated bootstrapped confidence interval, for Vietnam, using data from the 1992–1993 Vietnam Living Standards Survey. The Stata code is shown in Table 11.2, along with the results; Fig. 11.3 shows a histogram that summarizes the distribution of the SST measure.

It is worth noting that in this case, the bootstrapped values of the SST index can be computed with allowances for clustering. As we would expect, this produces wider, and more robust, standard errors than if clustering were ignored: the SST index was 0.309, with a bootstrapped standard error of 0.0053 when clustering is ignored, and 0.0149 with clustering. This also illustrates the flexibility of bootstrap techniques.

11.3.2 Measuring Vulnerability

An interesting application of bootstrapping may be found in a study by Kamanou and Morduch (2002) of vulnerability to poverty in Côte d'Ivoire. Vulnerability to poverty measures the probability that someone will be poor in the future – for instance next year, or within the next 5 years (see Haughton and Khandker 2009). While a poverty rate measures poverty in the past ("ex post"), vulnerability tries to assess the risk of poverty in the future ("ex ante"), as discussed in Chap. 10.

Let c_{it} be consumption by individual i in time t. If z is a poverty line, the person is poor if $c_{it} < z$, and is vulnerable to poverty in the next period if $V \equiv \Pr(c_{i,t+1} \leq z) > \gamma$, where γ is some threshold (e.g., 50%). The challenge that arises here is in measuring $c_{i,t+1}$, which is the expected value of individual i's consumption in the next period.

One approach is to estimate a model of consumption. A basic version might look like this:

$$\ln c_{it} = \mathbf{x}_{it} b + e_{it}, \tag{11.7}$$

Table 11.2 Bootstrapping the Sen–Shorrocks–Thon index, Incorporating sample design: Vietnam, 1992–1993

Stata code for generating bootstraps for simulated dataset

```
* Load the data from a file called statafile.dta
use statafile, clear
program sstrobust, eclass
tempname b
SST realpcex [aw=hhsize], line(1160.842)
matrix `b' = $S_6
ereturn post `b'
end
* Check that the routine sstrobust works
sstrobust
ereturn display
* Bootstrap the results
bootstrap _b, reps(100) seed(10101) saving(ss1.dta, replace):
     sstrobust
bootstrap _b, reps(100) seed(10101) strata(urban92) cluster(commune)
     saving(ss2.dta, replace): sstrobust
estat bootstrap
use "ss1.dta", clear
histogram _b_c1, bin(10) fcolor(gray) xtitle("SST index")
```

Bootstrap results for the SST, ignoring sample design (4,799 observations)

```
------------------------------------------------------------------------------
             |   Observed   Bootstrap                            Normal-based
             |      Coef.   Std. Err.      z    P>|z|     [95% Conf. Interval]
-------------+----------------------------------------------------------------
          c1 |  .3087849     .00529     58.37   0.000     .2984166    .3191531
------------------------------------------------------------------------------

             |   Observed                Bootstrap
             |      Coef.       Bias     Std. Err.   [95% Conf. Interval]
-------------+----------------------------------------------------------------
          c1 | .30878487     .0003842   .00529003    .2979622    .318597   (BC)
------------------------------------------------------------------------------
```

Bootstrap results for the SST, adjusting for stratification and clustering

```
                              (Replications based on 150 clusters in commune)
------------------------------------------------------------------------------
             |   Observed   Bootstrap                            Normal-based
             |      Coef.   Std. Err.      z    P>|z|     [95% Conf. Interval]
-------------+----------------------------------------------------------------
          c1 |  .3087849    .014926     20.69   0.000     .2795304    .3380393
------------------------------------------------------------------------------

             |   Observed                Bootstrap
             |      Coef.       Bias     Std. Err.   [95% Conf. Interval]
-------------+----------------------------------------------------------------
          c1 | .30878487    -.0003162   .014926      .2831463    .341656    (BC)
------------------------------------------------------------------------------
```

where $\mathbf{x}_{it}$ is a vector of observable characteristics of the individual (such as age and education), and the household and neighborhood in which the individual lives. The model in (11.7) can be estimated using cross-section data. Then we can use variables for the next period, $t + 1$, such as age in the next period, to obtain predictions $\hat{c}_{i,t+1}$ for each individual.

One further step is needed: for each individual, we need a value of $\hat{e}_{i,t+1}$ that reflects the idiosyncratic shock that an individual might face. If we are willing to assume a parametric distribution, such as $\hat{e}_{i,t+1} \sim N(0, \theta)$, then we can calculate

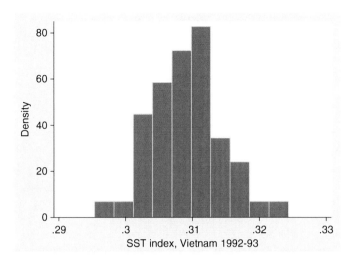

Fig. 11.3 Histogram of bootstrap values of Sen–Shorrocks–Thon index, Vietnam 1992–1993. (*Source*: As for Table 11.2)

the probability that $\hat{c}_{i,t+1} + \hat{e}_{i,t+1}$ will fall below the poverty line, thereby generating our measure of vulnerability; Haughton and Khandker (2009) provide further details.

An alternative, and elegant, approach is to sample randomly from the empirical distribution of the residuals $\hat{e}_{i,t}$. This generates a value of $\hat{\hat{c}}_{i,t+1}(= \hat{c}_{i,t+1} + \hat{e}^b_{i,t+1})$ for each individual, which we can compare to the poverty line to determine whether the individual is expected to be poor or not. However, this is just a single estimate of $\hat{\hat{c}}_{i,t+1}$, and in order to determine the *probability* of poverty, we need a distribution for $\hat{\hat{c}}_{i,t+1}$. This can be obtained by sampling repeatedly from $\hat{e}_{i,t}$, in other words, by using the bootstrap. Then, for each individual in the sample, we have a probability that the person will be poor in the next period, and we may tabulate the results, showing the proportion of the population that is highly vulnerable (i.e., have a greater than 50% probability of being poor in the next period), moderately vulnerable, and so on.

Kamanou and Morduch (2002) actually perform a double bootstrap. Using data from the 1985 Côte d'Ivoire Living Standards Survey, they randomly pick a bootstrap sample (with replacement) from the 1,600 households covered by the survey, and estimate the coefficients in (11.7). They then randomly pick from the residuals of this equation in order to construct a vector of $\hat{\hat{c}}_{i,t+1}, j = 1, \ldots, 1,600$, and measure the poverty rate. They repeat this 1,000 times, which produces what they refer to as the bootstrap headcount poverty rate. This may be compared with either the observed headcount in 1985, or the (newly) observed headcount measured based on a survey undertaken in 1986.

For example, they find that the headcount poverty rate in Abidjan in 1985 was 25%; their bootstrap estimate of the poverty rate for 1986 was 35%; and the actual poverty rate in 1986 was 23%. They thus conclude that more people in Abidjan were vulnerable to poverty than actually became poor.

11.4 Bootstrapping Inequality and Regression

The bootstrap does have some limitations, notably when attempting to estimate variation in measures such as the Gini coefficient, which tends to be sensitive to outlying values. We mention here recent attempts to remedy this situation by Davidson (2009) and Davidson and Flachaire (2007).

Davidson and Flachaire (2007) warn that even in large samples and large numbers of bootstrap samples, bootstrapping indices of inequality such as the Gini coefficient (or the Theil index) tends to be problematic, because of the influence of outlying values, although bootstrapping other poverty measures such as the SST (Sen–Shorrocks–Thon) index may work well enough. As remedies, they propose two nonstandard versions of the bootstrap, the "*m out of n*" bootstrap, and a bootstrap in which the upper tail is modeled parametrically.

More recently, Davidson (2009) has revisited the case of the Gini index, and proposes a bootstrap method that corrects for bias. His own tests indicate that his approach to measuring the asymptotic distribution of the Gini index behaves "at least as well as other proposed distributions" (p. 38). He also develops an expression for correcting for bias in bootstrap estimates of the distribution of the Sen–Shorrocks–Thon index of poverty.

11.4.1 Regression

There are a variety of possible resampling schemes that one may use when bootstrapping. Suppose that our interest is in bootstrapping standard errors for the coefficients of a regression equation. One possibility is to use a *paired bootstrap*, where we resample from the original data for the dependent variable y and the independent variables $\mathbf{x}$, with replacement. Each run will generate a slightly different estimate of the coefficient vector β, from which we may obtain confidence intervals or standard errors.

An alternative approach, if we may assume that the errors are iid, is to do a *residual* (or *design*) *bootstrap*. We first estimate the regression equation $y_i = \mathbf{x}'_i\beta + e_i$ from which we obtain the original residuals $\hat{e}_i$. We then make bootstrap draws from the residuals, and add them to $\mathbf{x}'_i\hat{\beta}$ to obtain a set of y_i^*, which we then regress on the $\mathbf{x}'_i$. Here again we obtain a distribution of the estimated coefficients, and the performance may be better than with a paired bootstrap.

In practice, we typically have heteroscedastic disturbances. In the case of linear regression this can be accommodated by using the *wild bootstrap*. As with the residual bootstrap, we first generate a set of original residuals $\hat{e}_i$. But now, we transform these residuals before adding them to $\mathbf{x}'_i\hat{\beta}$, by first multiplying them by an auxiliary distribution: a popular choice is to multiply either by -0.618034 (with probability 0.723607) or by -1.618034 (with probability 0.276393). Odd as this procedure might appear, the wild bootstrap has become increasingly popular; for further details, see Cameron and Trivedi (2009, p. 440), or Davidson and Flachaire (2008).

One of the more useful applications of bootstrapping is in the context of the Hausman test, which is used to determine whether the estimates from two different estimators – for instance, OLS and instrumental variables – are significantly different from one another. The standard test requires that one of the estimators be fully efficient. This strong and awkward assumption can be relaxed by bootstrapping the variance–covariance matrix of the difference in estimates; Cameron and Trivedi (2009, pp. 429–430) provide details and some Stata code.

11.5   Has Poverty Changed?

According to the 1992–1993 Vietnam Living Standards Survey, the headcount poverty rate in the country then stood at 55.2%. Using the same poverty line and a very similar questionnaire and sampling frame, the 1997–1998 VLSS found a poverty rate of 32.6%. The question to be asked here is this: was the reduction in the poverty rate between these two dates statistically significant?

A common approach to such a question is to apply a t-test.[1] In this example, the standard error of the difference in poverty rates is 0.94%, while the difference itself was 22.6%; the 95% confidence interval for this difference was therefore (20.8%, 24.4%), so there can be little doubt that the poverty rate fell. If we take into account clustering by commune, as we should, the confidence interval widens to (17.0%, 28.2%); further details are shown in Table 11.3.

But the issue is more interesting than this. Of the 4,800 households surveyed in 1992–1993, 4,306 were re-interviewed in 1997–1998. Thus the observations are not entirely independent between the two samples, and the application of the standard t-test is incorrect. Instead, one could apply a paired t-test to the subset of households that were surveyed in both years. This yields a standard error for the difference in poverty rates of 0.79%, which is tighter than the unpaired test, and yields a 95% confidence interval for the difference in poverty rate of (20.9%, 24.0%).

---

[1] The poverty rate is a proportion; because this distribution is nonnormal it would be more appropriate to use a χ^2 test in this case. For large samples, such as the one here, the use of a t-test will give a similar result, and for the purposes of this chapter we also wanted to illustrate the use of the t-test in this context.

Table 11.3 Conventional and bootstrap measures of confidence in differences in poverty rates, Vietnam 1993–1998

```
use "povobs.dta", clear

capture program drop povratediff
program povratediff, rclass
tempvar y diff z
sum poor93
gen `y'=r(mean)
sum poor98 [aw=wt]
gen `z' = r(mean)
gen `diff' = `z'-`y'
sum `diff'
return list
return scalar diff1=r(mean)
end

bootstrap r(diff1), reps(100) saving(keep1.dta): povratediff
bootstrap r(diff1), reps(100) cluster(comno) saving(keep2.dta):
        povratediff
estat bootstrap
```

	Difference (%)	se of diffence (%)	95% conf. interval	
			Lower	Upper
t-test, standard	22.6	0.94	20.8	24.4
t-test, clustering	22.6	2.86	17.0	28.3
Bootstrap, standard	22.6	0.77	21.1	24.1
Bootstrap, clustering	22.6	1.98	18.7	26.5
Panel: t-test unpaired	22.5	1.04	20.5	24.5
Panel: t-test, paired	22.5	0.79	20.9	24.1
Panel: t-test, bootstrap	22.5	0.79	20.9	24.1

Bootstrap results: without, and with, clustering

```
-----------------------------------------------------------------------
          |   Observed   Bootstrap                      Normal-based
          |     Coef.    Std. Err.      z    P>|z|    [95% Conf. Interval]
----------+------------------------------------------------------------
     _bs_1 |  -.2259238  .0077182   -29.27   0.000   -.2410513   -.2107964
-----------------------------------------------------------------------

          |   Observed   Bootstrap                      Normal-based
          |     Coef.    Std. Err.      z    P>|z|    [95% Conf. Interval]
----------+------------------------------------------------------------
     _bs_1 |  -.2259238  .0198047   -11.41   0.000   -.2647403   -.1871073
-----------------------------------------------------------------------
```

Neither approach is ideal. The unpaired *t*-test is not as precise as it could be, because it ignores the information that is included in the paired data, and is incorrect because it assumes the datasets are independent. On the other hand, the paired *t*-test ignores the information from all those households that were not sampled twice.

A solution is to bootstrap the results, using the code that is set out in Table 11.3. We have a partial panel, but have pooled the data for the 2 years; between the 4,800 observations in 1993 and 5,999 observations in 1998 we have a total of 6,496 different households. Some rows have observations for households surveyed in

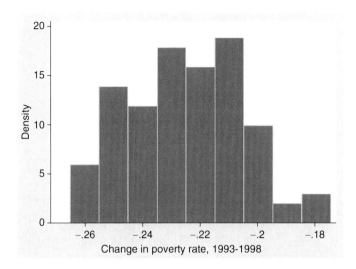

Fig. 11.4 Histogram of bootstrapped changes in poverty rate in Vietnam between 1993 and 1998. (*Source*: Vietnam Living Standards Surveys of 2003 and 2008)

1993 and not 1998, some rows for those surveyed in 1998 but not 1993, and many rows for those surveyed in both years. For each household we have a binary variable that is set to 1 if they were poor in the year in question, to 0 if they were not poor, and to "·" (missing) if they were not surveyed in that year.

Now we draw a sample with replacement from the total file of 6,496 observations, and compute the difference in the average poverty rate between these two periods; this is done by the povratediff program (see Table 11.3). The average poverty rates in each year are computed based on the non-missing observations for that year.

The results are set out in the bottom part of Table 11.3. If clustering is ignored, the bootstrapped standard error is 0.77, which is smaller than either the standard *t*-test, or the paired *t*-test applied to the panel. With clustering, the bootstrapped standard error is 1.98, which is substantially smaller than the value of 2.86 that applied in the standard *t*-test. In short, we have been able to use bootstrapping to optimize our use of information, and get the tightest plausible confidence intervals for measuring changes in poverty over time (Fig. 11.4).

11.6 Conclusion

Bootstrapping has quickly become an established part of the toolkit of anyone working with household survey data. Often, it is the only method that will work; and sometimes it is simply the easiest approach to measuring variability, although it cannot usually be applied mechanistically.

Clearly, there is no longer any excuse for not presenting measures of variability when publishing statistics on poverty, inequality, or for that matter any other measurable social or economic magnitude. Yet it is surprising how often poverty rates, for instance, are presented as single numbers, without confidence intervals or standard errors, leaving the reader with a false sense of security in the apparent accuracy of the data.

References

Cameron, Colin, and Pravin Trivedi. 2009. *Microeconometrics using Stata*. College Station: Stata Press.
Davidson, Russell. 2009. Reliable inference for the Gini index. *Journal of Econometrics* 150: 30–40.
Davidson, Russell, and Emmanuel Flachaire. 2007. Asymptotic and bootstrap inference for inequality and poverty measures. *Journal of Econometrics* 141: 141–166.
Davidson, Russell, and Emmanuel Flachaire. 2008. The wild bootstrap, tamed at last. *Journal of Econometrics* 146: 162–169.
Efron, B. 1979. Bootstrap methods: Another look at the jackknife. *Annals of Statistics* 7(1): 1–26.
Efron, B. 2003. Second thoughts on the bootstrap. *Statistical Science* 18(2): 135–140.
Efron, B., and R.J. Tibshirani. 1993. *An introduction to the bootstrap*. New York: Chapman & Hall/CRC.
Haughton, Jonathan, and Shahidur Khandker. 2009. *Handbook on poverty and inequality*. Washington, DC: World Bank.
Kamanou, Gisele, and Jonathan Morduch. 2002. Measuring vulnerability to poverty, Discussion Paper No. 2002/58. World Institute for Development Economics Research, United Nations University, Helsinki.
Osberg, Lars, and Kuan Xu. 1999. Poverty intensity: How well do Canadian provinces compare? *Canadian Public Policy-Analyse de Politiques* 25(2): 179–195.
Osberg, Lars, and Kuan Xu. 2000. International comparisons of poverty intensity: Index decomposition and bootstrap inference. *Journal of Human Resources* 25(1): 51–81.
Stata Corporation. 2009. *Stata 11.0 manual*. College Station: Stata Press.

Chapter 12
Impact Evaluation

12.1 Introduction

A government sets up a scheme for extending microcredit to farmers; or builds an irrigation canal; or provides free textbooks to 10-year-olds; or introduces supplemental nutrition for pregnant mothers; or strengthens the social security net with a food-for-work program.

All of these activities sound potentially promising. But do they really work? Increasingly, governments and donors want clear and rigorous answers before channeling funds into such schemes. And that calls for an impact evaluation.

Generally, an impact evaluation seeks to measure the changes in well-being that can be attributed to a particular project or policy (an "intervention" or "treatment"). The results of an impact evaluation can show which interventions have been effective, and so inform decisions on whether they should be eliminated, modified or expanded, and what priority they should be accorded. Impact evaluations are also essential pre-requisites for *ex post* cost–benefit or cost–effectiveness analyses, which weigh program costs against the benefits they deliver.

Impact evaluations are expensive and can be technically complex. Baker (2000, p.79) lists the expenses of undertaking seven high-quality impact evaluation studies: the average cost was $433,000, representing 0.56% of total project costs, with half of the expense going to data collection. It thus makes sense to undertake an impact evaluation only if (a) the policy or program is of strategic importance, or is innovative, and (b) the information from the evaluation is likely to fill gaps in current knowledge, and (c) someone might act on the basis of the results. This latter point is worth emphasizing, because not everyone welcomes impact evaluations. Every evaluation carries the risk that it will find that a program was ineffective or an organization might no longer be justified. In 2006 we were approached to undertake an impact evaluation of a large project in a middle-income country, but were then made to understand that such an evaluation would only be acceptable if it made the sponsoring agency look good (and ultimately the evaluation was not funded).

D. Haughton and J. Haughton, *Living Standards Analytics*, Statistics for Social
and Behavioral Sciences, DOI 10.1007/978-1-4614-0385-2_12,
© Springer Science+Business Media, LLC 2011

In this chapter, we set out and appraise the main approaches to impact evaluation. In addition to using illustrations from the academic literature, we draw extensively on a study of the impact of a major microcredit scheme in Thailand in order to show how the techniques of impact evaluation are applied. For a recent book-length treatment, see Khandker et al. (2010).

12.2   General Principles

The central idea of impact evaluation is straightforward: we need to compare the actual outcome of the intervention with our evaluation of what would have happened in the absence of the intervention (the *counterfactual*). The central challenge of impact assessment is constructing a plausible counterfactual.

The challenge is a difficult one. Consider the case of a program that provides additional food – maize, milk powder – to poor mothers with infants. Now suppose that the data show that the mothers and infants covered by the program are less well nourished than those who are not covered. Are we to conclude that the project is a failure?

Perhaps; but then again, it is likely that the project targeted poor mothers with malnourished infants – that was probably the whole point of the program! – so it is not surprising that households with underweight children are getting additional food. The problem here is one of estimating how malnourished the mothers and infants covered by the program would have been in the absence of the program, in other words, establishing an appropriate counterfactual (Ravallion 1999).

12.2.1   Case: The Thailand Village Fund

We illustrate many of the ideas of this chapter using as an example the evaluation of the impact of a major microcredit scheme in Thailand. In this section we provide the relevant background for this example, which is based on Boonperm et al. (2009).

In 2001 the newly elected government of Thaksin Shinawatra and the Thai Rak Thai Party established the Thailand Village and Urban Revolving Fund (VRF) program, which proposed to provide a million baht (about $22,500) to every village and urban community in Thailand as working capital for locally run rotating credit associations. Since there are almost 74,000 villages and over 4,500 urban communities in the country, this represented an injection of about 75 billion baht, equivalent to about $1.75 billion. The program was put into place rapidly, reaching over 90% of villages by 2004. By the end of May 2005 the TVF committees had lent a total of 258 billion baht ($6.9 billion) in 17.8 million loans, representing an average loan of $387. Total repayment of principal came to 168 million baht, leaving outstanding principal of 91 billion baht.

The question to be asked is whether the VRF had an impact on household expenditures, income, and asset accumulation. It is not self-evident that there

Table 12.1 Summary of use of Thailand Village Revolving Credit Fund, 2004

	All	Poorest fifth	Rural	Female
Number of observations (adults)	80,950	13,180	30,892	43,916
Expenditure per capita (baht/month)	3,398	1,060	2,578	3,427
Adult obtained ≥ 1 VRF loan since 2002 (%)	17	20	22	16
Reason for *not* borrowing from VRF				
No need (%)	29	16	25	29
Did not like to be in debt (%)	30	38	33	30
Amount borrowed (baht)	16,183	17,312	16,462	15,322
Annualized interest rate (%)	6.0	5.8	5.9	6.1
Main objective for obtaining loan				
Agricultural equipment/inputs (%)	40	45	42	35
Buy animals	10	12	10	8
Borrowed elsewhere to repay VRF loan (%)	16	19	17	17

Source: Boonperm et al. (2009)

would be any effect: If financial markets operate well – information is cheap and readily available, there are no policy distortions – then households should already have access to as much credit as they can productively use, and they would just substitute VRF credit for other sources of credit. On the other hand, it is not unreasonable to think that there are imperfections in the market for credit: credit markets have well-known informational asymmetries that village-level credit associations may be able to attenuate, given their (presumably) better knowledge about the ability of villager households to service loans.

The data for the impact evaluation come from the Thailand Socioeconomic Surveys of 2002 and 2004. The 2004 survey interviewed 34,843 households (representing 116,444 people) throughout the country. The data were collected in four rounds, spread throughout the year, and the survey used stratified random sampling (by province) with clustering. The 2002 survey used substantially the same questionnaire and covered 34,785 households. Both surveys collected information on income and expenditure, as well as an array of other socioeconomic variables. An effort was made in 2004 to resurvey all 6,309 households that had been surveyed in rural areas in rounds 2 and 3 of the 2002 survey; of these, 5,755 households were actually resurveyed, representing an annual attrition rate of 4.5%.

A selection of summary information on the VRF is shown in Table 12.1, and come from a special module that was included in the 2004 socioeconomic survey and that asked all adult members of households about their experiences with the VRF. By 2004 a sixth of all adults had borrowed at least once from the VRF, with higher proportions of borrowers among the poor and in rural areas. Adults in 31% of households had borrowed from the VRF by 2004, with an average loan of 16,183 baht ($390). Among those who did not borrow, 29% said they did not need a loan and 30% said that they did not want to be in debt. Proponents of the VRF had hoped and expected that it would mainly stimulate non-farm business, but in over half of all cases borrowers reported that their main objective for obtaining the loan was to purchase agricultural inputs, animals, or farm land.

It is striking that VRF borrowers had significantly lower incomes (3,209 baht per person per month) than the full sample (4,987 baht). But clearly one cannot conclude that the fund made people poorer. It follows that a more sophisticated method is needed to try to measure the impact of the VRF than a simple comparison of outcomes between the treated group (i.e., borrowers) and the comparators (i.e., nonborrowers).

12.2.2 A More Formal Treatment

It is helpful to treat the problem somewhat more formally. Let us suppose that we are interested in the impact of a program on some outcome variable Y_i. This will often be a standard monetary measure of well-being such as income or expenditure per capita, but there are many other possibilities, depending on the issue at hand, such as school performance, household assets, nutritional levels, and the like. We have observations of Y_i for each unit i (e.g., individual, household) from a sample of size n.

Some of the units have been subject to the intervention ("treated"), in which case we let $T_i = 1$; the remainder are untreated, in which case $T_i = 0$. Following the notation favored by Ravallion (2008), let Y_i^T be the value of the outcome for unit i under treatment and Y_i^C be the outcome for unit i if not treated (i.e., under the counterfactual). The gain from the treatment for any unit i is defined as

$$G_i \equiv Y_i^T - Y_i^C. \tag{12.1}$$

This is the impact (or "causal effect") of the program that we want to measure. But we cannot do this directly, because an individual is either in the treatment group (so we observe Y_i^T) or the comparison group (so we observe Y_i^C), but never in both. Thus we are faced with a problem of missing data.

In practice we are usually interested in estimating the average impact of a program or project. There is more than one way to construct an average based on (12.1). The commonest measure is the average treatment effect on the treated, given by the expected gain

$$G^{TT} = E(Y_i^T - Y_i^C \mid T_i = 1), \tag{12.2}$$

where $E(\cdot)$ is the expectations operator. The G^{TT} measure averages the impact over those who are actually treated, for whom $T_i = 1$. In these cases we observe Y_i^T but have to figure out a way to estimate Y_i^C. Analysts and politicians are most often interested in knowing whether a program benefited those for whom it was intended, in which case G^{TT} is the appropriate measure. Occasionally researchers are interested in the average treatment effect on the untreated:

$$G^{TU} = E(Y_i^T - Y_i^C \mid T_i = 0), \tag{12.3}$$

in which case we observe Y_i^C but not Y_i^T. The combined average treatment effect is a weighted average of these two effects, given by

$$G^{ATE} = G^{TT} \Pr(T = 1) + G^{TU} \Pr(T = 0), \tag{12.4}$$

and is also widely used.

A number of methods ("evaluation designs") have been developed to measure the average impacts, and we examine them in more detail below. But a natural place to start would be to try to measure the impact of a program by taking the difference in the outcome variable between the treated and the untreated. This unconditional single difference estimate is given by

$$D = E(Y_i^T \mid T_i = 1) - E(Y_i^C \mid T_i = 0). \tag{12.5}$$

In the case of our example of the Thailand Village Fund we have, for per capita income (in baht per month) in 2004

$$D = 3,209 - 6,088 = -2,879$$

and for per capita expenditure

$$D = 2,549 - 4,286 = -1,737.$$

Taken at face value, this would imply that borrowing from the Village Fund left households worse off, which is hardly credible.

The problem is that this simple difference is typically subject to bias. Quite generally,

$$D = G^{TT} + B \tag{12.6}$$

where the selection bias (B) is given by

$$B = E(Y_i^C \mid T_i = 1) - E(Y_i^C \mid T_i = 0). \tag{12.7}$$

The bias is given by the difference in outcomes, without the treatment, between those who are treated and those who are not. We note in passing that the first term in (12.7) is not observed, so the bias cannot be measured directly.

Consider the case of an anti-poverty program that is targeted at raising the incomes of poor households. Then, by design, the treated are likely to be poorer than the untreated, so

$$E(Y_i^C \mid T_i = 1) < E(Y_i^C \mid T_i = 0), \tag{12.8}$$

which means that the bias is negative. It follows from (12.6) that in such cases the simple difference in outcomes (such as income) between the treated and untreated group, given by D, will underestimate the impact G^{TT}.

The bias disappears if we can assume that the assignment of treatment, conditional on a set of covariates X, is independent of the value of the outcomes. This is the key assumption on which all impact evaluation rests. Imbens (2004, p. 7) formalizes it as the assumption of *unconfoundedness*:

$$(Y_i^T, Y_i^C) \perp T_i \mid X_i, \tag{12.9}$$

where $\perp$ is the independence operator. In other words, we need to assume that the treatments are not assigned in a way that is systematically related to the outcome variable, once we have controlled for the effects of the X covariates. Depending on the author and the literature, (12.9) is also referred to as the assumption of ignorable treatment assignment; or the conditional independence assumption; or the approach of selection on observables.

Every impact assessment has to make the case that unconfoundedness (or a slightly weaker version such as conditional exogeneity of treatment, addressed below) is plausible, because otherwise it is impossible to identify the effects of the treatment.

12.3   Experimental Design

One elegant way to ensure unconfoundedness, and thereby to solve the problem of bias, to assign treatments randomly. This *experimental design* approach ensures, by construction, that the expected value of the outcome variables can be assumed to be the same for the treatment group and the *control group* in the absence of treatment, which means that in this case

$$B = E(Y_i^C \mid T_i = 1) - E(Y_i^C \mid T_i = 0) = 0. \tag{12.10}$$

Having eliminated bias, the single difference in the mean values of the outcome variables between the control and treatment groups (12.5) can be attributed to the effects of the intervention, give or take some sampling error. Equivalently, the impact may be measured by the estimated coefficient $\hat{b}$ from the following regression:

$$Y_i = a + bT_i + \varepsilon_i \tag{12.11}$$

Table 12.2 Examination results (% of correct answers), practice exams for the Kenya Certificate of Primary Education, 8th grade, Busia and Teso districts

	School got flip charts	School did not get flip charts	Difference	SD of difference
July 1997	45.5	46.0	−0.5	12.5
July 1998	42.7	42.9	−0.3	11.2

Source: Glewwe et al. (2000)

where ε_i is an error term that is assumed to be normally distributed with variance σ^2, Y_i is defined as

$$Y_i \equiv Y_i^T T_i + Y_i^C (1 - T_i) \tag{12.12}$$

and T_i takes on a value of one if the unit is treated, and of zero otherwise. Estimating (12.11) makes it particularly easy to obtain a confidence interval for the treatment effect.

12.3.1 Case Study: Flip Charts in Kenya

Glewwe et al. (2000) present an interesting, if rare, example of pure randomization. The question that they address is whether flip charts – large, spiral-bound wall charts that can be used in high school classrooms – improve student learning, as measured by test scores. In 1997, a Dutch NGO provided funding for flip charts in 89 schools in the relatively poor Busia and Teso districts of western Kenya. The schools were chosen randomly from a total of 178 schools in these districts and the charts were distributed in early 1997.

The essential results of the study are shown in Table 12.2, and represent the percent of correct responses on standardized national tests given to eighth-graders. As one would expect with random assignment, in July 1997 the test scores did not differ between the schools that received flip charts and those that did not; this test was administered shortly after the flip charts were distributed and represents a benchmark position. Interestingly, there was no statistical difference in test scores between treatment and control schools in the July 1998 tests either, suggesting that the flip charts did not affect academic performance, even though Glewwe et al. found that teachers knew about the flip charts and used them regularly, and none of them had been lost. More complete regression results confirm the essential conclusion: the flip charts had no discernible effect.

The Dutch NGO also provided flip charts to a hundred schools elsewhere in Kenya, but the schools were not chosen randomly (although how they were selected is not entirely clear). Glewwe et al. compared the examination scores of schools that were given flipcharts with a comparison group of those that were not, and obtained the following regression results:

$$\text{Test scores} = 0.192 \text{ Number of flipcharts} + \text{School random effects},$$
$$\text{SE} = 0.080$$
$$+ \text{ Subject and grade fixed effects.}$$

The key point here is that flip charts in this case are associated with substantially higher test scores. Indeed the effect is twice as strong as that of providing textbooks, a measure that would cost ten times as much! Glewwe et al. argue that these latter results do not provide evidence that flip charts work; it is entirely possible that schools that received flipcharts were different in some systematic (but unobserved) way – perhaps they were more accessible, or richer – and these characteristics cannot be disentangled from the effects of the flip charts. This is a classic case of omitted variables bias, and underscores the importance of random assignment when conducting social experiments.

Another good example of a study that uses randomization is the research by Angrist et al. (2002) on school vouchers in Colombia. In 1991, the government of Colombia established the PACES (Programa de Ampliacion de Cobertura de la Educacion Secundaria[1]) program, which provided vouchers (i.e., scholarships) to students who had applied to and been accepted into private secondary schools. The vouchers were awarded based on a lottery; this provided the randomization that allowed the authors to compare the outcomes for applicants who received vouchers with the outcomes for those who did not.

One of the more interesting findings of this study is that voucher winners were 15–16 percentage points more likely to be in a private school when they were surveyed in 1998. It also appears that the program had a positive and significant effect on the number of years of schooling completed: Those who received vouchers in 1995 in the capital (Bogotá) completed 0.12–0.16 more years than those who did not. Furthermore, repetition rates fell significantly as a result of the project: In the 1995 Bogotá sample, the probability of repetition was reduced by 5–6 percentage points for lottery winners.

12.3.2 *Partial Randomization*

Pure randomization, which would be required for (12.11) to be appropriate, "is virtually inconceivable for anti-poverty programs" (Ravallion 2008, p. 19); after all, the point is that such programs should be geared to helping the poor, and so they are unlikely to be relevant or appropriate for a significant segment of society.

Thus in practice it is more common to find *partial randomization*, under which the treatment and control samples are chosen randomly, conditional on some

---

[1] "Program for the Expansion of Educational Coverage."

observable variables, X, that might include measures such as location, or age of the head of the household.

This *conditional exogeneity of program placement* may allow one to estimate the impact of a treatment using a parametric model with controls. Suppose that we may assume

$$Y_i^T = \alpha^T + X_i \beta^T + v_i^T, \quad i = 1, ..., n \quad (12.13a)$$

$$Y_i^C = \alpha^C + X_i \beta^C + v_i^C, \quad i = 1, ..., n \quad (12.13b)$$

where the error terms are normally distributed with zero means and constant variances. These two equations are often estimated together in the form of a switching regression using the pooled data from both the treatment and control samples, giving

$$Y_i = \alpha^C + (\alpha^T - \alpha^C)T_i + X_i \beta^C + X_i (\beta^T - \beta^C)T_i + \varepsilon_i^T, \quad i = 1, ..., n \quad (12.14)$$

where T_i takes on the values of one or zero and the error term now takes the form $\varepsilon_i = T_i(v_i^T - v_i^C) + v_i^C$.[2] If we may assume that the error term (the "latent effects") has zero mean conditional on the X covariates and treatment – a reasonable assumption if there is even partial randomization – then we have $E(v_i^T|X, T = t) = E(v_i^C|X, T = t) = 0$, $t = 0, 1$, and we can get consistent estimates of the average treatment effects by applying OLS to (12.14), and noting that[3]

$$G^{ATE} = E[\alpha^T - \alpha^C + X_i(\beta^T - \beta^C)]. \quad (12.15)$$

If we are also willing to assume (more problematically) that $\beta^T = \beta^C$ – the *common-impact model* – then the average treatment effect reduces to $\alpha^T - \alpha^C$.

12.3.3 Randomization Evaluated

Randomized experiments have been called "the gold standard for scientific experimentation" (Murray 2005, p. 17; Rubin and Waterman 2006, p. 210), but this overstates the case. Often the most serious problem with randomized experiments is that the withholding of treatment may be unethical. For instance, if we are trying to determine the effects of providing Vitamin A supplementation, which helps prevent blindness, it is likely to be unethical to withhold this very inexpensive treatment from significant numbers of young children. And once the treatment is applied universally there is no control group.

---

[2] Note that $Y_i^T = Y_i I_{T_i=1}$ where I_A denotes the indicator function of an event (1 if A occurs, 0 if not). We also have $Y_i^C = Y_i I_{T_i=0}$.

[3] We have that $G^{ATE} = E(Y_i I_{T_i=1}) - E(Y_i I_{T_i=0})$ since $G^{ATE} = E((Y_i I_{T_i=1} - Y_i I_{T_i=0})I_{T_i=1} + E((Y_i I_{T_i=1} - Y_i I_{T_i=0})I_{T_i=0}$ by the definition of conditional expectations.

The counterargument is that, when resources are limited, random assignment of treatment is fair and, moreover, it is also efficient inasmuch as it allows one to generate information that might steer more resources to a worthy program than would otherwise flow there.

In practice, it is often politically difficult to provide a treatment to one group and not to another. A recent proposal to provide $100 gifts to a random sample of Vietnamese households, with the eventual purpose of estimating a pure income effect on expenditure, was turned down by the national statistics office because it was considered to be invidious.

True random assignment is often difficult in practice, since it is rare to find an up-to-date and definitive list of all households (or individuals) in the population of interest. Moreover, even if eligibility for a program is assigned randomly, actual participation may not be, if those who decline to participate are nonrepresentative. For instance, a study of those eligible to borrow microloans from the Grameen Bank in Bangladesh found that those who did not borrow expressed more worry about their ability to repay loans than those who did borrow. Selective compliance of this kind compromises the internal validity of the impact evaluation.

Even when initial participation in a program is random, there is often selective attrition. There can also be selective uptake over time, for instance if people with sick children move to villages where health clinics were (randomly) established, again contaminating the results.

There are additional problems with randomized (or any) experiments, which sometimes limit their ability to yield worthwhile information for impact evaluation. Some experiments have spillover effects; for instance, a project to treat children against worms is likely to help untreated children too, since they are now less likely to come into contact with worms. But this makes it difficult to find a suitable control group. In other cases, projects could not be scaled up without creating macroeconomic effects – for instance, a small-scale job-training project might not affect overall wage rates, while a large-scale one would – in which case the impact as measured on the pilot project would be a poor guide to the impact of the project replicated on a national scale.

In some cases, the results of an experiment may be warped by the Hawthorne ("expectancy") effect, which occurs when the simple fact of being included in an experiment may affect behavior nonrandomly. And social experiments tend to be expensive, with the consequence that they are usually applied to small samples, which in turn makes inference less precise.

While (randomized) social experiments can be useful, they are no panacea for impact evaluation, and in practice most impact assessments have to rely on quasi-experimental methods, also referred to as "observational studies" or "nonexperimental evaluations," to which we now turn.

12.4   Quasi-Experimental Methods

If households are not assigned randomly to an intervention – such as food stamps, or vaccinations, or irrigation water – then those who benefit are unlikely to be typical of the eligible population. There are two main reasons for this. First, there may be nonrandom program placement, of which the researcher may or may not be aware; for instance, an anti-poverty program may be more likely to be set up in poor villages. This is the problem of *unobserved area heterogeneity*. Second, there may be self-selection into program participation; for instance, more-dynamic individuals may be the first to sign up, or program benefits may flow to those who are politically well-connected, or sick people may move to villages that have been equipped with clinics. Such effects are often hard to detect, and give rise to the problem of *unobserved individual and household heterogeneity*.

The presence of these unobservables immediately brings us back to the problem of selection bias. To see why it arises here, let us return to the case of the Thailand Village Fund. Our interest here is in determining whether this microcredit scheme has any impact on individual incomes.

A reasonable place to start would be to collect data on the outcome indicator (expenditure, for instance, given by Y_i), and on individual and household characteristics (X_i), for a sample of individuals that do $(T_i = 1)$, and do not $(T_i = 0)$, participate in the scheme, and to use this information to estimate a common-impact equation of the following form:

$$Y_i = \alpha^C + (\alpha^T - \alpha^C)T_i + X_i\beta + \varepsilon_i, \quad i = 1, ..., n \qquad (12.16)$$

This is the *common-impact model*, and may be derived from (12.14) by setting $\beta^T = \beta^C$. At first sight it would appear that the value of the estimated coefficient on participation (i.e., $\alpha^T - \alpha^C$) would measure the impact of the microcredit scheme on income.

Unfortunately this is unlikely to be the case, because program participation is often related to the other individual, household and village variables, some of which may not be observable. For instance, those who borrow money may be better educated, or younger, or live in villages with a loan office, or be more motivated. The degree of individual motivation is an unobservable; but a more motivated individual is more likely to participate in the program (a higher probability of $T_i = 1$) and to benefit more from it (a higher Y_i). This implies that there is a correlation between T_i and ε_i and so leads to a biased estimate of $\alpha^T - \alpha^C$. As a practical matter there will always be unobservables in such circumstances, and so there will always be some selection bias (which may also be thought of as a form of omitted variable bias).

Table 12.3 Treatment effects for Thailand Village Fund borrowing, common-impact equations, 2004

	Coefficient	t-statistic	Variables	R^2
1. All data: $N = 34{,}843$	−0.383	−47.42	1	0.060
2. All data: $N = 34{,}843$	−0.213	−30.42	6	0.331
3. All data: $N = 34{,}843$	−0.036	−5.47	28	0.497
4. All data: $N = 34{,}843$	0.023	3.69	103	0.558
5. Common support[a]: $N = 34{,}648$	0.023	3.69	103	0.555
6. P-score 0.2–0.8[b]: $N = 21{,}274$	0.031	4.53	103	0.399

[a]Common support refers to region of common support as determined by propensity score equation
[b]P-score indicates propensity score
Source: Based on data from Thailand Socioeconomic Survey, 2004

This point may be made more forcefully with the help of the numbers in Table 12.3, which are based on the estimation of the common-impact model using data from the Thailand Socioeconomic Survey of 2004. Each row in the table shows the key result from a separate regression, in which the dependent variable is the log of per capita household expenditure. The "coefficient" column reports the estimate of the impact of borrowing from the Village Revolving Fund; it is an estimate of $(\alpha^T - \alpha^C)$ in (12.16), using our terminology. The first regression includes only a dummy variable that indicated whether one borrows or not, and no other variables; in effect this shows that per capita expenditure levels are about 32% (i.e., $1 - e^{-0.382}$) lower for VRF borrowers than for nonborrowers. This comparison would only be a legitimate measure of the impact of borrowing if there were random assignment, which is not the case here.

In the second row of Table 12.3 we re-estimate (12.16), including five additional variables (the X_i), including the age and educational level of the head of the household. This improves the fit of the equation and reduces the measured impact of borrowing. As we add more covariates (rows 3 and 4) the equation fits better, of course, and the measured impact of borrowing changes dramatically. In the fourth equation, which includes dummy variables for each province in Thailand, the measured impact of borrowing appears to be positive – it raises per capita expenditure by about 2.3% – and statistically significant. We still do not know whether this is a correct measure of impact, since there may well be further relevant covariates that we have not observed, or cannot observe, but it is more plausible than the measures in rows 1 through 3.

Rows 5 and 6 of Table 12.3 show the effects of estimating the common-impact model using a subsample of the survey data, in effect retaining only those households that are in the area of "common support"; we define this more carefully below, but the essential idea is to exclude borrowing households whose predicted probability of borrowing is too high for there to be relevant nonborrowing comparators, and to exclude nonborrowing households whose predicted probability of borrowing is too low for there to be relevant borrowing comparators. The net result is to show a somewhat higher measured impact, on household per capita expenditure, of borrowing from the Village Fund.

At first sight, the presence of selection bias, whether due to unobserved area or household heterogeneity, might appear to doom all efforts to obtain an adequate measure of the impact of a project or program. But there are two possible directions that one can take, if not to solve the problem of selection bias, at least to attenuate it enough to arrive at usable estimates of program impact.

The first tack is to try to make the assumption of nonconfoundedness (or of the weaker assumption of conditional exogeneity of treatment, which says that $E(v_i^T \mid X, T = t) = E(v_i^C \mid X, T = t) = 0$, $t = 0, 1$, (Ravallion 2008)) more plausible, or at least more palatable. This may be attempted by using matching methods, or by using double or triple differences. An alternative tack is to assume that one can find instrumental variables that affect participation but not the outcome. We address the strengths and weaknesses of each of these approaches below.

12.4.1   Solution 1. Matching Comparisons

Even if treatment (or program participation) has not been assigned randomly, it may be possible to measure the impact of the program by using matched comparisons. In its purest form, the basic idea is to match each participant with an otherwise identical nonparticipant (the comparator) – based on observed pretreatment characteristics – and then to measure the average difference in the outcome variable between the participants and the comparison group.

Units that cannot be matched are usually discarded – this is central to good matching – because they "cannot support causal inferences about missing potential outcomes" (Diamond 2005, p. 9). The hope is that this allows one to mimic the effects of randomization, even though the treatments were not applied randomly in practice. The resulting measure of impact is only compelling to the extent that one believes that the matching has been done well and the treatment assignment is ignorable; in other words, we know that the treatment was not assigned randomly, but we believe that we may proceed as if it were.

The difficult part, of course, is finding the appropriate matches for participants. The ideal would be *exact matching*, which requires that for each unit (household, person) treated, one can find someone who did not receive treatment but who is otherwise identical in every relevant way – for instance, who is also 48 years old, father of two, illiterate, living in a small village, and working in construction. If there are many X_i covariates, or some of them are continuous, then exact matching is all but impossible. The two main solutions, discussed more fully below, are propensity score matching and covariate matching.

12.4.2 Propensity Score Matching

The problem of matching treatment with nontreatment units is much more tractable if we can create a summary measure of similarity in the form of a *propensity score*. Let $p(X_i)$ be the probability that unit i be assigned to the treatment group, conditional on X_i, and define

$$p(X_i) \equiv \Pr(T_i = 1 \mid X_i) = E(T_i \mid X_i). \tag{12.17}$$

This probability of participation – the propensity score – can be estimated using an *assignment model*. Given survey information, the commonest procedure starts by pooling the two samples (i.e., the participants and nonparticipants) and estimating a logit or probit model of program participation as a function of pretreatment variables that might influence participation. Diamond (2005) uses a robust logit estimator that reduces the influence of outliers. Some authors (e.g., Imbens 2004) favor the use of nonparametric binary response models, in order to constrain the assignment model as little as possible. Ironically, if the equation fits too well it is difficult to identify nonparticipants who are otherwise similar to participants.[4]

12.4.2.1 An Illustration

To illustrate, Table 12.4 shows the key elements of a propensity score equation estimated using data from the Thailand Socioeconomic Survey of 2004. In this case the dependent variable is set to 1 if the household had borrowed from the Village Rotating Fund at the time of the survey, so one may also think of this as a participation equation. The estimates are for a probit form and based on information from 34,752 households. Those households that are poor enough to get a subsidized health card, or that have more earners, are more likely to borrow. When the head of the household is older, or more educated, the household is initially more likely to borrow, but the negative coefficients on the squared terms show that these effects are gradually attenuated and eventually go into reverse (at an age of 44, and after 8 years of education).

Every village in Thailand was eligible for an initial injection of one million baht for the VRF, regardless of its population. Thus the probability of borrowing should be inversely proportional to the size of the village, here measured by the number of households. Table 12.4 shows that this effect is strong and highly statistically significant.

---

[4] To see this, consider an extreme case where all men borrow and no women borrow, so that gender perfectly predicts whether one will borrow. But then it will be impossible to match a borrower with an "otherwise identical" nonborrower.

Table 12.4 Propensity score equation for borrowing from Thailand Village Fund, 2004

	Coefficient	*p*-value	Full sample Mean	VRF borrowers Mean
Does household borrow from VRF? (Yes = 1)				
Age of head (in years)	0.017	0.00	49.7	50.4
Age of head squared (in years'00)	−1.935	0.00	26.9	27.1
Educational level of head (in years)	0.100	0.00	7.1	6.1
Educational level of head squared	−0.006	0.00	69.6	47.2
Number of adult males in household	−0.153	0.00	1.1	1.2
Number of adult females in household	−0.136	0.00	1.3	1.3
Size of household	0.100	0.00	3.5	3.8
Household has 30-baht medical card	0.223	0.00	0.83	0.93
Province 1 (metro Bangkok) (other provinces)[a]	−0.660	0.00		
1/(number of households per village, block) (other variables)[b]	29.810	0.00	0.007	0.008
Constant	0.395	0.57		
Memo items				
Number of observations	34,752			
Consumption (baht/capita/month)			3,622	2,549
Pseudo R^2	0.190			
Region of common support	0.004–0.985			

[a]There are 76 provinces in Thailand (including Bangkok), and dummy variables were included for all but one of these provinces
[b]Eighteen other variables were included; for details, see Boonperm et al. (2009), Table 2

12.4.2.2   Matching with Propensity Scores

The computation of propensity scores is only the first step in the process. Rosenbaum and Rubin (1983) prove that

$$(Y_i^T, Y_i^C) \perp T_i \mid X_i \quad \Rightarrow \quad (Y_i^T, Y_i^C) \perp T_i \mid p(X_i). \qquad (12.18)$$

Put plainly, this implies that conditional independence ("unconfoundedness") extends to the propensity score, so that treatment cases may be matched with comparison cases using just the propensity score rather than the entire set of predetermined covariates X_i. In other words, to find the nonparticipant that is most closely matched to the participant, one only needs to find the nonparticipant with the propensity score closest to that of the participant.

Rosenbaum and Rubin (1983) also show that

$$G^{TT} = E_{p(X)}[G_i|_{T=1,p(X)}|T_i = 1], \qquad (12.19)$$

where $G_i|_{T=1,p(x)}$ is the difference between the treatment outcome Y_i^T for treated unit i and the (control) outcome for the nontreated unit closest in propensity score to i.

This says that the average treatment effect (the gain for the treated) may be obtained by computing the expected value of the difference in the outcome variable between each treated household and the perfectly matched comparison household (as matched using the propensity score).

Perfect matching is not possible in reality, so in practice one needs to compute

$$\hat{G}_i \mid_{T=1} = \frac{1}{|N|} \sum_{i \in N} \left(Y_i - \frac{1}{|J_i|} \sum_{j \in J_i} Y_j \right), \qquad (12.20)$$

where Y_i is the observed outcome for the ith individual who is treated and J_i is the set of comparators for i, and N is the set of units for which the set of comparators is nonempty (the "common support," discussed in more detail below). The comparators are typically chosen with replacement – which means that they may be used in more than one matching – in which case the bias is lower but the standard error higher than without replacement. The key point here is that unmatched observations are simply dropped; without such pruning there would be little point to the exercise! This effort to create a useful dataset is not a method of estimation per se; it preprocesses the data so that we may draw causal inferences more satisfactorily (Ho et al. 2006, p. 12).

With nearest-neighbor matching one chooses the m closest comparators. It is common to use $m = 1$, but practice varies: some researchers prefer higher values of m (e.g., Abadie and Imbens 2002 favor $m = 4$), and others have used caliper matching (which uses all comparators within a given distance from the treatment), kernel matching, or Gaussian matching (both of which put more weight on closer comparators than those that are more distant). Dehejia and Wahba (2002) argue that the choice of matching mechanism is not as crucial as the proper estimation of the propensity scores, but this is not a settled issue.

In practice, the plausibility of propensity score matching depends on ensuring "common support" and "balancing."

In our example of the Thailand Village Fund, the highest propensity score (i.e., predicted value from the probit equation in Table 12.4) for a nonborrower in Thailand in 2004 was 0.985 while the lowest value for a borrower was 0.004. In between these extremes is the area of *common support*, where it is possible in principle to match borrowers with nonborrowers that have similar propensity scores.

Only in the area of common support is it possible to make comparisons that allow us to make inferences about causality (Rubin and Waterman 2006), so our comparisons need to be confined to this area, and an impact evaluation is not possible unless there is an area of common support (Imbens 2004, p. 7). Identifying the region of common support can be difficult in small samples. This is at the core of the debate about the extent to which nonexperimental methods can identify treatment effects (see for instance Dehejia and Wahba (2002) and Diamond (2005) who try to reproduce the results of an impact evaluation based on the randomized US National Supported Work Program using nonexperimental methods applied to fewer than 500 observations).

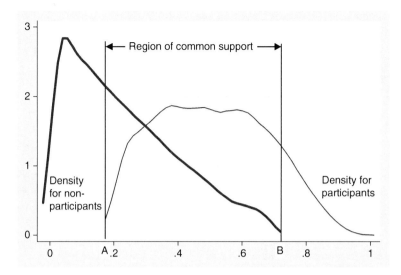

Fig. 12.1 The region of common support. This is the zone where the densities of the propensity scores for participants and nonparticipants overlap

The area of common support occurs where the densities of the estimated propensity scores for participants and for nonparticipants overlap, as shown in Fig. 12.1, which is based on a version of the propensity scores for the Thailand Village Fund study. Above point B there are no comparators for borrowers, so matching is not possible in this zone; below point A there are no borrowers that need to be matched.

In addition, for propensity score matching to work, the treatment and comparison groups need to be "balanced." A treated unit and matched comparator might both have essentially the same propensity scores, but this does not guarantee that they are similar: one household might be agricultural but young while the other might be urban but old. It is not necessary for every individual match to be close, but it is important for the distributions of covariates for the treated and the comparators to be similar, and this is what is meant by balance. More formally, in order to verify balance we need to check whether

$$\hat{p}(X \mid T = 1) = \hat{p}(X \mid T = 0) \tag{12.21}$$

where $\hat{p}$ gives the empirical (rather than population) density of the data.

Theoretically, the true (as opposed to estimated) propensity score ensures balance automatically. Unfortunately, we only have an estimate of the propensity score, and we do not know if the assignment model that generates the propensity scores is in fact the correct one, or even whether it is a consistent estimator of the true propensity scores. Thus we cannot invoke any theoretical results to help guide the choice of assignment model. However, Ho et al. (2006) argue that, paradoxically, we can make use of what they call the "propensity score tautology:" the estimated propensity score achieves balance when it provides a consistent estimate of the true score, but we only have a consistent estimate of the propensity score when matching balances the X_i covariates. One commonly used algorithm is to estimate a propensity score, match treated with nontreated units, and check for balance; if balance is not achieved, revise the assignment model. Repeat this process until balance is achieved.

It is common to use a formal test for balance. Since our interest is in comparing an entire distribution, one approach is to divide the data into ten or more strata ("blocks"), based on the estimated propensity score, and then use a series of t-tests or chi-square tests to check that, within each stratum, the values of each covariate (height, age, hair color) are on average the same. This allows one to "check the adequacy of the statistical model" of assignment (Imbens 2004, p. 18); if balance has not been achieved, the assignment model needs to be revisited and revised.

Ho et al. (2006) are critical of the use of formal statistical tests of balance, on the grounds that balance is a characteristic of the sample, not some underlying population. They also argue that it is likely to be important to achieve balance in some variables (which have large effects on the outcome, Y) while it is less essential for others. On the other hand, they also suggest that one compare each covariate between the treatment and comparison samples, and apply a rule of thumb that the difference should be no more than half a standard deviation! They conclude, and here we agree, that "evaluating balance should always be done in multiple ways" (p. 20).

12.4.2.3 Propensity Score Matching Illustrated

Given estimates of the propensity score, standard practice is to simply compare the outcomes of interest (such as expenditure or income) between the treatment group and the matched comparators; any difference between the two may reasonably be inferred to have been caused by the treatment, again provided that we believe that differences between the treated and matched groups are not contaminated by the effects of unobservables. Imbens (2004, p. 16) argues that the simple difference is not unbiased, and the outcomes should first be weighted by the inverse of the propensity scores. A more elaborate procedure is to use a "blocking-on-the-propensity-score" estimator (Rosenbaum and Rubin 1983), which estimates the treatment effect within each "block" and then obtains a weighted average for the overall effect.

An important advantage of these procedures is said to be that they are nonparametric, but of course this is only true conditional on the model used to generate the propensity scores.

At this point it is useful to return to our example of the Thailand Village Revolving Fund (VRF) to illustrate the application of propensity score matching. The estimations of the propensity score equation shown in Table 12.4 generate scores that yielded a wide region of common support (from 0.004 to 0.985).

To check for balance, the propensity scores were divided into 17 bins such that the estimated propensity score within each group was the same for borrowers and

Table 12.5 The effect of Thailand Village Fund borrowing on household income, expenditure and durable assets, using propensity score and covariate matching

	Sample means			Matched comparisons	
	Whole sample	VRF borrowers	Not VRF borrowers	VRF – non-VRF	t
Complete sample, provincial dummy variables					
Ln(expenditure/capita)[a]		2,549	4,286	0.033	2.67
Ln(income/capita)[b]				0.019	1.27
HH has VCR	0.60	0.61	0.60	0.036	4.04
HH has fridge	0.80	0.82	0.78	0.045	6.56
HH has washing machine	0.36	0.33	0.39	0.049	5.36
Rural households, regional dummy variables					
ln(exp/capita): propensity score matching				0.076	4.39
ln(exp/capita): covariate matching				0.013	1.02

[a]Means show levels, not logs
Source: From Boonperm et al. (2009), based on data from Thailand Socioeconomic Survey 2004

nonborrowers. Then within each bin we tested for significant differences in the values of the covariates between the borrowers and nonborrowers. In a total of 43 cases there were significant differences (at the 1% level), which is somewhat more than the 17 cases that might be expected randomly ($= 1\% \times 17$ bins $\times 102$ variables), but not so far out of line as to make the results implausible.[5]

Once satisfied that the balancing property is met, one measures the impact by taking each borrower, finding the nonborrower with the closest propensity score, and recording their outcome variables such as expenditure per capita. The difference, if any, between the average outcomes for these two matched groups measures the impact. The computation of the propensity score, and the tests for balance, can be done easily enough with the `pscore` command in Stata; and actual matching then uses `attnd` (for single nearest-neighbor matching) or a related command such as `attr` (for caliper or radius matching) or `attk` (for kernel matching).

A selection of results of this technique, applied to the Thailand VRF data for 2004, are shown in Table 12.5, along with the (unmatched) sample mean values of the outcomes. These results show, for instance, that borrower households had an average monthly expenditure per capita of 2,549 baht compared to 4,286 baht for nonborrowers. However, when borrowers are matched using the propensity score, with a single nearest neighbor, their expenditure per capita is 3.3% higher

---

[5] An earlier version of the model had used regional, rather than provincial, dummy variables in the propensity score equation; when it did not show adequate balance we revised the model, mainly by using the (more numerous) provincial dummy variables.

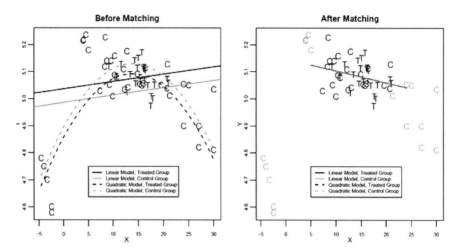

Fig. 12.2 Illustration of the effect of preprocessing, based on the propensity score, on the relationship between outcome Y and covariate X. The data come from a hypothetical example constructed by Ho et al. (2006); reproduced with permission. Treated units are marked T, comparison units are marked C. The best-fit lines are either *solid* (if linear) or *dashed* (if quadratic), *black* (if based on treated group), or *grey* (for the control group). The *right-hand panel* confines the estimation to observations based on the region of common support

($t = 2.67$) than for nonborrowers. Since we have, in effect, controlled for other observables, this difference may indeed be attributed to the microcredit program.

It is also clear from Table 12.5 that VRF borrowers were on average less likely than a typical household to have a phone or washing machine, but when matched with otherwise similar nonborrowers they had higher assets, which suggests that VRF borrowing enabled them to increase their assets.

Ho et al. (2006) make a strong case that the real value of propensity score matching lies in trimming ("preprocessing") the original dataset so that it is more appropriate for the usual type of parametric analysis. Thus, having matched and balanced the data, one could apply OLS or quantile regression to estimate the effect of the treatment on the outcome of interest, along the lines of (12.16). The results of such an approach are shown in the final two row of Table 12.3 and give results close to those generated by propensity score matching.

The importance of trimming the data is nicely illustrated in Fig. 12.2, which comes from Ho et al. (2006, Fig. 1) and is based on an artificial data set. In each of the two panels the values of the outcome variable (Y) are shown on the vertical axis and of a covariate (X) on the horizontal axis. Each observation is marked with either a T (for a treated unit) or C (for a comparison unit). The graphs show linear and quadratic fitted curves for treated cases (black) and comparison cases (grey). The left-hand panel fits the curves to all the data, while the right-hand panel fits the curves only to matched data in the zone of common support. The appropriate trimming of this data set leads to a very different conclusion about the relationship between X and Y.

12.4.2.4   Propensity Score Matching Cases

Propensity score matching has been used in a number of interesting impact evaluations. Jalan and Ravallion (1999) examined the effects of the *Trabajar II* program in Argentina, which was introduced in 1997 in response to a sharp rise in unemployment. The program provided low-wage work on community projects, and was intended to raise the incomes of the poor.

To analyze the impact of this "workfare" program, they used the results of the 1997 *Encuesta de Desarrollo Social* (Social Development Survey), coupled with a similar survey of participants in the Trabajar program. They estimated a logit model of program participation, using variables such as gender, schooling, housing, and subjective perceptions of welfare, and used it to derive propensity scores for participants and nonparticipants. They limited the sample of nonparticipants to those with common support.

Their key findings were that the program raised incomes by about half of the gross wages paid out, and that four-fifths of the participating workers came from the poorest quintile of the population.

The 1997 *Encuesta*, which surveyed 40,000 urban households, has also been used to assess the impact of Argentina's efforts to privatize the provision of water. By comparing data from the *Encuesta* with earlier data from the census, and comparing municipalities where the water supply was, and was not, privatized, Galiani et al. (2005) found that privatization increased access to water by 11.6%. Using data on child deaths, and applying propensity score matching to municipalities (rather than households), they also found that the privatization of water supply reduced child mortality by 6.7% on average, and by 24% in poor municipalities.

12.4.3   Covariate Matching

It is possible to match treated units with otherwise similar untreated units in a way that is more realistic than full matching but does not use propensity scores. One of the simplest forms of *nearest-neighbor matching* first normalizes all of the covariates (household size, age of household head, and so on) so that they have mean zero and unit variance. If each variable is given a weight of one, then one can match any treated unit with the closest untreated unit, where closeness may be defined as the minimum sum of squared differences across all covariates.

More formally, let

$$U_i = \frac{X_i - \bar{X}}{s_i} \tag{12.22}$$

be the normalized $k \times 1$ vector of covariates for unit i. Define the distance between normalized vectors U_i^{T} (for a treated unit) and U_i^{C} (for a comparison unit) to be

$$\left\| U_i^{\mathrm{T}} - U_i^{\mathrm{C}} \right\|_V \equiv \sqrt{(U_i^{\mathrm{T}} - U_i^{\mathrm{C}})'V(U_i^{\mathrm{T}} - U_i^{\mathrm{C}})}, \tag{12.23}$$

where V is a positive definite weight matrix. In the simplest case, V is the identity matrix I_k, which gives equal weight to the distance between each covariate.

This simple matching scheme may be used to check the robustness of the estimates of the impact of the Thailand Village Fund, with the results that are shown on the bottom rows of Table 12.5. It appears that VRF borrowing in rural Thailand raises expenditure per capita by 1.3%, compared to 7.6% using propensity score matching (and regional dummy variables). In this case, the measured effect was smaller with covariate matching and was not statistically significant at conventional levels.

A key issue in the use of direct matching of this type is the appropriate choice of the weight matrix, V. Let Σ_X be the covariance matrix of the covariates. Then it is common to use, as a weight matrix applied to the original (i.e., not normalized) magnitudes, the reciprocals of the variances, which is given by diag Σ_X^{-1}. This gives the results shown in Table 12.5. Some researchers prefer use the full inverse of the covariance matrix, Σ_X^{-1}, which gives the Mahalanobis distance, although there is no consensus that this represents an improvement over the simpler distance (Imbens 2004, footnote 6).

Diamond and Sekhon (2005) proposes the use of *genetic matching*. The basic idea is to start with a weight matrix V_0 and to adjust it iteratively until the best possible balance is achieved (Sekhon 2006). As usual, balance is achieved when the covariates (such as household size, age of head, and so on) do not differ, on average, between the treatment group and the sample with which they are matched; Sekhon recommends requiring every p-value associated with a t-test of the difference in the means of covariates to be 0.15 or higher, and likewise with Kolmogorov–Smirnov tests for the distributions of continuous variables. Whether genetic matching represents an improvement is not yet clear, but this is an active area of current research.

An interesting recent example of the creative use of matching may be found in a recent study by Cattaneo et al. (2007) of the impact of the *piso firme* program in Mexico. This is a large program, funded by the federal government but implemented by the states, that provides homeowners with ready-to-pour concrete to replace dirt floors. According to the 2000 census, three million Mexican households had dirt floors; by 2005 the government had provided concrete for over 300,000 of these.

A major justification given for the program is that it reduces the transmission of parasites to children, thereby improving their health, including their cognitive development. Cattaneo et al. set out to test this assertion, by surveying treatment and control households and comparing the outcomes. In doing this they are able to exploit a geographic discontinuity: the twin cities of Gómez Palacio/Lerdo and Torreón face each other across the border between states of Coahuila and Durango, and form part of a single urban area, but as of 2005 the *piso firme* program had only been implemented in Coahuila and not in Durango.

In order to construct a sample of households, Cattaneo et al. used data from the census blocks of the 2000 Census. They first chose census blocks in the treatment area (i.e., Gómez Palacio/Lerdo) and then matched these with similar census blocks in Torreón; similarity is measured by the smallest distance, which in turn is the maximum difference between any of four variables (including household size, and proportion of households with dirt floors). Having identified matching blocks, the researchers then sampled households that owned their house, had lived there since 2000, had at least one dirt floor in 2000, and had at least one child aged under six at the time of the survey. A total of 2,783 households were surveyed, more or less evenly divided between treatment and control areas, and information was collected on sociodemographic variables, anthropometric measurements, cognitive ability (for instance, using the Picture Peabody Vocabulary Test for children aged 36–71 months), and blood and stool quality.

To measure the impact of the program, Cattaneo et al. regressed the relevant outcomes, such as the parasite count in the blood, on the share of the cement floors (CF), and a large number of control variables.[6] Here is a typical finding:

$$\text{Parasite count} = -0.371\,CF + \text{ other variables}$$
$$[\text{SE} = 0.229]$$

The mean parasite count was 0.613, and this measures the number of different parasites found in a child's stool sample. The coefficient is significant at the 10% level, and is large, indicating that cement floors have a substantial effect in reducing parasitic infection in urban areas in Mexico.

In 2000, the proportion of rooms that had cement floors was 33% both for the treatment and the control sample; by 2005 this proportion had risen to 73% for the control sample and almost 100% for the treatment sample. Thus the *piso firme* program increased the proportion of cement floors by 27% (Cattaneo et al. 2007, p. 14). Thus it should be no surprise to find that when one regresses outcomes on a summary variable that measures whether an area has been treated, the result is about a quarter of the effect of a concrete floor. Thus

$$\text{Parasite count} = -0.078\,T + \text{ other variables},$$
$$[\text{SE} = 0.049]$$

where T is set equal to one if the area is covered by the program (i.e., if the household is in Coahuila) and zero otherwise.

---

[6] This variable was instrumented using a dummy variable that indicated whether the area was covered by the *piso firme* program; the rationale for and use of instrumental variables is discussed further below.

It is not surprising that the installation of concrete floors would reduce infection, but what is less obvious is the effect on the cognitive development of children. Here is another typical result from the Cattaneo et al. study:

$$\text{Picture Peabody Vocabulary Test} = 2.956\,T + \text{other variables.}$$
$$[\text{SE} = 1.477]$$

The mean value of the test, which gives a percentile score, was 30.7, so this result indicates that the program raised test scores by about a tenth. This is a large effect, and implies that the program was cost-effective even relative to programs that are aimed more directly at boosting educational performance (Cattaneo et al. 2007, p. 20).

12.4.4   Solution 2. Double Differences

To recapitulate, the problem we are addressing is how to measure the impact of a program ("treatment") when the units of interest (household, individuals) have not been randomly assigned to the program. The matching methods set out in the previous section were designed to reduce bias by selecting comparison units based on observable covariates ("selection on observables"). They are typically implemented in practice by using survey data collected after the program has been operating for some time.

More powerful measures of program impact are possible if we have panel data both from a baseline survey before the intervention occurs and a follow-up survey after the program is operating. Both surveys should be comparable in the questions used and the survey methods applied, and they must be administered both to participants and nonparticipants.

These requirements are not often met. An impact evaluation of, say, a single irrigation project may well be able to draw on baseline information from a national survey, but it is quite possible that the sample of those potentially affected by the irrigation project may be too small to serve as a useful baseline.

Given that we have the data, the simplest version of the double difference estimator consists of first computing the difference between the outcome variable after ($Y_{i,\text{after}}$) and before ($Y_{i,\text{before}}$) the intervention, both for the treatment and comparison samples. The difference between these two differences (the "double difference") gives an estimate of the impact of the program.

Figure 12.3 (from Khandker 2007) helps clarify the situation. When we have random assignment, we may compare the outcome for the beneficiaries ($Y = 30$ in Fig. 12.3) directly with the outcome for those who did not receive treatment ($Y = 17$ in the left-hand panel of Fig. 12.3). However, if the comparison group was not chosen randomly, and its outcome rose from 14 to 21 over time (right-hand panel of Fig. 12.3), then we might plausibly assume that the outcome for the treated group would also have risen by 7 over time, creating a counterfactual

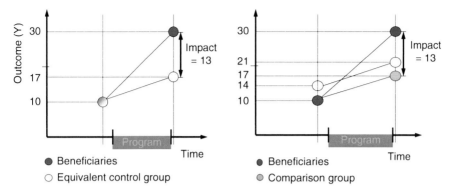

Fig. 12.3 Measuring program impact under randomization (*left*) and using double differences (*right*). The treatment sample starts with an outcome of 10 and finishes with an outcome of 30. With random assignment, the final level may compared with the control group (*left*); with a comparison group a counterfactual must be inferred

output of 17, which may be compared with the observed output of 30. This latter may be computed from the double difference

$$(30 - 10) - (21 - 14) = 13.$$

A fundamental advantage of panel data is that they allow one to eliminate unobserved variable bias, provided that this bias is linear and does not vary over time. These are not trivial conditions, but they are weaker than assuming that bias can be ignored (even conditional on the covariates). Consider the following model:

$$Y_{i,\text{before}} = a + cX_{ib} + \varepsilon_{ib} \tag{12.24}$$

and

$$Y_{i,\text{after}} = a + bT_i + cX_{ia} + \varepsilon_{ia}, \tag{12.25}$$

where the errors consist of a time-invariant component and an innovation error, so for time $t = a,b$ we have

$$\varepsilon_{it} = \eta_i + \mu_{it}. \tag{12.26}$$

With panel data we can take the difference between (12.25) and (12.24), to get

$$Y_{i,\text{after}} - Y_{i,\text{before}} = bT_i + c(X_{ia} - X_{ib}) + \mu_{ia} - \mu_{ib}. \tag{12.27}$$

Our double-difference measure of the impact of the treatment is given by the estimate of coefficient b, and we have swept away the effect of any unobservable

Table 12.6 Double difference estimates of the impact borrowing from the Thailand Village Revolving Fund, panel data for 2002 and 2004

	Expenditure per capita	Income per capita	Farm income per capita	Non-farm income per capita
	Means, 2002, baht per person per month			
Households that borrow from VRF	2,002	2,519	784	362
Households that do not borrow from VRF	2,205	2,984	551	403
	Impacts (in log form)			
Impact	0.020	−0.002	0.020	0.097
t-statistic	1.14	−0.11	0.25	1.36
Number of observations	6,966	6,966	992	2,681

Source: Based on panel component of Thailand Socioeconomic Surveys of 2002 and 2004 (which covers rural areas only). Each observation refers to one adult

(and observable) variables that do not vary over time – such as, for instance, the innate drive or ability of a farmer, or the social capital in a village, or the effects of nonrandom program placement – that would otherwise appear in the η_i terms.

The double difference method may be refined in a number of ways. One hybrid, which appears to perform well, first uses propensity score matching with data from the baseline survey to preprocess the data in order to ensure that the comparison group is similar to the treatment group, and then applies double differences; this helps deal with unobservable heterogeneity in the initial conditions. And more complex specifications of (12.27) could be used, for instance by including the levels of the X covariates (Ravallion 2008).

Double differencing is often very helpful in measuring impact effects, but it will give biased results if there is selective attrition of the treatment group – in other words, if some of the treatment group cannot be resurveyed a second time, and if those who drop out are not a random sample of the treatment group (for instance, if they are older or richer than their peers in the treatment group). The double difference method is typically relatively expensive to implement, inasmuch as it usually requires at least two rounds of survey data.

Returning to our example of microlending by the Thailand Village Revolving Fund, it was possible to apply double differences using data from the Thailand Socioeconomic Surveys of 2002 and 2004. The 2004 survey resurveyed 5,755 rural households, which created the necessary panel data.

Before computing the double differences, we first estimated the propensity scores using the 2002 data – as described above – and then confined the double differencing to the area of common support. We weighted the differences for each treated case (i.e., each adult who borrowed in 2004) by 1, and each comparison case by $p/(1-p)$ – where p is the propensity score – as recommended by Imbens (2004; see also Ravallion 2008). The results are summarized in Table 12.6, and show that the VRF had no statistically significant effect on income or farm

Table 12.7   Log(wage) and education in 1995 by age cohort and program intensity, Sekolah Dasar INPRES program, Indonesia

	Log(wages)			Years of education
	Level of program in region of birth			
	High	Low	Difference	Difference[a]
Aged 2–6 in 1974	6.61 (0.008)	6.73 (0.006)	−0.12 (0.010)	−1.27 (0.057)
Aged 12–17 in 1974	6.87 (0.009)	7.02 (0.007)	−0.15 (0.011)	−1.39 (0.067)
Difference	−0.26 (0.011)	−0.29 (0.010)	0.026 (0.015)	0.12 (0.089)

Source: Duflo (2001)
Notes: Terms in parentheses are standard errors
[a]Difference is in educational level attained by individuals between high- and low-intensity program areas

income; the effects on per capita expenditure and on non-farm income are only marginally stronger, and certainly not compelling.

12.4.4.1   Illustrations: Schools in Indonesia, Subsidies in Mexico

It is sometimes possible to apply double differences even without panel data, particularly where there is a "natural experiment" that has the effect of applying a treatment unexpectedly, or to a well-defined group. A good example is the study by Duflo (2001) of the impact on educational achievement and wages of Indonesia's massive push to build more schools in the mid-1970s under the Sekolah Dasar INPRES program. Between 1973–1974 and 1978–1979, Indonesia built and staffed 61,000 additional three-teacher primary schools, each capable of serving 120 children. This was equivalent to about two additional schools per thousand children of primary school age, and was associated with a rise in the gross primary school enrollment rate from 69% in 1973 to 83% in 1978.

One of the questions addressed by Duflo was whether the program had an impact on wages. Using data from the 1995 Intercensal Survey, she was able to compile information on wages, birthdates, and birthplaces for 60,633 individuals. The first cohort of people in a position to benefit from the Sekolah Dasar program were those aged 2–6 in 1974; on the other hand, anyone aged 12–17 in 1974 was too old to benefit from it. One can also distinguish those regions where the program was pursued with high intensity from those areas where it was less intensive. This allows one to construct a simple difference estimator, along the lines set out in Table 12.7.

Those aged 2–6 in 1974 in low-intensity regions had *higher* wages (as of 1995) than those regions where the Sekolah Dasar program was pursued intensively – not surprisingly, because the program was explicitly structured to build more schools in under-served parts of the country. But this gap in log wages was smaller for the cohort that benefited from the school building program (−0.12) than for those that did not (−0.15), as Table 12.7 shows. The difference between these differences, which comes to 0.026 (i.e., about 2.6%), is a measure of the impact of the program, although it should also be noted that the standard error of this double difference was

Table 12.8 Notation for enrollment rates, Progresa project, Mexico

	Poor households, eligible for Progresa grants	Nonpoor households, not eligible for Progresa grants
Progresa localities	$S_{1,t}$	$S_{3,t}$
Non-Progresa localities	$S_{2,t}$	$S_{4,t}$

Source: Schultz (2001, Fig. 1)

relatively high, at 0.015. It is worth emphasizing that this double difference estimator rests on the identification assumption that any increase in wages would not have differed systematically between regions in the absence of the Sekolah Dasar program; only if this seems plausible can we have much faith in the estimates. Duflo refines her estimates using regressions, but the identification strategy, and basic results, do not differ markedly from those summarized here in Table 12.7.

One of the most widely cited, and useful, studies to use differences to measure the impact of a program is Paul Schultz's analysis of the Progresa subsidies in Mexico. First implemented in 1998, the Progresa program made payments to poor mothers in rural Mexico provided that their children continued to attend school. The payments, which were indexed to inflation, initially varied from 70 pesos per month (about $7) for a child in third grade to 255 pesos per month for a girl in ninth grade. These amounts were substantial: the monthly wage for an adult male day-laborer was about 580 pesos, and for a child worker approximately 380 pesos.

The challenge here is to measure the impact, if any, that this program had on school enrollment rates. It helped that it was possible, at the start of the program, to set up a large-scale social experiment. First, 495 poor localities were identified in rural Mexico. Based on a census of households in these areas, conducted in October 1997, two-thirds of these households were deemed to be poor, and therefore eligible for Progresa grants. In the summer of 1998 the program was introduced in just 314 of the districts, chosen randomly, with a promise that the program would apply to the remaining districts 2 years later. A sample of households in all 495 localities were surveyed on four other occasions through November 1999. Table 12.9 shows that just prior to the program, although 95.1% of those who had completed fifth grade were still at school in the subsequent year, only 57.7% of those who had just completed the primary cycle (i.e., sixth grade) stayed on for the next grade.

In measuring the impact of the program it is useful to refer to the notation used by Schultz, reproduced here in Table 12.8. Let $S_{1,t}$ be the school enrollment rate for poor children in Progresa localities and $S_{2,t}$ the rate in non-Progresa localities. Then $D1_t \equiv S_{1,t} - S_{2,t}$ is the difference in outcome between the treatment and control samples in time t. When this is compared over time we have the double difference $DD1_t \equiv D1_2 - D1_1$. Measures of these single- and double-differences are shown in Table 12.9 and show that while enrollment rates for poor children did not differ significantly between Progresa and non-Progresa areas prior to the program, after the program was put in place these first differences became substantial, as did the double differences. Take, for instance, the case of those who

Table 12.9 Changes in enrollment rates, Progresa and Non-Progresa households, Mexico, 1997–1999

	Schooling year just completed		
	5	6	7
Proportion enrolled prior to Progresa program	0.951	0.577	0.956
Progresa – non-Progresa localities			
Difference in enrollment rates of poor before program	0.015	0.024	−0.012
p-value	0.129	0.345	0.894
Difference in enrollment rates of poor after program	0.047	0.111	0.013
p-value	0.001	0.002	0.147
Double difference	0.032	0.087	0.025
p-value	0.146	0.004	0.378
Progresa – non-Progresa localities			
Difference in enrollment gap[a] before program	−0.020	0.042	0.014
p-value	0.293	0.023	0.627
Difference in enrollment gap[a] after program	−0.047	−0.035	0.002
p-value	0.003	0.006	0.910
Triple difference	−0.027	−0.077	−0.012
p-value	0.279	0.001	0.738

[a]The enrollment gap is the enrollment rate of nonpoor children minus the enrollment rate of poor children
Source: Schultz (2001, Tables 2–4)

had just completed sixth grade: poor children in the areas with a Progresa program were more likely to be enrolled before the program (a difference of 2.4 percentage points, but not statistically significant) and much more likely to be enrolled after the program (an 11.1% point difference, and significant). The gap thus grew by 8.7 percentage points, an effect that is substantial and statistically significant.

An alternative approach is to measure the *differential* in enrollment rates between poor and nonpoor children (the "enrollment gap"), between Progresa and Non-Progresa localities. This is defined as $D2_t \equiv (S_{3,t} - S_{1,t}) - (S_{4,t} - S_{2,t})$. We would expect D2 to be close to zero before the program is introduced, and to become negative afterwards (as $S_{1,t}$ rises relative to the other terms). This is indeed what was observed, as the numbers in the lower half of Table 12.9 show. One can difference again, creating what is really the triple difference $DD2_t \equiv D2_2 - D2_1$. For the important case of those who have just finished sixth grade we have $DD2_t = -0.077$ and statistically significant; this indicates that the Progresa program increased the proportion of poor children who, having just completed primary school, continued on to lower secondary school, by 7.7 percentage points.

Although the key results of the study emerge clearly from the analysis of differences, Schultz also uses a probit regression to control for a limited number of covariates, but this does not alter the findings. He finds that the expected cumulative effect of the Progresa program is to increase the average length of time that children stay in school by 0.66 years, a 10% improvement. If viewed purely as a program to increase investment in human capital, Schultz estimates that it yields a real rate of return of about 8%.

12.4.5 Solution 3. Instrumental Variables

To repeat, our interest is in finding unbiased coefficients for the treatment term in the outcome regression, typically specified as in (12.16) (reproduced here):

$$Y_i = \alpha^C + (\alpha^T - \alpha^C)T_i + X_i\beta + \varepsilon_i, \quad i = 1, ..., n \qquad (12.16)$$

The problem is that for one of a number of reasons – an omitted, mis-measured, or endogenous explanatory variable – T_i may be correlated with ε_i. For instance, a dynamic individual might be more likely to participate in a program (a high T_i) and to benefit from it ($\varepsilon_i > 0$). Murray (2005) refers to T_i in this context as the "troublesome explanator;" without further adjustments, OLS estimation of (12.16) will yield biased estimates of the impact coefficients.

The idea behind instrumental variables (IV) estimation – also sometimes referred to as the statistical control method – is to try to find variables Z that are correlated with T_i but not with ε_i. In the jargon of instrumental variables, we ideally want strong instruments Z that have high "instrument relevance" so that they are closely correlated with T_i, but at the same time satisfy the "exclusion restriction" (or "instrument exogeneity") so that they play no direct role in the outcome regression (thus $\mathrm{cov}(Z_k,\varepsilon) = 0$ for all k instruments).

Given such instruments, it is common to estimate, as a first stage, a separate *participation equation* (or "assignment equation") of the form

$$T_i = Z_i\gamma + X_i\varphi + u_i. \qquad (12.28)$$

and then to use the estimated values of participation from (12.28) (i.e., $\hat{T}_i$) instead of T_i in estimating (12.16). In practice, (12.28) is typically estimated in logit or probit form, given the binary nature of the dependent variable.

To see why this technique works, return to the case of a dynamic individual who is both more likely to participate (so $u_i > 0$) and more likely to benefit from the program ($\varepsilon_i > 0$). By using $\hat{T}_i$ instead of T_i, the forces that influence ε_i and T_i now only affect ε_i, but not $\hat{T}_i$, so the correlation disappears, along with the bias. However, this is only true if there are influences on T_i that do not influence Y_i. The idea is to create variation in $\hat{T}_i$ so that we have some people in the sample who, even if they have the same X_i, may have different T_i; in effect we now have a source of variation in Y_i that is attributable to the program.

The major practical problem is finding appropriate instruments. They must influence program participation while somehow not influencing the outcome of the program once one is enrolled. This is difficult. In a useful review of IV estimation, Murray (2005, p. 18) writes, "all instruments arrive on the scene with a dark cloud of invalidity hanging overhead," and states, correctly, that "the credibility of IV estimates rests on the arguments offered for the instruments' validity" (p. 11).

It is not possible to test formally for unconditional instrument exogeneity – i.e., to test whether $\text{cov}(Z_k,\varepsilon) = 0$ – because ε is not known. Thus the case must be made using intuition, economic theory, and logical reasoning.

However, if there is more than one available instrument, it is possible to test, provided that one is already using a given instrument, whether additional instruments are justified (essentially by adding them to the instrumental version of (12.16) and testing for their statistical significance).

It is now considered good practice in applied work to report the results of the first state estimation (12.28), which allows the reader to judge whether the estimates look reasonable. A low value of a test of the joint significance of the coefficients of the instruments in this equation would signal weak instruments, and these in turn compromise the ability of IV to improve on the bias inherent in OLS estimation (Murray 2005; he also discusses the Stock–Yogo test for weak instruments and provides some critical values).

Instrumental variables estimation is widely used by economists, including in impact evaluations, and researchers have been imaginative in their search for suitable instruments. To take just one example: a recent study of the effect of famine relief on child growth in Ethiopia was able to use past climatic variation as an instrument in a model of the impact of the relief (Yamano et al. 2003).

The instrumental variables method is especially helpful if there is measurement error. Suppose that, because of measurement errors, observed program participation is more variable than true participation; this will lead to an underestimation of the impact of the program ("attenuation bias"), essentially because the noise of measurement error is getting in the way of isolating the effects of program participation. However, the predicted value of program intervention ($\hat{P}_{i1}$) is less likely to reflect measurement error, and can reduce the effects of attenuation bias.

12.4.5.1   An Illustration: Thai Microcredit

To illustrate the application of the instrumental variables approach we return again to our example of the Thailand Village Revolving Credit Fund (VRF). A feature of the VRF is that it provided a million baht to each Village Rotating Fund, regardless of the size of the village. Thus the probability of obtaining a VRF loan is approximately in inverse proportion to the size of the village ("nhinv"). Our measure of the size of the village is the number of households, which is likely to be closely correlated with the theoretically ideal measure (the number of people eligible for VRF loans, which is the number of adults aged 20 and above).

Some instrumental variables estimates of the impact of the VRF are summarized in Table 12.10. In each case the first-step equation is probit and the instruments are highly statistically significant at that point. The second-stage

Table 12.10 Instrumental variables estimates of the impact of borrowing from the Thailand Village Revolving Fund, 2004

	Expenditure per capita	Income per capita
2004 data		
	Mean, baht per household per month	
Borrowed from VRF in 2004	2,549	3,209
Did not borrow from VRF in 2004	4,286	6,088
	Impact (in log form)	
Instrument: nhinv[a]	0.016	0.017
z-statistic	0.36	0.33
Instruments: nhinv, anydebt[b]	0.196	0.163
z-statistic	15.6	10.8
Instruments: nhinv, non-VRF debt[b]	0.464	
z-statistic	24.2	
Panel Data		
	Mean, baht per household per month	
Borrow from VRF in 2004 only	2,376	3,179
Borrow from VRF in neither 2002 nor 2004	2,632	3,413
	Impact (in log form)	
VRF borrowing in 2004 vs. no VRF borrowing		
Instrument: nhinv[a], household fixed effects	0.179	0.152
z-statistic	3.19	2.24

Source: Based on data from the Thailand Socioeconomic Surveys of 2002 and 2004
Notes: nhinv is the inverse of the number of households per village.; anydebt is equal to 1 if a household has debt from any source, and to zero otherwise; non-VRF debt is 1 if a household has debt from any source other than the VRF, and is otherwise zero
[a]Used two-step estimator because maximum likelihood estimator did not converge
[b]Used maximum likelihood estimator

equation is linear. When the only instrument is *nhinv*, the measured impact is not statistically significant. However, when one also uses additional instruments – whether a household has any outstanding debt ("anydebt"), or whether it has any debt other than from the VRF ("non-VRF debt") – the measured impact becomes large and statistically significant. This underlines the general point that instrumental variables estimates are often highly sensitive to the choice of instruments, which can be disconcerting.

The bottom panel of Table 12.10 shows the results of applying the instrumental variables approach to the panel data that are available for some rural areas. The sample is confined to those households who either borrowed from the VRF both in 2002 and 2004, or borrowed in neither year. The second-stage equation uses household fixed effects – equivalent to a separate intercept for each household – which in principle should sweep away the effects even of unobserved differences between households ("household-level heterogeneity") provided that such effects do not vary over time. These estimates show the VRF having a large effect both on incomes and on expenditures in rural areas.

12.4.6   Other Solutions

Although matching, double differencing and instrumental variables estimation are the most widely used techniques in impact evaluation, a number of other techniques have been used, with more or less success.

Reflexive comparisons. In this approach, one first undertakes a baseline survey of the treatment group before the intervention, with a follow-up survey afterwards. The impact of the intervention is measured by comparing the before and after data; in effect the baseline provides the comparison group.

Such comparisons are rarely satisfactory. The problem in this case is that we really want a "with" and "without" comparison, not a "before" and "after." Put another way, in the reflexive comparison method there is no proper counterfactual against which the outcomes of the project may be compared. There is also a problem if attrition occurs, so that some of those surveyed before the project drop out in some systematic way. On the other hand, this may be the only option in trying to determine the impact of full-coverage interventions, such as universal vaccinations, where there is no possibility of a comparison or control group.

Discontinuity designs. The idea here is to make use of a sharp structural disconti-nuity in the data that is not caused by the outcome of interest. The approach is typically applied to time-series data – for instance, to measure the effect of a profit announcement on the market valuation of a firm. In this case, the data need to be available for small time units (e.g., weeks, days), and one typically restricts the data sample to a small neighborhood of the discontinuity – in this example, the period just before and immediately after the major exogenous event. The impact is then typically measured using a regression equation with appropriate dummy variables.

The approach can be applied in other contexts. For instance, Esther Duflo (2000) wanted to measure the effect of newly expanded old age pensions on child height and weight in the Republic of South Africa. She used the fact that men are eligible for a pension at 65, and women at 60, to compare the stature of children in households with members slightly below and slightly above pensionable age. She found that pensions received by women had a measurable positive effect on the anthropometric status of girls, but not boys; and pensions received by men had no such effects.

Qualitative methods. Some evaluations rely largely on qualitative information, which comes from focus groups, unstructured interviews, survey data on perceptions, and a variety of other sources. Such information complements, but does not supplant, the more quantitative impact evaluations, because qualitative methods are based on subjective evaluations, do not generate a control or comparison group, and lack statistical robustness.

12.5   Impact Evaluation: Macro Projects

It is much harder to evaluate the impact of an economy-wide shock (e.g., a devaluation) or macroeconomic policy change (e.g., increase in the money supply) than a project or program change, because the universal nature of the change makes it almost impossible to construct an appropriate counterfactual. But this challenge has not deterred researchers, so to finish this chapter we summarize some of the techniques that have been applied to this problem.

12.5.1   Time-Series Data Analysis: Deviations from Trend

One of the simplest, and commonest, methods used to measure the assumed effect of a shock is to use time-series data to extrapolate the outcome of interest – GDP growth, for instance – to create a counterfactual, and then to compare the actual outcome with this counterfactual. This is the approach taken by Kakwani and his co-authors in estimating the effects of the Asian financial crisis of 1997 on poverty and other indicators in South Korea and Thailand.

The first difficulty with this method is arriving at a robust counterfactual; for instance, how far back in time should one go when developing an equation that is used for the projections. And the second problem is linking the shock or program with the observed deviation from trend, because there are likely to be many other potentially plausible explanations. A good illustration of this is Datt and Hoogeveen's paper on the post-1997 slowdown of economic growth in the Philippines, which is titled "El Niño or El Peso?" Many observers claimed that the Asian financial crisis was largely to blame ("El Peso"), but they argued that more probably the slowdown was mainly due to drought ("El Niño") (Datt and Hoogeveen 1999).

12.5.2   CGE and Simulation Models

A computable general equilibrium (CGE) model of an economy is a set of equations that aims to quantify the main inter-relationships between households, firms and government in an economy. CGE models range from just a few to many hundreds of equations. In principle they may be used to simulate the effects of many types of policy interventions. Unfortunately, CGE models are technically difficult to build, are typically highly aggregated (which makes it difficult to identify the effects of policies on income distribution and poverty with much precision), require considerable data to construct the underlying social accounting matrix, and produce results that are sensitive to the assumptions made about the parameters. However, they have been used with some success to evaluate the economic and distributional effects of such interventions as programs to reduce HIV/AIDS, change food subsidies, alter taxes, or liberalize trade. The International Food Policy Research Institute (IFPRI) has developed a standard CGE model that has been applied with some success to a number of problems in developing countries (Loefgren et al. 2001), and has a comparatively short learning curve.

Heckman et al. (1998) argue that the incorporation of general equilibrium effects can greatly alter the conclusions of an impact evaluation. A partial-equilibrium analysis shows that a $500 per student college tuition subsidy in the USA would be expected to raise university attendance by 5.3%. However, this assumes that the relative wages of graduates to nongraduates remains unchanged, an assumption that is implausible if the subsidy were introduced nationwide. Using a general equilibrium model, Heckman et al. estimate that the $500 subsidy would raise university enrollment by just 0.46%. The smaller effect arises because rising university enrollments would lower the wages of graduates relative to nongraduates, thereby depressing the incentive to attend university, and offsetting the tuition subsidy to a substantial extent.

12.5.3 Household Panel Impact Analysis

If we have panel data on households then we could compare the situation of each household before and after the shock. By including household fixed effects in our estimating equation – equivalent to a separate dummy variable for each household – we can largely eliminate the effects of time-invariant household and area-specific heterogeneity (i.e., of the special or unique features of households, many of which are unobservable – such as whether the head is an alcoholic, or sick, or entrepreneurially inclined).

Again, the main difficulty here is that a before-and-after comparison does not establish an adequate counterfactual. For instance, if the income of a household in the Philippines fell between 1996 and 1998, how do we know that it was due to the 1997 financial crisis? It might have been caused by some other event; perhaps a family member fell ill, or the village suffered from a drought. No survey is ever complete enough to capture every conceivable relevant explanatory variable. Moreover, most household-level economic magnitudes (income, expenditure, even assets) do not follow regular or highly predictable trends from year to year.

12.5.4 Self-Rated Retrospective Evaluation

Another possibility is to ask the household to assess how much it has been affected by the crisis – as was done, for instance, in the APIS survey in the Philippines in 1998.

By definition, self-rated evaluations are subjective, which makes it difficult to assess whether the reported effects are indeed due to the shocks. In Vietnam, households reported higher levels of illness in 1998 than in 1993, despite being much better off in 1998; this is hardly plausible, unless one supposes that the definition of "illness" changes over time or with affluence. Whatever the reason, it makes the subjective evaluations untrustworthy. It is also optimistic to expect that most households have a clear enough grasp of the forces buffeting them to be able themselves to diagnose the root causes of variations in their incomes or expenditure.

A variant on this theme is to ask households whether they were hit by a shock. We then compare the situation of households that reported being affected with those that did not. Since self-reported shocks are highly endogenous – any household that has had a spell of bad luck is likely to report being hit by a shock – researchers often use the shock reported by a cluster (e.g., the village, the city ward) as an instrumental variable, to help resolve this endogeneity.

Even with this latter adjustment, we are left with the problem of unobserved community-level heterogeneity – for instance, for reasons that may not be apparent, some communities or clusters may report a shock more than others, even if objectively the shock hit all areas equally.

12.6   In Conclusion

Three simple points about impact evaluation are worth emphasizing. First, no method of impact evaluation is perfect, even randomization (although it can be helpful). The method used will depend on the problem, and the resources and time available, but will always face the problem of unobservables and hence the need to conjure up and rationalize a satisfactory counterfactual. Constructing a compelling impact evaluation is as much an art as a science; good econometric practice is helpful, but does not substitute for sensible, logical explanation.

Second, impact evaluation is more difficult with economy-wide policy interventions and crises than with micropolicies.

And third, program impact evaluation is important. It serves as a tool for learning whether and how programs matter, and has had a marked effect on public policy in a number of cases; Bamberger (2005) gives some interesting examples. Agencies such as the World Bank earmark as much as 1% of project funds for monitoring and evaluation, and increasingly, impact evaluations are being required in the name of accountability. This may be a passing fad; Ravallion (2008) doubts that impact evaluations will ever suffice for "informing future development projects and policies," because they are so dependent on the specific context of the programs whose impacts they are measuring. This may be unduly pessimistic: the impact of impact evaluations could often be enhanced by paying attention to creating adequate feedback mechanisms, so that policy makers do take the lessons to heart.

References

Abadie, Alberto, and Guido Imbens. 2002. Simple and bias-corrected matching estimators for average treatment effects. NBER Technical Working Paper No. 283.

Angrist, Joshua, Eric Bettinger, Erik Bloom, Elizabeth King, and Michael Kremer. 2002. Vouchers for private schooling in Colombia: Evidence from a randomized natural experiment. *American Economic Review* 92(5): 1535–1558.

Baker, Judy. 2000. *Evaluating the impact of development projects on poverty: A handbook for practitioners.* Washington, DC: World Bank [A useful handbook, with extensive examples.].

Bamberger, Michael. 2005. "Influential evaluations," presentation to the Monitoring and Evaluation Thematic Group, April 26. Washington, DC: World Bank.

Boonperm, Jirawan, Jonathan Haughton, and Shahid Khandker. 2009. Does the village fund matter in Thailand? Policy Research Working Paper 5011. Washington, DC: World Bank.

Cattaneo, Matias D., Sebastian Galiani, Paul J. Gertler, Sebastian Martinez, and Rocio Titiunik. 2007. Housing, health and happiness. Policy Research Working Paper 4214. Washington, DC: World Bank.

Datt, Gaurav, and J.G.M. Hoogeveen. 1999. "El Niño or El Peso? Crisis, poverty and income distribution in the Philippines." Policy Research Working Paper No. 2466. Washington, DC, World Bank.

Dehejia, Rajeev, and Sadek Wahba. 2002. Propensity score-matching methods for nonexperimental causal studies. *Review of Economics and Statistics* 84(1): 151–161.

Diamond, Alexis. 2005. Reliable estimation of average and quantile causal effects in non-experimental settings. Working draft, Harvard University, Cambridge, MA.

Diamond, Alexis, and Jasjeet Sekhon. 2005. Genetic matching for estimating causal effects. Harvard University and University of California Berkeley.

Duflo, Esther. 2001. Schooling and labor market consequences of school construction in Indonesia: Evidence from an unusual policy experiment. *American Economic Review* 91(4): 795–813.

Duflo, Esther. 2000. Grandmothers and granddaughters: Old age pension and intra-household allocation in South Africa. MIT.

Galiani, Sebastian, Paul Gertler, and Ernesto Schargrodsky. 2005. Water for life: The impact of the privatization of water services on child mortality. *Journal of Political Economy* 113: 83–120.

Glewwe, Paul, Michael Kremer, Sylvie Moulin, and Eric Zitzewitz. 2000. Flip charts in Kenya. NBER Working Paper 8018, Cambridge, MA.

Heckman, James J., Lance Lochner, and Christopher Taber. 1998. *General-equilibrium treatment effects: A study of tuition policy,* 381–386. May: American Economic Review.

Ho, Daniel, Kosuke Imai, Gary King, and Elizabeth Stewart. 2006. Matching as non-parametric preprocessing for reducing model dependence in parametric causal inference. http://gking.harvard.edu/files/matchp.pdf [An excellent and up-to-date guide for practitioners.]

Imbens, Guido. 2004. Nonparametric estimation of average treatment effects under exogeneity: A review. *Review of Economics and Statistics* 86(1): 4–29 [An essential reference for anyone planning to use propensity score matching.].

Jalan, Jyotsna, and Martin Ravallion. 1999. Income gains from workfare and their distribution. Policy Research Working Paper. Washington, DC: World Bank.

Khandker, Shahidur. 2007. Program impact evaluation, PowerPoint presentation. Washington, DC: World Bank.

Khandker, Shahidur, Gayatri Koolwal, and Hussain Samad. 2010. *Handbook on impact evaluation,* World Bank, Washington DC.

Loefgren, H, R.L. Harris, and S. Robinson. 2001. A standard computable general equilibrium model in GAMS. TMD Discussion Paper No. 75, International Food Policy Research Institute, Washington, DC.

Murray, Michael. 2005. The bad, the weak, and the ugly: Avoiding the pitfalls of instrumental variables estimation. Bates College. October.

Ravallion, Martin. 1999. The mystery of the vanishing benefits: Ms Speedy Analyst's introduction to evaluation. Policy Research Working Paper 2153. Washington, DC: World Bank. [A witty and accessible introduction to some of the finer points of impact evaluation.]

Ravallion, Martin. 2008. Evaluating anti-poverty programs. In *Handbook of development economics*, vol. 4, ed. Evenson Robert and T. Paul Schultz. Amsterdam: North Holland 3787–3846.

Rosenbaum, P., and D. Rubin. 1983. The central role of the propensity score in observational studies for causal effects. *Biometrika* 70(1): 41–55.

Rubin, Donald, and Richard Waterman. 2006. Estimating the causal effects of marketing interventions using propensity score methodology. *Statistical Science* 21(2): 206–222.

Schultz, T. Paul. 2001. School subsidies for the poor: Evaluating the Mexican PROGRESA Poverty Program. Economic Growth Center Discussion Paper No. 834. Yale University, New Haven.

Sekhon, Jasjeet. 2006. Multivariate and propensity score matching software for causal inference. http://sekhon.berkeley.edu/matching Accessed on August 1, 2011.

Yamano, Takashi, Harold Alderman, and Luc Christiaensen. 2003. Child growth, shocks and food aid in rural Ethiopia. Policy Research Working Paper No. 3128. Washington, DC: World Bank.

A growing number of impact evaluations are now available on the Web, and can serve as templates for new evaluations; for a useful list, see http://www.worldbank.org/poverty (and follow links Impact Evaluation and then Selected Evaluations).

Chapter 13
Multilevel Models and Small-Area Estimation

13.1 Introduction

Household surveys can provide a great deal of information about incomes, spending, crops grown, and other household and individual characteristics. This detail comes at a cost: given the expense of surveying each household, the number of households sampled is typically fairly modest, rarely exceeding 10,000. Samples of this size are adequate for estimating the magnitudes of interest at a national level, or at the level of broad regions, with a reasonable degree of accuracy.

Estimates that are made at the national or regional level are not satisfying for those who want or need more disaggregated "small-area" results – for instance, poverty rates by county, or the number of disabled adults by district. The desire for small-area estimates is often motivated by practical considerations. For instance, small-area poverty mapping holds the potential for more accurate geographic targeting of the poor: if we could identify poor districts, rather than just poor regions, then in principle we could target efforts at alleviating poverty more efficiently. This helps explain why poverty maps have been constructed in over 30 developing countries (Demombynes et al. 2007). Whether better geographic targeting of poverty is possible in practice is an issue to which we return later in this chapter.

Small-area estimation is by no means confined to poverty mapping. The excellent *Guide to Small Area Estimation* published by the Australian Bureau of Statistics (ABS) lists eighteen in-house studies related to small-area estimation, dating back to 1976. The variety of measures that ABS researchers have tried to disaggregate is impressive, and include the incidence of disability, water usage, tax collections, personal income, small-business clusters, agricultural output, health outcomes, crimes, household expenditures, and unemployment.

The purpose of this chapter is to review the main small-area methods that one might want to use. Most of these are relatively straightforward, but it has become increasingly common to use multilevel models as part of the small-area

D. Haughton and J. Haughton, *Living Standards Analytics*, Statistics for Social
and Behavioral Sciences, DOI 10.1007/978-1-4614-0385-2_13,
© Springer Science+Business Media, LLC 2011

estimation process, and this is technically more difficult (Rao 2003). That is why a substantial part of this chapter is devoted to explaining how to specify and implement such models.

13.2 Simple Small-Area Models

Small-area methods may conveniently be divided into "simple" models, and regression-based models, as the framework set out in Fig. 13.1 makes clear.

A possible starting point is to use the data from the sample survey to generate estimates at the small-area level – for instance, of incomes or poverty. This "direct" estimator will be unbiased, but the estimate will be noisy because of the small sample size in each small area.

A second strategy is to use a Broad Area Ratio Estimator (BARE). Suppose district A is in region R, and that we have a small number n_A of observations on income (y_i) in district A, and a substantial number n_R of observations for the region. Then, instead of using a direct estimator of average incomes in A – which would be given by $(1/n_A) \sum_{i=1}^{n_A} y_i$ – we might use the estimator from the broader region, given by $(1/n_R) \sum_{i=1}^{n_R} y_i$. This broad area ratio estimator may be quite precise, but to the extent that small areas are heterogeneous, will not adequately reflect these area-to-area differences.

A variant on the broad area ratio estimator is to use auxiliary data, which yields the Broad Area Ratio Estimator with Auxiliary Data (BARE-AD) model. Suppose that we have information from another source – a census, for instance – on the age of residents in an area. We may first use the broad area data to estimate income by age, and then for each small area we can construct an age-weighted measure of income based on these numbers. The estimated income will vary from area to area because of variations in the observed age structure of their populations.

This BARE-AD model is one of a class of "synthetic" estimators, a term that was first used in a report by the US Center for Health Statistics (1968; see too the

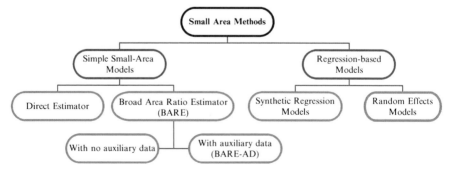

Fig. 13.1 Small-area modeling framework. (*Source*: Simplified version of Fig. 5.1 in Australian Bureau of Statistics 2006)

discussion by Moura 1994). In this application, the objective was to obtain state-level estimates of disability. The researchers had information on national rates of disability, gathered from a Health Interview Survey, that were broken down into 78 subgroups on the basis of variables that included age, sex, household size, income, and industry of employment. They then weighted these disability rates by the corresponding values (obtained from the 1960 population census) of the 78 subgroups in each of the states to arrive at their state-level estimates.

13.3   Synthetic Regression Models

A common approach to small-area estimation is to use a "synthetic regression" estimator. We suppose that we have relatively detailed information from a household survey of limited size, as well as auxiliary data from, for instance, a census. The auxiliary data contain a modest amount of information from a large number of households, but there are at least some variables – age, gender, household size, for instance – that are common both to the household survey and the auxiliary data.

In the first stage we construct and estimate a model using the household survey data. Our interest may be in measuring variable Y, as a function of some independent variables X. We may only choose regressors that are also found in the auxiliary data. As always, we hope for a tight-fitting equation.

In the second stage we use the estimated regression model, with the auxiliary data, to generate predicted values of Y for a large number of households. This will then allow us, if we so wish, to estimate averages or other measures based on Y for each of our small areas.

13.3.1   An Illustration: Poverty Mapping in Vietnam

A good example of the use of synthetic regression for poverty mapping comes from a study by Minot (2000), who used data from the Vietnam Living Standards Survey of 1992–1993 to estimate a probit model that estimated the likelihood that a (rural) household would be in poverty. He was able to find district-level means of the same regressors from the 1994 Agricultural Census, thereby generating estimates of the poverty rate for each of Vietnams 534 rural districts.

A subsequent study by Minot and Baulch (2002) built a similar model using data from the 1997–1998 Vietnam Living Standards Survey – this time with 6,000 observations – and applied the model to a 3% sample from the Population Census of 1999. An updated version of that study by Minot et al. (2006) was able to apply the model to a 33% sample from the same census. Cuong (2009) refined this approach by including GIS-based district-level data, including measures of elevation, soil quality, rainfall, and accessibility.

More recently, Swinkels and Turk (2007) re-estimated the poverty model using the data from the Vietnam Household Living Standards Survey of 2002, but still applied the model to the 33% sample from the 1999 census. These studies have produced attractive commune-level poverty maps. In passing, we note that Swinkels and Turk include an interesting discussion of the challenges involved in building local capacity for work of this nature.

The most serious drawback of synthetic models is that they assume that the variable of interest at the small-area level is determined by the auxiliary variables – i.e., the right-hand-side variables in the survey-based model, which are also available in the auxiliary data – in the same way for all areas. For instance, if the regression model shows that an extra year of age is associated with an additional $200 in annual income, the maintained assumption is that this same relationship holds in every small area. This is a strong assumption: local areas differ from one another for many reasons – remoteness, infrastructure, town spirit, and so on – and synthetic estimation tends to smooth out this variation. No model can expect to measure all of these factors completely, although the judicious choice of auxiliary variables can help, assuming that they are available (Moura 1994, p. 9).

13.4 Random Effects and Multilevel Models

13.4.1 Basic Idea

When the small areas are heterogeneous, and the differences are not adequately explained by the variables in the first-stage regression, it is usually more appropriate to use a model with random effects. Such models are also known as mixed models, or *multilevel models* (Goldstein 1999).

The term multilevel model originated in the education literature, and was popularized by the Center for Multilevel Modeling in the UK. The idea is that such models take into account the natural hierarchy that often exists in data sets, for example pupils in classes in schools in districts, through the use of random effects corresponding to the various levels (e.g., class random effects, school random effects, and so on).

The random effects capture some of the local variation, at least in the intercept of the regression model. The idea was first used by Fay and Herriott (1979), who were trying to estimate income for localities with less than a thousand inhabitants. An interesting early application was the study by Battese et al. (1988), who had data from a sample survey of farmers in Iowa who reported the areas devoted to growing corn and soybeans. They were able to wed this with satellite data in order to predict the areas devoted to these crops at the county level.

The dissertation and subsequent publications by Moura (1994) and Moura and Holt (1999) have yielded further results on the use of multilevel models for small-area estimation. More recently, Elbers et al. (2003) have used survey-cluster level random effects in the intercept of the first-stage regression model in the model of poverty mapping that they estimated for Ecuador. This paper also set out a simulation approach that has been widely imitated, and to which we return below.

13.4.2 Specifying and Estimating a Two-Level Model

Suppose we are interested in estimating some variable Y – for example, the log of expenditure per capita – at the level of a province or commune, but our household survey dataset is not large enough for direct estimation. Let i refer to the household (level 1), and j to the province (level 2) where the household is located. Then a basic multilevel model with a province-level random effect in the intercept can be represented by the equations:

$$Y_{ij} = \beta_{0j} + X'_{ij}\beta + e_{0ij} \tag{13.1}$$

$$\beta_{0j} = \beta_0 + u_{0j}. \tag{13.2}$$

Here, X_{ij} is a matrix of independent variables for household i in province j, and β denotes a vector of fixed parameters. Alternatively, we may write the model as

$$Y_{ij} = \beta_0 + X'_{ij}\beta + u_{0j} + e_{0ij}, \tag{13.3}$$

$$Y_{ij} = \beta_0 + X'_{ij}\beta + u_{ij}, \tag{13.4}$$

where $u_{ij} = u_{0j} + e_{0ij}$. The vector of disturbances in (13.4) consists of two parts, a location component u_{0j} that allows for spatial autocorrelation within a province, and a household component that picks up effects that are unique to each household. We assume for now that the u_{0j} are distributed normally with mean 0 and variance σ_{u0}^2, and that the e_{0ij} are distributed independently of the u_{0j} according to a normal distribution with mean 0 and variance σ_{e0}^2. Note that the variance of the Y_{ij} is then $\sigma_{u0}^2 + \sigma_{e0}^2$.

Mechanically, it is relatively straightforward to estimate this two-level model – for instance, using xtmixed or gllamm in Stata (GLLAMM 2009), or with the more-specialized MLwiN package (Center for Multilevel Modelling 2009). A strength of MLwiN is that it can estimate multilevel models using a Bayesian approach, which is particularly useful for problems that are not tractable with the restricted iterated generalized least squares (RIGLS) algorithm (Goldstein 1989); this arises, for instance, in extensions such as the case of multiple membership and cross-classified models (Browne et al. 2001; Moura and Migon 2002).

It is helpful to understand, intuitively at least, how the estimation works. First one estimates (13.4) using ordinary least squares, which generates residuals that serve as estimates, $\hat{u}_{ij}$, of the true errors. These may then be decomposed into estimates of the within-province means ($\hat{u}_{0j}$) and the household components ($\hat{e}_{0ij}$), which are the overall residuals net of the location components, since $\hat{u}_{ij} = \hat{u}_{0j} + \hat{e}_{0ij}$.

Table 13.1 Estimated coefficients of OLS and random intercept regression models of the log of real per capita expenditure, Vietnam, 2002

	Coefficient	Standard error	p-value
Ordinary least squares			
Dependent variable is Ln(real per capita expenditure)			
Constant	7.974	0.009	0.000
Household size	−0.085	0.002	0.000
Urban (yes = 1)	0.599	0.007	0.000
Years of education of head of household	0.037	0.001	0.000

Notes: $R^2 = 0.386$. No. of observations = 29,530.
Estimated using Stata command: `reg lrpcexp hhsize urban yearsedu`

	Coefficient	Standard error	p-value
Two-level model, random intercepts			
Dependent variable is Ln(real per capita expenditure)			
Constant	7.955	0.030	0.000
Household size	−0.083	0.001	0.000
Urban (yes = 1)	0.430	0.006	0.000
Years of education of head of household	0.043	0.001	0.000
Estimated standard error of $\hat{u}_{0j}$	0.223	0.020	
Estimated standard error of $\hat{e}_{0ij}$	0.418	0.002	

Notes: No. of observations = 29,530. Log likelihood = −16,271.327.
Estimated using Stata command: `xtmixed lrpcexp hhsize urban yearsedu || tinh`

Source: Data from Vietnam Household Living Standard Survey of 2002

One may then use $\hat{u}_{0j}$ and $\hat{e}_{0ij}$ to construct a variance–covariance matrix $\hat{V}$ that may be used to estimate (13.4) again, this time using generalized least squares. The process is iterated until the coefficient estimates converge. It is also possible to allow for heteroscedasticity in the $\hat{e}_{0ij}$ terms, and this is frequently useful; for an example see Elbers et al. (2003).

13.4.3   An Example: Expenditures in Vietnam

We illustrate the case of a basic two-level multilevel model using data from the 2002 Vietnam Household Living Standards Survey of 2002. Our interest is in estimating the level of per capita expenditure, first as an exercise at the level of each of the 61 provinces (as defined in 2002), and then more usefully at the level of 9,111 communes.

The 2002 VHLSS survey was actually quite large; it sampled 29,530 households, which would allow one to estimate per capita expenditure satisfactorily at the provincial level, but not at the level of each commune. Here we describe the application of the model to provinces, for expository purposes; for a four-level model that looks at households in communes in districts in provinces, see Phong et al. (2009).

The model is parsimonious: the dependent variable is the logarithm of household expenditure per capita, and the regressors are household size, a dummy variable set equal to 1 for urban areas, and the number of years of education of the head of household. The relevant results, generated by Stata, are shown in Table 13.1.

The top panel reports the OLS results: the signs and magnitudes of the coefficients are along the lines one would expect, and the small standard errors are due in part to the very large sample size. We should note, however, that this is not a model about inference; since our purpose is one of measurement (of magnitudes at the small-area level), rather than an attempt to identify causal relations, it is not particularly important that the model hew closely to economic theory, a point emphasized by Lanjouw (Zhao and Lanjouw 2009, p. 52).

The bottom panel of Table 13.1 shows the results of the random intercept model. With the exception of the coefficient on the urban dummy variable, the results look quite similar to the OLS estimates. However, we now have estimates of the standard errors of the two random effects.

The MLwiN package is designed to estimate multilevel models, uses a relatively intuitive interactive user interface, and presents the results in a very natural way. This may be seen in Table 13.2, which shows the MLwiN output for the OLS estimate at the top, and for the random-intercept model in the middle. Not surprisingly, these results are the same as those shown in Table 13.1. The bottom panel of Table 13.2 shows the MLwiN output for a more elaborate four-level multilevel version of the model, which also allows for random effects at the district and provincial levels in the coefficient of the urban dummy variable (Haughton and Phong 2010); this reflects the article's focus on the urban–rural gap. It is used as the basis for some of the maps shown later in this chapter (Phong et al. 2009).

In exploring the output of the two-level random intercept model, it is often useful to examine graphs such Fig. 13.2, which displays province-level random effects in increasing order, along with their 95% confidence intervals. It is clear from the graph that the random effects are significantly different from zero for almost all the provinces. Table 13.3 lists the provinces with their estimated random effects (i.e., $\hat{u}_{0j}$). Note the strong positive effect of location in urban centers such as Ho Chi Minh City, Hanoi, and Danang, despite the inclusion of an urban dummy variable in the model. Ba Ria-Vung Tau has a high random effect because it benefits from the presence of off-shore oil, and a strong tourism industry. There are strong negative effects for some of the more remote locations, including the provinces of Bac Kan, Hoa Binh, or Lai Chau, which are not only rural, but also relatively isolated and mountainous. It would be desirable to include additional variables that would pick up these patterns, as done by Cuong (2009).

13.4.4   Rationale for Using Multilevel Models for Small-Area Estimation

Having built the multilevel model, one applies it to the auxiliary data to arrive at the small-area estimates. In the illustrative case of the random-intercept model for Vietnam, the model set out in Table 13.2 was combined with data from the entire

Table 13.2 Estimated coefficients of OLS and random intercept regression models of the log of real per capita expenditure, Vietnam, 2002, generated by MLwiN

OLS model

$lrpcexp_{ij} \sim N(XB, \Omega)$

$lrpcexp_{ij} = \beta_{0i}cons + -0.085(0.002)hhsize_{ij} + 0.599(0.007)urban_{ij} + 0.037(0.001)yearsedu_{ij}$

$\beta_{0i} = 7.974(0.009) + e_{0ij}$

$\left[e_{0ij}\right] \sim N(0, \Omega_e) : \Omega_e = [0.226(0.002)]$

$-2*loglikelihood(IGLSDeviance) = 39838.863(29530$ of 29530 cases in use$)$

Random intercept model

$lrpcexp_{ij} \sim N(XB, \Omega)$

$lrpcexp_{ij} = \beta_{0ij}cons + -3(0.001)hhsize_{ij} + 0.430(0.006)urban_{ij} + 0.043(0.001)yearsedu_{ij}$

$\beta_{0ij} = 7.955(0.030) + u_{0j} + e_{0ij}$

$\left[u_{0j}\right] \sim N(0, \Omega_u) : \Omega_u = [0.050(0.009)]$

$\left[e_{0ij}\right] \sim N(0, \Omega_e) : \Omega_e = [0.175(0.001)]$

$-2*loglikelihood(IGLSDeviance) = 32542.662(29530$ of 29530 cases in use$)$

$lrpcexp_{ijkl} \sim N(XB, \Omega)$

$lrpcexp_{ijkl} = \beta_{0ijkl}cons + -0.039(0.009)\, female_{ijkl} + -0.441(0.011)\, children_{ijkl} +$
$\qquad -0.054(0.011)\, elderly_{ijkl} + -0.081(0.001)\, hhsize_{ijkl} + \beta 5kl\, urban_{jkl} +$
$\qquad 0.074(0.074)(0.007)\, safewater_{ijkl} + 0.287(0.007)\, toiletflush_{ijkl} +$
$\qquad 0.168(0.011)\, toiletsuilabh_{ijkl} + 0.190(0.006)\, housepermnt_{ijkl} +$
$\qquad -0.173(0.005)\, housetem_{ijkl} + 0.085(0.008)\, electricity_{ijkl} + 0.182(0.005)\, tv_{ijkl} +$
$\qquad 4.667(0.927)\, agerescale_{ijkl} + -41.759(8.886)\, agerescale\,2_{ijkl} +$
$\qquad hfill0.073(0.009)\, kinh_{ijkl} + 0.018(0.001)\, yearsedu_{ijkl} + 0.107(0.013)\, leader_{ijkl} +$
$\qquad 0.147(0.016)\, h.skilled_{ijkl} + 0.058(0.013)m.skilled_{ijkl} +$
$\qquad -0.047(0.005)\, noskilled_{ijkl} + 0.006(0.001)urbyearsed_{ijkl}$

$\beta_{0ijkl} = 7.893(0.035) + f_{0l} + v_{0kl} + u_{0jkl} + e_{0ijkl}$

$\beta_{5kl} = 0.076(0.018) + f_{5l} + v_{5kl}$

$\begin{bmatrix} f_{0l} \\ f_{5l} \end{bmatrix} \sim N(0, \Omega_f) : \Omega_f = \begin{bmatrix} 0.031(0.006) \\ -0.002(0.003)\ 0.008(0.003) \end{bmatrix}$

$\begin{bmatrix} v_{0kl} \\ v_{5kl} \end{bmatrix} \sim N(0, \Omega_v) : \Omega_v = \begin{bmatrix} 0.015(0.001) \\ -0.002(0.002)\ 0.006(0.003) \end{bmatrix}$

$\left[u_{0jkl}\right] \sim N(0, \Omega_u) : \Omega_u = [0.012(0.001)]$

$-2*loglikelihood(IGLSdeviance) = 14782.110(29530$ of 29530 cases in use$)$

Source: Data from Vietnam Household Living Standard Survey of 2002. *Notes*: The variables in the bottom panel that may require further explanation include female (=1 if head of household is female), children (number of children in household), elderly (number of elderly people in household), safewater (=1 if household has access to safe water), toiletsuilabh (=1 if a "suilabh" toilet is used), agerescale (age of head of household, rescaled), kinh (=1 if head of household is ethnic Vietnamese), leader (=1 if job has some leadership component), h_skilled (=1 if job requires university education), m_skilled (=1 if job requires medium skills such as high-school vocational education), and urbyearsed (interaction of urban and years of education)

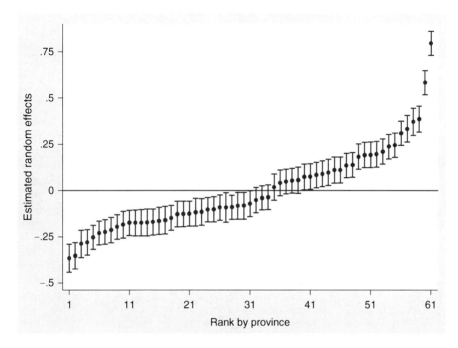

Fig. 13.2 Graph of province-level random effects (with approximately 95% confidence intervals) for two-level random intercept model of the log of per capita spending, Vietnam 2002. *Notes*: Model estimates are given in Table 13.1. This graph was generated by Stata, but MLwiN has a similar capability

1999 population census. The estimated random effects must be included in the estimates, of course (Moura 1994).

It is not self-evident that the use of random effects models improve the quality of small-area estimation, but Moura and Holt (1999) confirm it does in fact do so, in the sense that the mean square error approximation is smaller when the model includes them. Moura and Holt establish this formally by computing an approximation to the mean square error in the case of a two-level model.

However, in general, approximations of the mean square error, such as done by Moura and Holt, involve extremely complicated matrix computations. So it is useful to have at hand alternative validation methods, such as those proposed in Brown et al. (2001). One of their suggestions is to build a scatterplot of the direct estimates (directly estimated from the survey, with an unbiased estimator that is noisy, given the low small-area sample size in the survey) against the small-area estimates. If the small-area estimates are "close" to the true small-area values of interest, then the direct estimates should behave like random observations with the same mean as the small-area estimates. One can test whether an ordinary least squares line through this scatter plot differs significantly from the identity line.

Table 13.3 Estimated province-level random effects for a regression model of the log of per capita expenditure, Vietnam 2002

Province	Residual	Rank	Province	Residual	Rank	Province	Residual	Rank
Ha Noi	0.583	60	Quang Ninh	0.042	36	Ho Chi Minh	0.796	61
Hai Phong	0.054	38	Lai Chau	−0.287	3	Ninh Thuan	−0.117	22
Vinh Phuc	−0.126	20	Son La	−0.185	10	Binh Phuoc	0.056	39
Ha Tay	−0.039	33	Hoa Binh	−0.352	2	Tay Ninh	0.111	46
Bac Ninh	0.076	41	Thanh Hoa	−0.252	5	Binh Duong	0.333	57
Hai Duong	−0.103	24	Nghe An	−0.229	6	Dong Nai	0.309	56
Hung Yen	−0.092	26	Ha Tinh	−0.214	8	Binh Thuan	0.197	52
Ha Nam	−0.175	12	Quang Binh	−0.170	15	BaRia VungTau	0.387	59
Nam Dinh	−0.090	28	Quang Tri	−0.164	16	Long An	0.183	49
Thai Binh	−0.223	7	Hue	0.091	43	Dong Thap	0.049	37
Ninh Binh	−0.127	19	Da Nang	0.371	58	An Giang	0.245	55
Ha Giang	−0.159	17	Quang Nam	−0.125	21	Tien Giang	0.237	54
Cao Bang	−0.172	14	Quang Ngai	−0.101	25	Vinh Long	0.084	42
Lao Cai	−0.083	29	Binh Dinh	−0.036	34	Ben Tre	0.192	50
Bac Kan	−0.365	1	Phu Yen	0.018	35	Kien Giang	0.210	53
Lang Son	−0.082	30	Khanh Hoa	0.193	51	Can Tho	0.138	48
Tuyen Quang	−0.115	23	Kon Tum	−0.091	27	Tra Vinh	0.074	40
Yen Bai	−0.174	13	Gia Lai	−0.279	4	Soc Trang	0.111	45
Thai Nguyen	−0.052	32	Dak Lak	−0.196	9	Bac Lieu	0.098	44
Phu Tho	−0.175	11	Lam Dong	−0.071	31	Ca Mau	0.135	47
Bac Giang	−0.148	18						

Source: As for Table 13.2

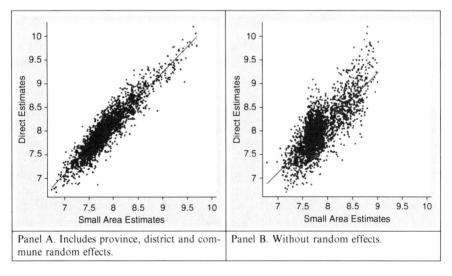

Panel A. Includes province, district and commune random effects.	Panel B. Without random effects.

Fig. 13.3 Scatter plots of direct estimates (*vertical axis*) vs. small-area estimates (*horizontal axis*) of the log of per capita expenditure, with and without random effects. (**a**) Includes province, district, and commune random effects. (**b**) Without random effects. (*Source*: Phong et al. 2009)

Fig. 13.4 Map of Vietnam
featuring small-area estimates
(with random effects) of the
log of expenditure per capita
at the commune level.
(*Source*: Phong et al. (2009)
based on VHLSS 2002 using
the four-level model set out in
Table 13.2)

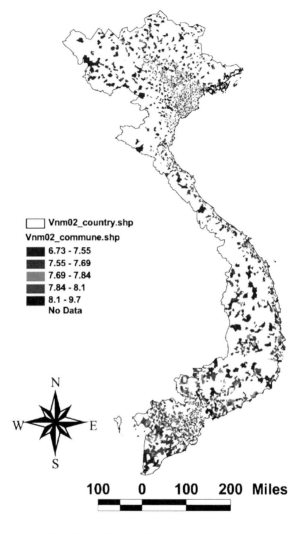

In Fig. 13.3, we display a pair of such graphs resulting from a model used in
Phong et al. (2009) that includes a number of predictors and four levels (household
in commune in district in province) to obtain commune-level means of the (logarithm
of) household expenditure per capita in Vietnam for 2002. The improvement that
arises from the inclusion of the random effects is quite clear, even to the naked eye.

Figures 13.4 and 13.5 show how one might display small-area estimates using
GIS (Geographic Information Systems) tools; here we use ArcView to map the log
of expenditure per capita for Vietnam for 2002 at the commune level, using the
four-level random effects model set out in the bottom panel of Table 13.2. One
observes a concentration of high estimates around the two main cities (Hanoi and
Ho Chi Minh City), and also in the Mekong Delta to the south of the country, and
along the East Coast. We note that the map presented in Fig. 13.4 displays small-

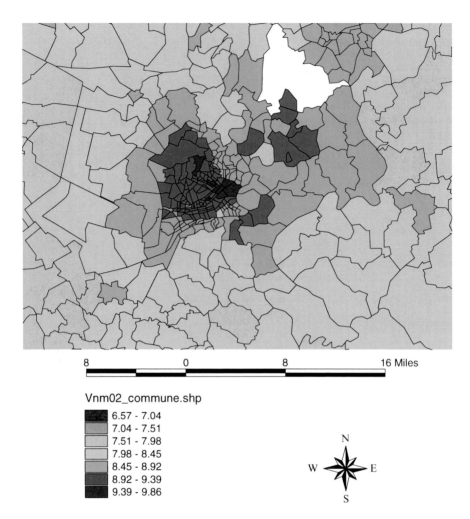

Fig. 13.5 Map featuring small-area estimates (with random effects) for Hanoi and immediate environs of the log of per capita expenditure. (*Source*: Phong et al. 2009)

area estimates only for communes that were covered by the VHLSS 2002. To obtain estimates for communes not covered by VHLSS 2002, a reasonable approach consists in averaging the commune random effects for the four communes geographically closest to a noncovered commune, keeping in mind that all districts and provinces (but not communes) were covered by the survey. This approach was implemented in Fig. 13.5.

Given a model (based on survey data) and auxiliary data, one obtains a single estimate of the variable of interest such as income or poverty, at the household level (and, by aggregation, at the small-area level). However, we are also interested in knowing how accurate these estimates are. This is important if, for instance, we plan to use the results to help target poverty interventions.

To obtain standard errors for each small-area estimate, an attractive approach is to simulate the results (Pfeffermann and Tiller 2005). This allows one to account for two sources of error: *model error* occurs because the parameters of the model itself are estimated using survey data; and *idiosyncratic error* is reflected in the household-level errors.

First one draws a set of model coefficients, $\tilde{\beta}_{0j}^r$ and $\tilde{\beta}^r$, from the multivariate normal distributions of β_{0j} and β, along with a measure of the standard error of $\hat{u}_{0j}$, where r is an index in $r = 1, \ldots, R$. These are then combined with the auxiliary (e.g., census) data to generate an estimate of the standard error of e_{0ij}. This allows one to draw values $\tilde{u}_{0j}^r$ and $\tilde{e}_{0ij}^r$ from their distributions, and so obtain a simulated value of the outcome variable $\tilde{y}_i^r$ for each household, based on the drawn parameters and disturbances, using $\tilde{y}_i^r = \mathbf{X}'_i \tilde{\beta} + \tilde{u}_{0j}^r + \tilde{e}_{0ij}^r$. Then, within each small area one may compute measures such as inequality or poverty, if desired. This parametric bootstrapping procedure is repeated R times, which then allows one to generate standard errors for the small-area measures of interest.

13.5 Conclusion

A great deal of recent effort has gone into poverty mapping, and the World Bank has developed a sophisticated tool, PovMap2, that is designed to make it comparatively easy to do the job well (Zhao and Lanjouw 2009). It is not clear that the poverty mapping project has lived up to its initial promise.

Some studies do find the small-area estimates to be potentially accurate enough to help guide policymakers in targeting interventions. Mistiaen et al. (2001) combine information from a 1993 household survey and the 1993 population census in Madagascar to produce estimates of poverty for each of the country's 1,248 *firaisanas* (communes). They find "considerable spatial heterogeneity in poverty levels across administrative levels within provinces," but also conclude that "on average most of the inequality in Madagascar is attributable to inequality within communes" (p. i). To the best of our knowledge, these findings have not been used in the design of poverty interventions in Madagascar.

A similar study, done in Mozambique, combines data from a 1996–1997 living standards survey with information from the 1997 population and housing census (Simler and Nhate 2005). Their conclusion is more pessimistic: "unfortunately, the notion of poor areas might not always be especially useful, as appears to be the case in Mozambique" (p. ii). They find that poverty is not strongly concentrated spatially; given that the poor and nonpoor live close to one another, geographically targeted interventions to alleviate poverty are likely to result in substantial leakage to the nonpoor.

Demombynes et al. (2007) are able to use data from rural Mexico to compare small-area estimates with the actual outcomes. They find a strong correlation between estimated and true values of measures of poverty and expenditure, but the small-area estimates do a poor job of measuring inequality. They also emphasize the importance of having a good predictive model, noting that "precision of estimates is shown to diminish markedly if unobserved location effects at the village level are not well captured in underlying consumption models" (p. 2).

This brings us back to the central theme of this chapter, which is that serious attention needs to be given to modeling the relationships that underlie small-area estimation. The multilevel (i.e., hierarchical) models introduced here represent a useful starting point.

References

Australian Bureau of Statistics. 2006. *A guide to small area estimation version 1.1*. Canberra: Australian Bureau of Statistics.

Battese, G.E., R.M. Harter, and W.A. Fuller. 1988. An error components model for prediction of country crop areas using survey and satellite data. *Journal of the American Statistical Association* 83: 28–36.

Brown, Gary, Ray Chambers, Patrick Heady, and Dick Heasman. 2001. Evaluation of small area estimation methods – An application to unemployment estimates from the UK LFS. *Proceedings of Statistics Canada Symposium 2001*.

Browne, W.J., H. Goldstein, and J. Rasbash. 2001. Multiple membership multiple classification (MMMC) models. *Statistical Modelling* 1: 103–124. http://www.cmm.bristol.ac.uk/team/mmmcm.pdf. Accessed April 2011.

Center for Multilevel Modelling. 2009. MLwiN; a Software Package for fitting multilevel models. http://www.cmm.bristol.ac.uk/MLwiN/index.shtml. Accessed April 2011.

Cuong, Nguyen Viet. 2009. Updating poverty maps without panel data: Evidence from Vietnam. *Asian Economic Journal* 23(4): 397–418.

Demombynes, Gabriel, Chris Elbers, Jean Lanjouw, and Peter Lanjouw. 2007. How good a map? Putting small area estimation to the test. Policy Research Working Paper 4155. Washington, DC: World Bank.

Elbers, Chris, Jean Lanjouw, and Peter Lanjouw. 2003. Micro-level estimation of poverty and inequality. *Econometrica* 71(1): 355–364.

Fay, R.E., and R.A. Herriott. 1979. Estimates of income for small places: An application of James-Stein procedures to census data. *Journal of the American Statistical Association* 74: 269–277.

Generalized Linear Latent and Mixed Models (GLLAMM). 2009. http://www.gllamm.org. Accessed April 2011.

Goldstein, H. 1989. Restricted unbiased iterative generalised least squares estimation. *Biometrika* 76: 622–623.

Goldstein, H. 1999. *Multilevel statistical models*. http://www.ats.ucla.edu/stat/examples/msm_goldstein/goldstein.pdf. Accessed April 2011.

Haughton, Dominique, and Nguyen Phong. 2010. Multilevel models and inequality in Vietnam. *Journal of Data Science* 8: 289–306.

Minot, Nicholas W. 2000. Generating disaggregated poverty maps: An application to Vietnam. *World Development* 28(2): 319–331.

Minot, Nicholas W., and Bob Baulch. 2002. The spatial distribution of poverty in Vietnam and the potential for targeting. MTID Discussion Paper 42. International Food Policy Research Institute, Washington, DC.

Minot, Nicholas, Bob Baulch, and Michael Epprecht. 2006. Poverty and inequality in Vietnam: Spatial patterns and geographic determinants. Research Report 148. IFPRI, Washington, DC.

Mistiaen, Johan, Berk Özler, Tiaray Razafimanantena, and Jean Razafindravonoma. 2001. Putting welfare on the map in Madagascar. Africa Region Working Paper Series No. 34. Washington, DC: World Bank.

Moura, Fernando Antonio da Silva. 1994. Small area estimation using multilevel models. PhD Thesis, University of Southampton.

Moura, Fernando Antonio da Silva, and David Holt. 1999. Small area estimation using multilevel models. *Survey Methodology* 25(1): 73–80.

Moura, F.A.S., and H.S. Migon. 2002. Bayesian spatial models for small area estimation of proportions. *Statistical Modelling* 2: 183–201.

National Center for Health Statistics. 1968. *Synthetic state estimates of Disability*. PHS Publication Number 1759. Washington, DC: Government Printing Office.

Phong, Nguyen, Dominique Haughton, Irene Hudson, and John Boland. 2009. Multilevel models and small area estimation in the context of Vietnam Living Standards Surveys. Federal Committee on Statistical Methodology Research Conference, Washington, DC.

Pfeffermann, D., and R. Tiller. 2005. Bootstrap approximation to prediction MSE for state-space models with estimated parameters. *Journal of Time Series Analysis* 26: 893–216.

Rao, J.N.K. 2003. *Small area estimation*. New York: Wiley.

Simler, Kenneth, and Virgulino Nhate. 2005. Poverty, inequality, and geographic targeting: Evidence form small-area estimates in Mozambique. FCND Discussion Paper 192. IFPRI, Washington, DC.

Swinkels, Rob and Carrie Turk. 2007. Poverty mapping in Vietnam. In: *More than a pretty picture: Using poverty maps to design better policies and interventions*, eds., Tara Bedi, Aline Coudouel, and Kenneth Simler, Chap. 14. Washington, DC: World Bank.

Zhao, Qinghua, and Peter Lanjouw. 2009. Using PovMap2: A user's guide. Draft. Washington, DC: World Bank. http://econ.worldbank.org/WBSITE/EXTERNAL/EXTDEC/EXTRESEARCH/EXTPROGRAMS/EXTPOVRES/0,,contentMDK:22717057~pagePK:64168182~piPK:64168060~theSitePK:477894,00.html. Downloaded 16 March 2011.

Chapter 14
Duration Models

14.1 Introduction

We are often interested in modeling the time that elapses between one event and another – for instance, between one birth and the next, between a medical treatment and recovery, or between losing a job and finding the next one. Duration models are concerned with describing and explaining these spells.

Duration models are widely used in engineering studies of reliability, where the issue of concern is determining how long a machine or component will last until it fails. Much of the terminology used in duration models comes from the widespread use of such models in medical research, where the effectiveness of a treatment may be measured by the length of time that the patient lives (the duration function), whether he is still alive (the survival function), and the risk of dying (the hazard function).

The fundamental problem in almost all duration problems, and the main reason that simple regression techniques are not generally applicable, is that the data are censored. Suppose, for instance, that we wish to evaluate a job-training program by measuring the amount of time (the duration, or spell) that it takes for someone who has undertaken the training to obtain a job. We can measure the duration for those who, at the time of the survey, have found employment; but for those who have not yet found a job we only know that the duration is at least as long as the time between the end of the training and the time of the survey. Many of the observations are therefore incomplete, and so are censored.

14.2 Basics

It is helpful to begin by setting out the terminology and essential principles in a somewhat more formal manner. Let T be a random variable representing duration, such as the time until failure of a unit, and let $P(x)$ refer to the probability of event x.

D. Haughton and J. Haughton, *Living Standards Analytics*, Statistics for Social
and Behavioral Sciences, DOI 10.1007/978-1-4614-0385-2_14,
© Springer Science+Business Media, LLC 2011

The survival function $S(t)$, sometimes referred to as the reliability function, is defined as

$$S(t) = P(T \geq t), \tag{14.1}$$

and it gives the probability that the spell is at least as long as time t. This is also the probability that one has "survived." If T has a continuous probability distribution $f(t)$, then the cumulative probability, $F(t)$, is given by

$$F(t) = P(T \leq t) = 1 - S(t), \tag{14.2}$$

since $P(T = t) = 0$, and the density function is therefore

$$f(t) = F'(t) = -S'(t). \tag{14.3}$$

It follows that the probability that a unit fails in a short time interval $[t, t + \Delta t]$ is

$$P(t \leq T \leq t + \Delta t) \approx f(t)\, \Delta t. \tag{14.4}$$

In practice, it is often helpful to measure the probability of imminent failure, given that a unit has not yet failed. This "proneness to failure" is measured by the *hazard function*, or failure rate function, $h(t)$, given by

$$h(t) = \lim_{\Delta t \to 0} \frac{P(t \leq T < t + \Delta t \mid T \geq t)}{\Delta t} \tag{14.5}$$

so

$$h(t) = \lim_{\Delta t \to 0} \frac{P(t \leq T < t + \Delta t)}{P(T \geq t)} \frac{1}{\Delta t} = \lim_{\Delta t \to 0} \frac{1}{\Delta t} \frac{F(t + \Delta t) - F(t)}{S(t)} = \frac{f(t)}{S(t)}. \tag{14.6}$$

The survival function S, cumulative density function F, density f and hazard function h are alternative ways of describing T, but they are mathematically equivalent in the sense that given any one of these functions, the others may be derived (Crowder et al. 1991, p. 14).

If the hazard function is constant, so that $h(t) = \rho$, then the probability of imminent failure does not change over time: the process does not age, or alternatively, has no memory. In this case, the survivor function is given by $S(t) = e^{-\rho t}$ and the density function is exponential, taking on the form $f(t) = \rho\, e^{-\rho t}$. Graphs of density and hazard functions are discussed in more detail below, and for the exponential case are shown in the top row of Fig. 14.3.

The hazard rate could rise over time, in which case it is said to have positive duration dependence, or an increasing failure rate. This is to be expected, for instance, if a unit is subject to aging, so the older it is, the greater the hazard of failure (or dying). In some situations it is more likely that $h(t)$ should be a decreasing function of t, in which case we have negative duration dependence, or a decreasing failure rate. For instance, the probability that an unemployed person will find a job in the coming week might be expected to fall, the longer the time that the person remains unemployed. More complex patterns are also possible – such as the "bathtub" case where the hazard rate first falls and then rises over time – but, as will be seen below, such cases are generally more difficult to model.

14.3   An Exploratory Analysis of Duration Data

A good place to begin the analysis of duration data is with the nonparametric estimation of the survival function $S(t)$; in subsequent sections we turn to the semiparametric Cox model and then to fully parametric estimators of duration models.

To fix ideas, in what follows, we make extensive use of data from the Vietnam Living Standards Survey of 1993 (VLSS93) on the interval (denoted by int23) between the birth of a second and a third child. The sample consists of households with at least two children, except for those few cases of households that were interviewed less than 9 months after the birth of their second child. Thus the duration variable, int23, is measured in months, and never takes on a value below 9. Observations for which there was no third child by the time of the interview are censored: we only know that the interval between the second and third child is greater than int23.

This interval is of particular interest because state policy in Vietnam stipulates that families should have at most two children, separated by 2–5 years. For further background and a discussion of this policy, see the article by Hoa et al. (1996).

Households were selected by a stratified double cluster design; details of the sample design are available at the World Bank Living Standards Measurement Survey site.[1] The two strata are rural and urban areas of Vietnam. Communes are selected from each stratum, with probability proportional to the number of households, then villages (rural areas) or wards (urban areas), again with probability proportional to the number of households, then households (randomly with equal probability). Note that VLSS93 is self-weighing (see aforementioned World Bank site).

The survey features quite an extensive questionnaire, covering a number of areas; we focus here on a few variables of interest included in the section on fertility.

---

[1] http://www.worldbank.org/html/prdph/lsms/country/vn98/VIE14.pdf

14.3.1   The Kaplan–Meier Estimator

It is possible to estimate the survival function, $S(t)$, nonparametrically. The procedure is first to sort all the observations from the smallest to the largest duration. Let n_j be the number of observations of households at risk just before time t_j, and d_j be the number of those households who "died" at time t_j. Then the Kaplan–Meier estimator of the survival function is given by

$$\hat{S}(t) = \prod_{j|t_j \leq t} \left(\frac{n_j - d_j}{n_j} \right). \tag{14.7}$$

The Kaplan–Meier estimator is a step function, with steps at the observed values of the duration variable, and $S(t)$ represents the probability that the duration variable is at least t.

To illustrate, consider our example, where n_j is the number of households that have only two children and have not yet been interviewed just before time t_j, and d_j is the number of these that had a third child at time t_j. The duration variable, int23, is the interval between the birth of the second and the third child, or between the birth of the second child and the time of the survey if the family had only two children when interviewed.

The mechanics of constructing the Kaplan–Meier estimator in this case are set out with the help of Table 14.1, where we show the computations for the first 20 observations from the VLSS93 survey. The first three columns present the raw data from the survey; these are then sorted by duration (column 4) and ties are removed (e.g., the value 29 of int23 appears twice in column 2 and once in column 4), the number of households at risk is determined (column 5), and the number who "die" – i.e., have a third child – is computed (column 6). The estimate of the survival function is given in the final column. These results may usefully be summarized in a graph of the survival function against time, as in the top panel of Fig. 14.1.

The second panel of Fig. 14.1 shows a more substantive use of the survival function. Surveys of attitudes in Vietnam consistently find that parents express a preference for having a son (Haughton and Haughton 1995). There may be a rational economic basis for this, as parents are traditionally supported in their old age by their son(s), while daughters usually move away from their families when they marry. There is also a belief, in the Confucian tradition, that sons are needed to maintain the family line.

But does an attitude of son preference actually change fertility behavior? One might suppose that if households have son preference, then those with two daughters will move more quickly to have a third child than those who already have a son. A first cut at determining whether this might be so comes from the survival functions at the bottom of Fig. 14.1; the dotted line shows the function for households with two children and at least one son while the lower, solid line shows the function for households with two children and no son. In this case, "survival" measures the

Table 14.1 Illustrative computation of the Kaplan–Meier estimator of the survival function, interval between second and third child, Vietnam, 1993

Unsorted raw data			Data sorted from lowest to highest duration (by int23)				
Observation number	int23	third	int23	Households at risk (n_j)	Households having 3rd child (d_j)	$(n_j - d_j)/n_j$	Product $\hat{S}(t)$
(1)	(2)	(3)	(4)	(5)	(6)	(7)	(8)
1	29	1	10	20	0	1.00	1.00
2	96	1	15	19	1	0.95	0.95
3	36	1	17	18	1	0.94	0.89
4	31	1	18	17	1	0.94	0.84
5	20	1	19	16	1	0.94	0.79
6	29	1	20	15	1	0.93	0.74
7	18	1	24	14	0	1.00	0.74
8	76	0	29	13	2	0.85	0.62
9	32	1	30	11	1	0.91	0.57
10	60	1	31	10	1	0.90	0.51
11	15	1	32	9	1	0.89	0.45
12	17	1	36	8	1	0.88	0.40
13	10	0	45	7	1	0.86	0.34
14	19	1	46	6	1	0.83	0.28
15	48	1	48	5	2	0.60	0.17
16	24	0	60	3	1	0.67	0.11
17	48	1	76	2	0	1.00	0.11
18	30	1	96	1	1	0.00	0.00
19	46	1					
20	45	1					

Note: The data come from the Vietnam Living Standards Survey of 1993. The int23 variable gives the time, in months, between the birth of the second child and the birth of the third child (or the date of interview, if that comes sooner). "third" is equal to 1 if the household has a third child and to 0 otherwise

probability that the household does not have a third child. It is clear from the graph that two-child households without sons are more likely to have a third child, and to have that child sooner, than households that already have a son. In other words, there is some evidence that fertility behavior in Vietnam is influenced by son preference.

14.4   Cox Proportional Hazards Model

One of the most popular approaches to analyzing the effects of relevant variables on the hazard rate uses the semiparametric proportional hazards model first proposed by Cox (1972). The model specifies the hazard function $h(t)$ for individual i, conditional on the covariates $\mathbf{x}$, as

$$h(t_i, \mathbf{x}_i) = h_0(t_i) \cdot \exp(\mathbf{x}_i \beta). \qquad (14.8)$$

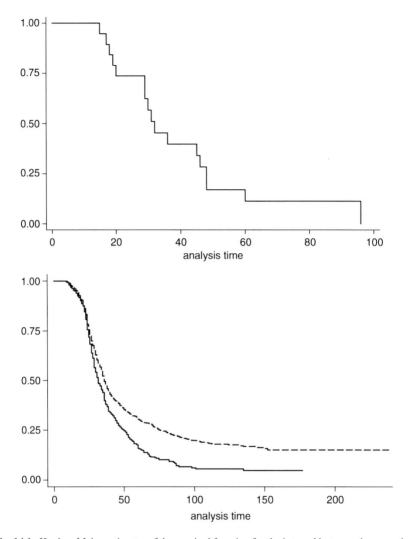

Fig. 14.1 Kaplan–Meier estimates of the survival function for the interval between the second and third child, Vietnam, 1993. The *top panel* shows the estimates for the first 20 observations; the *bottom panel* shows the survival function for two-child households with no sons (*solid line*) and with at least one son (*dotted line*)

Here, β is a vector of unknown parameters and $h_0(t_i)$ is the "baseline" hazard, which is the hazard function when all predictors are equal to zero. A virtue of this technique is that no assumption needs to be made about the distribution of the birth intervals, but the cost is that it yields relative, but not absolute, hazard rates. The β coefficients can be estimated without needing to estimate the baseline hazard function.

Implicit in the equation above is the proportional hazard assumption, which states that if a covariate x_j increases by one unit while the other variables are held

Table 14.2 Proportional hazards model of the risk of giving birth, for households with two children, Vietnam, 1993

Variable	Coefficient	SE	Z-statistic	p-value
Household has a son	−0.246	0.060	−4.10	0.000
Years of education of household head	−0.046	0.008	−6.01	0.000
Age of mother in years, squared	−0.00051	0.00015	−3.47	0.001
Real expenditure per capita p.a. (m dong)	0.00051	0.00005	−5.05	0.000
Household lives in an urban area	−0.402	0.085	−4.72	0.000
Region 2 (Hanoi and surrounds)	−0.322	0.070	−4.60	0.000

Notes: Based on 2,061 observations, of which 605 were censored. Log likelihood = −9,894.9765.
Source of data: Vietnam Living Standards Survey 1992–1993

constant, the hazard is multiplied by e^{β_j}, and this multiplicative factor does not change over time. This is a fairly strong assumption, which needs to be verified.

To illustrate the Cox model at work we return to our example of the interval between second and third births in Vietnam in 1993. The results, which were generated using the stcox command in Stata, are shown in Table 14.2, where the dependent variable is the interval between the second and third births, and censoring is taken into account. The imminent probability (i.e., hazard) of giving birth is substantially lower in urban areas, in Region 2 (the area that includes Hanoi), and for households that already have a son. This provides formal statistical evidence of the presence of son preference in Vietnam in 1993.

Note that the output from a proportional hazard model is similar to that of a linear regression in its format. The Z-statistic equals the estimated coefficient divided by its standard error. The likelihood (the logarithm of which is given in the notes below Table 14.2) represents how likely it is that the data would have arisen from the estimated model. The higher the likelihood, the better the fit. The p-values in the last column are those for testing that each population parameter is zero (or not).

It is important to check that the proportional hazard assumption is reasonable. A useful visual way to do this is as follows: Recalling that

$$h(t) = \frac{f(t)}{S(t)} = -\frac{S'(t)}{S(t)}, \tag{14.9}$$

and that

$$h_0(t) = \frac{f_0(t)}{S_0(t)} = -\frac{S'_0(t)}{S_0(t)}, \tag{14.10}$$

it follows that

$$-\frac{S'(t)}{S(t)} = -\frac{S'_0(t)}{S_0(t)} e^{x_i \beta}. \tag{14.11}$$

Integrating (14.11) over the interval $[0, t]$, and taking logarithms, yields

$$\ln(-\ln(S(t))) = \ln(-\ln(S_0(t))) + \mathbf{x}_i \beta. \tag{14.12}$$

Since the second term on the right hand side does not depend on time, it follows that by drawing graphs of $\ln(-\ln(S(t)))$ against time (t) for different values of the regressors $(\mathbf{x}_i)$ we should get curves that are close to being parallel with one another.

This property can be appreciated visually in the top panel of Fig. 14.2, where the curves for two-child households with and without a son, based on (14.12), are close to parallel.

The bottom panel of Fig. 14.2 shows the estimated survival function for two-child households with and without a son, based on the proportional hazard model estimates. The step functions are computed using the Kaplan–Meier estimator and the smooth lines are obtained from the Cox model. The two sets of curves are close to one another, and so the model fit appears to be adequate.

14.5   Parametric Regression Models

Many duration studies use fully parametric models, which are elegant and relatively simple but impose more structure on the data than the semiparametric Cox proportional hazards model. These models use the time interval until an event as a dependent variable, and take censoring into account by incorporating it into the likelihood function, a function of the unknown parameters that evaluates how likely it is that the model with these parameters would have generated these data. Maximum likelihood estimation, used here, estimates the parameters by finding values for them that maximize the likelihood function.[2] The most popular of the parametric specifications is the Weibull model, which is both flexible and easy to use, and includes the exponential model as a special case.

14.5.1   Weibull Regression Models

The survival function for the Weibull distribution may be written as

$$S(t) = e^{-(\lambda t)^p}, \tag{14.13}$$

---

[2] See http://en.wikipedia.org/wiki/Maximum_likelihood for more formal definitions and examples.

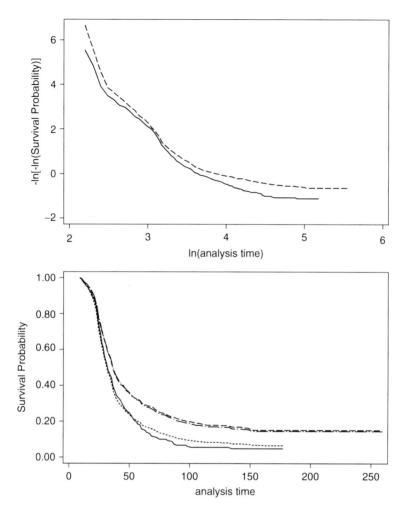

Fig. 14.2 Check for proportionality, and survival function, for the interval between the second and third child, Vietnam, 1993. The *top panel* shows that the relationship between $-\ln(-\ln(S(t)))$ and $\ln(t)$ for households without a son (*solid line*) is parallel to that for households with a son (*dotted line*), suggesting proportionality. The *bottom panel* shows survival functions for households with a son (*upper lines*) and without a son (*lower lines*); the jagged lines are Kaplan–Meier estimates and the *smooth lines* are based on the Cox proportional hazard model

and the associated hazard function is given by

$$h(t) = \lambda p(\lambda t)^{p-1}. \tag{14.14}$$

The Weibull distribution has three major advantages for studies of duration: it is concentrated on positive values, it is straightforward, and it is quite flexible. There are two parameters, a scaling parameter λ, and a shape parameter p. A set of Weibull densities and the associated hazard rates are shown in Fig. 14.3, for four different values of p.

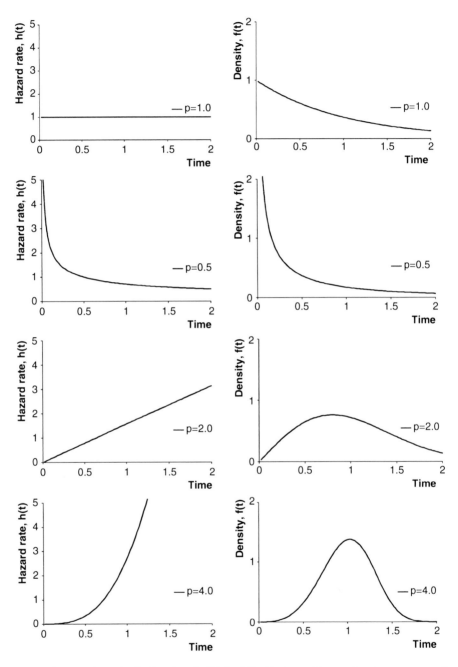

Fig. 14.3 Hazard and density functions for Weibull distributions with mean 1 and p parameters of 1.0, 0.5, 2.0, and 4.0

When $p = 1$, the hazard rate is constant over time and the Weibull collapses to the exponential distribution, which is shown in the top two panels in Fig. 14.3. For values of $p < 1$ the hazard rate falls as time passes (negative duration dependence); this case is displayed in the second row of Fig. 14.3. In the case where $p = 2$, the hazard rate rises linearly over time and the Weibull density has a clear single peak, as the third row of diagrams in Fig. 14.3 shows; for $1 < p < 2$ the hazard rate also rises over time, but at a decreasing rate. Finally, when $p > 2$, the hazard rate rises more than linearly over time; the case for $p = 4$ is shown in the bottom row of Fig. 14.3.

One does not need to specify the parameters of the Weibull model in advance, and so the data can be allowed to determine the shape parameter p. On the other hand, the hazard rate for the Weibull distribution is always monotonic; to construct a "bathtub" model where the hazard rate first falls and then rises one would need for example a mixture of Weibull models, an issue to which we return in Sect. 14.5.2 below.

The standard way to introduce covariates into the Weibull model is to allow λ to be a function of the relevant regressors, so that

$$\lambda_i = e^{-\mathbf{x}_i \beta}. \tag{14.15}$$

The $\mathbf{x}_i$ variables are assumed to remain unchanged in the course of the spell under consideration, from $T = 0$ until $T = t_i$. In practice, these variables – such as education, or even per capita income – are often measured at the point when the survey was undertaken, which is when $T = t_i$. By allowing λ to vary with the covariates, the hazard function now becomes

$$h(t, \mathbf{x}_i) = p \cdot t^{p-1} \cdot e^{-p \cdot (\mathbf{x}_i \beta)}. \tag{14.16}$$

The effect of the covariates is to "stretch" or "compress" the units of measurement on the time axis, which is why such models are sometimes referred to as accelerated failure time models (Greene 2003, p. 796).

In empirical work we are usually interested in the sign and significance of the estimated β coefficients. Estimation is typically done by forming the likelihood function, taking censoring into account. Practically speaking, this can be done with a number of statistical packages, whose strengths and weaknesses are reviewed in Haughton (1997).

Returning to our Vietnamese example, where we model the interval between the second and third births in a family using data collected in 1993, the estimated coefficients based on a Weibull model are shown in Table 14.3. The first point to note is that the estimate of p is 1.60, which implies that the hazard rate (of having a third child, for households that already have two children) rises over time, but at a decreasing rate.

Since $\partial h(t)/\partial x_k = -p\beta_k h(t)$, a positive value of β is associated with a *fall* in the hazard rate. Thus the results in Table 14.3 show that urban households have a lower

Table 14.3 Weibull model of the risk of giving birth, for households with two children, Vietnam, 1993

Variable	Coefficient	SE	Z-statistic	p-value
Household has a son	0.198	0.038	5.28	0.000
Years of education of household head	0.030	0.005	6.32	0.000
Age of mother in years, squared	0.00042	0.00009	4.78	0.000
Real expenditure per capita p.a. (m dong)	0.00024	0.00003	7.95	0.000
Household lives in an urban area	0.320	0.054	5.99	0.000
Region 2 (Hanoi and surrounds)	0.236	0.044	5.39	0.000
Constant	3.067	0.067	46.1	0.000
p	1.602	0.030		

Notes: Based on 2,061 observations, of which 605 were censored. Log likelihood $= -2,045.3893$
Source of data: Vietnam Living Standards Survey 1992–1993

imminent probability of having a third child, and the same is true of families that already have a son. Once again there is evidence of son preference.

It is useful to compare the results of the Weibull estimator with those of the Cox proportional hazards model. For the latter, $\partial h(t)/\partial x_k = \beta_k h(t)$, so we might expect the estimated coefficients in the Cox model to be approximately $-p$ times those in the Weibull model; the effect will be approximate because the two models make different parametric assumptions. For instance, the coefficient on the edlevel variable – the number of years of education of the head of household – is 0.030 in the Weibull model and -0.046 for the Cox model, which is approximately 0.030×-1.60. Even the coefficients on the binary variable that measures whether a two-child household has a sun (surson2), at 0.198 for the Weibull model and -0.246 for the Cox model, are of the relative magnitude that we would expect. It is reassuring that the two models give comparable results, and suggests that the finding of son preference, as reflected in statistically significant coefficients on surson2, is relatively robust. It is not uncommon to find that the results of duration models are robust with respect to the model that is used.

Like the Cox model, the Weibull model implicitly assumes proportional hazards, so it is advisable to check that this assumption is reasonable, as in the case of Cox models. Because it is fully parameterized, the Weibull model includes a constant coefficient while in the Cox model this contribution is included in the nonparametric base hazard function.

14.5.2   A Mixture of Two-Weibull Regression Models

In many cases the results from a Cox proportional hazards or a Weibull regression lead to similar conclusions. But one advantage of a parametric model such as the Weibull is that it is more amenable to an extension that would take into account the fact that the population may not be homogeneous; in such a case it may be sensible to fit a mixture of two-Weibull regressions.

In our Vietnamese example, we are interested in measuring the extent of son preference, which we hypothesize leads to shorter birth intervals for households that do not yet have a son. But it may be more plausible to suppose that there are two types of parents in the population, for whom the process of deciding to have a third child may differ. Perhaps one group exhibits son preference and the other does not.

If this is true, then it is not appropriate to use a single-Weibull distribution to summarize the duration effect for the whole population, and it would be more desirable to use a mixture of two Weibulls. Haughton and Haughton (1996) take this approach, and propose the following survival function $S(t)$:

$$S(t) = \mu\, e^{-(\lambda_i^1 t)^p} + (1 - \mu)\, e^{-(\lambda_i^2 t)^q} \tag{14.17}$$

where μ is a positive number between 0 and 1, and the pairs of parameters λ_1 and p, and λ_2 and q, define survival functions for two sets of Weibull distributions. The weight parameter μ represents the proportion of the sample that can be assigned to the first group.

This model can be fitted with maximum likelihood methods, although as a general rule, fitting mixture models can be challenging. Among the difficulties encountered is the possibility of nonconvergence, as well as the risk of convergence to a local rather than global maximum of the likelihood function. These problems have been well documented in the literature on statistical mixtures, and in general a judicious choice of initial values can be very helpful. Many researchers favor the use of the E-M (Expectation-Maximization[3]) algorithm, which has now become standard for fitting finite mixtures to data, or more generally for fitting models to incomplete data. The E-M algorithm has the advantage that the likelihood increases at each step of the algorithm, but it is known to be fairly slow and can be sensitive to the choice of the initial values.

For the Vietnamese data we maximized the likelihood using a more traditional Newton–Raphson method (a classical optimization method),[4] but followed suggestions made by Crowder et al. (1991) in the procedure we used to pick initial values (the Stata code for fitting a mixture of two Weibull regressions is available in Haughton 1997). We chose an initial value for μ of 0.1, initial values for p of 1.6 (from the single-Weibull regression model), and for q of 1.2 (close to but not equal to 1.6), and first fitted the mixture model with only constant terms. We then used the new estimated coefficients obtained from this first step, and starting values equal for both groups to that from the single-Weibull regression model, to add one predictor at a time to the model until all the covariates had been included. This procedure yielded the results in Table 14.4 below, reproduced from Haughton and Haughton (1996).

---

[3] See http://en.wikipedia.org/wiki/Expectation-maximization_algorithm for a fuller discussion.

[4] See, for instance, http://en.wikipedia.org/wiki/Newton's_method or any calculus textbook.

Table 14.4 Two-Weibull mixture model of the risk of giving birth, for households with two children, Vietnam, 1993

Variable	Group 1		Group 2	
	Coefficient	SE	Coefficient	SE
Household has a son	0.278	0.063	0.0252	0.028
Years of education of household head	0.032	0.008	0.004	0.004
Age of mother in years, squared	0.00049	0.00014	0.00010	0.00007
Real expenditure per capita p.a. (m dong)	0.00036	0.00006	0.00003	0.00002
Household lives in an urban area	0.363	0.097	−0.011	0.044
Region 2 (Hanoi and surrounds)	0.350	0.079	0.014	0.033
Constant	3.201	0.116	3.472	0.052
p	1.706	0.062		
q			4.292	0.211
μ	0.523	0.023		

Notes: Based on 2,052 observations, of which 600 were censored. Log likelihood $= -7{,}037.716$. From Haughton and Haughton (1996)
Source of data: Vietnam Living Standards Survey 1992–1993

This model implies that two groups (of about equal size since μ was estimated at 0.52) exist, with different mechanisms for the decision whether to have a third child or not. Son preference is significant for the first group, since the estimated coefficient for the variable indicating whether the two-child household had a son is statistically significant; at 0.278 it is larger than the value of 0.198 found in the single-Weibull case, indicating an even shorter interval between the second and third child for those households without a living son. On the other hand, the second group exhibits no son preference, and indeed none of the other covariates appear to play a role for this "colorless" group.

The estimated value of p is greater than 1, so the hazard rate for Group 1 households rises over time (positive duration dependence) but less and less quickly. Curiously perhaps, for the second group, the estimated value of q is much larger, at 4.29, which implies both positive and acceleration duration dependence.

Although we cannot identify with certainty who, in our sample, belongs to Group 1 and who to Group 2, two interesting studies of son preference in Malaysia fitted separate models to Malay and to Chinese-Malaysian households (Leung 1988 and Pong 1994). They found that Chinese-Malaysians exhibited son preference but had smaller families than Malays, who exhibited no son preference but had larger families.

14.6   Other Applications

At first sight it might seem surprising that living standards survey data, which are typically cross-sectional, are often well-suited for duration models. But there is a growing body of work that makes use of the information on the spells of breastfeeding, the times between births, the lifetimes of household enterprises, the duration of unemployment, and other measures that call for the use of the techniques set out in this chapter. In this section we summarize a sampling of this work.

Duration models have been used since the 1980s to model mortality in less-developed countries. One of the earlier papers, by Trussell and Hammerslough (1983), uses a proportional hazards model of infant and child mortality in Sri Lanka. An interesting feature of their model is that it includes, as covariates, dummy variables corresponding to various age categories of the children. This is no doubt to try to take into account the notorious nonlinearity in the link between age and mortality.

A number of papers make use of duration models to study contraceptive use in developing countries. One strand of this literature focuses on the duration of use of a particular contraceptive method until contraceptive failure; Wang et al. (1998) use a method similar to that in Trussell and Hammerslough (1983) to model the hazard of contraceptive failure (see Wang et al. 1998, for the exact definition of contraceptive failure). They model the logarithm of the hazard of contraceptive failure as a linear function of covariates, inclusive of dummy variables for categories of duration intervals (which implies that the constant in the linear function can differ at different points of the duration range).

Another strand in the literature on contraception examines the length of time between the birth of a first child and the adoption of a contraceptive method. Maples et al. (2002) propose an extension of the proportional hazard model to a "multi-level" situation where duration, here between the birth of the first child and the adoption of a contraceptive method, is expected to be influenced not only by individual-level variables, such as the level of education of the mother, but also by neighborhood-level variables, such as whether a school is available within a 5-min walk of the village where the mother lives. This model has a nonparametric specification of the baseline hazard function, as in a Cox model, but also allows random effects, which allow multiplicative random shifts of the baseline hazard function according to neighborhoods, and also random coefficients (depending on the neighborhood) for covariates such as the education of the mother. The methodology is applied to a data set of Nepalese mothers from 171 neighborhoods in the Chitwan Valley in south-central Nepal.

Many applications of duration models arise in health-related problems. Here we mention just two papers. The first, by Nagelkerke et al. (1995), seeks to determine an optimal breastfeeding duration for mothers who have been infected with the HIV-1 virus, notably in Africa. The issue here is one of balancing the risks of mortality related to the use of unclean alternatives to breastfeeding as well as the loss of antibodies present in the mother's milk if breastfeeding is eliminated, against the risk of mortality from an HIV-1 infection via the mother's milk, assumed in the paper to be fatal to the infant.

Nagelkerke et al. model the hazard of HIV-1 transmission via the mother's milk using an exponential model, which has a constant hazard rate. The hazard of mortality for non-breastfed children, on the other hand, is modeled by a Weibull model, for which the authors argue the parameter p should be about 0.5; this would imply negative duration dependence, as the hazard rate falls over time. A recommendation for a suitable length of breastfeeding then arises from the identification of the point where the hazard of mortality due to lack of breastfeeding falls below the constant hazard of HIV-1 transmission; this is found to occur somewhere between about 3 and 7 months.

Another health-related study is the examination by Long et al. (1994) of the onset of diarrhea in children in Guadalajara, Mexico. They find that an exponential model of duration, which has a constant hazard rate (but varies seasonally), fits best for the time that elapses between infections of *Escherichia coli*, a major source of diarrheal disease. On the other hand, the best model for the duration between the infection by *E. coli* and the onset of diarrhea was a Weibull model with an increasing hazard rate over time. This hazard rate was reduced by the use of traditional medicinal teas, and by higher levels of certain antibodies conveyed by the mother's milk.

Another important area of application of duration models in less-developed countries is to the spells of employment, or of unemployment, or of self-employment. Nziramasanga and Lee (2001) make use of a unique data set of small enterprises in Zimbabwe that registered between 1984 and 1996. The data provide dates of entry and exit from the business as well as demographic information on the business owner. Kaplan–Meier estimates of hazards of exiting the business are plotted against time to evaluate the impact of macroeconomic conditions on the hazards of exit. Then the data are partitioned by year of entry to control for macroeconomic conditions, and the effect of the personal characteristics of the owner on the hazard of exiting the business are evaluated using a Weibull model for each subdataset. The authors report trying a number of distributions aside from the Weibull distribution to model exit hazards, and found that this choice made very little difference to the results.

References

Cox, D.R. 1972. Regression models and life tables. *Journal of the Royal Statistical Society, Series B* 34: 187–220.

Crowder, M.J., A.C. Kimber, R.L. Smith, and T.J. Sweeting. 1991. *Statistical analysis of reliability data*. London: Chapman and Hall.

Greene, William H. 2003. *Econometric analysis*, 5th ed. Upper Saddle River: Prentice Hall.

Haughton, Dominique. 1997. Packages for estimating finite mixtures: A review. *The American Statistician* 51: 194–205.

Haughton, Dominique, and Jonathan Haughton. 1996. Using a mixture model to detect son preference in Vietnam. *Journal of Biosocial Science* 28: 355–365.

Haughton, J., and D. Haughton. 1995. Son preference in Vietnam. *Studies in Family Planning* 26(6): 325–337.

Hoa, H.T., N.V. Toan, A. Johansson, V.T. Hoa, B. Hojer, and L.A. Persson. 1996. Child spacing and two child policy in practice in rural Vietnam: Cross sectional survey. *British Medical Journal* 313: 1113–1116.

Leung, Siu Fai. 1988. On tests for sex preferences. *Journal of Population Economics* 1: 95–114.

Long, Kurt Z., James W. Wood, Edgar Vasquez Gariby, Kenneth M. Weiss, John J. Mathewson, Francisco J. de la Cabada, Herbert L. Dupont, and Richard A. Wilson. 1994. Proportional hazards analysis of diarrhea due to enterotoxigenic *Escherichia coli* and breastfeeding in a cohort of urban Mexican children. *American Journal of Epidemiology* 139(2): 193–205.

Maples, Jerry J., Susan A. Murphy, and William G. Axinn. 2002. Two-level proportional hazards models. *Biometrics* 58: 754–763.

Nagelkerke, Nico J.D., Stephen Moses, Joanne E. Embree, Françoise Jenniskens, and Francis A. Plummer. 1995. The duration of breastfeeding by HIV-1-infected mothers in developing countries: Balancing benefits and risks. *Journal of Acquired Immune Deficiency Syndromes and Human Retrovirology* 8: 176–181.

Nziramasanga, Mudziviri, and Minsoo Lee. 2001. Duration of self-employment in developing countries: Evidence from small enterprise in Zimbabwe. *Small Business Economics* 17: 239–253.

Pong, Suet-Ling. 1994. Sex preference and fertility in peninsular Malaysia. *Studies in Family Planning* 25(3): 137–148.

Trussell, James, and Charles Hammerslough. 1983. A hazards-model analysis of the covariates of infant and child mortality in Sri Lanka. *Demography* 20(1): 1–26.

Wang, Duolao, Ian Diamond, and Siàn L. Curtis. 1998. Contraceptive failure and its subsequent effects in China: A two-stage event history analysis. *Asia-Pacific Population Journal* 13(1): 45–64.

Index

A

Abidjan, 230
Absolute poverty, 194, 196, 197, 227
Adult equivalents, 193–194, 209
Africa, 19, 20, 130, 144, 145, 195, 196, 303
Agglomeration schedule. *See* Clustering
Agglomerative. *See* Clustering
Akaike information criterion (AIC), 32, 69, 71, 74, 167–169
Anscombe's quartet, 1, 2
ArcGIS, 18
ArcView, 18, 283
Argentina, 255
Armenia, 204
Asia, 176, 212, 268
Assignment equation. *See* Instrumental variables (IV)
Assignment model. *See* Propensity score matching
Asymptotic variance–covariance matrix of the estimator, 27
ATT. *See* Average treatment effect on the treated (ATT)
Attenuation bias, 29, 265
Attrition, 175, 178, 180, 237, 244, 260, 267
Average treatment effect on the treated (ATT), 238

B

Bagplot
depth median, 14
halfspace location depth, 14–15
inner bag, 15
outer bag, 15
Bandwidth. *See* Kernel densities
Bangladesh, 161, 162, 244

BARE. *See* Broad Area Ratio Estimator (BARE)
BARE-AD. *See* Broad Area Ratio Estimator with Auxiliary Data (BARE-AD)
Basis function. *See* Multiple adaptive regression spline (MARS)
Bayes factors, 130, 140–145
Bayesian analysis
Bayes factors, 130, 141, 142
credible intervals, 129, 130, 133, 136, 150
diffuse prior, 133, 140, 143
eliciting priors, 137–139
non-informative prior, 132, 139
posterior distribution, 129–131, 133–137, 139, 142, 143, 146, 147
posterior predictive checking, 130, 140–145
prior, 129–134, 136–142, 146, 147
Bayesian model averaging, 130, 146–148, 151
Bayesian network, 117
Bayesian techniques. *See* Bayesian analysis
Bayes information criterion (BIC), 32, 69, 71, 146, 168, 169
Bayes' theorem, 131
Best linear unbiased estimates (BLUE), 26, 160
Beta distribution, 132–134, 136, 139, 149
BIC. *See* Bayes information criterion (BIC)
Bins. *See* Histogram
Bin width. *See* Histogram
Birth weights, 3, 4
BLUE. *See* Best linear unbiased estimates (BLUE)
Bolivia, Santa Cruz, 158, 159
Bootstrap confidence interval, 63
Bootstrapping, 42, 183, 203, 206, 217, 221–234, 285
Box-and-whisker plot. *See* Boxplot

D. Haughton and J. Haughton, *Living Standards Analytics*, Statistics for Social and Behavioral Sciences, DOI 10.1007/978-1-4614-0385-2, © Springer Science+Business Media, LLC 2011